To Ilene, Lauren, Julie, Sam, and Erica Jacobs and
Laurie, Kara, Max, Brenda, and Hannah Levy
For their love, patience, and support

EQUITY MANAGEMENT

EQUITY MANAGEMENT

Quantitative Analysis for Stock Selection

BRUCE I. JACOBS
KENNETH N. LEVY

With a Foreword by
Harry M. Markowitz, Nobel Laureate

McGraw-Hill

New York San Francisco Washington, D.C. Auckland Bogotá
Caracas Lisbon London Madrid Mexico City Milan
Montreal New Delhi San Juan Singapore
Sydney Tokyo Toronto

McGraw-Hill

A Division of The McGraw·Hill Companies

1 2 3 4 5 6 7 8 9 0   DOC/DOC   9 0 9 8 7 6 5 4 3 2 1 0 9

ISBN 0-07-134686-4

The sponsoring editor for this book was Stephen Isaacs, the editing supervisor was Patricia V. Amoroso, and the production supervisor was Elizabeth J. Strange. It was set in Palatino by Carol Barnstable of Carol Graphics.

Printed and bound by R. R. Donnelley & Sons Company.

This publication is designed to provide accurate and authoritative information in regard to the subject matter covered. It is sold with the understanding that neither the author nor the publisher is engaged in rendering legal, accounting, futures/securities trading, or other professional service. If legal advice or other expert assistance is required, the services of a competent professional person should be sought.

> —*From a declaration of principles jointly adopted by a committee of the American Bar Association and a committee of publishers.*

 This book is printed on recycled acid-free paper containing a minimum of 50% recycled, de-inked fiber.

McGraw-Hill books are available at special quantity discounts to use as premiums and sales promotions, or for use in corporate training programs. For more information, please write to the Director of Special Sales, Professional Publishing, McGraw-Hill, 2 Penn Plaza, New York, NY 10121-2298. Or contact your local bookstore.

C O N T E N T S

Foreword by Harry M. Markowitz, Nobel Laureate   xiii

Acknowledgments   xix

Introduction

Life on the Leading Edge   1

PART ONE

Selecting Securities   19

Chapter 1

The Complexity of the Stock Market   25

The Evolution of Investment Practice   26

Web of Return Regularities   26

Disentangling and Purifying Returns   29

Advantages of Disentangling   30

Evidence of Inefficiency   31

Value Modeling in an Inefficient Market   33

Risk Modeling versus Return Modeling   34

Pure Return Effects   35

Anomalous Pockets of Inefficiency   37

Empirical Return Regularities   39

Modeling Empirical Return Regularities   40

Bayesian Random Walk Forecasting   41

Conclusion   43

Chapter 2

Disentangling Equity Return Regularities: New Insights and Investment Opportunities   47

Previous Research   48

Return Regularities We Consider   55
    Methodology   59

The Results on Return Regularities   61
    P/E and Size Effects   62
    Yield, Neglect, Price, and Risk   65
    Trends and Reversals   67
    Some Implications   72

January versus Rest-of-Year Returns   73

Autocorrelation of Return Regularities   77

Return Regularities and Their Macroeconomic Linkages   81

Conclusion   85

Chapter 3

On the Value of 'Value'   103

Value and Equity Attributes   104

Market Psychology, Value, and Equity Attributes   105
    The Importance of Equity Attributes   108

Examining the DDM   110
    Methodology   110
    Stability of Equity Attributes   113

Expected Returns   114
    Naïve Expected Returns   116
    Pure Expected Returns   117

Actual Returns   118
    Power of the DDM   120
    Power of Equity Attributes   120

Forecasting DDM Returns   121

Conclusion   123

Chapter 4

Calendar Anomalies: Abnormal Returns at Calendar Turning Points   135

The January Effect   136
    Rationales   137
The Turn-of-the-Month Effect   140
The Day-of-the-Week Effect   141
    Rationales   143
The Holiday Effect   145
The Time-of-Day Effect   148
Conclusion   151

Chapter 5

Forecasting the Size Effect   159

The Size Effect   159
    Size and Transaction Costs   160
    Size and Risk Measurement   161
    Size and Risk Premiums   163
    Size and Other Cross-Sectional Effects   164
    Size and Calendar Effects   166
Modeling the Size Effect   169
    Simple Extrapolation Techniques   171
    Time-Series Techniques   173
    Transfer Functions   175
    Vector Time-Series Models   176
    Structural Macroeconomic Models   178
    Bayesian Vector Time-Series Models   179

Chapter 6

Earnings Estimates, Predictor Specification, and Measurement Error   193

Predictor Specification and Measurement Error   194
    Alternative Specifications of E/P and Earnings Trend for Screening   196

Alternative Specifications of E/P and Trend for Modeling Returns   204
Predictor Specification with Missing Values   209
Predictor Specification and Analyst Coverage   212
The Return-Predictor Relationship and Analyst Coverage   216
Summary   221

PART TWO

Managing Portfolios   229

Chapter 7

Engineering Portfolios: A Unified Approach   235

Is the Market Segmented or Unified?   236
A Unified Model   238
A Common Evaluation Framework   240
Portfolio Construction and Evaluation   241
Engineering "Benchmark" Strategies   242
Added Flexibility   243
Economies   245

Chapter 8

The Law of One Alpha   247

Chapter 9

Residual Risk: How Much Is Too Much?   251

Beyond the Curtain   252
Some Implications   257

Chapter 10

High-Definition Style Rotation   263

High-Definition Style   267
Pure Style Returns   270

Implications 272

High-Definition Management 276

Benefits of High-Definition Style 278

PART THREE

Expanding Opportunities 283

Chapter 11

Long-Short Equity Investing 289

Long-Short Equity Strategies 289

Societal Advantages of Short-Selling 290

Equilibrium Models, Short-Selling, and Security Prices 291

Practical Benefits of Long-Short Investing 293

Portfolio Payoff Patterns 294

Long-Short Mechanics and Returns 297

Theoretical Tracking Error 300

Advantages of the Market-Neutral Strategy over Long Manager plus Short Manager 301

Advantages of the Equitized Strategy over Traditional Long Equity Management 301

Implementation of Long-Short Strategies: Quantitative versus Judgmental 303

Implementation of Long-Short Strategies: Portfolio Construction Alternatives 303

Practical Issues and Concerns 304

Shorting Issues 304

Trading Issues 305

Custody Issues 306

Legal Issues 306

Morality Issues 307

What Asset Class Is Long-Short? 307

Concluding Remarks 309

Chapter 12

20 Myths about Long-Short 311

Chapter 13

The Long and Short on Long-Short 321

Building a Market-Neutral Portfolio 322
A Question of Efficiency 326
Benefits of Long-Short 328
Equitizing Long-Short 331
Trading Long-Short 334
Evaluating Long-Short 339

Chapter 14

Long-Short Portfolio Management: An Integrated Approach 349

Long-Short: Benefits and Costs 350
   The Real Benefits of Long-Short 352
   Costs: Perception versus Reality 353
The Optimal Portfolio 355
   Neutral Portfolios 358
   Optimal Equitization 361
Conclusion 364

Chapter 15

Alpha Transport with Derivatives 369

Asset Allocation or Security Selection 370
Asset Allocation and Security Selection 372
Transporter Malfunctions 374
Matter-Antimatter Warp Drive 377
To Boldly Go 379

Index 381

FOREWORD

by Harry M. Markowitz, Nobel Laureate

This volume presents 15 pioneering articles by Bruce Jacobs and Kenneth Levy. In particular, it includes the Jacobs and Levy (1988) seminal work on "Disentangling Equity Return Regularities: New Insights and Investment Opportunities." Such disentangling of multiple equity attributes improves estimates of expected returns. Other articles in this volume, especially in Part 1, spell out some of the implications of this disentangling for various investment issues. Parts 2 and 3 are concerned with how to make the most effective use of investment insights, such as those provided by disentangling. In particular, Part 2 is concerned with the construction of long portfolios; Part 3, with long-short portfolios. In the introductions to the three parts, Jacobs and Levy present background and highlights.

It may be fairly asserted that Jacobs and Levy's work is based on mine, and my work is based on theirs. Specifically, Markowitz (1956 and 1959) presented the "general mean-variance portfolio selection model," extending an earlier Markowitz (1952) proposal. The portfolio selection models discussed in Parts 2 and 3 of this volume are special cases of the Markowitz "general" model. This is the sense in which their work is based on mine.

Mean-variance analysis requires, as inputs, estimates of the means and variances of individual securities and covariances between pairs of securities. Markowitz (1952, 1956, and 1959) does not specify how to estimate these inputs. When colleagues and I built DPOS (the Daiwa Portfolio Optimization System) in 1990, however, our expected return estimation procedures were based on Jacobs and Levy (1988) [see Bloch et al. (1993)]. Thus our work was based on theirs.

Markowitz (1952) begins:

> The process of selecting a portfolio may be divided into two stages. The first stage starts with observation and experience and ends with beliefs about the future performances of available securities. The sec-

ond stage starts with the relevant beliefs about future performances and ends with the choice of portfolio.

In other words: Estimate first, optimize second. Two steps must precede "estimate" and "optimize": (1) choose criteria and (2) list the universe of stocks available to the optimizer.

In Markowitz (1952), the criteria are assumed to be mean and variance. Today, mean and semivariance [Markowitz (1959), Chapter 9] are sometimes used instead. Either variance or semivariance could be used to measure tracking error (variability of returns minus benchmark), rather than the variability of return itself. The universe might include stocks, bonds, currencies, asset classes, money managers, and derivatives.

Suppose criteria and universe have been chosen and estimates have been made. Specifically, assume that mean and variance have been chosen as criteria and, in the first instance, it is mean and variance of return, rather than tracking error, that are considered. A basic theoretical principle, illustrated in Jacobs and Levy's (1999) "Long-Short Portfolio Management: An Integrated Approach," is that, given the estimates, in order to maximize mean for given variance, or minimize variance for given mean, one should not impose on the optimizer any constraints that are not required legal or physical constraints.

For example, Jacobs and Levy define a "minimally constrained portfolio" that maximizes expected investor utility and argue that imposition of any other constraints will result in a portfolio with (the same or) lower utility. Utility-reducing constraints include the following: not shorting; creating the long-short portfolio as a combination of an optimized long portfolio and a separately optimized short portfolio; forcing the number of dollars invested long to equal that sold short; and forcing the net beta of the securities held long to equal the net beta of those sold short. Jacobs and Levy analyze conditions under which one or another of these constraints would be optimal. Under such conditions, the investor will arrive at the same answer whether or not the particular constraint is imposed; otherwise the optimizer will find a portfolio with greater expected utility if the constraint is *not* imposed. In short, tell the optimizer the objectives, the universe, the estimates, and the minimal constraints required, and let it take it from there.

In practice, of course, additional constraints are often imposed. For example, DPOS, which had tracking error versus a Japanese market index as its measure of risk, constrained the optimizer not to hold individual positions that were "too much" different from their benchmark weights, and not to hold sector totals that deviated too much from the corresponding benchmark totals. I am not privy to the models used in practice by Jacobs and Levy, but I imagine that the outputs of even their most sophisticated model of expected returns, when run through an optimizer subject to minimal constraints, will sometimes result in *ex ante* efficient portfolios with uncomfortably large positions. To avoid this, the optimizer can be told to restrict maximum holdings.

But such constraints result in (the same or) less efficient portfolios, *ex ante,* given estimated means, variances, and covariances of security returns. How are we to reconcile theory and practice?

Chapter 13 of Markowitz (1959) presents the mean-variance investor as approximating a rational decision maker acting under uncertainty. Examination of this analysis highlights limits of the approximation, and suggests reasons why one might add constraints in practice beyond minimally required restraints.

1. The mean-variance analysis may implicitly be less averse to an extreme downside move than the true expected utility maximization. [See Table 1 in Levy and Markowitz (1979).] It is therefore possible that adding constraints to a minimally constrained mean-variance analysis may produce a portfolio that gives higher true expected utility, even though it gives a lower value to a mean-variance approximation.

2. The rational decision maker (RDM) of Markowitz (1959) is like a human decision maker (HDM) in that both must make decisions under uncertainty. It differs, however, in that the former is assumed to have unlimited computing capability; for example, it can instantly compute the billionth place of π. Nor does the RDM make up hypotheses about the world as it goes along. Rather, it has an astronomically long list of possible hypotheses about the nature of the world, attaches probability beliefs to these hypotheses, and alters these beliefs according to Bayes's rule as evidence accumulates.

In choosing between two possible decisions, the RDM does not act as if the hypothesis that it currently considers most probable is, in fact, certain. Rather, with its unlimited computing capacity, for each decision the RDM evaluates the expected utility of that decision if each alternative hypothesis were true. For a given decision, the RDM computes a weighted sum of these expected utilities, weighting each hypothesis by its probability. The (grand total) utility the RDM attaches to the decision is this probability-weighted sum. In particular, if one decision (for example, choice of portfolio) would have high utility if the hypothesis that is considered most likely were true, but would be disastrous if some different, not too implausible, hypothesis were true, the decision's (grand total) expected utility would be less than that of a decision that would do almost as well if the more likely hypothesis were true and not too badly if the less likely hypothesis were true.

The human decision maker cannot perform a similar calculation, at least not on an astronomically long list of alternative models of the world. By imposing constraints that rule out extreme solutions, like too large bets on particular securities, the HDM may be seen as intuitively emulating the RDM by avoiding actions with dire consequences under not-too-implausible scenarios and hypotheses.

3. Chapter 13 of Markowitz (1959) discusses a many-period consumption-investment game assuming perfectly liquid assets. Lip service is given to the illiquid case, but only to recognize that the problem is important and hard. In practice (for example, with DPOS), transaction costs, including estimated market impact, and constraints, such as upper bounds on portfolio turnover and on the increase or decrease in holdings of a security at any one time, attempt to achieve reasonable, if not optimal, policies in light of illiquidity.

The inability of human decision makers to fully emulate RDMs in maximizing expected utility in the face of uncertainty and illiquidity is a manifestation of what Herbert Simon (1997) calls "bounded rationality." The imposition of more than minimally required constraints, however, is not an example of what Simon calls "satisficing" behavior. The investor does not add constraints that lower *ex ante* efficiency because the investor is "satisfied" with less efficiency. Constraints are added (in part, at least) because the investor seeks protection against contingencies whose probability of "disutility" is underrated by mean-variance approximation or, possibly, by the parameter estimation procedure. We may view such constraints as an effort by the HDM to achieve intuitively a policy that an RDM would consider superior to that provided by the minimally constrained mean-variance procedure.

By and large, I still believe, as I did in 1952, that mean-variance analysis can provide "the 'right kind' of diversification for the 'right reason.'" Diversification makes sense, and proper diversification depends on a consideration of covariances. This is in contrast to the view that the decision to "buy, sell, or hold" can be determined by studying the security itself and not in relation to other securities. It seems to me obvious, as well as an implication of mean-variance analysis, that the buy-hold-sell decision should depend on the desirability of alternative investments and the investor's risk aversion, as well as the covariances of the security in question with other available securities, subject to the caveat that mean-variance analysis should not be considered a black box that can be set on automatic and allowed to run portfolios on its own.

The virtues of an "integrated portfolio approach" are further described in Parts 2 and 3 of this volume. Jacobs and Levy are to be acknowledged for bridging the gap between theory and practice in the world of money management and thanked for bringing together their cogent observations on the virtues of integrated portfolios and the estimation of required inputs.

REFERENCES

Bloch, M. et al. 1993. "A comparison of some aspects of the U.S. and Japanese equity markets." *Japan and the World Economy* 5 (1): 3–26.

Jacobs, B. and K. Levy. 1988. "Disentangling equity return regularities: New insights and investment opportunities." *Financial Analysts Journal* 44 (3).

Jacobs, B., K. Levy and D. Starer. 1999. "Long-short portfolio management: An integrated approach." *Journal of Portfolio Management* 26 (2).

Levy, H. and H. Markowitz. 1979. "Approximating Expected Utility by a Function of Mean and Variance." *American Economic Review* 69: 308–317.

Markowitz, H. 1952. "Portfolio selection." *Journal of Finance* 7 (2): 77–91.

———. 1956. "The optimization of a quadratic function subject to linear constraints." *Naval Research Logistics Quarterly* III: 111–133.

———. 1959. *Portfolio Selection: Efficient Diversification of Investments.* New York: John Wiley & Sons.

Simon, H. 1997. *Models of Bounded Rationality.* Cambridge, Massachusetts: MIT Press.

ACKNOWLEDGMENTS

The articles collected here first saw light in the pages of *Financial Analysts Journal*, the *Journal of Investing*, and the *Journal of Portfolio Management*. We are indebted to editors Charles D'Ambrosio and Van Harlow at *FAJ*, Brian Bruce at *JOI*, and Peter Bernstein and Frank Fabozzi at *JPM* for recognizing the worth of our efforts and for providing us with outlets to the broader investment community.

Two of the articles here were coauthored with colleagues at Jacobs Levy Equity Management. Our many thanks to Mitchell Krask, Ph.D., for his contributions to "Earnings Estimates, Predictor Specification, and Measurement Error," and to David Starer, Ph.D., for his contributions to "Long-Short Portfolio Management: An Integrated Approach."

Judith Kimball, also at Jacobs Levy Equity Management, provided valuable editorial advice and support for much of the work in this book. Stephen Isaacs, Senior Acquisitions Editor at McGraw-Hill, has shepherded the book through the publication process.

Thanks to all our associates at Jacobs Levy Equity Management for their teamwork and dedication. And thank you to our clients for providing us with the opportunities of our lifetimes, and for always challenging us to stay on the leading edge of investment research.

Readers may send comments or questions via e-mail to jacobslevy@jlem.com or visit our website at www.jlem.com.

Life on the Leading Edge

Prior to founding Jacobs Levy Equity Management in 1986, we had spent 5 years managing U.S. equity portfolios at the asset management arm of Prudential Insurance Company of America. Experience and intuition had led us to believe that new and emerging technologies could be used to detect profitable investment opportunities and to exploit them for the benefit of institutional clients.

Our seminal insight was that U.S. equity market returns were driven by complex combinations of company fundamentals, macroeconomic conditions, and psychological factors. That is, security prices respond to fundamentals, such as return on equity, and to the economic backdrop, including inflation and interest rates; but they also respond to behavioral elements such as investors' tendencies to overreact to news and events. As a result, the market is permeated by a complex web of interrelated return effects. We believed that detecting and exploiting these inefficiencies could lead to profitable opportunities for investment.

We devoted the first 3 years of our new firm to developing the tools needed to find and exploit these opportunities. We started by modeling a broad universe of U.S. stocks, combining our leading-edge financial research and intuition with the best available statistical and computer technology to build a system capable of analyzing numerous stock-specific, industry-related, market-related, and macroeconomic forces. The variables chosen for modeling had to capture both the concrete, fundamental characteristics of stocks and markets and their more abstract behavioral characteristics; the modeling process itself had to capture both differences across different types of stocks and evolutions over time.

We were the first to analyze these numerous inefficiencies in a multivariate framework, pioneering a proprietary process of "disentangling" return-predictor relationships. Disentangling allows us to examine the effect on return of individual attributes—small market capitalization, for example—controlling for the impact of other attributes such as low share price or the number of analysts following the stock. The resulting "pure" returns amplify predictive power by clarifying stock price responses to changes in underlying variables.

We have also devoted considerable efforts to the portfolio construction and trading processes, as both can have substantial impacts on investment outcomes. It is, after all, portfolio construction that translates the insights from stock selection into actual performance; improper construction can lead to loss of potential return or introduction of unintended risk. Our proprietary portfolio optimization methods, designed to be fully congruent with our stock selection process, help to ensure that expected portfolio returns are maximized at controlled levels of risk. Our innovative trading techniques, designed to exploit lower-cost electronic trading venues, minimize the impact of trading costs on portfolio returns.

Jacobs Levy Equity Management currently manages over $5 billion for more than 20 clients, including many of the world's largest corporate pension plans, public retirement systems, multiemployer funds, endowments, and foundations. We offer large- and small-capitalization core portfolios and style portfolios, such as large-cap growth or small-cap value, that have been able to deliver consistent, superior returns relative to benchmarks, at controlled levels of risk. We also offer more aggressive approaches, including long-short portfolios, designed to deliver value added consistent with model insights at higher levels of risk.

The 15 articles in this collection represent over a dozen years of research. The first was published in 1988, the most recent in 1999. Over this period, our insights and strategies have been honed by experience, but our basic philosophy has remained intact. Before going into more detail, however, it may be useful to review the history of investment practice from which our philosophy emerged.

A VERY BRIEF HISTORY OF MODERN INVESTING

The publication of *Security Analysis* by Benjamin Graham and David L. Dodd in 1934 inaugurated the era of professional money management. Graham and Dodd introduced a systematic approach to evaluating securities. That system was based on the philosophy that investors could arrive at an estimate of the fair value of a company, based on in-depth analysis of underlying fundamentals—information about the company, its industry, the overall market, and the economy—and that actual market prices were prone to diverge from those values. Divergences represented investment opportunities; buying (or selling) securities that were trading away from fair values would yield profits over time as market prices eventually corrected to reflect actual company performance.

By the 1970s, however, fundamental analysis à la Graham and Dodd was on the verge of being supplanted by a new paradigm. The years since the publication of the first edition of *Security Analysis* had witnessed explosive growth in information technology. Computer power, advancing at exponential rates, had revolutionized data collection and data analysis, giving rise to new and larger databases and new statistical techniques for parsing those data.

Over the same period, investing had become more and more institutionalized, with professional investors overtaking individual investors in the trading arena. This had two results. First, market prices were increasingly being set by professional investors, many of whom were presumably engaged in the systematic analysis of fundamental data. Second, as ownership and control of investment assets began to diverge, with control being vested more and more in the hands of professional managers, those managers began to be held to stricter account and higher disclosure standards. As a result, more data on actual investment performance became available for analysis.

These developments gave birth to a new theory of market price behavior and a new approach to investing. The new theory was the Efficient Market Hypothesis. The new approach was passive, or indexed, investing.

Computer-enabled dissection of actual market prices led to the belief that price changes follow a random walk; analyses of past or current prices alone could not be used to predict future prices. Efficient market enthusiasts argued that security analysis itself was futile, at least in terms of providing profits from forecasting, as market prices already incorporated all information available and relevant to stock prices. As proof, they pointed to the newly available performance records of professional managers; on average, these managers had not outperformed their benchmarks, despite their in-depth analyses—or because of them.

It seemed reasonable to conclude that, in a market dominated by professional investors armed with the tools for sophisticated analysis of an ever-increasing flood of data, security prices would become more efficient. Ironically, the vast improvement in investment tools over this period, including the dissemination and collection of data, as well as its analysis, may have created conditions that made profiting from those tools more difficult, if not impossible.

If analysis aimed at selecting individual securities that could provide superior returns was futile, active investing was a loser's game. In that case, the solution seemed to be to shift the emphasis from security selection to the task of constructing portfolios that would offer the market's return at the market's level of risk. If you can't outperform the market, passive investing held out the possibility of becoming one with the market.

Passive management uses portfolio construction techniques that utilize statistical sampling or full index replication to deliver portfolios that mimic the returns and risks of an underlying market benchmark. As the trading required to keep portfolios in line with underlying indexes is typically less than that required to beat the indexes, transaction costs for passive management are generally lower than those incurred by active investment approaches. As much of the investment process can be relegated to computers, the management fees for passive management are also modest. For the same reason, the number of securities that can be included in any given passive portfolio is virtually unlimited.

Passive management thus has the scope to match the risk-return profiles of any number of underlying market benchmarks. Today, there are passive, or index, funds tied to market indexes such as the S&P 500 or Russell 3000. There are also specialized index funds designed to deliver the performance of market style subsets such as growth, value, or smaller-capitalization stocks.

Passive management has no insight, however. It does not attempt to pursue or offer any return over the return of the relevant benchmark. If the market is as efficient as passive managers assume, of course, such excess returns are unattainable.

Where Traditional Active Management Fails

The inability of traditional active managers on average to perform up to expectations suggested to efficient market theorists that the market could not be bested, that pricing was so efficient as to preclude the possibility of doing any better than the aggregate of investors setting those prices. But what if the observed failure of traditional active management stems not from the insurmountable hurdle of market efficiency, but from inherent weaknesses in traditional active management?

Traditional investment managers focus on stock picking. They look for individual securities that will perform well over the investment horizon. Their search requires in-depth examinations of companies' financial statements and investigations of companies' managements, products, and facilities. No matter how exhaustive their selection process is, however, it is bounded by the limitations of the human mind.

A human mind can consider only a limited number of variables at any given time. In-depth analyses of large numbers of securities are thus not practical for any one manager. Traditional active analysts have instead tended to focus on subsets of the equity market, looking for streams of earnings that promise significant growth (growth stocks), for example, or assets that can be bought on the cheap (value stocks).

Narrowing the focus of analysis reduces the stock selection problem to human dimensions, but it also introduces significant barriers to superior performance. Most critically, it can limit the sheer number of potentially profitable insights that can be incorporated into a portfolio. From a universe of, say, 750 large-cap value stocks, a traditional active manager's closely followed universe may constitute only 200 issues. This effectively excludes profit opportunities that may be available from other stocks.

Traditional active management essentially relies on the ability of in-depth fundamental research to supply insights that are good enough to overcome the severe limitation on the number of insights a traditional manager can generate. But just how good must those forecasts be to compensate for their lack in number?

Figure I-1 plots the combinations of breadth and depth of insights necessary to achieve a given level of investment performance, as measured by the ratio of annual excess return to annual residual risk (information ratio).[1] Breadth may be understood as the number of independent insights incorporated in the portfolio; depth, or goodness, of insights is measured as the information coefficient, the correlation between a stock's forecast and actual returns.

F I G U R E   I—1

Combination of Breadth (Number) of Insights and Depth, or "Goodness," of Insights Needed to Produce a Given Investment Return/Risk Ratio

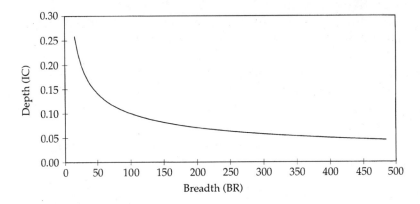

Note that the depth requirement starts to increase dramatically as the number of insights falls below 100; the slope gets particularly steep as breadth falls below 50. The insights of traditional analysts must be very, very good indeed to overcome the commensurate lack of breadth. Traditional active management is like the baseball team that relies on home runs, rather than strings of singles, to deliver a winning season—a problematic game plan. In 1998, despite Mark McGwire's record-setting 70 home runs, contributing to a league-leading 223 for the team, the St. Louis Cardinals wound up the season 19 games out of their divisional lead. The New York Yankees, placing only fourth in the American League in home runs, but tying for league lead with a .288 batting average, took their division and went on to win the World Series.

What's more, the constricted breadth of inquiry of the traditional manager can have detrimental effects on the *depth* of attainable insights. It results not only in the exclusion of profit opportunities available from stocks outside the closely followed universe, but also in the exclusion of information that may affect the stocks within that universe. The behavior of growth stocks not followed by a traditional growth manager, even the behavior of value stocks, may contain information relevant to the pricing of those stocks that do constitute the manager's universe. Ignoring this information can reduce the predictive power (the goodness) of the forecasts for the stocks the manager does follow.

The performance of traditional active management may suffer not only from limitations on the amount of information that can be processed by the human mind alone, but from errors in interpreting information. All humans are subject to cognitive biases, in-grown habits of thought that can lead to systematic errors in decision making. Most of us, for example, remember our successes more readily than our mistakes, hence we tend to approach problems with more confidence than may be warranted. We are also apt to give more credit to news that confirms our preconceived views, while ignoring news that contradicts those views.

A growing body of research suggests that investors often act under the influence of cognitive biases that warp their decisions.[2] Investors appear to be as susceptible as any other consumers to fads and fashions, hence to bidding up prices of hot stocks and ignoring out-of-favor issues. Investors tend to overemphasize new information if it appears to confirm their existing opinions. An investor who believes a particular firm's management is good may thus be biased toward earnings estimates that are on the high side. Such biases can erode the discipline of security analysis and, in turn, portfolio performance.

Traditional active management's reliance on the subjective judgments of individual analysts makes it susceptible to cognitive biases. It also makes it difficult to transform the output from the stock selection process into coherent input for systematic construction of portfolios. However on target an analyst's buy or sell recommendations may be, for example, it is difficult to combine them with the (also largely qualitative) output from other analysts, let alone firm economists and investment strategists, each of whom may be following his or her own idiosyncratic approach to valuation. It is also difficult to translate them into quantifiable portfolio performance goals such as expected portfolio return and risk estimates.

Nor does traditional active management look to underlying benchmarks to provide portfolio construction guidelines. While the return on a traditional active portfolio may be measured against a selected market index, that index does not serve as a benchmark in the sense of defining portfolio performance. Unlike passive managers, who are held to strict account by the need to match the risk and return of their underlying benchmarks, traditional active managers are generally given wide leeway to pursue return. This leaves the door open to cognitive errors and ad hoc portfolio construction, which can detract from return and add to risk.

Traditional management's focus on return over risk and on security selection over portfolio construction can result in portfolios that are poorly defined with regard to the underlying investment benchmarks, and this may create problems for clients. Without explicit guidelines that tie a portfolio to an underlying benchmark, a traditional manager may be tempted to stray from the fold. A traditional value manager averse to analyzing utilities, for instance, may simply exclude them from the portfolio. Or, if value stocks are currently underperforming, the manager may seek to bolster portfolio performance by buying some growth stocks instead.

A client using this manager cannot expect performance consistent with value stocks in general. If utilities outperform, for example, the value portfolio that excludes this sector will lag the benchmark. Nor can the investor comfortably combine this manager's portfolio with, say, a growth stock portfolio; if the value portfolio already includes growth stocks, the investor's overall portfolio will be overweighted in growth and overly susceptible to the risk that growth stocks will fall out of favor. Thus lack of discipline in traditional active management's security selection and portfolio formation processes can be compounded at the level of the client's overall investment funds.

Given their heavy reliance on human brainpower and their primary focus on return, with little consideration of risk control, traditional active approaches tend to suffer from a lack of breadth and a lack of discipline. These shortcomings, in turn, can translate into diminished return, increased risk, and inconsistencies in portfolio composition and performance. Perhaps it is for these reasons that traditional active portfolios have not tended to turn in superior performances.

It is, in any case, difficult to ascribe that failure to the utter efficiency of capital markets. In fact, the very shortcomings of traditional management would seem to foster inefficiencies in price setting—and opportunities for investors savvy enough to exploit them.

Quantifying Risk and Return for Profit

Investment managers who use quantitative analysis, like managers who use traditional analysis, seek to outperform the market, but their search is engineered to combine human insight and intuition with modern computing power, finance theory, and statistical techniques—instruments that have the potential to extend the reaches (and discipline the vagaries) of the human mind. While human brainpower continues to provide the creativity, computer modeling of stock price behavior and quantitative portfolio construction techniques provide the discipline to ensure that return opportunities are maximized at controlled levels of risk.

A quantitative stock selection process can deal with as wide a universe as passive management can. It can thus approach the investment problem with an unbiased philosophy, unhampered, as is traditional active management, by the need to reduce the equity universe to a tractable subset of stocks. Analysis of a particular style subset can take advantage of information gleaned from the whole universe of securities, not just stocks of that particular style (or a subset of that style, as in traditional management). The increased breadth of inquiry should lead to improved insights vis-à-vis traditional style portfolios.

Quantitative management also delivers *numerical* estimates for the expected returns and anticipated risks of the stocks in that universe. Unlike the largely subjective judgments of traditional active management, such numerical estimates are eminently suitable for portfolio construction via optimization techniques.

The goal of optimization is to maximize the portfolio's return while controlling its risk level. Portfolio risk will typically reflect the risk of the underlying benchmark (systematic risk) and the risk incurred in pursuing returns in excess of the benchmark return. This incremental, or residual, risk should be no more than is justified by the expected excess portfolio return.

The nature of quantitative stock selection and portfolio construction processes imposes discipline on active portfolios. With individual stocks defined by expected performance parameters, and portfolios optimized along those parameters to provide desired patterns of expected risk and return, portfolios can be defined in terms of preset performance goals. Adherence to stock selection models and underlying benchmark risk-return guidelines helps to immunize the manager from cognitive errors. Still better, engineered strategies can be designed to exploit the cognitive biases that can lead traditional active managers astray.

Furthermore, the discipline imposed by engineering portfolios to benchmark standards ensures portfolio integrity. Properly constructed quantitative active portfolios can be combined without fear that the combination will result in dilution or distortion of expected performance. Most importantly, portfolio integrity offers some consistency of benchmark-relative expected return and risk. The investor faced with the task of having to select managers (portfolios) to meet overall fund objectives can have more certainty of the contributions likely to be made by quantitative, as opposed to traditional, active managers. Manager selection can thus be more systematic and overall fund performance more predictable.

Of course, passive portfolios offer even more certainty of benchmark-relative performance, because they are designed to track underlying benchmarks closely. But passive portfolios offer no opportunity for superior performance. Only active quantitative management has the potential for both breadth and depth of analysis, as well as the imposed discipline, to deliver outperformance on a consistent basis.

ATTAINING INSIGHTS

While at the asset management arm of Prudential Insurance Company of America, we worked extensively with commercially available systems for measuring and controlling risk. These systems drew on earlier models for pricing risk, including the Capital Asset Pricing Model and Arbitrage Pricing Theory, and covered multiple risk factors, based on accounting and economic data. They provided us and other portfolio managers with tools for constructing portfolios that could meet quantitative risk control goals.

These systems were risk-oriented, not return-oriented. Their value came from the control of overall portfolio risk, rather than the enhancement of stock selection. But superior portfolio performance requires insights that can deliver returns, as well as tools for controlling risk. We felt we could develop return-oriented proprietary systems having the power to deliver significant value added.

By the early 1980s, the Efficient Market Hypothesis was already beginning to show signs of wear. For example, researchers had documented significant abnormal (that is, excess of market) returns accruing, over a number of years, to firms with low price-earnings ratios or small market capitalizations.[3] These findings were anomalies within the context of the Efficient Market Hypothesis. They indicated patterns of stock price behavior that investors could have exploited to earn above-average returns.

As the evidence in contradiction of the Efficient Market Hypothesis mounted, it became increasingly apparent that, in theory, a useful construct from which to view some broad truths about the market, the Efficient Market Hypothesis was, in practice, a viewpoint so reductionist as to rival the nineteenth-century "science" of phrenology, whereby a person's entire intellect and character could be deduced from the bumps on his or her head.

Unfortunately, many of the contradictions to the theory seemed, to us, equally simplistic—and equally incapable of guiding investors to superior returns. If profits were to be had simply by buying low-P/E stocks or small-capitalization stocks, why weren't investors taking advantage of these opportunities? If it was so easy, why wasn't everyone rich?

It seemed to us that, in fact, the implications of these early findings on market inefficiencies were too easy. As research uncovers exploitable opportunities, investors learn about them and act on them, causing the opportunities to disappear. And the easier the lesson, the faster investors learn it, and the more quickly the opportunity vanishes. It is hardly surprising that the observed superior return to small-cap versus large-cap stocks at the turn of the year began to disappear shortly after the documentation of the January effect.

As it reflects human activity, the market is changeable and not subject, like the physical sciences, to hard-and-fast laws. Simple rules don't apply, or don't apply long enough to offer superior returns with any consistency. Investing on the basis of such rules is like "investing" in a Ponzi scheme; the rewards accrue only to those in on the ground floor.

Another problem that we had with many of the studies of market anomalies was their tendency to ignore the implicit interrelationships between factors. Low-P/E stocks, for example, also tend to be small-cap stocks. Did abnormal returns accrue to both low-

P/E stocks and small-cap stocks? Or was one stock attribute merely proxying for the other? And what of the numerous other variables that had the potential to impact stock returns? Arriving at answers would require a simultaneous analysis of returns and stock attributes on an unprecedented scale.

Our start-up of Jacobs Levy Equity Management was followed by 3 years of intensive research into market price behavior aimed at detecting profitable pricing inefficiencies. We began with the philosophy that the market is a complex system. Market pricing is not totally efficient. But neither is it the product of a small number of variables, which can be exploited by relatively simple rules, such as "buy low-P/E stocks" or "buy high-earnings-growth stocks." Rather, pricing is a result of a very large number of variables, all of which interact in complex ways.

The stock selection process thus requires both breadth of inquiry and depth of analysis. We achieve breadth of inquiry by starting with a full range of stocks and examining variables that intersect many dimensions, from the fundamental to the psychological, and from the stock-specific to the macroeconomic. Breadth of inquiry is likely to increase the number of insights from the stock selection model, hence the profit opportunities that can be incorporated into a portfolio.

Stock price can be related in systematic ways not only to historical earnings, for example, but also to earnings announcements and to analysts' earnings estimates and revisions in earnings estimates, for psychological as well as fundamental reasons. Each inefficiency may provide its own opportunity for profit. If analysts have substantially underestimated a company's earnings, for example, they may be loath to revise future estimates upward sharply, preferring to ease out of their mistake by making smaller incremental adjustments; stock prices may thus be slow to change, providing an opportunity to invest "cheaply."

Furthermore, return-predictor relationships vary over different types of stocks and different market environments. We find, for example, that earnings surprises and earnings estimate revisions are more important for growth than for value stocks. Stocks with high dividend-discount-model values tend to perform better in bull markets than bear markets, whereas high-yield stocks experience the reverse.

It is also important to take into account nonlinearities in relationships between stock returns and relevant variables. For example, stock prices may be quick to reflect the effects of positive earnings surprises, but slower to reflect the effects of negative earnings surprises. One reason could be that sales of stock are limited to investors who already own the stock and to a relatively small number of short sellers.

By taking into account such intricacies of stock price behavior, and by disentangling return-variable relationships through multivariate analysis, we achieve depth of analysis. Depth improves the reliability, or goodness, of the insights incorporated in portfolios.

Putting Insights to Work

While breadth of inquiry and depth of analysis can improve the number of insights and the strength of the insights obtained from security research, it is the implementation of those insights via the portfolio construction process that translates insights into actual performance. Portfolio construction is thus a critical link in the investment process.

The development of multifactor risk models, as noted, had been vital to achieving control of portfolio risk. We built on the ideas and technology behind such models to design a portfolio construction process that is customized to our security selection process. Customization is vital; if a given factor is in the return model, but not the risk model, the optimization process will not deliver the best possible trade-off between risk and return.

Customized optimization procedures ensure that the portfolio takes advantage of all the profit opportunities detected by the stock selection process. To use our earlier example, suppose the stock selection model indicates that prices respond to historical earnings, earnings announcements, and analysts' earnings estimates. A portfolio construction process that does not account for all these earnings attributes will result in a portfolio that fails to fully benefit from them. At the same time, customized optimization ensures that the portfolio incurs no more risk than is justified by its expected return. Any risk in excess of this level would constitute a cost that detracts from portfolio performance.

Transaction costs also diminish performance, and so must be accounted for in the portfolio optimization process. Innovative trading methods and exploitation of electronic trading venues can reduce these costs. Electronic trading generally entails lower commissions and less market impact than traditional trading alternatives, and is also able to incorporate more factors, including trade urgency and market conditions, than a trader can be expected to bear in mind. Nevertheless, traditional trading is helpful at times when liquidity is not available electronically.

Although our investment process demands intensive computer modeling, for us computer modeling does not mean the type of "black box" models used by some quantitative approaches. Selection of variables to be modeled, for example, relies heavily on an intuitive understanding of how stock prices respond to factors such as changes in interest rates or announcements of earnings revisions. It also relies critically on the generation of new ideas, whether motivated by new data that open up new vistas, or by new statistical and modeling techniques that provide better predictive tools.

Furthermore, our performance attribution process provides transparency to the investment process. A performance attribution system that is customized to the stock selection and portfolio construction processes allows the manager to see how each component of the investment engine is working. Continuous monitoring of each portfolio determines whether selected insights are paying off as expected. A feedback loop between performance attribution and research helps to translate the information gleaned from performance attribution into improvements in stock selection and to ensure that the system remains dynamic, adjusting to the market's changing opportunities.

Profiting from Complexity

John Maynard Keynes (1936) observed, more than half a century ago, that the stock market is like a beauty contest in which the objective is to pick the contestant the judges deem to be the most beautiful. Success in such an endeavor requires more than your own subjective evaluation of beauty. You might study historical depictions of beauty in art and literature to arrive at a more universal standard of beauty. You might seek to adapt historical standards to contemporary tastes by studying current movies, magazines, and television. But it will also help to learn something about the idiosyncrasies of the contest judges. What characteristics does each of them find beautiful? What do their spouses look like? What are their tastes in art?

The stock market is a beauty contest with tens of thousands of contestants and tens of millions of judges, so succeeding is a bit more complicated than handicapping the next Miss America pageant. The task is beyond the capacity of the human mind alone. It requires computers and statistical techniques that can organize and make sense of vast amounts of disparate information. It requires insights into psychology as well as fundamentals. It requires a means of evaluating these insights so that their usefulness is maximized. It requires the adaptability to stay on the leading edge of new developments and the creativity to hone that edge with new ideas and new research.

As H. L. Mencken allegedly said, "For every complex problem, there's a simple solution, and it's almost always wrong." Investing is a complex problem, and it demands a complex solution. Arriving at that solution requires painstaking effort, but is ultimately rewarding.

Paradoxically, if the market were simpler, and investing were easier, the rewards would be smaller, because everyone would buy low and sell high. It is the market's very complexity that offers the opportunity to outperform—to those intrepid investors able to combine the breadth of inquiry and depth of analysis needed to disentangle and make sense of that complexity.

THE BOOK

For those readers unfamiliar with our articles, this book provides an introduction to the concepts that form the foundation of our approach to equity investing. For those of you who may have read these articles as they first appeared in print, the book provides an overall context within which the contributions of each article to our overall philosophy are clarified. In either case, we hope it will provide an enjoyable and valuable addition to your investment library.

The book groups the articles into three main sections. The articles in Part 1 focus primarily on security analysis in a complex market. The first two articles define complexity and discuss the importance of disentangling and purifying return-predictor relationships. The next three take a closer look at some of the anomalies that we have found to be exploitable, including departures from model-defined value, calendar effects, and the size effect. The last article in this section discusses some of the practical problems that arise in building predictors to include in a stock selection model.

In Part 2, the emphasis shifts from security selection to portfolio construction. The first two articles here investigate the benefits for both stock selection and portfolio construction of a "holistic" approach to the investment task, one that views the market from a broad, unified perspective, rather than focusing more narrowly on individual segments of the market. The third article discusses the limits of portfolio risk, arguing that there may be such a thing as a portfolio that is too safe. The fourth provides a case-study example of a portfolio construction process that aims to maximize the insights of our stock selection system by allowing portfolio weights to change aggressively as underlying economic and market conditions evolve.

The articles in Part 3 explore some recent developments in quantitative portfolio management. The first four articles concentrate on long-short portfolios, which can enhance the implementation of investment insights by enabling managers to sell short securities they expect to perform poorly. In these articles, we debunk some of the myths surrounding shorting and long-short portfolios, in particular, including the perceptions that long-short portfolios are necessarily riskier and costlier than long-only portfolios. We describe the mechanics of constructing market-neutral and "equitized" long-short portfolios, and the trading required to maintain them. And we introduce the concept of "integrated optimization" for maximizing the opportunities available from long-short management.

The final article in this section looks at how derivatives can be used in both long-only and long-short management to enhance performance. Derivatives have the potential to revolutionize investment management by allowing clients and managers to separate the security selection decision from the asset allocation decision.

ENDNOTES

1. The plot reflects the relationship:

$$IR = IC\sqrt{BR}$$

where IC is the information coefficient, BR is the breadth, or the number of independent insights, and IR (in this case assumed to be equal to 1), the information ratio, is the ratio of annual excess return to annual residual risk. Other values of IR will produce curves of similar shape, but below or above the curve illustrated. See Grinold and Kahn (1999). Also, for further discussion, see Jacobs and Levy (1998).

2. See, for example, Kahneman and Tversky (1979), Arrow (1982), Shiller (1984), and Thaler (1993).

3. See Basu (1977) and Banz (1981).

REFERENCES

Arrow, K. J. 1982. "Risk perception in psychology and economics." *Economic Inquiry* 1 (1): 1–8.

Banz, R. W. 1981. "The relationship between return and market value of common stock." *Journal of Financial Economics* 9 (1): 3–18.

Basu, S. 1977. "Investment performance of common stocks in relation to their price/earnings ratios: A test of the Efficient Market Hypothesis." *Journal of Finance* 32 (3): 663–682.

Graham, B. and D. L. Dodd. 1934. *Security Analysis.* New York: McGraw-Hill.

Grinold, R. C. and R. N. Kahn. 1999. *Active Portfolio Management.* 2d ed. New York: Mc-Graw-Hill, Chapter 6.

Jacobs, B. I. and K. N. Levy. 1998. "Investment management: An architecture for the equity market." In *Active Equity Portfolio Management,* F. J. Fabozzi, ed. New Hope, Pennsylvania: Frank J. Fabozzi Associates.

Kahneman, D. and A. Tversky. 1979. "Prospect theory: An analysis of decision under risk." *Econometrica* 47 (2): 263–292.

Keynes, J. M. 1936. *The General Theory of Employment, Interest, and Money.* New York: Harcourt Brace, 1964 reprint.

Shiller, R. J. 1984. "Stock prices and social dynamics." *Brookings Papers on Economic Activity* 15 (2): 457–498.

Thaler, R. H., ed. 1993. *Advances in Behavioral Finance.* New York: Russell Sage Foundation.

Selecting Securities

An active quantitative equity manager expects to benefit from returns in excess of those on an underlying benchmark, whether a broad market index such as the Wilshire 5000, a large-capitalization index such as the S&P 500, a small-capitalization index such as the Russell 2000, or a growth or value subset of the market. Whether those expectations will be met depends on how well the manager does at two basic related tasks. The first task is to detect mispriced securities. The articles here in Part 1 focus primarily on that task. The articles in Parts 2 and 3 of the book have more to do with the second task of the manager—combining those securities in portfolios that preserve the superior returns without incurring undue risk.

Mispriced securities have the potential to provide superior returns as their prices correct, over time, to fair values. Of course, the Efficient Market Hypothesis and Random Walk Theory would say that mispricing, if it exists at all, is so fleeting or so random as to defy exploitation. And elegant Ivory Tower theories, such as the Capital Asset Pricing Model and Arbitrage Pricing Theory, would say that any apparent superior returns are merely the investor's compensation for bearing various kinds of risk.

Certainly, both research and reality have shown that simple rules don't work. Buying stocks with low price/earnings (P/E) ratios or high dividend discount model values won't deliver superior returns on a consistent basis, over changing economic and market environments. Successful investing isn't that easy.

The difficulty of the task stems from the nature of the market itself. Random walk enthusiasts would have one believe that the market is a random system, that stock prices meander like a stumbling drunkard. Trying to predict their path is a futile task.

Other investors—those who screen on fundamentals such as low P/E, or technicals such as moving averages—apparently believe the market to be an ordered system. Ordered systems, such as the structure of diamond crystals or the dynamics of pendulums, are definable by a relatively small number of variables and predictable by relatively simple rules. But if the stock market is predictable on the basis of such simple laws, why isn't everyone profiting from them?

We believe that the stock market is a complex system. Complex systems, such as the weather and the workings of DNA, can be modeled and partly predicted, but only with great difficulty. The number of variables that must be modeled, and their interactions, are beyond the capacity of the human mind alone. Identifying these variables, and detecting exploitable profit opportunities, requires extensive computer-based statistical modeling across a broad range of stocks. Robust insights into stock price behavior emerge only from an analysis that carefully considers numerous factors simultaneously.

In defining "value," say, a model that grapples with the market's complexity does not confine itself to a dividend discount model (DDM) measure of value, but also examines earnings, cashflow, sales, and dividend yield value, among other attributes. Growth measurements to be considered include historical, expected, and sustainable earnings growth, as well as the momentum and stability of that growth. Share price, volatility, and analyst coverage are among the elements to be considered along with market capitalization as measures of size.

These variables are often closely correlated with each other. Small-cap stocks, for example, tend to have low P/Es; low P/E is correlated with high yield; both low P/E and high yield are correlated with DDM estimates of value. Furthermore, they may be correlated with a stock's industry affiliation. A simple low-P/E screen, for example, will tend to select a large number of bank and utility stocks. Such correlations can distort naïve attempts to relate returns to potentially relevant variables. A true picture of the return-variable relationship emerges only after disentangling the variables via appropriate multivariate analysis.

More common methods of measuring return effects, such as quintiling or univariate (single-variable) regression, are "naïve" because they assume, naïvely, that prices are responding only to the single variable under consideration—low P/E, say. But a number of related variables may be affecting returns. Because small-cap stocks and banking and utility industry stocks all tend to have low P/Es, a univariate regression of return on low P/E will capture, along with the effect of P/E, a great deal of noise related to firm size, industry affiliation, and other variables.

Simultaneous analysis of all relevant variables takes into account and adjusts for such interrelationships. The result is the return to each variable separately, controlling for all related variables. A properly controlled, multivariate analysis of low P/E, for example, will provide a measure of the excess return to a portfolio that has a lower-than-average P/E ratio, but is marketlike in all other respects, including its exposures to company capitalization and industries. Such disentangled returns are "pure" returns.

Disentangling distinguishes real effects from mere proxies and thereby distinguishes between real and spurious investment opportunities. Disentangling shows, for example, that returns to small firms in January are not abnormally high; the apparent January seasonal merely proxies for year-end tax-loss selling and subsequent bounceback. Not all small firms will benefit from a January rebound; indiscriminately buying small firms at the turn of the year is not an optimal investment strategy. Ascertaining true causation leads to more profitable strategies.

Disentangling can also reveal hidden opportunities. Small-cap stocks, for example, may be characterized by low price and analyst neglect, as well as capitalization. Only a multivariate analysis can distinguish the extent to which returns accrue to each of these characteristics separately. Furthermore, the resulting pure returns are additive. If analysis shows that positive returns accrue to both small capitalization and analyst neglect, the investor may benefit from both attributes by investing in small-cap stocks that are covered by relatively few analysts.

Pure returns also tend to be much less volatile than their naïve counterparts, because they capture more signal and less noise. Consider a naïve analysis of returns to book-to-price (B/P) ratios. As most utilities have high B/P ratios, a naïve return to high B/P will be affected by events such as oil price shocks, which are relevant to the pricing of utility stocks, but not necessarily to the pricing of other stocks with high B/Ps. By contrast, a pure return to B/P controls for the static introduced by industry-related (and other) effects. By providing a clearer picture of the precise relationships between stock price behavior, company fundamentals, and macroeconomic conditions, disentangling improves return predictability.

In considering possible variables for inclusion in a model of stock price behavior, it is important to recognize that pure stock returns are driven by a combination of economic fundamentals and investor psychology. That is, economic fundamentals, such as interest rates, industrial production, and inflation, can explain only part of the behavior of stock returns. Psychology, including investors' tendency to overreact, their desire to seek safety in numbers, and their selective memories, plays a substantial role in security pricing. Signals by corporate management, including stock splits, earnings preannouncements, changes in dividend policy, share repurchases or secondary offerings, and insider trading activity, may also prove productive.

It is also important to allow for the fact that price responses may be nonlinear. For instance, a stock might be expected to react twice as favorably to a 2-cent positive earnings surprise as to a 1-cent surprise. It is highly unlikely, however, that a 57-cent surprise will elicit 57 times the response of a 1-cent surprise. Investor enthusiasm tends to taper off because of satiation, suspicion that such a large surprise is a nonrecurring event, or fear that it reflects a data error.

Return-predictor relationships are likely to differ across different types of stocks. Because the value sector includes more financial stocks than the growth sector, for example, value stocks in general tend to be more sensitive than growth stocks to changes in interest rate default spreads. Earnings surprises and earnings estimate revisions, by contrast, appear to be more important for growth than for value stocks. Thus, Intel shares can take a nosedive when earnings come in a penny under expectations, whereas Ford shares remain unmoved by similar departures of actual earnings from expectations.

Relationships between risk and predictors as well as between return and predictors may differ across different types of stock. Small-cap stocks generally have more idiosyncratic risk than large-cap stocks, so diversification is more important for small-stock than for large-stock portfolios. Oil price increases may be positive news for the oil industry, but are likely to have a negative impact on airlines.

A rich model containing multiple variables is likely to turn up a number of promising return-predictor relationships. But are these perceived profit opportunities real, or mere artifacts of data mining? Are some too ephemeral? Too small to survive frictions such as trading costs? Answering this last question requires adjusting estimates of expected returns by estimates of trading costs to arrive at realistic returns net of trading costs.

Return-predictor relationships change over time. The world is constantly evolving, and old inefficiencies disappear, giving way to new ones. The market is not simply ordered; merely tilting a portfolio toward historical anomalies does not produce consistent returns. Ongoing research on new inefficiencies, new sources of data, and new statistical techniques, however, can keep the model in sync with evolving opportunities.

The articles in this section discuss our approach to security analysis in a complex market. "The Complexity of the Stock Market" provides an introduction to our view of market complexity and the ways in which market inefficiencies, hence opportunities, arise from a complex web of interrelated return effects. This article, which first appeared in the fifteenth anniversary issue of the *Journal of Portfolio Management* (Fall 1989), was chosen for *Streetwise: The Best of the Journal of Portfolio Management* (Princeton University Press, 1997).

"Disentangling Equity Return Regularities: New Insights and Investment Opportunities" describes our pioneering methodology for disentangling and purifying return effects. The findings here demonstrate the existence of return anomalies that contradict the Efficient Market Hypothesis and constitute a core tenet of our investment philosophy and a prime motivation for active equity management. This article, which first appeared in the May/June 1988 issue of *Financial Analysts Journal*, won a Graham and Dodd Award for that year, and appeared in translation in the March and April 1990 issues of the *Security Analysts Journal of Japan*.

"On the Value of 'Value'" (*Financial Analysts Journal*, July/August 1988) examines the ability of the dividend discount model to explain market prices. We find that "value" can explain but a small part of the security pricing story. Furthermore, returns to DDM value are heavily dependent on the underlying market and economic environments.

"Calendar Anomalies: Abnormal Returns at Calendar Turning Points" (*Financial Analysts Journal*, November/December 1988) strikes another blow against rational pricing and market efficiency. Since the early 1930s, investors have observed a tendency for market prices to follow certain calendar-based patterns. A review and investigation of time-related anomalies, such as the turn-of-the-year, turn-of-the-week, and holiday effects, suggest that investor behavior can, at times, be outright irrational.

By the time we wrote "Forecasting the Size Effect" (*Financial Analysts Journal*, May/June 1989), investors had recognized that market capitalization played a substantial role in stock price performance. In this article, we look at some factors that might be used to forecast the relative returns to small-capitalization stocks. This investigation of the small-cap effect presents an interesting case study of the ways in which macroeconomic factors influence certain return effects.

With "Earnings Estimates, Predictor Specification, and Measurement Error" (*Journal of Investing*, Summer 1997), we focus on some of the important problems and issues that arise when specifying a predictor. When using analysts' earnings estimates to predict stock returns, for example, how does the timeliness of the estimates matter? Do results vary depending on related stock attributes such as the number of analysts covering a company? Are the results robust to different statistical estimation procedures? How does one deal with missing data? For proper model specification, attention to detail is critical.

CHAPTER 1

The Complexity of the Stock Market*

A web of interrelated return effects.

Investment theory and practice have evolved rapidly and tumultuously in recent years. Many placed the Efficient Market Hypothesis (EMH) and the Capital Asset Pricing Model (CAPM) on pedestals in the 1970s, only to see them come crashing down in the 1980s. In explaining why such theories cannot represent the true complexity of security pricing, we suggest new approaches to coping with the market's complexity. To do so, we follow a taxonomy from the sciences.

Scientists classify systems into three types—ordered, complex, and random.[1] Ordered systems are simple and predictable, such as the neatly arranged lattice of carbon atoms in a diamond crystal. Similarly, Newton's Laws of Motion are a simple set of rules that accurately describe the movement of physical objects. At the other extreme, random systems are inherently unpredictable; an example is the random behavior, or Brownian motion, of gas molecules.

Complex systems fall somewhere between the domains of order and randomness.[2] The field of molecular biology exemplifies complexity. The mysteries of DNA can be unraveled only with the aid of computational science. The human mind alone cannot cope with DNA's complexity, nor do simple theories suffice.

The stock market, too, is a complex system.[3] Security pricing is not merely random, nor are simple theories adequate to explain

---

* Originally published in the *Journal of Portfolio Management* 16 (1): 19–27.

market operation. Rather, the market is permeated by a web of interrelated return effects. Substantial computational power is needed to disentangle and model these return regularities.

THE EVOLUTION OF INVESTMENT PRACTICE

Before the 1970s, the investment norm was security analysis and stock selection. In a traditional, compartmentalized approach, security analysts, technicians, and economists all funneled their insights to portfolio managers. The market was viewed as complex, in the sense that no single human mind could master all the knowledge needed for optimal decision making. Coordinating the insights of multiple participants, however, is not a simple task. Needless to say, this approach has generally produced unsatisfactory results.

The EMH mounted a frontal assault on the traditional mode of investment management. In an efficient market, prices fully reflect all available information. With its flood of information and countless participants, the U.S. stock market was regarded by academicians as highly efficient. It was thought that no one could beat the market, with the possible exception of insiders. By the mid-1970s, the EMH had substantial empirical support, and was a central paradigm in finance.

The revolutionary concept of passive management was a natural outgrowth of the EMH. If security returns are random and unpredictable, then only a passive approach makes sense. Index funds that were introduced to the investment community in the mid-1970s soon blossomed in popularity.

Since the late 1970s, though, there has been a proliferation of empirical results uncovering security pricing patterns, or return regularities. In fact, many of these effects have long been part of market folklore. These include the low-P/E, small-firm, and January effects.

Thomas Kuhn (1970), the scientific historian, refers to such evidence of departure from conventional theory as "anomalies." In his words (p. 52), "discovery commences with the awareness of anomaly, i.e., with the recognition that nature has somehow violated the paradigm-induced expectations that govern normal science." In recent years, investment theory has been undergoing such a process of discovery.[4]

At first, academics rallied to defend the EMH. Tests of market efficiency are joint tests of the effect studied and the validity of the asset pricing model used to adjust for risk. Perhaps anomalies were due solely to deficiencies in risk measurement. Yet anomalies have been shown to be robust to asset pricing models, including the CAPM and Arbitrage Pricing Theory (APT). By the early 1980s, there were undeniable chinks in the armor of the EMH.

Investors have also sought to benefit from market anomalies by using simple rules such as buying low-P/E stocks. Others have tilted toward smaller-size or higher-yielding stocks. These investors consider the stock market an ordered system; they believe that simple rules will provide consistent and predictable returns.

What has recently become evident, however, is that the market is not a simple, ordered system. In a number of instances, we have documented a pervasive and complex web of interrelated return effects. This web must first be disentangled to allow us to distinguish real effects from mere proxies. Moreover, some return effects do not produce consistent rewards. Thus, the optimal investment strategy is not as simple as tilting toward yesterday's anomalies.

Nevertheless, the indexers' nihilistic view of the market as a random system is unjustified. The market is not random, but rather complex. Computational systems can be designed to grapple with its complexity. Besides being objective and rigorous, such systems are also fully coordinated, unlike the more traditional compartmentalized approaches. Beneath the complexity of the market lie enormous inefficiency and substantial investment opportunity.

WEB OF RETURN REGULARITIES

Figure 1-1 displays some interrelated return effects. The various connections shown between pairs of effects have been reported by previous studies.[5] For example, the small-size effect and the January effect are related, as it has been claimed that much of the annual outperformance of small stocks occurs in the month of January. The small-size and low-P/E effects also are related. Because stocks with lower-than-average P/E ratios tend to be smaller in size, a natural question arises as to whether the size effect and P/E effect are two separate forces, or merely two different ways of measuring the same underlying phenomenon.

FIGURE 1-1

A Web of Some Interrelated Return Effects

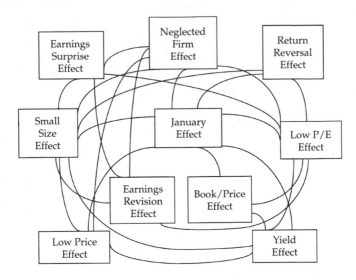

Many researchers have addressed this issue by examining the two return effects jointly. Some conclude that the superior performance of small-capitalization stocks relates to their tendency to have lower P/E ratios, while others find that low-P/E stocks outperform simply because they are smaller in size. Still another viewpoint maintains that neglected securities outperform, and that low P/E and small size both proxy for this underlying effect.

While some previous academic studies have examined two or three return effects simultaneously, their findings often conflict with one another. This arises from the use of different methodologies, different time periods, and different company samples. But more fundamentally, conflicting results arise from failure to disentangle other related effects. Only a joint study of return effects in a unified framework can distinguish between real effects and illusory ones.

Consider the determinants of an individual's blood pressure. A medical researcher would not limit the analysis arbitrarily to just one or two explanatory variables such as age and weight. More accurate evaluation can be obtained by including additional variables such as exercise and diet. Of course, all these measures are somewhat correlated with one another. But they may all have independent predictive content.

The same holds true for the stock market: Many forces affect stock returns; some of them may be correlated, but considering only a few can produce highly misleading results.

DISENTANGLING AND PURIFYING RETURNS

The standard approach to measuring a return effect, such as low P/E, first screens for a set of stocks below a given P/E ratio, or selects the lowest quintile of stocks as ranked by P/E. Portfolio returns are then calculated and compared to those of the universe. Any differences are ascribed to the low-P/E effect. But, a low-P/E portfolio by its nature will be biased unintentionally toward certain related attributes, such as higher yield, and show heavy representation in certain industries such as utilities. Screening or quintiling procedures consider only one attribute at a time, while assuming that related effects do not matter at all. We refer to the returns produced by such methods as "naïve."

The low-P/E effect, measured naïvely, is contaminated by other forces. An oil price shock or an accident at a nuclear power plant, for instance, will have a major impact on utilities, which will be reflected in the returns of the low-P/E portfolio. While fundamentals, such as oil prices, have no intrinsic relationship to the low-P/E effect, they can confound its naïve measurement.

In two papers we have introduced the alternative approach of disentangling and purifying return effects [Jacobs and Levy (1988b and 1988c)]. "Pure" return attributions result from a simultaneous analysis of all attribute and industry effects using multiple regression. Returns to each equity characteristic are purified by neutralizing the impact of all other effects. For example, the pure payoff to low P/E is disentangled from returns associated with related attributes such as higher yield.

Conceptually, the pure return to low P/E arises from a lower-P/E portfolio that is marketlike in all other respects; that is, it has the same industry weights and the same average characteristics, such as yield and capitalization, as the market. Hence, any differential returns to such a portfolio must be attributable to the low-P/E characteristic, because it is immunized from all other exposures that might contaminate returns.

ADVANTAGES OF DISENTANGLING

The pure returns that arise from disentangling eliminate the proxying problems inherent in naïve returns. The unique insights from studying pure returns have many practical benefits for investment management.

When we distinguish between real effects and proxies, we find that some closely related effects are, in fact, distinct from one another. For instance, small size, low P/E, and neglect exist as three separate return effects in pure form. Each should be modeled individually, which provides greater explanatory power.

Conversely, some naïve return effects merely proxy for one another, and vanish in pure form. Half of the outperformance of small stocks, for example, is reported to occur in January. But the small-firm effect, measured naïvely, arises from a bundle of related attributes. Smaller firms tend to be more neglected, and informational uncertainty is resolved at year end as these firms close their books. This year-end reduction in uncertainty might induce a January seasonal return. Furthermore, smaller firms tend to be more volatile and are more commonly held by taxable investors, so they may be subject to heavier year-end tax-loss selling pressure. The abatement of selling pressure in January may lead to a price bounceback.

We find the January small-firm seasonal vanishes when measured properly in pure form. Purifying the size effect of related characteristics, such as tax-loss selling, reveals the January size seasonal to be a mere proxy. The optimal investment approach models the underlying causes directly. Because not all small firms benefit from tax-loss rebound, a strategy that directs the purchase of smaller firms at year end is only second best.

While we find some return effects to be real, and others to be illusory, we also find the power of some pure return effects to exceed their naïve counterparts by far. This is true, for example, of the return-reversal effect. This effect represents the tendency of prices to overshoot and then correct, hence the term "reversal." Yet if a jump in price is due to a pleasant earnings surprise, the superior performance will persist and not reverse. Hence, disentangling return reversal from related effects, such as earnings surprise, results in a stronger, more consistent reversal measure.

Disentangling also reveals the true nature of the various return effects. For example, low-P/E stocks are usually considered defensive. But pure returns to low P/E perform no differently in down markets than in up markets. The defensiveness of low P/E in naïve form arises because it proxies for defensive attributes, such as high yield, and defensive industries, such as utilities. In fact, low-P/E stocks are not the safest harbor in times of uncertainty. Rather, low P/E is an imperfect surrogate for truly safe havens such as higher yield.

Additionally, pure returns are more predictable than their naïve counterparts. Pure returns possess cleaner time-series properties because they are not contaminated by proxying. For example, a time series of naïve returns to the low-P/E effect is buffeted by many extraneous forces such as oil price shocks to low-P/E utility stocks. In contrast, pure returns are immunized from such incidental forces, and thus can be predicted more accurately.

A major benefit of disentangling is that pure return effects avoid redundancies, and hence are additive. This allows us to model each return effect individually, and then to aggregate these attribute return forecasts to form predicted security returns. Moreover, by considering a large number of return effects, we obtain a very rich description of security pricing.

EVIDENCE OF INEFFICIENCY

Previous research on market anomalies taken one at a time has not added to the weight of evidence contravening market efficiency. That is, if the size, P/E, and neglect effects, all measured naïvely, proxy for the same underlying cause, they all represent "photographs" of the same anomaly taken from different angles. We have documented, however, the existence of many contemporaneous "pure" return effects. These separate photographs of many distinct anomalies, all taken from the same angle, constitute the strongest evidence to date of market inefficiency.

Calendar-related anomalies represent additional evidence of market inefficiency. We find that return patterns, such as the day-of-the-week and January effects, cannot be explained by consider-

F I G U R E   1–2

Cumulative Return to Beta

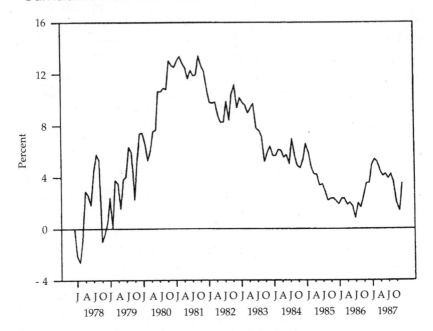

ations of risk or value, and thus cast further doubt on the EMH [see Jacobs and Levy (1988*a*)].

Return effects are also contrary to current asset pricing theories, such as the CAPM, the multifactor CAPM, and the APT. For example, the CAPM posits that systematic risk, or beta, is the only characteristic that should receive compensation. Other considerations, such as a firm's size, or the month of the year, should be unrelated to security returns.

Figure 1-2 displays cumulative pure returns to beta in excess of market returns for the years 1978 through 1987. These returns derive from a 1 cross-sectional standard deviation of exposure to high beta, roughly equivalent to a sixteenth percentile ranking. While in the early years the beta attribute provided positive returns, its returns were negative thereafter. These pure returns may differ from other studies because of our control for related attributes such as price volatility. The fact that pure returns to beta did not accumulate positively over the period from July 1982 to August 1987, one of the strongest bull markets in history, casts serious doubt on the CAPM.

The existence of return effects also poses a challenge to the multifactor CAPM.[6] Even the APT cannot account for the existence of several market anomalies. In fact, it appears doubtful that any meaningful definition of risk is as transient as some return effects. Thus, the weight of recent empirical evidence has buried the EMH. Also, while current asset pricing theories may contain elements of truth, none is fully descriptive of security pricing.

VALUE MODELING IN AN INEFFICIENT MARKET

In a reasonably efficient market, prices tend to reflect underlying fundamentals. An investor superior at gathering information or perceiving value will be suitably rewarded.

In an inefficient market, prices may respond slowly to new information and need not reflect underlying fundamentals. Given the substantial evidence of market inefficiency, the efficacy of value modeling is an open question. We have examined this issue by exploring the quintessential value model—the dividend discount model (DDM) [Jacobs and Levy (1988d and 1989b)].

We find the DDM to be significantly biased toward stocks with certain attributes such as high yield and low P/E.[7] In fact, some have argued that the only reason such attributes have positive payoffs is because they are highly correlated with DDM value. Further, they maintain that a properly implemented DDM will subsume these return effects.

We test this notion directly by incorporating a DDM in our disentangled framework. We find the DDM's return predictive power to be significantly weaker than that of many other equity attributes. Hence, return effects such as P/E are not subsumed by the DDM. Rather, equity attributes emerge important in their own right, and the DDM is shown to be but a small part of the security pricing story.

The DDM embodies a particular view of the world, namely, "going concern" value. But there are other sensible notions of value. For instance, current yield is an important consideration for endowment funds with restrictions against invading principal. Such endowments may be willing to pay up for higher-yielding stocks. And, in today's market environment, breakup value and leveraged buyout value have taken on increased significance. Thus, there are several competing and legitimate notions of value.

Also, we find the efficacy of value models varies over time, and often predictably. For instance, the effectiveness of the DDM depends on market conditions. Because the DDM discounts future dividends out to a distant horizon, it is a forward-looking model. When the market rises, investors become optimistic and extend their horizons. They are more willing to rely on DDM expectations. When the market falls, however, investors become myopic, and prefer more tangible attributes such as current yield.

In a price-inefficient market, the blind pursuit of DDM value is a questionable approach. Moreover, other value yardsticks clearly matter. We find that some rather novel implementations of value models offer substantial promise.

RISK MODELING VERSUS RETURN MODELING

While the existence of anomalies remains a puzzle for asset pricing theories, substantial progress has been made in the practice of portfolio risk control. In recent years, several equity risk models have become commercially available. Some are APT-based, and rely on factors derived empirically from historical security return covariances. These unnamed factors are sometimes related to pervasive economic forces.

Another, perhaps more common, approach relies on prespecified accounting and market-related data. Intuitive notions of risk, such as arise from company size or financial leverage, are first identified. Then, composite risk factors are formed by combining a number of underlying fundamental data items selected to capture various aspects of that type of risk. One well-known system, for instance, defines a successful firm risk factor in terms of historical price, earnings, dividend, and consensus expectational data.

Multifactor risk models work quite well for risk measurement, risk control (portfolio optimization), and related tasks such as performance analysis. Both APT and composite factors are fairly stable over time. This is desirable, because meaningful definitions of a firm's risk do not change from day to day. Hence, such measures are eminently sensible for risk-modeling purposes.

However, we find that the various components of composite factors often behave quite differently. For instance, each of the components of the successful company risk factor has a unique relationship to security returns. While historical relative price strength exhibits a strong January seasonal (because historical price weakness proxies for potential tax-loss selling), other fundamental components, such as earnings growth, have no seasonal pattern. Rather than combining these measures into one composite factor, we can model them more effectively individually.

Moreover, effects like return reversal and earnings surprise are ephemeral in nature, and thus unrelated to firm risk. Yet, they represent profitable niches in the market. These return-generating factors must be modeled individually, because their information content would be lost through aggregation. Hence, disaggregated measures are superior for return modeling. The use of numerous and narrowly defined measures permits a rich representation of the complexity of security pricing.

PURE RETURN EFFECTS

We find that pure returns to attributes can be classified into two categories. The distinction is best shown graphically. Figure 1-3 displays cumulative pure returns in excess of the market to the return-reversal and small-size effects for the period 1978 through 1987.[8] Clearly, return reversal provides very consistent payoffs, while the small-size effect does not. Our classification system relates not only to the consistency of the payoffs, but also to the inherent nature of the attributes. This will become apparent shortly.

The pure payoff to return reversal is remarkably powerful. It provided a cumulative return, gross of transaction costs, of 257 percent in excess of the market, and "worked" in the right direction over 95 percent of the time. We refer to these market niches that produce persistent rewards as "anomalous pockets of inefficiency" (APIs), because they are anomalous to the EMH and represent instances of opportunity.

API strategies can require very high portfolio turnover, because the particular stocks exhibiting the desired characteristics change constantly. Such strategies include purchasing recent lag-

F I G U R E   1–3

Cumulative Pure Returns

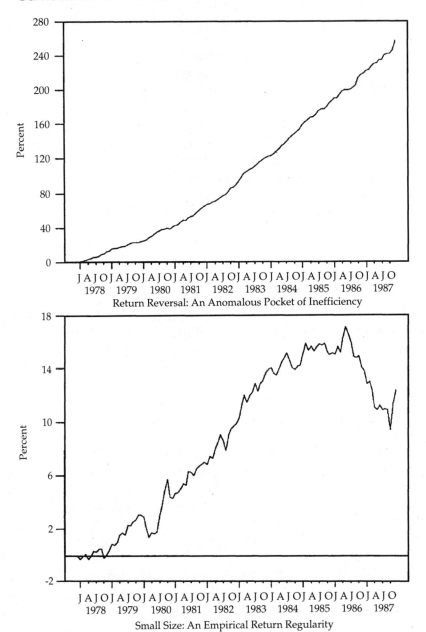

Return Reversal: An Anomalous Pocket of Inefficiency

Small Size: An Empirical Return Regularity

gards to capture return reversal, or emphasizing stocks with recent pleasant earnings surprises.

We suggest exploiting these effects as trading overlays, because no additional transaction costs are incurred if trades are to be made regardless. For instance, an investor purchasing energy stocks would benefit by focusing on recent laggards. Moreover, APIs such as return reversal can be exploited even more effectively with real-time trading strategies. APIs appear to be psychologically motivated, as we illustrate in the following paragraphs.

The pure payoff to the smaller-size attribute illustrates the second type of return effect. Unlike APIs, the payoffs to smaller size are not consistent. For instance, the pure returns were positive in 1983 but negative in 1986. While such effects are not regular to the naked eye, they are regular and predictable in a broader empirical framework, with the use of macroeconomic information. Hence, we refer to them as "empirical return regularities" (ERRs).

Because characteristics such as size are fairly stable over time, directly exploiting ERRs requires less turnover than following an API strategy. Nonetheless, optimal exploitation of ERRs, such as the size effect, still requires portfolio turnover, because small stocks should be emphasized at times and large stocks at other times.

ANOMALOUS POCKETS OF INEFFICIENCY

Return reversal relates to the concept of "noise" in security prices, that is, price movements induced by trading unrelated to fundamentals. The return-reversal effect has psychological underpinnings. Investors tend to overreact to world events and economic news, as well as to company-specific information. Moreover, technical traders exacerbate price moves by chasing short-term trends. These types of behavior lead to overshooting and subsequent reversion in stock prices.

Another API relates to the earnings estimate revisions of Wall Street security analysts. We refer to this as the "trends in analysts' earnings estimates effect," for reasons that will soon become apparent. Upward revisions in a stock's consensus earnings estimates generally are followed by outperformance, as are downward revisions by underperformance.

The trends in estimates effect may be attributable in part to slow investor reaction to earnings estimate revisions. But it also relates to the psychology of Wall Street analysts, specifically to their herd instinct. When leading analysts raise their earnings estimate for a stock, clients will buy. Secondary analysts will then follow suit, and there will be more buying pressure.

Also, individual analysts tend to be averse to forecast reversals. Suppose an analyst had been forecasting $2 of earnings per share, but now believes the best estimate to be $1. Rather than admitting to a bad forecast, the analyst often shaves the estimate by a nickel at a time and hopes no one notices.

These psychological factors give a momentum to earnings revisions. Upward revisions tend to be followed by additional revisions in the same direction. The same is true for downgrades. This persistence of estimate revisions leads to a persistence in returns.

The earnings surprise effect closely relates to the trends in estimates effect. Stocks with earnings announcements exceeding consensus expectations generally outperform, and those with earnings disappointments underperform. This API relates to the tendency for earnings surprises to repeat in the following quarter. Also, we find evidence of anticipatory revisions in analysts' estimates up to 3 months ahead of an earnings surprise, and reactive revisions up to 3 months subsequent to a surprise, so there is an interplay between earnings revisions and earnings surprises.

Another analyst bias is a chronic tendency to overestimate the earnings of growth stocks. Such optimism leads, on average, to negative surprises, or "earnings torpedoes." Conversely, stocks with low growth expectations tend, on average, to produce pleasant surprises. This analyst bias arises from cognitive misperceptions. Analysts place too much emphasis on recent trends, and consistently underestimate the natural tendency toward mean reversion. For instance, during the energy crunch in the early 1980s, many analysts predicted that oil prices would continue to rise unabated.

Year-end tax-loss selling pressure also has psychological underpinnings. We find evidence of tax-loss-taking in depressed stocks near year end, and the proceeds are often "parked" in cash until the new year. The abatement of selling pressure, combined with the reinvestment of the cash proceeds, produces a bounceback in January. Investors often defer selling winners until the new year, thereby deferring tax-gain recognition. This exerts downward pressure on winners in January.

But, waiting until year end to take losses is not optimal. Before the 1986 Tax Reform Act, the optimal tax-avoidance strategy was to realize losses short term throughout the year, prior to their becoming long term, because short-term losses sheltered more taxable income. Yet investors are loath to admit mistakes and often defer loss-taking until year end, when tax planning can be used as an excuse for closing out losing positions.

We find long-term tax-loss selling pressure to be stronger than short-term, which is surprising, given the greater tax sheltering provided by short-term losses. But it is understandable in light of the investor disposition to ride losers too long in hopes of breaking even. Investor psychology thus leads to various predictable return patterns at the turn of the year.

The turn-of-the-year effect does not arise solely from tax-motivated trading. Institutional investors often dump losers and buy winners prior to year end to "window-dress" their portfolio. Window dressing is not sensible from an investment viewpoint, but may serve to deflect embarrassing questions at the annual review.

EMPIRICAL RETURN REGULARITIES

While APIs provide persistent payoffs, ERRs, like the size effect, do not. Nevertheless, we find these effects predictable in a broader framework, with the use of macroeconomic information.

Market commentators regularly discuss the "numbers that move the market." The focus in the early 1980s was on the money supply. Today, the emphasis is on the trade deficit and foreign exchange rates. Clearly, the stock market is driven by macroeconomic news. Moreover, macroeconomic events drive returns to some equity attributes.

Consider the linkage between foreign exchange rates and the size effect. The recent and substantial Japanese investments in U.S. stocks generally have been concentrated in more esteemed, bigger companies such as IBM and Coca-Cola. Fluctuations in the dollar/yen exchange rate alter the attractiveness of U.S. stocks to Japanese investors, which affects investment flows, thereby inducing a return differential between large and small companies.

The size effect is strongly linked to the default spread between corporate and government yields. The default spread, a business cycle indicator, widens as business conditions weaken and narrows as the economy strengthens. Smaller companies are especially susceptible to business cycle risk, as they are more fragile, less diversified, and have tighter borrowing constraints than larger firms. We find small stocks perform better when business conditions are improving; the converse is true as well. Hence, the default spread is a useful macro driver for predicting the size effect.

MODELING EMPIRICAL RETURN REGULARITIES

We can illustrate the predictability of ERRs by discussing the size effect in greater detail. We utilize pure returns to smaller size, thereby avoiding the confounding associated with other cross-sectional and calendar effects related to size.

We consider a variety of forecast techniques, as they pertain to the size effect, and utilize several statistical criteria for measuring "out-of-sample" forecast accuracy [Jacobs and Levy (1989a)]. That is, we estimate our models over a portion of the historical time series, leaving a more recent holdout sample for testing predictions. This differs fundamentally from "in-sample" data fitting.

We have categorized the size effect as an ERR, which suggests that predictive models should utilize macroeconomic drivers. Thus, univariate forecasting techniques, which model only the historical returns to the size effect, are inappropriate.

Multivariate time-series techniques can take explicit account of the macroeconomic forces that drive the size effect. Multivariate approaches, like vector autoregression (VAR), model a vector, or group, of related variables. A joint modeling permits an understanding of the dynamic relationships between the size effect and macroeconomic variables.

We constructed a monthly VAR model of the size effect using six economic measures as explanatory variables: (1) low-quality (BAA) corporate bond rate, (2) long-term Treasury bond rate, (3) Treasury bill rate, (4) S&P 500 total return, (5) Industrial Production Index, and (6) Consumer Price Index. We chose these macro drivers because of their importance in security valuation. Other considerations, such as the dollar/yen exchange rate, may be helpful in modeling the size effect, but we limited our investigation to these six valuation variables.

While we found the VAR model to fit the size effect quite well in-sample, it provided poor forecasts out-of-sample. Because it has a large number of coefficients available to explain a small number of observations, a VAR model can explain historical data well. But it is likely to "overfit" the data. That is, it will fit not only systematic or stable relationships, but also random or merely circumstantial ones. The latter are of no use in forecasting, and may be misleading.[9]

One solution to the overfitting problem of vector time-series approaches is to incorporate economic theory. Such structural econometric models include only those variables and relationships suggested by theory. Simple theories, however, are no more descriptive of the economy than they are of the stock market, and structural models generally have not performed well. An alternative solution involves a novel Bayesian technique.

BAYESIAN RANDOM WALK FORECASTING

Many economic measures are difficult to predict, but their behavior can often be approximated by a random walk. A random walk model for interest rates assumes it is equally likely that rates will rise or fall. Hence, a random walk forecast of next month's interest rate would be simply this month's rate of interest.

That it is difficult to predict stock returns is no secret. But stock prices, like other economic data, can be approximated by a random walk. As early as 1900, Bachelier proposed a theory of random walks in security prices. A random walk is thus an eminently sensible first approximation, or "prior belief," for modeling security returns.[10]

Prior beliefs about the coefficients of a forecast model can be specified in many ways. One Bayesian specification imposes a random walk prior on the coefficients of a VAR model. This prior belief acts as a filter for extracting signals (meaningful relationships in the data), while leaving accidental relationships behind. Such a specification results in a powerful forecasting tool.

The results of modeling the size effect with a Bayesian random walk prior belief are displayed in Figure 1-4. The upper chart shows cumulative pure returns to small size for the period January 1982

FIGURE 1–4

Forecasting Returns to Small Size

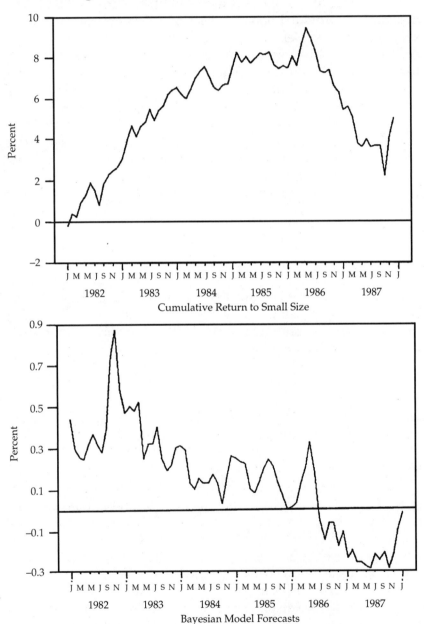

Cumulative Return to Small Size

Bayesian Model Forecasts

through December 1987. The lower chart shows out-of-sample return forecasts for 1 month ahead. The forecasts for small stocks are positive during the early years when small stocks performed well; they gradually decline and turn negative during the last 2 years, as small stocks faltered.

Moreover, the Bayesian model forecasts have statistically significant economic insight. Also, the results are quite intuitive. For instance, we find that smaller firms falter as the default spread between corporate and Treasury rates widens.

CONCLUSION

The stock market is a complex system. Simple rules, such as always buy smaller-capitalization stocks, clearly do not suffice. At the same time, the nihilism of indexing is equally unjustified.

Proper study of the market requires the judicious application of computational power. Disentangling reveals the true crosscurrents in the market. Only by exposing the underlying sources of return can we hope to understand them. And only through understanding can we hope to model and exploit them.

ENDNOTES

An expanded version of this article appears in *Managing Institutional Assets,* edited by Frank Fabozzi, Harper & Row, New York, 1990.

1. See Pagels (1988).
2. The emerging field of catastrophe theory, or "chaos," should not be confused with randomness. Chaos theory has been applied to such diverse phenomena as the motion of smoke rings and the incidence of bank failures. In fact, chaos theory is a form of complexity. Ostensibly random behavior is sometimes well defined by a series of nonlinear dynamic equations. An important characteristic of chaotic systems is that small changes in the environment can cause large, discontinuous jumps in the system. For instance, because the weather is chaotic, a butterfly stirring the air today in Japan can produce storms next month in New York.
3. As Nobel laureate Herbert Simon (1987) has asserted (p. 39), the emerging laws of economic behavior "have much more the

complexity of molecular biology than the simplicity of classical [Newtonian] mechanics."

4. Science progresses through recurring cycles of (a) conventional theory, (b) discovery of anomalies, and (c) revolution. Anomalies in the Newtonian dynamics model, for example, were resolved in 1905 by Einstein's revolutionary theory of relativity.

5. See Table I in Jacobs and Levy (1988c) for a listing of previous studies on interrelationships.

6. Time-series regressions of pure returns to attributes on market excess (of Treasury bills) returns result in significant nonzero intercepts, indicating abnormal risk-adjusted payoffs. The nonzero intercepts could be due to nonstationary risk for these attributes, but we reject this explanation based on an examination of high-order autocorrelation patterns in the pure return series. Hence, these findings are anomalous in a multifactor CAPM framework.

7. Such biases represent incidental side bets inherent in the DDM. We suggest various methods for controlling these biases in Jacobs and Levy (1989b).

8. It has often been reported that the small-size effect peaked in mid-1983. This observation is correct for naïve small size, which is a bundle of several related attributes, including low price per share and high volatility. While these attributes peaked in 1983, the pure small-size effect continued to pay off positively until 1986.

9. Vector autoregression moving-average (VARMA) models attempt to overcome the overfitting problem inherent in VAR models through a more parsimonious, or simpler, representation. But VARMA models are quite difficult to identify properly. As the number of explanatory variables increases, VARMA models face what statisticians call "the curse of higher dimensionality." In these cases, VARMA forecasting is not only extremely expensive, but also rather foolhardy.

10. Technically, a random walk model implies that successive price changes are independent draws from the same probability distribution. That is, the series of price changes has no memory and appears unpredictable. In fact, short-run stock returns are approximated well by a random walk. However, there is some evidence of a mean reversion tendency for longer-run returns.

REFERENCES

Jacobs, Bruce and Kenneth Levy. 1986. "Anomaly capture strategies." Paper presented at the Berkeley Program in Finance Seminar on the Behavior of Security Prices: Market Efficiency, Anomalies and Trading Strategies, September.

———— and ————. 1987. "Investment management: Opportunities in anomalies?" *Pension World*, February, pp. 46–47.

———— and ————. 1988*a*. "Calendar anomalies: Abnormal returns at calendar turning points." *Financial Analysts Journal* 44 (6): 28–39.

———— and ————. 1988*b*. "Disentangling equity return regularities." In *Equity Markets and Valuation Methods*. Charlottesville, Virginia: Institute of Chartered Financial Analysts.

———— and ————. 1988*c*. "Disentangling equity return regularities: New insights and investment opportunities." *Financial Analysts Journal* 44 (3): 18–43.

———— and ————. 1988*d*. "On the value of 'value.'" *Financial Analysts Journal* 44 (4): 47–62.

———— and ————. 1988*e*. "Web of 'regularities' leads to opportunity." *Pensions & Investment Age*, March 7, pp. 14–15.

———— and ————. 1989*a*. "Forecasting the size effect." *Financial Analysts Journal* 45 (3): 38–54.

———— and ————. 1989*b*. "How dividend discount models can be used to add value." In *Improving Portfolio Performance with Quantitative Models*. Charlottesville, Virginia: Institute of Chartered Financial Analysts Continuing Education Series.

———— and ————. 1989*c*. "Trading tactics in an inefficient market." In *A Complete Guide to Securities Transactions: Controlling Costs and Enhancing Performance*, Wayne Wagner, ed. New York: John Wiley.

———— and ————. 1990. "Stock market complexity and investment opportunity." In *Managing Institutional Assets*, Frank Fabozzi, ed. New York: Harper & Row.

Kuhn, Thomas. 1970. *The Structure of Scientific Revolutions*. 2d ed. Chicago: University of Chicago Press.

Pagels, Heinz. 1988. *The Dreams of Reason: The Computer and the Rise of the Sciences of Complexity*. New York: Simon & Schuster.

Simon, Herbert. 1987. "Rationality in psychology and economics." In *Rational Choice: The Contrast between Economics and Psychology*, R. Hogarth and M. Reder, eds. Chicago: University of Chicago Press.

Disentangling Equity Return Regularities

New Insights and Investment Opportunities[*]

Disentangling returns gives rise to profit opportunities.

Over the last decade, a growing body of literature has documented equity return regularities (or "anomalies") that seem contrary to the Capital Asset Pricing Model (CAPM), the Efficient Market Hypothesis (EMH), and even Arbitrage Pricing Theory (APT).[1] While some of these effects appear to represent true pockets of stock market inefficiency, others, such as the small-size effect, may be driven by the macroeconomy.

Nevertheless, a growing amount of assets has been targeted to the exploitation of various sectors of the stock market perceived to be inefficient.[2] For instance, index funds tilted toward higher-yielding or smaller-capitalization stocks have become increasingly popular in the last few years [Hawthorne (1984)]. Many active managers are also riding the anomaly bandwagon, but often in an ad hoc fashion. For example, a recent survey revealed that 29.3 percent of institutional equity managers regard low P/E as an integral part of their investment strategy (*Pensions & Investment Age,* November 10, 1986, p. 92).

Whether these equity return patterns represent true mispricing or are empirical regularities only in a broader macroeconomic framework, efficacious equity management requires that they be properly identified and measured. Unraveling their

---

[*] Originally published in *Financial Analysts Journal* 44 (3):18–44.

interrelationships is a critical part of the process. It has not yet been conclusively determined whether these effects are mere proxies for one another or whether they are independent and hence additive. This article focuses on these issues. We disentangle returns associated with 25 different anomaly measures and compare our results with earlier findings. Several interesting insights emerge. For example, previous research has generally been baffled by the presence of a January seasonal in the small-size anomaly. We find that this seasonal effect vanishes once year-end tax-loss selling is properly controlled for.

We also present substantial evidence contravening market efficiency, document significant autocorrelations in the time series of equity return effects, and analyze the relationship of these return effects to stock market returns. The findings suggest some equity strategies based on empirical return regularities.

PREVIOUS RESEARCH

Recent articles examining the interrelationships of equity return regularities generally consider only two or three anomalies at once. Unfortunately, a study drawing conclusions based on only a few explanatory variables may yield highly misleading results. For example, if one wanted to study the determinants of a person's blood pressure, one would not arbitrarily limit the explanatory variables to marital status and years of education. Other factors, such as exercise, diet, and income, are clearly important. Furthermore, many of these factors are highly correlated.

A similar situation holds for stock market return regularities. Many studies have considered the interrelationship of the size and P/E effects to determine if one subsumes the other. Is it size that really matters, or P/E, or some combination of the two effects? Or, given the high correlation between both these attributes and a firm's degree of institutional neglect, is it really neglect that drives anomalous returns, with size and P/E being mere proxies for the underlying cause [Arbel (1985)]? Any effort to disentangle size and P/E without considering and controlling for other effects is incomplete and potentially confusing. This may partially account for the high frequency of conflicting results from previous studies.

Box 2-1 categorizes and provides references for empirical studies that have examined the interrelationships of equity return regularities. Their results will be discussed in light of our findings.

B O X   2–1

INTERRELATIONSHIPS OF EQUITY RETURN REGULARITIES: SOME PREVIOUS STUDIES

SIZE AND PRICE/EARNINGS RATIO

Banz, R. and W. Breen. 1986. "Sample-dependent results using accounting and market data: Some evidence," *Journal of Finance* 41 (4): 779–793.

Basu, S. 1983. "The relationship between earnings yield, market value and return for NYSE common stocks: Further evidence." *Journal of Financial Economics* 12 (1): 129–156.

Cook, T. and M. Rozeff. 1984. "Size and earnings/price ratio anomalies: One effect or two?" *Journal of Financial and Quantitative Analysis* 19 (4): 449–466.

Goodman, D. and J. Peavy. 1986. "The interaction of firm size and price-earnings ratio on portfolio performance." *Financial Analysts Journal* 42 (1): 9–12.

Peavy, J. and D. Goodman. 1982. "A further inquiry into the market value and earnings yield anomalies." Southern Methodist University Working Paper #82–114, Dallas.

Reinganum, M. 1981. "Misspecification of capital asset pricing: Empirical anomalies based on earnings' yields and market values." *Journal of Financial Economics* 9 (1): 19–46.

SIZE AND NEGLECT

Arbel, A., S. Carvell, and P. Strebel. 1983. "Giraffes, institutions and neglected firms." *Financial Analysts Journal* 39 (3): 57–62.

Arbel, A. and P. Strebel. 1982. "The neglected and small firm effects." *Financial Review* 17 (4): 201–218.

———— and ————. 1983. "Pay attention to neglected firms." *Journal of Portfolio Management* 9 (2): 37–42.

B O X   2–1 Continued

SIZE AND JANUARY

Blume, M. and R. Stambaugh. 1983. "Biases in computed returns: An application to the size effect." *Journal of Financial Economics* 12 (3): 387–404.

Constantinides, G. 1984. "Optimal stock trading with personal taxes: Implications for prices and the abnormal January returns." *Journal of Financial Economics* 13 (1): 65–90.

Givoly, D. and A. Ovadia. 1983. "Year-end tax-induced sales and stock market seasonality." *Journal of Finance* 38 (1): 171–185.

Keim, D. 1983. "Size-related anomalies and stock return seasonality: Further empirical evidence." *Journal of Financial Economics* 12 (1): 13–32.

Keim, D. and R. Stambaugh. 1986. "Predicting returns in the stock and bond markets." *Journal of Financial Economics* 17 (2): 357–390.

Lakonishok, J. and S. Smidt. 1984. "Volume and turn-of-the-year behavior." *Journal of Financial Economics* 13 (3): 435–455.

——— and ———. 1986. "Trading bargains in small firms at year-end." *Journal of Portfolio Management* 12 (3): 24–29.

Reinganum, M. 1983. "The anomalous stock market behavior of small firms in January: Empirical tests for tax-loss selling effects." *Journal of Financial Economics* 12 (1): 89–104.

Rogalski, R. and S. Tinic. 1986. "The January size effect: Anomaly or risk mismeasurement?" *Financial Analysts Journal* 42 (6): 63–70.

Roll, R. 1983. "Vas ist das? The turn of the year effect and the return premia of small firms." *Journal of Portfolio Management* 9 (2): 18–28.

Schultz, P. 1985. "Personal income taxes and the January effect: Small firm stock returns before the War Revenue Act of 1917: A note." *Journal of Finance* 40 (1): 333–343.

SIZE AND RESIDUAL RISK

Basu, S. and S. Cheung. 1982. "Residual risk, firm size, and returns for NYSE common stocks: Some empirical evidence." McMaster University Working Paper, Montreal, January.

B O X   2–1 Continued

Lakonishok, J. and A. Shapiro. 1984. "Stock returns, beta, variance and size: An empirical analysis." *Financial Analysts Journal* 40 (4): 36–41.

Tinic, S. and R. West. 1986. "Risk, return and equilibrium: A revisit." *Journal of Political Economy* 94 (1): 127–147.

SIZE AND EARNINGS SURPRISE

Foster, G., C. Olsen, and T. Shevlin. 1984. "Earnings releases, anomalies and the behavior of security returns." *The Accounting Review* 59 (4):574–603.

Freeman, R. 1986. "The association between accounting earnings and security returns for large and small firms." CRSP Working Paper #192, Center for Research in Security Prices, University of Chicago, October.

Rendleman, R., C. Jones, and H. Latane. 1986. "Further insight into the S.U.E. anomaly: Size and serial correlation effects." University of North Carolina at Chapel Hill Working Paper, April.

SIZE, YIELD, AND CO-SKEWNESS

Cook, T. and M. Rozeff. 1982. "Size, dividend yield and co-skewness effects on stock returns: Some empirical tests." University of Iowa Working Paper #82–20, Ames.

SIZE, JANUARY, AND DAY OF THE WEEK

Keim, D. 1987. "Daily returns and size-related premiums: One more time." *Journal of Portfolio Management* 13 (2): 41–47.

Rogalski, R. 1984. "New findings regarding day-of-the-week returns over trading and non-trading periods: A note." *Journal of Finance* 39 (5): 1603–1614.

SIZE AND RETURN REVERSAL

Fama, E. and K. French. 1987. "Permanent and temporary components of stock prices." CRSP Working Paper #178, Center for Research in Security Prices, University of Chicago, February.

B O X   2–1 Continued

SIZE, JANUARY, AND NEGLECT

Barry, C. and S. Brown. 1986. "Limited information as a source of risk." *Journal of Portfolio Management* 12 (2): 66–72.

SIZE, JANUARY, AND YIELD

Keim, D. 1983. "The interrelation between dividend yields, equity values and stock returns: Implications of abnormal January returns." Ph.D. dissertation, University of Chicago, 1983.

————. 1985. "Dividend yields and stocks returns: Implications of abnormal January returns." *Journal of Financial Economics* 14: 473–489.

————. 1986. "Dividend yields and the January effect." *Journal of Portfolio Management* 12 (2): 54–60.

SIZE, NEGLECT, AND PRICE/EARNINGS RATIO

Dowen, R. and S. Bauman. 1986. "The relative importance of size, P/E, and neglect." *Journal of Portfolio Management* 12 (3): 30–34.

SIZE, NEGLECT, PRICE/EARNINGS RATIO, AND JANUARY

Arbel, A. 1985. "Generic stocks: An old product in a new package." *Journal of Portfolio Management* 11 (4): 4–13.

PRICE/EARNINGS RATIO AND RESIDUAL RISK

Goodman, D. and J. Peavy. 1985. "The risk universal nature of the P/E effect." *Journal of Portfolio Management* 11 (4): 14–16.

PRICE/EARNINGS RATIO, CONTROVERSY, AND NEGLECT

Carvell, S. and P. Strebel. 1984. "A new beta incorporating analysts' forecasts." *Journal of Portfolio Management* 11 (1): 81–85.

PRICE/EARNINGS RATIO AND PRICE/SALES RATIO

Senchack, A. and J. Martin. 1987. "The relative performance of the PSR and PER investment strategies." *Financial Analysts Journal* 43 (2): 46–56.

B O X   2–1 Concluded

PRICE/EARNINGS RATIO AND NEGLECT

Dowen, R. and S. Bauman. 1984. "A test of the relative importance of popularity and price-earnings ratio in determining abnormal returns." *Journal of the Midwest Finance Association* 13 (1): 34–47.

YIELD AND LOW PRICE

Elton, E., M. Gruber, and J. Rentzler. 1981. "A simple examination of the empirical relationship between dividend yields and deviations from the CAPM." New York University Working Paper #240, August.

DAY OF THE WEEK AND TIME OF THE DAY

Harris, L. 1986a. "A transaction data study of weekly and intradaily patterns in stock returns." *Journal of Financial Economics* 16 (1): 99–117.

———. 1986b. "How to profit from intradaily stock returns." *Journal of Portfolio Management* 12 (2): 61–64.

Smirlock, M. and L. Starks. 1986. "Day-of-the-week and intraday effects in stock returns." *Journal of Financial Economics* 17 (1): 197–210.

EARNINGS SURPRISE AND TRENDS IN ANALYSTS' EARNINGS ESTIMATES

Arnott, R. 1985. "The use and misuse of consensus earnings." *Journal of Portfolio Management* 11 (3): 18–27.

Benesh, G. and P. Peterson. 1986. "On the relation between earnings changes, analysts' forecasts and stock price fluctuations." *Financial Analysts Journal* 42 (6): 29–39.

RESIDUAL RISK AND JANUARY

Gultekin, M. and B. Gultekin. 1987. "Stock returns and the tests of the APT." *Journal of Finance* 42 (5): 1213–1224.

Tinic, S. and R. West. 1986. "Risk, return and equilibrium: A revisit." *Journal of Political Economy* 94 (1): 126–147.

In addition to studies of equity return interrelationships in the U.S. stock market, a small but growing body of literature has considered foreign stock market anomaly interrelationships.[3] International studies are especially useful for gaining perspective on the January/size connection, because tax laws (hence optimal trading strategies) vary widely across countries.

Some major multifactor studies of the U.S. equity market consider multiple factors (such as industry affiliation or financial leverage) that have strong cross-sectional explanatory power for returns within a month.[4] Some of these factors may also be anomalous in that they have provided accumulating payoffs over time. The first of these models, developed by BARRA over a decade ago, is widely used in the investment community [see Rosenberg and Marathe (1976) and Rudd and Clasing (1982)].[5] Two other multifactor models by Sharpe (1982) and Reid (1982) study a much longer time span, but lack data on accounting-based factors such as P/E.[6] We present a comprehensive analysis of equity return regularities in the spirit of these multifactor studies.

Because our analysis is based on monthly returns, we do not consider "faster" time-related anomalies, such as time-of-the-day, day-of-the-week, and week-of-the-month effects, despite evidence of their interrelationships with anomalies we do consider [see Jacobs and Levy (1988 and 1989)]. Prior research has indicated, for example, that: (1) much of the size effect occurs on Fridays [Keim (1987)], (2) much of the size effect occurs in the first few trading days of January [Keim (1983a) and Roll (1983b)], and (3) time-of-day and day-of-the-week effects interact [Harris (1986a and 1986b) and Smirlock and Starks (1986)].

Some recent empirical work ties several seemingly unrelated anomalies to the human disposition to delay announcing bad news [Penman (1987)]. This tendency may partially account for three anomalies:

1. The day-of-the-week effect may relate to management's disposition to delay reporting bad news until after the market closes, especially over the weekend. This bunching of negative news would help explain weak Friday-to-Monday returns.

2. The week-of-the-month effect may relate to management's proclivity for announcing good earnings reports quickly (generally during the first 2 weeks of a calendar month) and sitting on bad reports longer.

3. Because companies long overdue for an earnings announcement may be delaying the release of bad news, there might be a "late reporter" anomaly, whereby late announcements are often negative and cause a price decline.

RETURN REGULARITIES WE CONSIDER

In this section, we describe briefly each return regularity considered in this article. The method of constructing and normalizing each measure is explained more fully in the next section.

Low P/E. It has been well documented that stocks with lower price/earnings ratios tend to outperform those with higher P/E ratios.[7] We used the reciprocal of P/E, E/P, measured as the trailing year's fully diluted earnings divided by price. This measure allowed us to accommodate negative and zero earnings in a continuous fashion.

Small size. Smaller size has a pronounced correlation with future performance.[8] We found, as did many previous researchers, that the effect is roughly linear in the log of size. Hence we used the negative of the natural log of market capitalization.

Dividend yield. Because U.S. tax law has treated capital gains more favorably than dividends, taxable investors may have demanded a higher pretax return on higher-yielding stocks to compensate for the increased tax liability. (Even under the Tax Reform Act of 1986, taxes on capital gains are not taxed until realized, although they no longer enjoy a preferential rate.) Alternatively, investors may have a psychological preference for cash dividends.[9] There are conflicting empirical studies on these propositions.[10] In addition, zero-yielding stocks have been shown to have unusually high returns, especially in January.[11] We used a dividend-divided-by-price measure, as well as a binary indicator of zero yield, to model these relationships.

Neglect. Neglected stocks have tended to outperform the market [see, for example, Arbel (1985)].[12] Neglect has been modeled by measures of institutional ownership, the intensity of Wall Street security analyst coverage, and the extent of information availability. We used the negative of the natural log of one plus the number of analysts.

Low price. Some researchers have found low-priced stocks to produce extra rewards [Blume and Husic (1973), Bachrach and Galai (1979), and Edmister and Greene (1980)].[13] The measure we used is the negative of the natural log of price.

Book/price. Stocks with high book value in relation to price have outperformed the market [Rosenberg, Reid, and Lanstein (1985)]. We used common equity per share divided by price to measure this effect.

Sales/price. Some have suggested that sales/price may be superior to E/P as an investment criterion.[14] We use the trailing year's sales per share divided by price, relative to the capitalization-weighted average sales/price for that stock's industry. This is the only variable we calculated as an industry relative, because of: (1) the enormous disparity across industries for this particular measure and (2) the looser theoretical link between sales and value than between earnings or dividends and value across industries.

Cashflow/price. It can be argued that, because of disparate accounting practices, cashflow is superior to earnings as a measure of value.[15] The definition we used is trailing year's earnings plus depreciation and deferred taxes per share divided by price.

Sigma. The CAPM maintains that only systematic (or undiversifiable) risk should be rewarded. But many studies have found an apparent compensation for unsystematic risk.[16] Such risk is often referred to as *residual risk,* or *sigma.* We calculated sigma as the standard error of estimate, or dispersion of error terms, from a rolling historical 60-month regression of excess stock return (that is, return over the Treasury bill rate) on the S&P 500 excess return.

Beta. The finance literature is replete with empirical tests of the CAPM. Many findings on the reward to bearing systematic risk have been contrary to theory [see Tinic and West (1986)]. We included a historical beta measure in our model, not merely for risk adjustment, but also to explore the payoff to beta when controlling for multiple anomalies. We calculated beta for each security from the rolling 60-month regression described previously. We then applied Vasicek's (1973) Bayesian adjustment, in light of the well-known tendency of historical betas to regress over time toward the mean [see Klemkosky and Martin (1975)].

Co-skewness. Investors may prefer positive skewness in their portfolios. Because the market has positive skewness, investors might pay more for securities having positive co-skewness with the market [Kraus and Litzenberger (1976), Friend and Westerfield (1980), and Barone-Adesi (1985)].[17] We calculated co-skewness on a rolling 60-month basis as follows:

$$\sum \frac{(R_i - \overline{R}_i)(R_m - \overline{R}_m)^2}{\sum (R_m - \overline{R}_m)^3}$$

where R_i is stock excess return, R_m is the S&P 500 excess return, and $\overline{R}_i$ and $\overline{R}_m$ are rolling 60-month arithmetic averages.

Earnings controversy. Some maintain that stocks with more uncertainty about future prospects produce superior returns, perhaps as compensation for information deficiency or even as a proxy for systematic risk [Cragg and Malkiel (1982), Arnott (1983), and Carvell and Strebel (1984)]. We used the standard deviation of next year's analysts' earnings estimates normalized by stock price.

Trends in analysts' earnings estimates. There is substantial empirical support for the proposition that stocks whose earnings estimates have been recently upgraded by analysts tend to produce abnormal returns [Hawkins, Chamberlin, and Daniel (1984), Kerrigan (1984), Arnott (1985), and Benesh and Peterson (1986)]. Some possible explanations are imperfect information dissemination and the psychology of Wall Street analysts (notably, their "herd instinct" and aversion to substantial earnings-estimate revisions). We

measured the trend separately for each of the three most
recently completed months as the change in next fiscal year's
consensus estimate normalized as a percentage of stock price
(rather than normalized by earnings), to avoid problems
caused by near-zero or negative divisors. By employing three
distinct monthly lags, we could observe the time decay in
information content.

Earnings surprise. Stocks that have experienced recent
earnings surprises tend to produce abnormal returns.[18]
Reasons advanced include imperfect information
propagation, a tendency for surprises to repeat quarter to
quarter, and analysts' inclination to be reactive to earnings
announcements. We measured surprises separately for each
of the three most recent calendar months, calculated as the
difference between the actual earnings announcement and
the consensus estimate on that date, normalized by stock
price. Again, by using three monthly lags, we could observe
the time decay in information content.

The "earnings torpedo" effect. Stocks expected to have high
future earnings growth may be more susceptible to negative
surprises (or "torpedoes"); those with low expected earnings
may be more likely to experience positive surprises. There is
some empirical support for the proposition that low-
expectation stocks on average outperform their high-
expectation counterparts [Rainville (1983), Hagin (1984), and
Benesh and Peterson (1986), Table V]. We used the change
from the earnings per share last reported to next year's
consensus estimate and normalized by stock price.

Relative strength. Market technicians have long claimed that
the market is not efficient, even in the "weak-form" sense
(that is, past prices alone may have predictive content). Some
recent studies support the investment merit of relative price
strength, while finding perverse results for 1-month relative
strength and for January.[19] The measure we used is the alpha
intercept from our rolling 60-month beta regression.

Residual reversal. As noted, near-term relative price strength
tends to reverse. This effect is not an artifact of pricing errors,
bid/ask spreads, or infrequent trading, and it may persist for

up to 2 months.[20] We examined the predictive power of residuals (from our beta regression) separately, for each of the previous 2 months, to study the decay pattern.

January. From as early as 1942, studies have documented the effects of year-end tax-loss selling on January returns.[21] Some have found investors' behavior to be irrational in light of traditional finance theory; others have sought novel explanations for the observed effects.[22] In addition, recent studies have documented January seasonals in returns to small size, neglect, dividend yield, P/E, and sigma, as listed in Box 2-1. We utilized separate proprietary measures of potential long-term and short-term tax-loss selling pressure for each stock. These were designed to capture price rebounds in January after year-end tax-loss selling abates. We also examined the January versus rest-of-year behavior of all our measures in light of the substantial previous evidence.

Methodology

Two common methodologies have been applied in previous anomaly research. The first, which often implicitly assumes a stationary return-generating process, usually groups stocks into portfolios based on a particular characteristic such as firm size.[23] Time-series regressions of each group's returns on the market are followed by an analysis of portfolios' regression intercepts to test for significant differences. If this approach is extended to cross-classification on two anomalies, however, care must be taken to randomize the experimental design [see, for example, Basu (1983)]. Such an approach becomes unwieldy as the number of anomalies to be studied increases.

The second methodology involves cross-sectional regressions of returns on predetermined attributes. Here, a stationary generating process need not be presumed. The return observations can be either on a stock-by-stock basis or on a portfolio basis. Grouping reduces dimensionality, which may permit application of Zellner's (1962) seemingly unrelated regression model (SURM).[24] It has been demonstrated, however, that results can be sensitive to the grouping procedure.[25] In any case, with a large number of anomalies studied simultaneously, grouping becomes intractable.[26]

We modeled the return regularities linearly and utilized cross-sectional regression analysis (as did the previously cited multifactor studies).[27] For each month from January 1978 through December 1986, we ran a generalized least-squares (GLS) regression for our universe of the 1500 largest-capitalization stocks. The dependent variable was excess return for each security; the independent variables were its anomaly exposures, normalized as described later in this section. We calculated the GLS weights, updated monthly, as the squared reciprocal of each stock's residual risk, as measured by sigma; each stock's weight was limited to a maximum of 10 times and a minimum of one-tenth the average GLS weight.

The use of GLS produces more statistically efficient estimates than ordinary least-squares regression in the presence of heteroscedasticity [Theil (1971), Chapter 6]. Intuitively, stocks that exhibit relatively lower residual risk have a higher percentage of their returns explained by anomalies, hence greater estimation accuracy is achieved by placing more weight on them. Because higher residual risk is correlated with small size, GLS weights generally lie between capitalization and equal weights.

Data errors, especially in historical prices, can cause severe problems.[28] Our data were examined for extreme outliers. A normalization and truncation process, described later, diminished this concern. Additionally, we lagged the price used to calculate anomalies, such as P/E, by 1 month. By lagging price, we controlled for spurious returns to low-P/E stocks that would otherwise result if a price were incorrect one month and correct the next [see Rosenberg, Reid, and Lanstein (1985).] Also, by lagging price we avoided the accidental capture of bid/ask spreads in our estimates of anomaly payoffs.[29] Lagging price does induce a slightly conservative bias to the payoffs of price-related anomalies, because the price used to construct each is slightly stale.

We also controlled for survivorship bias. If the population is defined retrospectively as those companies that survived and prospered, then bankrupt, merged, and shrinking firms are omitted from the analysis. This can severely bias the results. Additionally, we controlled for look-ahead bias. If one constructs P/E using earnings that were as yet unknown, because of announcement lags, a positive return bias is induced for low-P/E stocks. To control for this bias, we lagged all accounting variables 3 months. Thus, the P/E for IBM as of 12/31/80 was calculated using its price as of 11/30/80 and its earnings as of 9/30/80. Another deficiency that several anomaly studies suffer from is the arbitrary restriction to companies with December fiscal years. Such a constraint, imposed for computational simplicity, may induce industry and other biases.[30]

We normalized each measure (including beta) by subtracting its capitalization-weighted average and dividing by its cross-sectional standard deviation, with outliers truncated.[31] The payoff coefficients to each anomaly were thus scaled consistently. Each coefficient, or return attribution, represents the marginal return to a stock with an exposure to that factor of 1 cross-sectional standard deviation. For example, if the distribution of book/price across stocks in a particular month has a capitalization-weighted average of 1.1 and a standard deviation of 0.2, then an attribution of −0.15 implies that a stock with a book/price ratio of 1.3 (that is, a book/price ratio 1 standard deviation higher than the capitalization-weighted average of book/price) would have underperformed the market by 15 basis points that month. This analysis assumes neutral (or average market) exposures to all other anomalies.

In addition to normalized anomaly measures, we included a zero-yield indicator in the form of a binary dummy variable. In total, we have 25 anomaly measures. We also used binary variables to assign each company to one of 38 industries, based on Standard Industry Classification (SIC) code. The binary industry variables were utilized to purify anomaly return attributions from the impact of industry return comovement. (As noted, industry assignments were also used to calculate industry-relative sales/price ratios.) Payoffs to the binary variables have the simple interpretation of being the marginal return arising from that attribute.

THE RESULTS ON RETURN REGULARITIES

We ran two sets of GLS cross-sectional regressions of excess stock return on normalized anomaly measures for the 108-month period from January 1978 to December 1986. The first set consisted of 25 univariate cross-sectional regressions each month, treating each of our measures individually. The second set consisted of 1 multivariate cross-sectional regression each month, treating all 25 anomaly and 38 industry variables simultaneously.

The multivariate regressions measure all anomaly and industry effects jointly, thereby "purifying" each effect so that it is independent of other effects. We refer to the multivariate return attributions as "pure" returns and to the univariate attributions as "naïve" returns. The univariate regressions naïvely measure only one anomaly at a time, with no effort to control for other related effects. A single anomaly will often be a proxy for several related effects; a multivariate anomaly framework properly attributes return to its underlying sources.

Table 2-1 presents summary statistics for the monthly cross-sectional regressions over the period January 1978 to December 1986. The average monthly return and associated t-statistic for each anomaly are shown in both naïve and pure forms.[32] A paired t-test on the difference between naïve and pure returns is also displayed.[33] In several instances (notably residual reversals), the difference in returns is significant. These differences are due to the substantial proxying that muddies the waters in simple univariate regressions because of omitted-variable bias [see Kmenta (1971) pp. 392–395). A regression of return on just cashflow/price, for example, may unintentionally pick up part of the low-P/E effect, as the average correlation between a stock's cashflow/price and earnings/price ratios is 0.65 for our sample.

The use of multivariate regression to disentangle highly correlated effects may, however, raise the specter of multicollinearity. Does our use of so many closely related regressors somehow cause inefficiency, or are potential problems obviated by our large sample size? One simple diagnostic test is a comparison of the time-series standard deviation of payoffs to each naïve versus pure anomaly. Because "both strategies have the same standardized exposure . . . a reduction in time-series variability can occur only if the risk reduction from immunizing the effects of other common factors has exceeded the risk increase due to higher specific variance" [Rosenberg, Reid, and Lanstein (1985), p. 14].[34] In fact, the time-series risk of all 25 anomalies is lower in the multivariate regression, often by over 50 percent. Thus multicollinearity is not a serious problem.

P/E and Size Effects

The results displayed in Table 2-1 reveal significant return regularities during the period studied. First, low P/E paid off handsomely, on average, from 1978 to 1986. The naïve return attribution aver-

TABLE 2–1

Monthly Average Returns to Anomalies

Anomaly	Naïve Anomaly Monthly Average (%)	Naïve Anomaly t-Statistic	Pure Anomaly Monthly Average (%)	Pure Anomaly t-Statistic	Differential (Pure–Naïve) Monthly Average (%)	Differential (Pure–Naïve) t-Statistic
Low P/E	0.59	3.4**	0.46	4.7**	−0.13	−1.4
Small size	0.15	2.3*	0.12	2.7**	−0.03	−0.7
Yield	−0.01	−0.1	0.03	0.5	0.04	0.4
Zero yield	0.00	0.0	0.15	1.3	0.15	0.6
Neglect	0.14	1.9*	0.10	1.7*	−0.04	−0.7
Low price	−0.01	−0.1	0.01	0.2	0.02	0.3
Book/price	0.17	1.4	0.09	1.2	−0.08	−0.7
Sales/price	0.17	3.1**	0.17	3.7**	−0.01	−0.2
Cash/price	0.36	2.7**	0.04	0.6	−0.32	−2.3*
Sigma	0.16	0.6	0.07	0.6	−0.09	−0.4
Beta	−0.01	−0.0	0.04	0.3	0.05	0.4
Co-skewness	0.09	0.6	0.04	0.7	−0.05	−0.3
Controversy	−0.33	−2.1*	−0.05	−0.8	0.27	2.0*
Trend in estimates (−1)	0.48	4.8**	0.51	8.1**	0.03	0.3
Trend in estimates (−2)	0.40	4.4**	0.28	4.9**	−0.12	−1.3
Trend in estimates (−3)	0.29	3.0**	0.19	3.8**	−0.10	−1.3
Earnings surprise (−1)	0.44	2.1*	0.48	3.7**	0.04	0.2
Earnings surprise (−2)	0.47	1.8*	0.18	0.8	−0.28	−1.8*
Earnings surprise (−3)	−0.03	−0.1	−0.21	−1.1	−0.18	−1.0
Earnings torpedo	−0.00	−0.0	−0.10	−1.7*	−0.10	−1.2
Relative strength	0.30	1.4	0.34	3.5**	0.04	0.3
Residual reversal (−1)	−0.54	−4.9**	−1.08	−17.8**	−0.54	−7.3**
Residual reversal (−2)	−0.13	−1.4	−0.37	−8.1**	−0.23	−3.3**
Short-term tax	−0.08	−0.4	−0.04	−0.4	0.04	0.3
Long-term tax	−0.29	−1.6	−0.00	−0.1	0.28	1.7*

*Significant at the 10 percent level.
**Significant at the 1 percent level.

aged 59 basis points per month, while the pure return attribution averaged 46 basis points. The naïve return to low P/E was confounded by other related effects such as sales/price. Because the payoff to sales/price was positive for this period, part of it, and other related effects, was unintentionally picked up by the naïve low-P/E anomaly.

Despite the lower average return of the pure low-P/E series, its *t*-statistic of 4.7 was higher than the 3.4 of the naïve series; this can be attributed to its greater consistency. While the pure return was positive in 76 out of 108 months, or 70.4 percent of the time, the naïve return was positive in only 70 months, or 64.8 percent of the time. Also, the volatility of the pure low-P/E series, as measured by standard deviation, was 1.01 percent, while that of the naïve series was 1.82 percent.

Because *t*-statistics this large would be expected to occur by chance alone much less than 1/100th of the time if P/E truly did not matter, we conclude that low P/E is a statistically significant effect at the 1 percent confidence level. The significance of the pure return to low P/E, furthermore, refutes the assertion that low P/E is merely a surrogate for some other effect such as size or neglect.[35]

While pure returns to low P/E were significant, on average, over the period studied, there were, nonetheless, stretches when these pure returns were negative. For instance, Figure 2-1, which illustrates the cumulative pure payoff to low P/E, shows negative returns from mid-1982 to early 1984. It appears that the low-P/E effect has been unstable.[36]

The small-size effect was also more significant, on average, in its pure than in its naïve form, albeit with a slightly lower average monthly return of 12 basis points versus 15 for the naïve effect. The existence of a size effect in its pure form demonstrates that small size is not just a proxy for some other underlying effect.[37]

While pure returns to small size peaked in 1984, as illustrated in Figure 2-2, naïve returns to size peaked earlier, in 1983. This divergence may be caused by naïve returns to size picking up some of the low-price effect, which also peaked in 1983 (as discussed later). Additionally, the lack of persistence in returns to small size may be evidence of nonstationarity.[38] Furthermore, the size effect and other return regularities may be related to macroeconomic events.[39]

F I G U R E   2–1

Cumulative Return to Low Price/Earnings

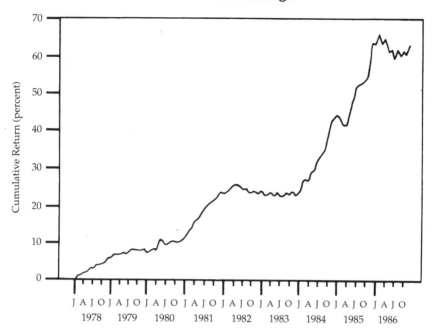

Yield, Neglect, Price, and Risk

Yield and zero yield on average were not statistically significant over this period. However, a clearer picture emerges when January seasonals are examined (as discussed later).

Neglect was a significant effect both in its naïve form, where it added an average of 14 basis points per month, and in its pure form, where it added 10. Because the neglect effect survives the purification process, it appears to exist independently of the low-P/E and small-size anomalies.

We found no significant accumulation of returns to low price over the period. This is in contrast to previous research on naïve returns to low price, as well as Reid's (1982) finding of a significant effect in his multifactor model. The difference is due primarily to our use of a more recent sample period. We observed significant naïve and pure return accumulations from this effect until mid-1983, but

F I G U R E   2–2

Cumulative Return to Small Size

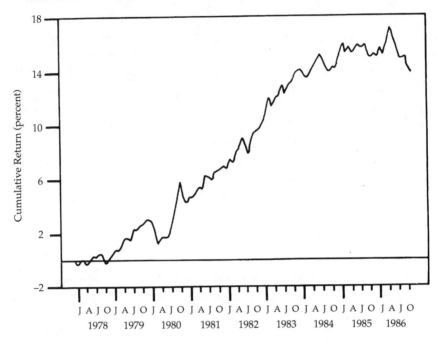

decumulations thereafter. Another reason may be our practice of lagging price 1 month, which abstracts return attributions from pricing errors and bid/ask spread biases. The low-price measure is especially sensitive to such problems.

Both naïve and pure returns to book/price had the expected positive sign, but did not achieve statistical significance. While this might appear surprising in view of the research by Rosenberg, Reid, and Lanstein (1985), which highlighted the power of book/price, it is consistent with the BARRA finding that the introduction of sales/price and cashflow/price measures significantly weakens the return attribution to book/price.[40]

Sales/price experienced a strong payoff. Both naïve and pure returns averaged 17 basis points monthly, significant at the 1 percent confidence level. Conversely, the 36 basis point naïve return to cashflow/price dissipated in the multivariate anomaly setting (as evidenced by the significant differential-returns t-test), indicating that it acted as a surrogate for other factors, primarily low P/E, in the univariate regression.

Sigma, beta, and co-skewness all had negligible average monthly payoffs. While these measures do not accumulate over time, they generally have statistically significant cross-sectional explanatory power within a month, thereby further purifying return attributions to other effects. The lack of any cumulative return to beta during one of the most extended bull markets in history is especially interesting. While seemingly inconsistent with the CAPM (which is couched, however, in expectational terms), it is not inconsistent with other empirical findings.[41] Figure 2-3 illustrates the cumulative pure payoff to beta. These returns appear unstable, as they cumulate positively in the early years and negatively in the later years. This change in trend may be evidence of nonstationarity.[42]

Stocks with controversial earnings prospects did poorly in a naïve sense and produced insignificant results in a pure sense. This is inconsistent with the previous research on controversy, which demonstrated a positive naïve payoff. It is, however, another illustration that for the period we considered, there was an absence of ex post compensation for bearing many forms of risk.

Trends and Reversals

Trends in analysts' estimates for individual stocks emerge as powerfully in their pure form as in their naïve form. Thus, it is not true, for example, that this anomaly is due to any tendency of analysts systematically to underestimate and then upgrade estimates on low-P/E stocks (in which case it might merely be a proxy for low P/E). Figure 2-4 plots cumulative pure payoffs to analyst revisions made 1, 2, and 3 months previously. While there is a marked decay in the value of this measure over time (as evidenced by the t-statistics, which decline from 8.1 to 4.9 to 3.8), even 3-month-old data are significant at the 1 percent level.

Returns to earnings surprise exhibit a quicker decay than do returns to analyst revisions. Only 1-month-old surprises were statistically significant in their pure form; by the time surprises were 3 months old, results were perverse. Naïve returns to earnings surprise were significant for 2 monthly lags.

F I G U R E   2–3

Cumulative Return to Beta

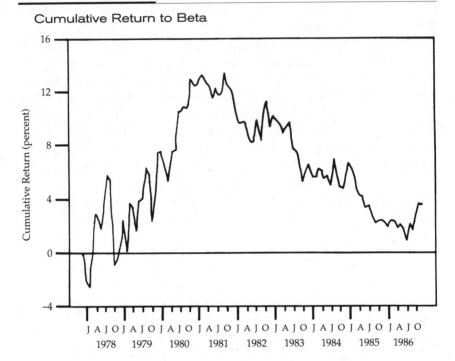

Our univariate regression provided no evidence of a torpedo stock effect. The pure effect was present, however, and with the predicted sign. There was a statistically significant and negative pure average monthly payoff of 10 basis points to higher predicted earnings growth.

Relative strength paid off handsomely. Its pure return of 34 basis points per month was strongly significant statistically in the multivariate regression. Reid's (1982) multifactor model included a 1-year relative-strength measure that was also quite powerful. Sharpe's (1982) multifactor relative-strength measure, a 60-month alpha similar to ours, had negative return attribution, perhaps because of the absence of related measures, such as residual reversal.

Residual reversal turned out to be by far the most powerful effect we found, especially in the multivariate regression. The *t*-statis-

F I G U R E   2-4

Cumulative Return to Trends in Earnings Estimates

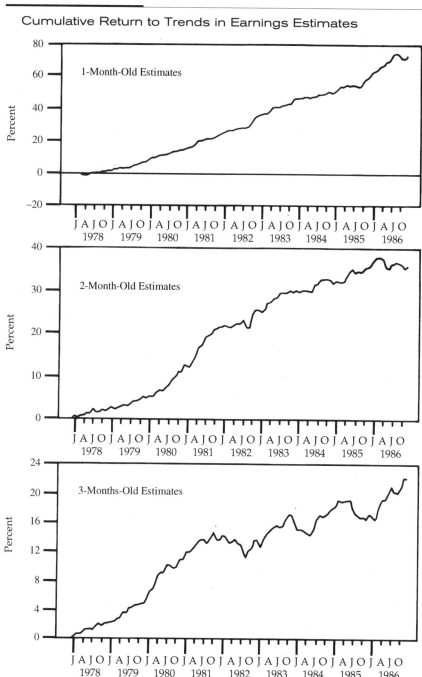

tic of 17.8 for 1-month reversals is in line with the findings of previous researchers.[43] The paired t-test on differential returns showed a significant increase in the strength of pure versus naïve residual reversal. Pure returns to residual reversal emerged more powerfully, because related effects such as earnings surprise were disentangled. Figure 2-5 illustrates cumulative returns to 1- and 2-month-old residual returns. The negative payoffs demonstrate the strong tendency for these residuals to reverse partially over the next 2 months. The relative stability of returns to these measures over time is in marked contrast to the less regular patterns noted in some of the earlier figures.

Reid's multifactor model considered 1-month and 1-quarter returns subsequent to a 1-month-old residual and found a roughly equal reversal after either holding period. Rosenberg and Rudd (1982) examined 1- and 2-month-old reversals separately and found persistence from 2 months ago to be about 26 percent as strong as that from 1 month ago. We found reversal persistence from 2 months ago to be about 34 percent as strong as that from 1 month ago. We can reconcile our results and those of Rosenberg-Rudd with Reid's as follows: We found that the 3-month-old residual had a payoff about equal in magnitude and opposite in sign to the 2-month-old residual; thus the total 1-quarter return examined by Reid should be of roughly the same magnitude as his 1-month return, as months 2 and 3 cancel each other out.

Finally, on average, there was no significant payoff to our tax measures. A clearer picture of tax effects emerges, however, when we examine the January effect.

The time series of returns to our 38 industries exhibited nothing unusual. Seven industries had average returns that were significantly different from zero at the 10 percent level, versus the four that would be expected by chance alone. Only one (media) was significant at the 1 percent level, perhaps because of the recent wave of takeovers in that industry. Also, a cluster analysis of returns to industries revealed expected patterns such as the existence of an interest rate sensitive financial sector.[44] Furthermore, the industry return series appear to be related to macroeconomic events. For example, returns to the most volatile industry, precious metals, were closely related to gold prices.

F I G U R E 2–5

Cumulative Return to Residual Reversal

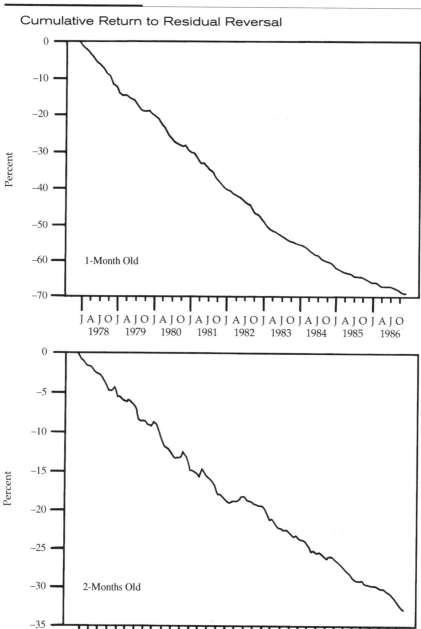

Some Implications

How much explanatory power does our multivariate anomaly framework possess? The average R-squared from our 108 monthly cross-sectional regressions was 39 percent.[45] (Adjusted for degrees of freedom used up by all our measures, the variance explained was 36 percent.) This corresponds very favorably with the R-squared of 10 percent achieved by Sharpe's model [Sharpe (1982), p. 9].[46]

To summarize, there is strong evidence that the stock market was rife with return regularities during the period from 1978 to 1986. Our evidence documents several statistically significant and independent return regularities, which often differed substantially from their naïve manifestations. The failure of beta to be priced is further evidence that conventional theory is unable to explain observed stock returns.

The EMH is strongly contradicted. We examined only publicly available information. Thus, we do not test directly the contention that the market is "strong-form" efficient—that is, that prices fully reflect all information (including private or "insider" information). We are, however, able to reject narrower definitions of efficiency, which is even more indicative of market inefficiency. Consider, for instance, the predictive power of the measure of trends in analysts' earnings estimates, which documents "semistrong" inefficiency; that is, prices do not fully and instantaneously reflect all publicly available information. The ability of residual reversal, which is derived solely from past returns, to explain future returns represents prima facie evidence that the stock market is weak-form inefficient: Past prices alone have predictive power.

The significant return accumulations to our purified anomalies independently add to the weight of evidence contravening the EMH. The same cannot be said of previous studies. For instance, separate studies of trends in analysts' estimates and earnings surprise do not represent independent evidence of inefficiency, because these effects are closely related and may proxy for one another.

While some anomalies provided consistent excess performance, month by month, others were less stable in nature. The stationarity of some return effects is questionable. Granted, many of these return regularities have been exhibited as far back as data are available. Also, the underlying causes, such as institutional features of the stock market and the quirks of human nature, are slow to change.[47] An issue of vital concern to investors is whether the returns to anomalies were of sufficient magnitude and stability to have been exploitable for profit, net of transaction costs.

The costs of trading consist of both market impact and commissions. As a first approximation, market impact is a function of a stock's market capitalization, while commission (expressed as a percentage) is a function of stock price. Recall that capitalization and price are two of the factors we control for in our multivariate regression. Hence payoffs to other anomalies, such as low P/E, represent the return to a low-P/E stock that has average market size and price. In other words, our return attribution to low P/E can be captured, on average, by trading stocks of average price and size, implying approximately average transaction costs.

The various return regularities studied obviously require differing amounts of trading to maintain a given portfolio exposure. At one extreme, heavy monthly trading would be necessary to maintain a big portfolio bet on residual reversal. Conversely, relatively little trading would be needed to maintain a more stable characteristic, such as small size.

Although not reported here, there is substantial evidence that "anomaly capture strategies" have the potential to generate above-market returns (net of transaction costs) that are both economically and statistically significant [Jacobs and Levy (1986)]. These strategies are designed to utilize Stein-James estimators, which are superior to historical averages as estimates of true payoffs to anomalies. This estimation technique, sometimes referred to as *Empirical Bayes,* is applicable when the number of measures to be estimated exceeds two, and works better the larger the number of measures.[48] Such diversified anomaly exploitation strategies can also benefit from the January effect, which is discussed in the next section.

JANUARY VERSUS REST-OF-YEAR RETURNS

As mentioned earlier, several studies have found significant January seasonals in the returns to anomalies. Our findings transcend much of the previous work because of our substantial purification and our careful abstraction from both potential long-term and short-term tax-loss selling pressure.

Table 2-2 displays the average monthly returns and associated *t*-statistics for each attribute, in both naïve and pure form, for January and non-January months. Also shown is a difference-of-means test for January versus non-January months.[49]

Our findings of significantly different January versus non-January naïve returns to small size, low price, book/price, sales/price, earnings controversy, and tax measures agree with earlier anomaly studies.[50] For neglect, however, while the difference-of-means test showed no January seasonal at even a 10 percent significance level, the average January return of 53 basis points is significantly nonzero.[51] Our results for naïve returns to yield (including zero yield), sigma, and relative strength, although not statistically significant, are in accord with earlier reported results.[52]

Of all the naïve anomaly results displayed in Table 2-2, only low P/E is at variance with some of the previous studies, which found low P/E to be more powerful in January than in other months [see, for example, Cook and Rozeff (1984)]. This difference may arise from our use of a more recent time period than those used in previous studies.

Purifying anomalies and controlling for potential tax-loss selling in our multivariate regressions reveals several noteworthy features. The January yield effect, including zero yield, remains powerful and strongly nonlinear in our multivariate framework. Interestingly, the significant January return attributable to zero-yield stocks is not subsumed by sigma, small size, low price, or other related attributes.

The pure January seasonals for low price and book/price are attenuated in magnitude compared with their naïve counterparts, while the pure January seasonals for small size, sales/price, and earnings controversy vanish completely. Perhaps the most striking result in Table 2-2 relates to small size. While the naïve January return to smallness of 57 basis points is significantly different from the non-January naïve return of 11 basis points, the pure returns to smallness exhibit no discernible seasonality. Apparently, the January size seasonal observed by the researchers cited in Box 2-1 is merely a proxy for tax-related effects.

While both pure tax-effect measures are significant in January, the long-term tax-loss measure has a rebound effect of 78 basis points, about twice the magnitude of the short-term measure. This

TABLE 2-2

Monthly Average Returns to Anomalies: January versus Non-January

Anomaly	Naive Anomaly					Pure Anomaly				
	Average January (%)	t-Statistic	Average Non-January (%)	t-Statistic	t-Statistic of Difference	Average January (%)	t-Statistic	Average Non-January (%)	t-Statistic	t-Statistic of Difference
Low P/E	0.19	0.3	0.63	4.0**	−0.9	0.09	0.5	0.49	4.7**	−1.1
Small size	0.57	2.5*	0.11	1.7*	1.9*	0.14	1.3	0.12	2.5*	0.2
Yield	0.25	0.4	−0.03	−0.2	0.5	0.67	3.4**	−0.03	−0.4	2.9**
Zero yield	1.42	1.5	−0.13	−0.5	1.6	1.00	1.9*	0.08	0.6	2.1*
Neglect	0.53	2.3*	0.10	1.4	1.6	0.36	1.8*	0.08	1.3	1.3
Low price	0.94	2.5*	−0.10	−1.1	3.1**	0.38	2.0*	−0.02	−0.4	2.1*
Book/price	0.97	2.0*	0.10	0.8	2.0*	0.51	2.4*	0.05	0.7	1.9*
Sales/price	0.71	3.2*	0.13	2.3*	2.9**	0.05	0.2	0.18	4.1**	−0.8
Cash/price	0.28	0.6	0.37	2.6*	−0.2	−0.15	−2.0*	0.05	0.8	−1.0
Sigma	1.32	1.3	0.06	0.2	1.3	0.62	2.1*	0.02	0.2	1.4
Beta	0.15	0.2	−0.02	−0.1	0.3	−0.05	−0.1	0.05	0.4	−0.2
Co-skewness	0.34	0.6	0.07	0.4	0.5	0.10	0.5	0.04	0.6	0.3
Controversy	0.89	2.5*	−0.44	−2.7**	2.4*	−0.01	−0.1	−0.06	−0.8	0.2
Trend in earnings (−1)	0.25	0.9	0.50	4.7**	−0.7	0.60	3.8**	0.50	7.5**	0.5
Trend in earnings (−2)	0.15	0.5	0.42	4.4**	−0.8	0.25	1.6	0.29	4.7**	−0.2
Trend in earnings (−3)	−0.18	−0.4	0.33	3.5**	−1.5	0.13	0.6	0.19	3.8**	−0.4

Continued

TABLE 2-2

Concluded

Anomaly	Naïve Anomaly					Pure Anomaly				
	Average January (%)	t-Statistic	Average Non-January (%)	t-Statistic	t-Statistic of Difference	Average January (%)	t-Statistic	Average Non-January (%)	t-Statistic	t-Statistic of Difference
Earnings surprise (−1)	0.18	0.2	0.46	2.0*	−0.3	1.36	1.6	0.42	3.4**	1.8*
Earnings surprise (−2)	−0.48	−0.6	0.53	2.0*	−1.0	0.14	2.0	0.18	0.7	−0.1
Earnings surprise (−3)	−0.39	−0.3	−0.01	0.0	−0.3	−0.01	0.0	−0.22	−1.1	0.3
Earnings torpedo	0.15	0.5	−0.02	−0.2	0.5	0.08	0.3	−0.12	−1.9*	0.9
Relative strength	−0.66	−0.6	0.39	1.9*	−1.4	−0.13	−0.2	0.39	4.0**	−1.4
Residual reversal (−1)	−0.51	−1.7	−0.83	−4.6**	−0.8	−1.38	−6.0**	−1.06	−16.8**	−1.5
Residual reversal (−2)	−0.64	−1.5	−0.09	−0.9	−1.6	0.56	−2.5*	−0.35	−7.7**	−1.3
Short-term tax	1.06	1.3	−0.19	−0.8	1.6*	0.38	1.8*	−0.08	−0.7	1.2
Long-term tax	1.43	2.9*	−0.44	−2.5*	2.9**	0.78	3.2**	−0.07	−1.2	3.6**

* Significant at the 10 percent level.

** Significant at the 1 percent level.

is somewhat surprising, in view of the lower tax rate on long-term versus short-term capital gains during the period studied. Greater short-term loss-taking might be expected, because it shelters more income. However, our results are consistent with other empirical findings.[53] Furthermore, irrational investor behavior may offer a potential explanation; investors are often more averse to admitting recent mistakes than to admitting older ones [see Shefrin and Statman (1985)]. The attenuation of non-January returns to our tax-loss measures in their pure forms provides further evidence that they are sensibly constructed.

Although the difference between January and non-January returns is not quite statistically significant for our relative-strength measure, the average January return is negative while the average non-January return is significantly positive. The negative returns in January likely arise from increased profit taking among stocks with positive relative strength, motivated by a desire to defer gain recognition until the following tax year. Our tax measures, in contrast, are designed only to capture rebounds from year-end tax-loss-taking.

There is no solid theoretical explanation for a January seasonal to yield, size, or any other security characteristic other than to tax-related measures.[54] Thus, while our results showing a January seasonal in yield remain a puzzle, the dissipation of pure January seasonals for other anomalies, such as small size, is gratifying.

AUTOCORRELATION OF RETURN REGULARITIES

Earlier, we asserted that the evidence presented strongly contradicts both the weak and semistrong forms of the EMH. A more subtle test of weak-form efficiency entails an examination of the time series of returns to equity characteristics for autocorrelation. If returns between adjacent months are correlated (first-order autocorrelation), then an optimal prediction for next month's return uses the product of the correlation coefficient and the past month's return. Past prices alone would have predictive content. The sequence of first- and higher-order autocorrelations can be used to measure the "memory" of the return-generating process and may be useful in forecasting.

We examined the time-series properties of the returns to each anomaly. There is some prior evidence of patterns in these series, with most previous work having focused on naïve returns to stock characteristics.[55]

Rosenberg and Rudd (1982), using a multifactor framework, reported significantly positive monthly first-order, and negligible second-order, autocorrelation in the total factor-related return component of each stock. They discussed various possible explanations: (1) underresponse of the market to exogenous (macroeconomic) shocks, (2) nonsynchronous response of individual assets to a factor, and (3) changing risk premiums for various stock attributes.[56] We extended their approach. First, we calculated results for both naïve and pure anomalies. Second, rather than aggregating anomalies up to the individual stock level, we analyzed the autocorrelations of the return series to each pure anomaly separately. Third, we tested each return effect's overall autocorrelation structure for significance. Table 2-3 reports the results.

Note that most anomalies, both naïve and pure, exhibit positive first-order autocorrelation, with several being statistically significant.[57] A t-test of the hypothesis that the average anomaly's lag-1-month autocorrelation is zero is strongly rejected, with a t-statistic of 4.9 for the naïve and 3.1 for the pure case. Pure anomaly autocorrelations of lag-2 are on average not significantly different from zero (consistent with Rosenberg-Rudd).

The naïve autocorrelations for lag-1 are stronger than the pure anomaly results, and the naïve lag-2 results are significantly negative. One explanation for these differences from the pure results is the impact of related naïve anomalies acting as proxies for one another. For example, P/E, book/price, cash/price, sales/ price, and yield are all closely related. In the naïve analysis, the returns (hence autocorrelations) to any one of them contain information from all the other related effects. The positive first-order autocorrelations in each of these pure series are, thus, partially additive for each naïve anomaly. Similarly, past trends in analyst estimates have negative second-order autocorrelations and are also highly correlated; hence the negative second-order autocorrelation in any one naïve series is stronger than that in the associated pure anomaly.

Table 2-3 also displays a test for nonrandomness in the time series of returns to each attribute.[58] The autocorrelations at many different monthly lags (including and beyond the two shown) are strong enough that returns to several naïve and pure anomalies are

TABLE 2-3

Autocorrelation of Anomaly Returns

Anomaly	Naïve Anomaly					Pure Anomaly				
	Autocorrelation Lag of 1 Month	t-Statistic	Autocorrelation Lag of 2 Months	t-Statistic	Q-Statistic	Autocorrelation Lag of 1 Month	t-Statistic	Autocorrelation Lag of 2 Months	t-Statistic	Q-Statistic
Low P/E	0.16	1.7*	−0.01	−0.1	61.2**	0.06	0.6	0.25	2.6**	45.1*
Small size	0.03	0.3	0.08	0.8	31.3	0.09	0.9	−0.06	−0.6	30.5
Yield	0.23	2.4*	−0.05	−0.5	35.0	0.22	2.3*	0.04	0.4	22.8
Zero yield	0.19	2.0*	0.06	0.6	48.6*	0.07	0.7	0.03	0.3	29.2
Neglect	−0.20	−2.1*	0.10	1.0	29.7	−0.12	−1.2	−0.05	−0.5	18.0
Low price	0.14	1.5	−0.03	−0.3	40.7*	0.21	2.2*	0.16	1.7*	32.0
Book/price	0.14	1.5	−0.01	−0.1	24.0	0.06	0.6	0.09	0.9	32.9
Sales/price	0.14	1.5	−0.06	−0.6	32.2	0.07	0.7	−0.03	−0.3	21.9
Cash/price	0.13	1.4	−0.03	−0.3	39.1	0.13	1.4	0.06	0.6	43.1*
Sigma	0.20	2.1*	0.02	0.2	34.8	0.21	2.2*	0.16	1.7*	74.2**
Beta	0.14	1.5	−0.09	−0.9	25.7	−0.10	−1.0	−0.22	−2.3*	42.1*
Co-skewness	0.23	2.4*	0.00	0.0	20.2	0.02	0.2	0.03	0.3	26.7
Controversy	0.00	0.0	−0.11	−1.1	24.8	−0.18	−1.9*	−0.13	−1.4	30.2
Trend in earnings (−1)	0.02	0.2	−0.11	−1.1	36.4	0.13	1.4	−0.01	−0.1	24.4
Trend in earnings (−2)	0.07	0.7	−0.26	−2.7**	46.5*	0.07	0.7	−0.08	−0.8	20.6
Trend in earnings (−3)	0.05	0.5	−0.25	−2.6**	50.9**	0.13	1.4	−0.08	−0.8	32.9

Continued

T A B L E 2-3

Concluded

Anomaly	Naïve Anomaly					Pure Anomaly				
	Autocorrelation Lag of 1 Month	t-Statistic	Autocorrelation Lag of 2 Months	t-Statistic	Q-Statistic	Autocorrelation Lag of 1 Month	t-Statistic	Autocorrelation Lag of 2 Months	t-Statistic	Q-Statistic
Earnings surprise (−1)	0.14	0.8	−0.01	−0.1	13.6	0.03	0.2	0.17	1.0	15.2
Earnings surprise (−2)	−0.04	−0.2	0.03	0.2	31.7*	−0.02	−0.1	−0.03	−0.2	24.8
Earnings surprise (−3)	0.14	0.8	−0.02	−0.1	37.6**	−0.02	−0.1	−0.09	−0.5	37.5**
Earnings torpedo	0.29	3.0**	0.17	1.8*	47.6*	0.18	1.9*	0.25	2.6**	46.8*
Relative strength	0.24	2.5*	−0.04	−0.4	17.4	0.39	4.1**	0.12	1.2	39.4
Residual reversal (−1)	−0.03	−0.3	−0.06	−0.6	31.7	0.08	0.8	0.01	0.1	30.1
Residual reversal (−2)	0.05	0.5	−0.07	−0.7	30.5	0.02	0.2	−0.13	−1.4	35.3
Short-term tax	0.01	0.1	−0.10	−1.0	37.5	−0.03	−0.3	−0.07	−0.7	28.5
Long-term tax	0.21	2.2*	0.02	0.2	28.2	0.15	1.6	−0.17	−1.8*	36.7
Average anomaly	0.11	4.9**	−0.03	−1.8*		0.07	3.1**	0.01	0.4	

*Significant at the 10 percent level.
**Significant at the 1 percent level.

statistically nonrandom, as shown by their significant Q-statistics. We leave it to the interested reader to compare results for anomalies in their naïve and pure forms. We simply want to point to this demonstration of meaningful patterns in the returns to various anomalies over time as further evidence of departures from randomness.

As mentioned previously, significant autocorrelations can arise from changing risk premiums—that is, from time-varying expected returns to equity characteristics. Risk premiums may fluctuate because of macroeconomic events. Because risk premiums are likely to evolve slowly over time, autocorrelation patterns consistent with such variation would exhibit persistence over many lags, and thus need not contravene weak-form efficiency. Careful examination of the lag structures of our measures reveals persistence for some. For the majority of anomalies, however, no such persistence is observed. We thus have further evidence of weak-form inefficiency. Irrespective of the issue of market efficiency, the presence of autocorrelation suggests that time-series modeling of the individual return effects might have investment merit.

RETURN REGULARITIES AND THEIR MACROECONOMIC LINKAGES

We have suggested that exogenous forces, such as macroeconomic events, might play a role in driving returns to various equity characteristics. A full investigation of such linkages is beyond the scope of this article. However, we note some possible connections here.

One special macroeconomic measure is the return to the stock market. At the economywide level, this measure is useful, as indicated by its inclusion in the Index of Leading Indicators. It may also have explanatory power for returns to stock market attributes. In fact, market folklore maintains that low-P/E and high-yield stocks are generally "defensive" in nature. One might, thus, suppose that their payoffs are dependent on the direction of the stock market.

A simple method of testing this possibility would be to examine anomaly returns in up and down markets separately [see, for example, Lakonishok and Shapiro (1984)]. A more rigorous approach, taken here, is a time-series regression of monthly anomaly returns on monthly market excess returns.[59] Table 2-4 displays the results of these time-series regressions for both naïve and pure anomalies. The *intercept* refers to each anomaly's payoff in a flat market month (that is, a month providing no market excess return). The *slope,* or *market sensitivity,* refers to the incremental return to an anomaly above (below) the intercept, given a 1 percent market excess return.

Conventional wisdom holds that low-P/E stocks are defensive; indeed, the significantly negative slope coefficient shown in Table 2-4 indicates that low-P/E stocks do relatively less well in bull than in bear markets. However, it would take a 1-month excess market return of 6 percent ($-0.11 \times 6\% = -0.66\%$) to offset fully the 0.66-percent advantage of (a 1 cross-sectional standard deviation exposure to) low-P/E stocks. This defensiveness does not carry over to the pure low-P/E anomaly, which has a zero slope coefficient. In other words, the pure return to the low-P/E anomaly is not affected by the direction of the market. A glance at Figure 2-1 confirms this: While pure low P/E did not add value in the mid-1982 to mid-1983 roaring bull market, it did add value during other up market periods, such as mid-1984 to late 1985.

Conventional wisdom is confirmed for the yield attribute: Returns to higher yield have a strong negative slope in both naïve and pure regressions, indicating that their relative payoffs move inversely with the market's direction. Other attributes, however, are strongly procyclical. For example, monthly naïve and pure returns to historical beta are intimately and positively tied to excess market returns. Also, a significant positive relationship exists between market movements and returns to earnings controversy and to relative strength.

These fitted time-series relations represent a simple mechanism for making forecasts of returns to equity characteristics conditional on market returns. Also, the significant market-related components highlight the power of various prespecified attributes in forming a prediction of a stock's beta.[60] For example, because the pure returns to low yield and neglect are negatively related to market action (both having slopes of -0.05), individual stocks with these attributes will tend to exhibit lower systematic risk than otherwise. Note that our analysis controls for historical beta in deriving each pure anomaly return series. Not unexpectedly, our Vasicek-adjusted historical beta in the pure case is the dominant contributor to predictive beta, having a slope coefficient of 0.21 with a *t*-statistic

TABLE 2-4

Regressions of Anomaly Returns on Market Returns

	Naïve Anomaly				Pure Anomaly			
	Intercept (%)	t-Statistic	Slope	t-Statistic	Intercept (%)	t-Statistic	Slope	t-Statistic
Low P/E	0.66	4.4**	-0.11	-2.8**	0.46	4.6**	0.00	0.2
Small size	0.16	2.4*	-0.01	-0.4	0.12	2.7**	-0.00	-0.2
Yield	0.13	1.1	-0.23	-8.4**	0.06	1.0	-0.05	-3.5**
Zero yield	-0.17	-0.7	0.27	4.9**	0.15	1.2	0.01	0.2
Neglect	0.18	2.6**	-0.07	-4.1**	0.13	2.3*	-0.05	-3.7**
Low price	0.02	0.2	-0.05	-2.5*	-0.00	-0.1	0.03	2.1*
Book/price	0.25	2.4*	-0.13	-5.5**	0.08	1.1	0.02	0.9
Sales/price	0.15	2.7**	0.05	3.8**	0.15	3.4**	0.02	2.2*
Cash/price	0.44	3.5**	-0.13	-4.5**	0.04	0.7	-0.01	-0.4
Sigma	-0.07	-0.3	0.38	7.2**	0.05	0.4	0.05	1.7*
Beta	-0.21	-1.6	0.33	10.7**	-0.09	-0.9	0.21	9.7**
Co-skewness	-0.02	-0.2	0.13	5.3**	0.04	0.6	0.00	0.2
Controversy	-0.38	-2.4*	0.07	2.2*	-0.07	-1.0	0.03	1.7*
Trend in earnings (-1)	0.49	4.9**	-0.02	-0.8	0.49	7.9**	0.02	1.6
Trend in earnings (-2)	0.40	4.3**	-0.00	-0.0	0.28	4.8**	0.01	0.4
Trend in earnings (-3)	0.27	2.8**	0.03	1.2	0.18	3.6**	0.01	0.9
Earnings surprise (-1)	0.11	1.6	-0.01	-0.4	0.52	3.5**	-0.01	-0.1
Earnings surprise (-2)	0.16	1.8*	-0.02	-0.8	0.17	0.6	-0.01	-0.2
Earnings surprise (-3)	-0.06	-0.6	-0.00	-0.2	-0.21	-1.0	-0.04	-0.8
Earnings torpedo	-0.02	-0.2	0.03	1.3	-0.10	-1.6	-0.00	-0.3
Relative strength	0.15	0.8	0.17	4.9**	0.28	3.1**	0.09	4.5**
Residual reversal (-1)	-0.53	-4.7**	-0.01	-0.6	-1.08	-17.5**	-0.01	-0.7
Residual reversal (-2)	-0.16	-1.7*	0.05	2.3*	-0.37	-8.2**	0.02	1.5
Short-term tax	-0.15	-0.8	0.12	2.6**	-0.09	-0.8	0.06	2.6*
Long-term tax	-0.25	-1.8	0.04	1.3	0.02	0.3	-0.02	-1.0

* Significant at the 10 percent level.
** ignificant at the 1 percent level.

of 9.7. The reader may wonder why this slope coefficient differs so much from one; the answer lies in our use of a normalized historical beta measure, which is scaled differently from the predictive, raw-form beta.

We noted previously that the purification of the low-P/E effect caused its market-related component to dissipate. Similar diminution occurred for the market sensitivity of zero yield, cash/price, and co-skewness. The market sensitivities of the low-price and book/price measures actually reverse sign when purified. Unlike their pure counterparts, naïve anomalies are clearly unsuitable for beta prediction, because they serve as proxies for each other and their market sensitivities are not additive.

A comparison of the naïve and pure anomaly intercepts in Table 2-4 with the average monthly anomaly returns in Table 2-1 indicates that the statistically significant anomalies are generally robust to market-return adjustment. For example, the pure sales/price intercept is 15 basis points, with a t-statistic of 3.4, while the naïve monthly average return is 17 basis points, with a t-statistic of 3.7. This similarity holds despite the statistically significant slope coefficient for pure sales/price.

Also, our earlier findings on the pure January seasonality of various anomalies are robust to market-return adjustment. In fact, our results become more conclusive for the relative-strength measure. Earlier, we found the difference between January and non-January returns to be in the expected direction, but not statistically significant. However, once we adjust for the average excess market return in January of 2.3 percent, the difference between January and non-January intercepts is significant at the 1 percent level. This further supports our contention that negative pure returns to relative strength in January arise from profit taking associated with tax-gain deferral.

As we indicated earlier, the presence of equity return regularities calls into question the EMH and current asset pricing models, including the CAPM and APT. Also, the existence of significant pure anomaly intercepts, in the time-series regressions of anomaly returns on excess market returns, raises questions about the validity of a multifactor CAPM.[61]

CONCLUSION

Anomalies such as residual reversal and trends in analysts' earnings estimates appear to be true pockets of stock market inefficiency. Other effects, such as low P/E and small size, appear nonstationary; they may be anomalous, or they might represent empirical return regularities only in a broader macroeconomic framework. The future holds open the potential of uncovering new return regularities, as better databases (such as real-time pricing) and greater computer power are brought to task. At the same time, however, as we develop better ways of measuring risk and newer asset pricing models, new theories will undoubtedly arise to fit the observed facts. It will be exciting to observe the progress on both fronts.

ENDNOTES

The authors thank The Dais Group, Interactive Data Corporation, Institutional Brokers Estimate System (I/B/E/S), and Standard & Poor's Compustat for data and systems support.

1. For a review of the anomaly literature, see Keim (1986b). See Fama (1976) for a discussion of the CAPM and tests of market efficiency. While still controversial, some recent research finds anomalies even in an APT framework [Reinganum (1981b); Lehmann and Modest (1985); Chen, Copeland, and Mayers (1987); and Connor and Korajczyk (1987)]. While Lehmann and Modest show that the size-related rejection of APT is not an artifact of infrequent trading or solely due to the month of January, they also find that the dividend-yield and own-variance effects are not anomalous in their APT framework (while they are CAPM anomalies). Connor and Korajczyk find APT performs better in explaining the January seasonality in returns to small size, but no better than CAPM in non-January months. Chen, Copeland, and Mayers show that the size effect and Value Line enigmas are not explained by an APT framework. Value Line uses a composite of several measures, such as earnings surprise and price and earnings momentum. Gultekin and Gultekin (1987) find that APT cannot explain January, size, or sigma return regularities.

2. There are contrary opinions as to the advisability of doing so. On one
   hand, Joy and Jones (1986) conclude (p. 54) that "until we have
   incontrovertible knowledge of the true state of market efficiency,
   adoption of the anomalies-based strategies is justified." [See also
   Jacobs and Levy (1987) for thoughts on the philosophy of anomaly
   investing, and Einhorn, Shangkuan, and Jones (1987) for a view from
   Wall Street.] On the other hand, Merton (1987b) suggests that, since
   all researchers are essentially analyzing the same data set and since
   only interesting anomaly articles get published, it "creates a fertile
   environment for both unintended selection bias and for attaching
   greater significance to otherwise unbiased estimates than is
   justified." Nevertheless, Merton (1987a) constructs a theoretical
   model positing the existence of multiple anomalies (including the
   neglected-firm and size effects) and discusses some investment
   implications.

3. For the January/size connection in Australia, see Brown et al. (1983);
   for Canada, see Tinic, Barone-Adesi, and West (1987); for Japan, see
   Terada and Nakamura (1984) and Kato and Schallheim (1985); for
   the United Kingdom, see Beckers, Rosenberg, and Rudd (1982).

4. For a comparison of multifactor models with the CAPM and Ross'
   Arbitrage Pricing Theory, see Sharpe (1984). For a demonstration
   that multifactor models may explain stock returns better than APT
   models, see Blume, Gultekin, and Gultekin (1986).

5. The original BARRA model, termed "E1," consists of six composite
   risk factors—market variability, earnings variability, low valuation
   and unsuccess, immaturity and smallness, growth orientation, and
   financial risk—and 39 industry classifications. The second generation
   BARRA model, "E2," consists of 13 composite risk factors—
   variability in markets, success, size, trading activity, growth,
   earnings/price, book/price, earnings variation, financial leverage,
   foreign income, labor intensity, yield, and a low-capitalization
   indicator—and 55 industry classifications.

6. Sharpe (1982) examines five attributes—beta, yield, size, bond beta
   (or interest rate sensitivity), and alpha—and six broad industry
   classifications. Reid (1982) examines the following attributes—
   cumulative stock price range, co-skewness, beta, price, sigma,
   relative strength, and several measures each of size, yield, and
   residual return—and eight broad industry classifications.

7. Early studies include McWilliams (1966), Miller and Widmann
   (1966), Breen (1968), Breen and Savage (1968), and Nicholson (1968).
   The first to test carefully in a CAPM framework was Basu (1977). For

an updated study of industry-relative P/E ratios, see Goodman and Peavy (1983). For a test that circumvents potential CAPM pitfalls, see Levy and Lerman (1985). For a practitioner's view, see Dreman (1982).

8. For evidence on the size effect, see Banz (1981); Brown, Kleidon, and Marsh (1983); and Reinganum (1983a). For an overview of some size-related anomaly issues, see Schwert (1983). For a discussion of transaction costs as a potential explanation, see Stoll and Whaley (1983) and Schultz (1983). For evidence that the size anomaly is not a proxy for industry effects, see Carleton and Lakonishok (1986). For a discussion of deficient risk adjustment, see Roll (1981); Reinganum (1982); Booth and Smith (1985); Chan and Chen (1986); Ferson, Kandel, and Stambaugh (1987); and Handa, Kothari, and Wasley (1987). Blume and Stambaugh (1983) and Roll (1983a) find the size effect halved in magnitude when the bid/ask bias in daily pricing is controlled for, while Amihud and Mendelson (1983) find it totally subsumed. For a discussion of the size effect in an APT framework, see endnote 1.

9. Shefrin and Statman (1984) articulate theories of choice behavior that lead to results contrary to standard financial theory.

10. Black and Scholes (1974) and Miller and Scholes (1982) find an effect not significantly different from zero. Litzenberger and Ramaswamy (1979) report a significant and positive relationship between yield and return. Blume (1980) finds a discontinuity, with zero-yielding stocks earning an abnormally high return.

11. Keim (1985) shows the entire nonlinear yield anomaly to occur in the month of January.

12. For a theoretical model of the neglect effect, see Merton (1987a).

13. Stoll and Whaley (1983) report the low-price effect to be almost as powerful as the small-size effect.

14. Senchack and Martin (1987) test this claim and find earnings/price superior. It was reported that sales/price is significant in a multifactor framework at the BARRA Research Seminar, Berkeley, California, June 1986.

15. BARRA has tested this measure contemporaneously with E/P, sales/price, and book/price, and finds it significant; reported at the BARRA Research Seminar, Berkeley, California, June 1986.

16. If investors do not hold well-diversified portfolios, they may demand compensation for bearing residual risk [Levy (1978) and Mayshar (1981)]. However, price volatility confers on the taxable investor a valuable timing option for recognizing losses short term

and deferring gains [as per Constantinides (1984)], which could cause a lower required return for higher sigma. Also, Benston and Hagerman (1974) found sigma to be strongly and positively related to the bid/ask spread. This raises the issue of whether a significant excess return can be achieved from high-sigma stocks net of transaction costs. Empirically, a positive payoff to sigma was found by Douglas (1969). His methodology was criticized by Miller and Scholes (1972). Fama and MacBeth (1973) found sigma to be positively but insignificantly related to risk-adjusted return. Later, Friend, Westerfield, and Granito (1978) found sigma significant. Finally, Tinic and West (1986) replicated the Fama–MacBeth study on a longer time period and found sigma to be significant and to subsume beta, especially in January.

17. Singleton and Wingender (1986), however, find that individual stock skewness is not persistent and thus conclude that one should not bet on historical skewness.

18. For an early literature review, see Ball (1978). For more recent results, see Jones, Rendleman, and Latane (1984 and 1985) and Rendleman, Jones, and Latane (1986).

19. A recent paper noting these results is Brush (1986). Earlier studies include Greene and Fielitz (1977), Arnott (1979), Bohan (1981), and Brush and Boles (1983).

20. See Schwartz and Whitcomb (1977); Rosenberg and Rudd (1982); Rosenberg, Reid, and Lanstein (1985); and Howe (1986). A longer cycle (3- to 5-year) return reversal is documented in Fama and French (1987).

21. See Wachtel (1942); McEnally (1976); Rozeff and Kinney (1976); Branch (1977); Dyl (1977); and Jones, Pearce, and Wilson (1987). In addition, see the January/size studies referenced in the sidebar.

22. Constantinides (1984) demonstrates that the observed tax-trading pattern is irrational. Lakonishok and Smidt (1986b) show trading volume to be inconsistent with rational tax trading. Chan (1986) finds the January effect as strong for long-term losses as for short-term, contrary to optimal tax trading. DeBondt and Thaler (1985 and 1987) suggest that investor "overreaction," in violation of Bayes' rule, may explain anomalies such as the January effect. Shefrin and Statman (1985) develop Kahneman and Tversky's (1979) Prospect Theory, as well as notions of mental accounting, regret aversion, and self-control, to explain investors' observed January tax-loss behavior.

23. Portfolio grouping helps to resolve the econometric problem of measurement error [Fama and MacBeth (1973)].

24. See Brown, Kleidon, and Marsh (1983) for an application of SURM to the size effect. While SURM is more efficient asymptotically, it is only feasible if the number of assets (stocks or portfolios) is small in relation to the number of time periods [Maddala (1977)]. Since we cannot compact our stocks into portfolios because of the large number of attributes studied simultaneously, this approach is inapplicable here. We also consider it inappropriate for another reason—we take the perspective of an investor seeking to exploit anomalies, and thus could not have claimed ex ante knowledge of the future error covariance structure.

25. For example, Lakonishok and Shapiro (1984) cite this as a reason their results contradict Fama and MacBeth (1973). Also see Litzenberger and Ramaswamy (1979) and Warga (1987) for other arguments against grouping stocks.

26. To partition simultaneously into quintiles on the basis of our 25 anomalies results in 5^{25}, or 310^{17}, separate classifications. Using monthly returns on our 1500 stocks, it would take over 16.6 trillion years to generate just one observation per cell.

27. See Grinold (1987) for a discussion of the appropriateness of modeling expected returns linearly in equity characteristics.

28. See McElreath and Wiggins (1984) for an overview of potential methodological pitfalls.

29. Blume and Stambaugh (1983) demonstrate this problem in the context of the small-size and low-price effects.

30. Banz and Breen (1986) provide a comprehensive discussion of methodological problems and a stark example of the potential for survivorship and look-ahead biases to confound the disentangling of the size and P/E effects.

31. This type of normalization belongs to the general class of "winsorised M-estimators" [Judge et al. (1985), pp. 829–834]. This concept was first applied in common stock research by BARRA in their E1 model (see endnote 5).

32. Ratcliffe (1968) demonstrates this test to be robust in samples of over 80 observations. Because of data availability constraints, our earnings surprise series commences in 1984. Significance levels shown for this anomaly reflect the lesser degrees of freedom.

33. For a description of paired t-tests, see Snedecor and Cochran (1967), pp. 91–100.

34. Also, for a general discussion of multicollinearity, see Kmenta (1971), pp. 380–391.

35. For example, Arbel (1985) suggested that P/E might be a proxy for neglect; Reinganum (1981a) and Banz and Breen (1986) found the size effect to subsume P/E. Our results are more consistent with those of Cook and Rozeff (1984) and Dowen and Bauman (1986), who identify an independent P/E effect.

36. In fact, an arbitrary split of the sample period into two subperiods of equal length reveals significantly different (at the 1 percent level) pure return variances across time for 8 of our 25 anomaly measures, and significantly different pure average monthly returns for three of our measures. These frequencies of rejecting equality are, of course, much greater than expected from chance alone at the 1 percent level if the series were truly stationary. An F-test was used to check for equality of variances across subperiods for each attribute. A difference-of-means test was then performed using the stricter Cochran criteria in those cases where equality of variances was rejected. These tests were two-sided. For a discussion of these tests, see Snedecor and Cochran (1967).

37. This contradicts Basu (1983), who found the P/E effect to subsume the size effect. Consistent with our findings, however, all three previously cited multifactor models indicate a significant size effect.

38. Brown, Kleidon, and Marsh (1983) document major time periods when small size was deleterious to returns.

39. See Chan, Chen, and Hsieh (1985) for an analysis of linkages between the size effect and macroeconomic measures. See Keim and Stambaugh (1986) for linkages to several ex ante risk premiums. For analyses of various univariate return effects and their macroeconomic correlates, see Arnott and Copeland (1985); for an analysis with multivariate factors, see Marathe (1979).

40. See BARRA Research Seminar, Berkeley, California, June 1986.

41. Lakonishok and Shapiro (1984) find that the size effect subsumes returns to both beta and sigma. Tinic and West (1986) report that the interaction of returns to beta, sigma, and size depends on whether or not the month is January. We will examine January separately later. Sharpe's (1982) multifactor beta did accumulate significantly over time; Reid's (1982) multifactor beta also had a positive total payoff, but a t-statistic test that was not quite significant. In addition, Reid's model included co-skewness and sigma factors. His co-skewness factor had a significantly positive accumulation; sigma had a marginally significant negative payoff.

42. Nonstationarity of returns to systematic risk has been demonstrated by Tinic and West (1986).

43. Rosenberg, Reid, and Lanstein (1985) report a t-statistic of –13.8 and Reid's (1982) multifactor residual reversal achieves a –15.0; our –17.8 is slightly stronger, despite our shorter time period. Rosenberg, Reid, and Lanstein (RRL) report a consistency rate of 91.3 percent, while 103 out of 108 of our monthly payoffs were negative, for a consistency of 95.4 percent. Note, however, that the RRL measure is specific return (net of factor-return attributes), while ours and Reid's are residual of the beta-adjusted market return. As Reid noted, the two approaches produce reversals of similar magnitude. Note also that it is impossible to abstract from pricing errors and bid/ask spreads by lagging price in constructing this measure. However, RRL do some diagnostics that indicate the measure is robust with respect to such concerns. Furthermore, the observed second-month reversal persistence is by construction free from any pricing concerns.

44. For an early application of cluster analysis to finance, see Farrell (1974).

45. The explanatory power was generally much higher in months with unusual stock returns. This stems from the increased cross-sectional variation of returns explained by beta in such months. See the discussion of beta in Table 2-4 for quantification of its market sensitivity.

46. Sharpe's model has a time-series RZ of 40 percent versus a cross-sectional R-squared of 10 percent. The former is an average across stocks (regressed over time); the latter is an average across months (regressed over stocks). Sharpe discusses the difference between the two measures.

47. For example, the salient features of tax laws and their effects on optimal trading strategies are usually relatively constant. Human nature is even less fluid; hence observed "irrational" behavior (inconsistent with the CAPM and EMH) need not become rational in the future. For a discussion of human irrationality and security markets, see Arrow (1982).

48. When the number of means to be estimated jointly exceeds two, using each historical average individually is "inadmissible." An estimator is inadmissible if there is another that has smaller risk (in terms of mean square error) independent of the true unknown means. Stein-James estimators shrink all individual historical averages toward the grand average. The shrinking factor for each historical average varies inversely with its standard deviation. The shrinking factor is thus positively correlated with the degree of randomness or uncertainty in each measure [James and Stein (1961)].

49. Before applying the difference-of-means test, we used an F-test to check for equality of variances in January and non-January months for each attribute. Equality of variances could only be rejected in three cases, and the subsequent difference-of-means tests were robust to the stricter Cochran criteria in all three cases. Hence the t-tests shown for January versus non-January differences are based on a pooled estimate of January and non-January return variance. These tests were two-sided with the exception of the tax-loss measures. Because theory predicted positive January tax measure coefficients, one-sided tests were used. (See endnote 36.)

50. For example, on size, see Keim (1983a); on controversy, see Arnott and Copeland (1985); on tax measures, see Reinganum (1983b).

51. Compare this with Arbel (1985).

52. For example, on yield, see Keim (1986a); on sigma, see Tinic and West (1986); on relative strength, see Brush (1986). These authors focus on fewer anomalies than we do, thereby facilitating a longer sample period and hence greater statistical power. Their findings are consistent with ours, but are also statistically significant.

53. Chan (1986) reports that a loss from two calendar years prior has about as much January impact as a loss from the most recent calendar year. As our long-term measure is broader than Chan's, an even larger impact from long-term losses is not unexpected.

54. Arbel (1985) cites year-end release of information as a potential explanation of a neglect seasonal. However, Chari, Jagannathan, and Ofer (1986) find no excess returns at fiscal year end for non-December fiscal year reporters, casting doubt on Arbel's thesis. Kato and Schallheim (1985) suggest additional liquidity in the economy as a possible explanation for the Japanese January/June seasonals and the U.S. January/size anomaly. However, our finding that the January/size seasonal is subsumed after properly controlling for tax-loss selling appears to belie this rationale.

55. Grant (1984), Fama and French (1987), Lo and MacKinlay (1987), and Morgan and Morgan (1987) document periodicity in naïve returns to the size effect.

56. The concept of changing expected risk premiums inducing autocorrelation in returns was discussed earlier by Fama (1976), p. 149.

57. The t-statistic for each attribute is calculated using the Bartlett approximation [Box and Jenkins (1976), pp. 34–36].

58. The metric we use is the Portmanteau statistic Q given in Ljung and Box (1978). The first 31 autocorrelation lags for each attribute were tested for nonstationarity (18 lags for earnings surprise).

59. Specifically, the independent variable is monthly S&P 500 excess (over Treasury bills) return. This type of analysis is also implemented in the multifactor works of Sharpe (1982) and Reid (1982).

60. This approach was pioneered by Rosenberg and McKibben (1973).

61. See Sharpe (1982), pp. 17–18. Fluctuations in risk premiums could induce significant intercepts, which would not contravene a multifactor CAPM. But as noted earlier, our autocorrelation results are not generally supportive of changing anomaly risk premiums. In fact, it is doubtful that any meaningful definition of risk is as transient as some of our return effects. Furthermore, fleeting return effects, such as residual return reversal, should be immune to Roll's (1977) CAPM critique, because they are likely robust to any reasonable definition of the market portfolio.

REFERENCES

Amihud, Y. and H. Mendelson. 1983. "Asset pricing and the bid-ask spread." *Journal of Financial Economics* 17 (2): 223–249.

Arbel, A. 1985. "Generic stocks: An old product in a new package." *Journal of Portfolio Management* 11 (4): 4–13.

Arbel, A., S. Carvell, and P. Strebel. 1983. "Giraffes, institutions and neglected firms." *Financial Analysts Journal* 39 (3): 57–62.

Arbel, A. and P. Strebel. 1982. "The neglected and small firm effects." *Financial Review* 17 (4): 201–218.

―――― and ――――. 1983. "Pay attention to neglected firms." *Journal of Portfolio Management* 9 (2): 37–42.

Arnott, R. 1979. "Relative strength revisited." *Journal of Portfolio Management* 5 (3): 19–23.

――――. 1983. "What hath MPT wrought: Which risks reap rewards?" *Journal of Portfolio Management* 10 (1): 5–11.

――――. 1985. "The use and misuse of consensus earnings." *Journal of Portfolio Management* 11 (3): 18–27.

Arnott, R. and W. Copeland. 1985. "The business cycle and security selection." *Financial Analysts Journal* 41 (2): 26–32.

Arrow, K. 1982. "Risk perception in psychology and economics." *Economic Inquiry* 20 (1): 1–9.

Bachrach, B. and D. Galai. 1979. "The risk return relationship and stock prices." *Journal of Financial and Quantitative Analysis* 14 (2): 421–441.

Ball, R. 1978. "Anomalies in relationships between securities' yields and yield-surrogates." *Journal of Financial Economics* 6 (2–3): 103–126.

Banz, R. 1981. "The relationship between return and market value of common stocks." *Journal of Financial Economics* 9 (1): 3–18.

Banz, R. and W. Breen. 1986. "Sample-dependent results using accounting and market data: Some evidence." *Journal of Finance* 41 (4): 779–793.

Barone-Adesi, G. 1985. "Arbitrage equilibrium with skewed asset returns." *Journal of Financial and Quantitative Analysis* 20 (3): 299–313.

Barry, C. and S. Brown. 1986. "Limited information as a source of risk." *Journal of Portfolio Management* 12 (2): 66–72.

Basu, S. 1977. "Investment performance of common stocks in relation to their price-earnings ratios: A test of the efficient market hypothesis." *Journal of Finance* 32 (2): 663–682.

———. 1983. "The relationship between earnings yield, market value and return for NYSE common stocks: Further evidence." *Journal of Financial Economics* 12 (1): 129–156.

Basu, S. and S. Cheung. 1982. "Residual risk, firm size, and returns for NYSE common stocks: Some empirical evidence." Working Paper, McMaster University, Montreal, January.

Beckers, S., B. Rosenberg, and A. Rudd. 1982. "The January or April effect: Seasonal evidence from the United Kingdom." In *Proceedings of the Second Symposium on Money, Banking and Insurance,* H. Goppi and R. Henn, eds. University of Karlsruhe, Germany, December. New York: Athenuem, pp. 537–550.

Benesh, G. and P. Peterson. 1986. "On the relation between earnings changes, analysts' forecasts and stock price fluctuations." *Financial Analysts Journal* 42 (6): 29–39.

Benston, G. and R. Hagerman. 1974. "Determinants of bid-asked spreads in the over-the-counter market." *Journal of Financial Economics* 1(4): 353–364.

Black, F. and M. Scholes. 1974. "The effects of dividend yield and dividend policy on common stock prices and returns." *Journal of Financial Economics* 1(1): 1–22.

Blume, M. 1980. "Stock returns and dividend yields: Some more evidence." *Review of Economics and Statistics* 62 (4): 567–577.

Blume, M., M. Gultekin, and B. Gultekin. 1986. "On the assessment of return generating models." Rodney White Working Paper #13, University of Pennsylvania, Philadelphia.

Blume, M. and F. Husic. 1973. "Price, beta and exchange listing." *Journal of Finance* 28 (2): 283–299.

Blume, M. and R. Stambaugh. 1983. "Biases in computed returns: An application to the size effect." *Journal of Financial Economics* 12 (3): 387–404.

Bohan, J. 1981. "Relative strength: Further positive evidence." *Journal of Portfolio Management* 7 (1): 36–39.

Booth, J. and R. Smith. 1985. "The application of errors-in-variables methodology to capital market research: Evidence on the small-firm effect." *Journal of Financial and Quantitative Analysis* 20 (4): 501–515.

Box, G. and G. Jenkins. 1976. *Time Series Analysis: Forecasting and Control.* Rev. ed. San Francisco: Holden-Day.

Branch, B. 1977. "A tax loss trading rule." *Journal of Business* 50 (2): 198–207.

Breen, W. 1968. "Low price-earnings ratios and industry relatives." *Financial Analysts Journal* 24 (6): 125–127.

Breen, W. and J. Savage. 1968. "Portfolio distributions and tests of security selection models." *Journal of Finance* 23 (5): 805–819.

Brown, P., et al. 1983. "Stock return seasonalities and the tax-loss selling hypothesis: Analysis of the arguments and Australian evidence." *Journal of Financial Economics* 12 (1): 105–127.

Brown, P., A. Kleidon, and T. Marsh. 1983. "New evidence on the nature of size-related anomalies in stock prices." *Journal of Financial Economics* 12 (1): 33–56.

Brush, J. 1986. "Eight relative strength models compared." *Journal of Portfolio Management* 12 (1): 21–28.

Brush, J. and K. Boles. 1983. "The predictive power in relative strength and CAPM." *Journal of Portfolio Management* 9 (4): 20–23.

Carleton, W. and J. Lakonishok. 1986. "The size anomaly: Does industry group matter?" *Journal of Portfolio Management* 12 (3): 36–40.

Carvell, S. and P. Strebel. 1984. "A new beta incorporating analysts' forecasts." *Journal of Portfolio Management* 11 (1): 81–85.

Chan, K. 1986. "Can tax-loss selling explain the January seasonal in stock returns?" *Journal of Finance* 41 (5): 1115–1128.

Chan, K. and N. Chen. 1986. "Estimation error of stock betas and the role of firm size as an instrumental variable for risk." Working Paper #179, Center for Research in Security Prices, University of Chicago, June. [Subsequently published as "An unconditional asset-pricing test and the role of firm size as an instrumental variable for risk." *Journal of Finance* 43 (2): 309–325.]

Chan, K., N. Chen, and D. Hsieh. 1985. "An exploratory investigation of the firm size effect." *Journal of Financial Economics* 14 (3): 451–471.

Chari, V., R. Jagannathan, and A. Ofer. 1986. "Fiscal year end and the January effect." Working paper #20, Kellogg Graduate School of Management, Northwestern University, Evanston, Illinois, July.

Chen, N., T. Copeland, and D. Mayers. 1987. "A comparison of single and multifactor portfolio performance methodologies." Working Paper, University of California at Los Angeles, February. [Published in *Journal of Financial and Quantitative Analysis* 22 (4): 401–418.]

Connor, G. and R. Korajczyk. 1987. "Risk and return in an equilibrium APT." Working Paper #9, Kellogg Graduate School of Management, Northwestern University, Evanston, Illinois, April. [Published in *Journal of Financial Economics* 21 (2): 255–290.]

Constantinides, G. 1984. "Optimal stock trading with personal taxes: Implications for prices and the abnormal January returns." *Journal of Financial Economics* 13 (1): 65–89.

Cook, T. and M. Rozeff. 1982. "Size, dividend yield and co-skewness effects on stock returns: Some empirical tests." Working Paper #82–20, University of

Iowa, Ames. [See "Coskewness, dividend yield and capital asset pricing." *Journal of Financial Research* 7 (3):231–241.]

———— and ————. 1984. "Size and earnings/price ratio anomalies: One effect or two?" *Journal of Financial and Quantitative Analysis* 19 (4): 449–466.

Cragg, J. and B. Malkiel. 1982. *Expectations and the Structure of Share Prices.* Chicago: University of Chicago Press.

DeBondt, W. and R. Thaler. 1985. "Does the stock market overreact?" *Journal of Finance* 40 (3): 793–805.

———— and ————. 1987. "Further evidence on investor overreaction and stock market seasonality." *Journal of Finance* 42 (3): 557–581.

Douglas, G. 1969. "Risk in the equity markets: An empirical appraisal of market efficiency." *Yale Economic Essays* (Spring): 3–45.

Dowen, R. and S. Bauman. 1984. "A test of the relative importance of popularity and price-earnings ratio in determining abnormal returns." *Journal of the Midwest Finance Association* 13 (1): 34–47.

———— and ————. 1986. "The relative importance of size, P/E and neglect." *Journal of Portfolio Management* 12 (3): 30–34.

Dreman, D. 1982. *The New Contrarian Investment Strategy.* New York: Random House.

Dyl, E. 1977. "Capital gains taxation and year-end stock market behavior." *Journal of Finance* 32 (1): 165–175.

Edmister, R. and J. Greene. 1980. "Performance of super-low-price stocks." *Journal of Portfolio Management* 6 (1): 36–41.

Einhorn, S., P. Shangkuan, and R. Jones. 1987. "A multifactor model." Goldman Sachs Portfolio Strategy, April 10.

Elton, E., M. Gruber, and J. Rentzler. 1981. "A simple examination of the empirical relationship between dividend yields and deviations from the CAPM." Working Paper #240, New York University, New York, August. [Published in *Journal of Banking and Finance* 7 (1): 135–146.]

Fama, E. 1976. *Foundations of Finance.* New York: Basic Books.

Fama, E. and K. French. 1987. "Permanent and temporary components of stock prices." Working Paper #178, Center for Research in Security Prices, University of Chicago, Chicago, February. [Published in *Journal of Political Economy* 96 (2): 246–273.]

Fama, E. and J. MacBeth. 1973. "Risk, return and equilibrium: Empirical tests." *Journal of Political Economy* 81 (3): 607–636.

Farrell, J. 1974. "Analyzing covariation of returns to determine homogeneous stock groupings." *Journal of Business* 47 (2): 186–207.

Ferson, W., S. Kandel, and R. Stambaugh. 1987. "Tests of asset pricing with time-varying expected risk premiums and market betas." *Journal of Finance* 42 (2): 201–220.

Foster, G., C. Olsen, and T. Shevlin. 1984. "Earnings releases, anomalies and the behavior of security returns." *The Accounting Review* 59 (4): 574–603.

Freeman, R. 1986. "The association between accounting earnings and security returns for large and small firms." Working Paper #192, Center for Research in Security Prices, University of Chicago, Chicago, October. [Published in *Journal of Accounting and Economics* 9 (2): 195–228.]

Friend, I. and R. Westerfield. 1980. "Co-skewness and capital asset pricing." *Journal of Finance* 35 (4): 897–913.

Friend, I., R. Westerfield, and M. Granito. 1978. "New evidence on the Capital Asset Pricing Model." *Journal of Finance* 33 (2): 903–920.

Givoly, D. and A. Ovadia. 1983. "Year-end tax-induced sales and stock market seasonality." *Journal of Finance* 38 (1): 171–185.

Goodman, D. and J. Peavy. 1983. "Industry relative price-earnings ratios as indicators of investment returns." *Financial Analysts Journal* 39 (4): 60–66.

———— and ————. 1985. "The risk universal nature of the P/E effect." *Journal of Portfolio Management* 11 (4): 14–16.

———— and ————. 1986. "The interaction of firm size and price-earnings ratio on portfolio performance." *Financial Analysts Journal* 42 (1): 9–12.

Grant, J. 1984. "Long-term dependence in small firm returns." Working Paper #84–10, Boston College, Boston, March.

Greene, M. and B. Fielitz. 1977. "Long-term dependence in common stock returns." *Journal of Financial Economics* 4 (3): 339–349.

Grinold, R. 1987. "Multiple factor risk models and exact factor pricing." Working Paper #166, University of California at Berkeley, February.

Gultekin, M. and B. Gultekin. 1987. "Stock return anomalies and the tests of the APT." *Journal of Finance* 42 (5): 1213–1224.

Hagin, R. 1984. "An examination of the torpedo effect." Paper presented at the Institute for Quantitative Research in Finance, Fall.

Handa, P., S. Kothari, and C. Wasley. 1987. "Bias in estimation of systematic risk and its implications for tests of the CAPM." Working Paper #404, New York University, New York, January. [See "The relation between the return interval and betas: Implications for the size effect." *Journal of Financial Economics* 23 (1): 79–100.]

Harris, L. 1986a. "A transaction data study of weekly and intradaily patterns in stock returns." *Journal of Financial Economics* 16 (1): 99–117.

————. 1986b. "How to profit from intradaily stock returns." *Journal of Portfolio Management* 12 (2): 61–64.

Hawkins, E., S. Chamberlin, and W. Daniel. 1984. "Earnings expectations and security prices." *Financial Analysts Journal* 40 (5): 24–38.

Hawthorne, F. 1984. "When is an index fund not an index fund?" *Pensions & Investment Age*, November 10, p. 92.

Howe, J. 1986. "Evidence on stock market overreaction." *Financial Analysts Journal* 42 (4): 74–77.

Jacobs, B. and K. Levy. 1986. "Anomaly capture strategies." Paper presented at the Berkeley Program in Finance, Berkeley, California, September.

———— and ————. 1987. "Investment management: Opportunities in anomalies?" *Pension World*, February, pp. 46–47.

———— and ————. 1988. "Calendar anomalies: Abnormal returns at calendar turning points." *Financial Analysts Journal* 44 (6): 28–39.

———— and ————. 1989. "Trading tactics in an inefficient market." In *A Complete Guide to Securities Transactions: Controlling Costs and Enhancing Performance*, W. Wagner, ed. New York: John Wiley.

James, W. and C. Stein. 1961. "Estimation with quadratic loss." In *Proceedings of the 4th Berkeley Symposium on Probability and Statistics.* Berkeley: University of California Press.

Jones, C., D. Pearce, and J. Wilson. 1987. "Can tax-loss selling explain the January effect? A note." *Journal of Finance* 42 (2): 453–561.

Jones, C., R. Rendleman, and H. Latane. 1984. "Stock returns and SUEs during the 1970's." *Journal of Portfolio Management* 10 (2): 18–22.

——, ——, and ——. 1985. "Earnings announcements: Pre- and post-responses." *Journal of Portfolio Management* 11 (3): 28–32.

Joy, O. and C. Jones. 1986. "Should we believe the tests of market efficiency?" *Journal of Portfolio Management* 12 (4): 49–54.

Judge, G., et al. 1985. *The Theory and Practice of Econometrics.* 2d ed. New York: John Wiley.

Kahneman, D. and A. Tversky. 1979. "Prospect Theory: An analysis of decision under risk." *Econometrica* 47 (2): 263–292.

Kato, K. and J. Schallheim. 1985. "Seasonal and size anomalies in the Japanese stock market." *Journal of Financial and Quantitative Analysis* 20 (2): 243–260.

Keim, D. 1983a. "Size-related anomalies and stock return seasonality: Further empirical evidence." *Journal of Financial Economics* 12 (1): 13–32.

——. 1983b. "The interrelation between dividend yields, equity values and stock returns: Implications of abnormal January returns." Ph.D. dissertation, University of Chicago, Chicago.

——. 1985. "Dividend yields and stock returns: Implications of abnormal January returns." *Journal of Financial Economics* 14 (3): 473–489.

——. 1986a. "Dividend yields, size, and the January effect." *Journal of Portfolio Management* 12 (2): 54–60.

——. 1986b. "The CAPM and equity return regularities." *Financial Analysts Journal* 42 (3): 19–34.

——. 1987. "Daily returns and size-related premiums: One more time." *Journal of Portfolio Management* 13 (2): 41–47.

Keim, D. and R. Stambaugh. 1986. "Predicting returns in the stock and bond markets." *Journal of Financial Economics* 17 (2): 357–390.

Kerrigan, T. 1984. "When forecasting earnings, it pays to watch forecasts." *Journal of Portfolio Management* 10 (4): 19–26.

Klemkosky, R. and J. Martin. 1975. "The adjustment of beta forecasts." *Journal of Finance* 30 (4): 11–23.

Kmenta, J. 1971. *Elements of Econometrics.* New York: Macmillan.

Kraus, A. and R. Litzenberger. 1976. "Skewness preference and the valuation of risk assets." *Journal of Finance* 31 (4): 1085–1100.

Lakonishok, J. and A. Shapiro. 1984. "Stock returns, beta, variance and size: An empirical analysis." *Financial Analysts Journal* 40 (4): 36–41.

Lakonishok, J. and S. Smidt. 1984. "Volume and turn-of-the-year behavior." *Journal of Financial Economics* 13 (3): 435–455.

—— and ——. 1986a. "Trading bargains in small firms at year-end." *Journal of Portfolio Management* 12 (3): 24–29.

———— and ————. 1986b. "Volume in winners and losers: Taxation and other motives for stock trading." *Journal of Finance* 41 (4): 951–974.

Lehmann, B. and D. Modest. 1985. "The empirical foundations of the Arbitrage Pricing Theory I: The empirical tests." Working Paper, Columbia University Business School, New York, August. [Published in *Journal of Financial Economics* 21 (2): 243–254.]

Levy, H. 1978. "Equilibrium in an imperfect market: A constraint on the number of securities in the portfolio." *American Economic Review* 68 (4): 643–658.

Levy, H. and Z. Lerman. 1985. "Testing P/E ratio filters with stochastic dominance." *Journal of Portfolio Management* 10 (2): 31–40.

Litzenberger, R. and K. Ramaswamy. 1979. "The effect of personal taxes and dividends on capital asset prices: Theory and empirical evidence." *Journal of Financial Economics* 7 (2): 163–195.

Ljung, G. and G. Box. 1978. "On a measure of lack of fit in time series models." *Biometrika* 65: 297–303.

Lo, A. and C. MacKinlay. 1987. "Stock market prices do not follow random walks: Evidence from a simple specification test." Working Paper #2168, National Bureau of Economic Research, Boston, February. [Published in *Review of Financial Studies* 1 (1): 41–66.]

Maddala, G. 1977. *Econometrics*. New York: McGraw-Hill.

Marathe, V. 1979. "Elements of covariance in security returns and their macroeconomic determinants." Ph.D. dissertation, University of California at Berkeley.

Mayshar, J. 1981. "Transaction costs and the pricing of assets." *Journal of Finance* 36 (2): 583–597.

McElreath, R. and D. Wiggins. 1984. "Using the Compustat tapes in financial research: Problems and solutions." *Financial Analysts Journal* 40 (1): 71–76.

McEnally, R. 1976. "Stock price changes induced by tax switching." *Journal of Business* 49 (1): 47–54.

McWilliams, J. 1966. "Prices, earnings and P.E. ratios." *Financial Analysts Journal* 22 (3): 137–142.

Merton, R. 1987a. "A simple model of capital market equilibrium with incomplete information." *Journal of Finance* 42 (3): 483–510.

————. 1987b. "On the current state of the stock market rationality hypothesis." In *Macroeconomics and Finance: Essays in Honor of Franco Modigliani*, S. Fischer and R. Dornbusch, eds. Cambridge: MIT Press.

Miller, M. and M. Scholes. 1972. "Rates of return in relation to risk: A reexamination of some recent findings." In *Studies in the Theory of Capital Markets*, M. Jensen, ed. New York: Praeger.

———— and ————. 1982. "Dividends and taxes: Some empirical evidence." *Journal of Political Economy* 90 (6): 1118–1141.

Miller, P. and E. Widmann. 1966. "Price performance outlook for high & low P/E stocks." *Commercial & Financial Chronicle*, September 29, pp. 26–28.

Morgan, A. and I. Morgan. 1987. "Measurement of abnormal returns from small firms." *Journal of Business and Economic Statistics* 5 (1): 121–129.

Nicholson, F. 1968. "Price ratios in relation to investment results." *Financial Analysts Journal* 24 (1): 105–109.

Peavy, J. and D. Goodman. 1982. "A further inquiry into the market value and earnings yield anomalies." Working Paper #82–114, Southern Methodist University, Dallas.

Penman, S. 1987. "The distribution of earnings news over time and seasonalities in aggregate stock returns." *Journal of Financial Economics* 18 (2): 199–228.

Rainville, H. 1983. "Earnings momentum in equities." Paper presented at the Institute for Quantitative Research in Finance, Spring.

Ratcliffe, J. 1968. "The effects on the *t*-distribution of nonnormality in the sampled population." *Applied Statistics* 17: 42–48.

Reid, K. 1982. "Factors in the pricing of common equity." Ph.D. dissertation, University of California at Berkeley.

Reinganum, M. 1981a. "Misspecification of capital asset pricing: Empirical anomalies based on earnings' yields and market values." *Journal of Financial Economics* 9 (1): 19–46.

———. 1981b. "The Arbitrage Pricing Theory: Some empirical results." *Journal of Finance* 36 (2): 313–321.

———. 1982. "A direct test of Roll's conjecture on the firm size effect." *Journal of Finance* 37 (1): 27–35.

———. 1983a. "Portfolio strategies based on market capitalization." *Journal of Portfolio Management* 9 (2): 29–36.

———. 1983b. "The anomalous stock market behavior of small firms in January: Empirical tests for tax-loss selling effects." *Journal of Financial Economics* 12 (1): 89–104.

Rendleman, R., C. Jones, and H. Latane. 1986. "Further insight into the S.U.E. anomaly: Size and serial correlation effects." Working Paper, University of North Carolina at Chapel Hill, April. [Published in *Financial Review* 22 (1): 131–144.]

Rogalski, R. 1984. "New findings regarding day-of-the-week returns over trading and non-trading periods: A note." *Journal of Finance* 39 (5): 1603–1614.

Rogalski, R. and S. Tinic. 1986. "The January size effect: Anomaly or risk mismeasurement?" *Financial Analysts Journal* 42 (6): 63–70.

Roll, R. 1977. "A critique of the asset pricing theory's tests, Part I: On past and potential testability of the theory." *Journal of Financial Economics* 4 (2): 129–176.

———. 1981. "A possible explanation of the small firm effect." *Journal of Finance* 36 (4): 371–386.

———. 1983a. "On computing mean returns and the small firm premium." *Journal of Financial Economics* 12 (3): 371–386.

———. 1983b. "Vas ist das? The turn of the year effect and the return premia of small firms." *Journal of Portfolio Management* 9 (2): 18–28.

Rosenberg, B. and V. Marathe. 1976. "Common factors in security returns: Microeconomic determinants and macroeconomic correlates." In *Proceedings of the Seminar on the Analysis of Security Prices,* May 1976. Chicago: University of Chicago Press, pp. 61–115.

Rosenberg, B. and W. McKibben. 1973. "The prediction of systematic and specific risk in common stocks." *Journal of Financial and Quantitative Analysis* 8 (2): 317–333.

Rosenberg, B., K. Reid, and R. Lanstein. 1985. "Persuasive evidence of market inefficiency." *Journal of Portfolio Management* 11 (3): 9–17.

Rosenberg, B. and A. Rudd. 1982. "Factor-related and specific returns of common stocks: Serial correlation and market inefficiency." *Journal of Finance* 37 (2): 543–554.

Rozeff, M. and W. Kinney. 1976. "Capital market seasonality: The case of stock returns." *Journal of Financial Economics* 3 (4): 379–402.

Rudd, A. and H. Clasing. 1982. *Modern Portfolio Theory: The Principles of Investment Management.* Homewood, Illinois: Dow Jones–Irwin.

Schultz, P. 1983. "Transaction costs and the small firm effect: A comment." *Journal of Financial Economics* 12 (1): 81–88.

————. 1985. "Personal income taxes and the January effect: Small firm stock returns before the War Revenue Act of 1917: A note." *Journal of Finance* 40 (1): 333–343.

Schwartz, R. and D. Whitcomb. 1977. "Evidence on the presence and causes of serial correlation in market model residuals." *Journal of Financial and Quantitative Analysis* 12 (2): 291–313.

Schwert, W. 1983. "Size and stock returns, and other empirical regularities." *Journal of Financial Economics* 12 (1): 3–12.

Senchack, A. and J. Martin. 1987. "The relative performance of the PSR and PER investment strategies." *Financial Analysts Journal* 43 (2): 46–56.

Sharpe, W. 1982. "Factors in NYSE exchange security returns, 1931–1979." *Journal of Portfolio Management* 8 (4): 5–19.

————. 1984. "Factor models, CAPM, and the APT." *Journal of Portfolio Management* 11 (1): 21–25.

Shefrin, H. and M. Statman. 1984. "Explaining investor preference for cash dividends." *Journal of Financial Economics* 13 (18): 253–282.

———— and ————. 1985. "The disposition to sell winners too early and ride losers too long: Theory and evidence." *Journal of Finance* 40 (3): 777–790.

Singleton, C. and J. Wingender. 1986. "Skewness persistence in common stock returns." *Journal of Financial and Quantitative Analysis* 21 (3): 335–341.

Smirlock, M. and L. Starks. 1986. "Day-of-the-week and intraday effects in stock returns." *Journal of Financial Economics* 17 (1): 197–210.

Snedecor, G. and W. Cochran. 1967. *Statistical Methods.* 6th ed. Ames: Iowa State Press.

Stoll, H. and R. Whaley. 1983. "Transaction costs and the small firm effect." *Journal of Financial Economics* 12 (1): 57–79.

Terada, N. and T. Nakamura. 1984. "The size effect and seasonality in Japanese stock returns." Paper presented at the Institute for Quantitative Research in Finance, May.

Theil, H. 1971. *Principles of Econometrics.* New York: John Wiley.

Tinic, S., G. Barone-Adesi, and R. West. 1987. "Seasonality in Canadian stock prices: A test of the 'tax-loss selling' hypothesis." *Journal of Financial and Quantitative Analysis* 22 (1): 51–63.

Tinic, S. and R. West. 1986. "Risk, return and equilibrium: A revisit." *Journal of Political Economy* 94 (1): 126–147.

Vasicek, O. 1973. "A note on using cross-sectional information in Bayesian estimates of security betas." *Journal of Finance* 28 (5): 1233–1239.

Wachtel, S. 1942. "Certain observations in seasonal movements in stock prices." *Journal of Business* 15 (July): 184–193.

Warga, A. 1987. "Experimental design in tests of linear factor models." Working Paper, Columbia University Business School, New York, January. [Published in *Journal of Business and Economic Statistics* 7 (2): 191–198.]

Zellner, A. 1962. "An efficient method of estimating seemingly unrelated regressions and tests for aggregation bias." *Journal of the American Statistical Association* 57 (298): 348–368.

CHAPTER 3

On the Value of "Value"[*]

The dividend discount model does not fully define value.

In an efficient market, prices reflect information instantaneously and unbiasedly and are good indicators of value [see, for example, Fama (1976), p. 33, and Sharpe (1985), pp. 67–69]. We find, however, substantial evidence contravening stock market efficiency.[1] There is also a growing body of literature suggesting that prices deviate from value, and that such departures can be substantial and long-lasting. This accumulating evidence calls into question the blind pursuit of value in a marketplace that is not price-efficient.

This article investigates the usefulness of value modeling. For purposes of exposition, we use the dividend discount model, or DDM, because it is the quintessential value model and currently enjoys widespread acceptance among practitioners [see Donnelly (1985)]. The DDM's theoretical appeal derives from its all-encompassing nature, as it discounts the entire anticipated stream of future cashflows to arrive at fair, or intrinsic, value. It is the equity counterpart to the yield-to-maturity concept for bonds.

In theory, a strong case can be made for focusing on value to the exclusion of other equity characteristics such as price/earnings ratio and yield. In practice, we find, matters are much less clear-cut. The evidence indicates that value is but a small part of the security pricing story.

---

[*] Originally published in *Financial Analysts Journal* 44 (4): 47–62.

VALUE AND EQUITY ATTRIBUTES

The DDM was first articulated by John Williams in 1938. It posits
that the value, V, of any asset equals the present value of all future
dividends, D, discounted at a rate, r, as follows:

$$V = \frac{D_1}{1+r} + \frac{D_2}{(1+r)^2} + \frac{D_3}{(1+r)^3} \cdots$$

If dividends are assumed to grow at a constant rate, g, this formula
reduces to:[2]

$$V = \frac{D_1}{r-g}.$$

Assuming the denominator $(r-g)$ is the same for all firms, value is
just a constant multiple of dividends. In this simplified world, high-
yielding stocks sell below fair value, while low-yielding stocks are
overpriced.

Miller and Modigliani (1961) demonstrated the equivalence of
discounting dividends, earnings, or cashflow. Thus valuation models can be defined in terms of alternative accounting measures. With
appropriate (if sometimes heroic) simplifying assumptions, such
models can also be reduced to simple financial ratios.

For example, if value is a constant multiple of dividends, and if
the payout ratio (dividends/earnings) is also assumed constant,
then value is just a fixed multiple of earnings. In this case, low-P/E
stocks would be undervalued. Similarly, if depreciation as a percentage of earnings is assumed constant, value is a fixed multiple of
cashflow; if net profit margin is assumed constant, value is a fixed
multiple of sales; and if return on equity is assumed constant, value
is a fixed multiple of book. In these cases, low-price/cashflow, low-
price/sales, and low-price/book stocks would be undervalued.

Reasons can be proposed for why these financial ratios might
be important indicators of value. Current yield, for example, may
interest endowment funds restricted from invading principal. The
price/book ratio may interest corporate raiders concerned with
breakup value, assuming a relation between book and resale value.
The price/cashflow ratio may interest investors prospecting for leveraged buyouts, as excess cashflow may be synonymous with un-
used debt capacity.

Although these ratios clearly differ from the "going concern" notion of value embodied in the DDM, equity characteristics and valuation modeling are intimately related. Some have asserted that low-P/E, high-yield, and antigrowth biases "explain" the DDM's performance, and that DDM forecasts are statistically indistinguishable from those obtained from a low-P/E model [Michaud and Davis (1982)].[3] Others argue that equity attributes, such as low P/E, are associated with anomalous returns simply because they are incomplete proxies for value and conclude that they are not useful measures.[4]

In the next section, we compare the efficacy of the DDM with that of the simple financial ratios discussed previously, plus other equity attributes. First, however, we review existing evidence, which suggests that value may not be the linchpin of asset pricing. Rather, human behavior may violate many of the assumptions underlying conventional financial theory, and market psychology may result in "irrational" pricing [see, for example, Hogarth and Reder (1987)].

MARKET PSYCHOLOGY, VALUE, AND EQUITY ATTRIBUTES

The DDM can be implemented for individual stocks or for the aggregate market. At the individual stock level, DDMs using consensus earnings estimates usually show some securities to be mispriced by a factor of 2 or greater (that is, the price is more than double or less than half the estimated value). Entire groups of stocks often appear to be mispriced for long spans of time.[5] While this degree of mispricing is not inconsistent with Black's (1986) "intuitive" definition of an efficient market, it does suggest that more than just value matters.[6]

As an asset allocation tool, the DDM appears to be useful in valuing equities relative to alternative asset classes.[7] But the DDM is far from omniscient. The market often departs widely from its underlying value. The year 1987 provides a stark example. During the first three quarters, stocks outperformed bonds by 46.7 percent, despite the prediction of value-based asset allocation models that bonds would provide higher returns.[8] Equilibrium was practically restored in just one cataclysmic day—October 19. In the words of Summers (*The Wall*

Street Journal, October 23, 1987, p. 7), "If anyone did seriously believe that price movements are determined by changes in information about economic fundamentals, they've got to be disabused of that notion by Monday's 500-point [Dow] movement."

While this particular market overvaluation was corrected quickly, mispricing can be longer-lasting. Modigliani and Cohn maintained, in 1979, that the stock market had been 50 percent undervalued for as long as a decade because of inflation illusion. The emergence of a bull market after inflation subsided was consistent with their hypothesis.

Such significant and long-lasting departures from value run counter to conventional theory, which suggests that the competitive efforts of many diverse investors are sufficient to restrain prices to some small corridor around fair value.[9] They are more in line with the perspectives of such market observers as Shiller (1984), who argues (p. 497) that "social movements, fashions or fads are likely to be important or even the dominant cause of speculative asset price movements."[10] Moreover, Summers (1986), has pointed out (p. 598) that the whole litany of empirical tests supporting market efficiency is also consistent with an alternative "fads" hypothesis; he takes issue with the notion that market prices must represent rational assessments of fundamental value.

In the context of arguing that the stock market is inefficient because it is too volatile, Shiller (1981) documented wide departures of historical prices from theoretical value and cited these departures as evidence for the existence of fads.[11] Fama and French (1987a) found that dividend yields can explain only 25 percent of the variance in future 2- to 4-year returns and suggested, as one possible explanation, that prices behave whimsically in an irrational market.

Furthermore, the market appears to overreact to world news (such as presidential illnesses), dividends, and other financial news, and may systematically overreact during panics.[12] Several studies, including those by DeBondt and Thaler (1985) and Fama and French (1987b), have documented long-run reversals in security prices, which seem to be due to investor overreaction.[13] DeBondt and Thaler showed reversals lasting up to 5 years, which occurred primarily in January. Fama and French demonstrated that up to 40 percent of the variance of 3- to 5-year returns is a predictable reversal of previous returns. Others, extending these findings, have generally concluded that such reversals represent evidence of serious market inefficiency [see, for example, O'Brien (1987) and Poterba and Summers (1987)].

How can such "mispricing" persist in the face of "smart money"? Summers (1986) concluded that irrationality may be difficult to identify and risky to exploit, hence irrational prices need not be eliminated in time. Black (1986) has argued that trading by those who do not possess useful information creates "noise"—that is, deviations of price from value.[14] These deviations induce information-based traders to enter the market, but the time required for them to correct pricing errors caused by noise traders "is often measured in months or years."[15] As evidence from economic theory, experimental markets, and the real world (such as racetrack betting behavior) has indicated, learning, competition, and arbitrage may be insufficient to eliminate irrationality and market inefficiencies.[16]

Furthermore, institutional investors may be particularly susceptible to fads. Bernstein (1987b) has suggested that value models move in and out of favor with portfolio managers, based on their current effectiveness. Such "style" fads might affect prices. Camerer and Weigelt (1986) have maintained that the relative performance goal of professional money managers is conducive to price bubbles. Friedman (1984) noted that the close-knit professional investment community shares the same research sources and suggested that the asymmetry of rewards in money management leads to "herd" opinions and decisions. In a similar vein, Treynor (1987) has demonstrated that "shared errors" can decrease price accuracy. A shared error results, for example, if all investors accept the imperfect opinion of one Wall Street expert. Ironically, the ubiquitous application of the DDM using analysts' consensus earnings estimates may lead to more, rather than less, misvaluation.

Finally, fads and other departures of price from valuation fundamentals may last because they represent return-maximizing behavior. As Arrow (1982) has noted (p. 7), "If everyone else is 'irrational,' it by no means follows that one can make money by being rational, at least in the short run. With discounting, even eventual success may not be worthwhile."[17] It can be demonstrated that, under certain conditions, irrational traders actually earn higher returns than their more rational counterparts.[18]

This is not inconsistent with Keynes' observation, made over 50 years ago, that the market is like a beauty contest, in which each investor's goal is not to pick the prettiest contestant but, rather, the contestant other judges deem the prettiest. In this view, investors find it more profitable to anticipate the opinions of others than to focus on value. It has, in fact, been demonstrated that foreknowledge of future consensus earnings estimates is more valuable than foreknowledge of actual earnings [see Elton, Gruber, and Gultekin (1979) and Zacks (1979)]. Keynes (1936) may well have been correct in asserting (p. 157) that "investment based on genuine long-term expectations is so difficult . . . as to be scarcely practicable. He who attempts it must surely . . . run greater risks than he who tries to guess better than the crowd how the crowd will behave."[19]

The Importance of Equity Attributes

The power of the DDM appears diminished when it is combined in a multivariate framework with P/E and dividend yield measures [Lanstein (1987)].[20] This suggests that equity attributes are more than just surrogates for value.

There are several reasons why equity attributes might be related to subsequent returns. First, attributes have long been recognized as important determinants of investment risk [see Rosenberg and Marathe (1975)]. Attributes associated with greater riskiness should command higher expected returns. Second, the effects of macroeconomic forces may differ across firms, depending on the firms' equity attributes [Rosenberg and Marathe (1976)]. For instance, changes in inflation affect growth stocks differently from utility stocks. Furthermore, like the overall market, attributes may be mispriced. Mispricing might manifest itself in the form of persistent, anomalous pockets of inefficiency, such as the residual-return-reversal effect [Jacobs and Levy (1988c)]. Or it may, just like fads in the stock market, be psychologically motivated, hence mean-reverting over time.

Because individual stocks are less universally scrutinized than the overall market, one might presume them to be relatively less efficiently priced. Indeed, there is growing evidence that fads cut across stocks sharing a common attribute. As these fads ebb and flow, abnormal returns accrue.

Anomalous returns to some attributes, such as neglect, sigma, and earnings controversy, may arise because investors demand compensation for perceived risk.[21] In conventional theory, such a demand would be irrational, because the risks are diversifiable, hence should earn no abnormal returns. More recent theories that incorporate the effects of incomplete information posit abnormal returns to such attributes [see Merton (1987)].

The novel cognitive psychological approach termed Prospect Theory by Kahneman and Tversky (1979) has been applied by Shefrin and Statman (1984, 1985, and 1987) to explain the dividend-yield, small-size, low-P/E, neglected-firm, and January anomalies, and by Arrow (1982) to explain anomalies associated with investor overreaction. Arrow's argument can be generalized to encompass a host of anomalies, including the earnings torpedo and residual-return-reversal effects.

As noted previously, DeBondt and Thaler (1985) and Fama and French (1987b) cite overreaction as a potential explanation of long-term price reversals. Overreaction can also explain low-P/E, yield, and other effects related to simple financial ratios.[22] Overreactions have also been related to stock splits, earnings, and news events.[23]

The human tendency to avoid, or at least delay, announcing bad news may explain day-of-the-week and week-of-the-month anomalies [Penman (1987)]. Human psychology may also underlie analysts' tendency to overestimate growth stock earnings, which accounts for the earnings torpedo effect [Elton, Gruber, and Gultekin (1984)].[24] Other behavioral predilections appear to explain the trends in analysts' earnings estimates effect. The persistence of analysts' revisions is consistent with the "herd instinct" on Wall Street and analysts' tendency to avoid reversing forecasts [Arnott (1985)].

Simon's (1987) "procedural rationality," a psychological decision-making framework, has been useful in understanding the January, size, yield, and other effects [see Miller (1986)]. Noise in securities prices may explain low-P/E and other simple financial ratio effects [Black (1986), p. 534]. It may also account for the seemingly inexplicable discount to net asset value of many closed-end funds [DeLong et al. (1987)].

Once we loosen the strict rationality assumptions of conventional theory, we find cognitive psychological models capable of explaining seemingly anomalous pricing. Equity characteristics other than theoretical value thereby become important in understanding stock returns.

EXAMINING THE DDM

While previous evidence thus suggests that DDM is a useful construct, it appears to be far from the complete answer to modeling returns. We provide further insight on this issue. First, we examine the relation between DDM expected, or ex ante, security return and other equity attributes. We thereby ascertain whether certain attributes tend to be favored by DDM models. We next examine the relation between actual, or ex post, security return and equity attributes, including the DDM. This provides an empirical assessment of the value of "value" modeling.

Methodology

We used the 25 equity attributes analyzed in our previous article [Jacobs and Levy (1988c)]. Table 3-1 defines these measures.[25] We also utilized expected stock returns from a commercially available three-stage DDM.[26] These expected returns are based on consensus earnings forecasts, and were collected quarterly, in real time, to avoid potential biases such as look-ahead and survivorship.

We employed cross-sectional regression of returns on predetermined attributes. Both DDM expected returns and actual stock returns were tested as the dependent variable. The independent variables were the attribute exposures, normalized as described here.

We utilized both univariate and multivariate regressions, as appropriate. Multivariate regression measures several effects jointly, thereby "purifying" each effect so that it is independent of the others. We refer to multivariate return attributions as "pure" returns and to univariate attributions as "naïve" returns. Univariate regression naïvely measures only one attribute at a time, with no control for other related effects. A single attribute will often proxy for several related effects; a multivariate analysis properly attributes return to its underlying sources.

We analyzed the 20 quarters of the 5-year period from June 1982 to June 1987. For each quarter, we ran a generalized least-squares

T A B L E 3-1

Equity Attributes

Attribute	Definition
Low P/E	Trailing year's fully diluted earnings per share divided by price
Book/price	Common equity per share divided by price
Cashflow/price	Trailing year's earnings plus depreciation and deferred taxes per share divided by price
Sales/price	Trailing year's sales per share divided by price, relative to the capitalization-weighted average sales per share for that stock's industry
Yield	Indicated annual dividend divided by price, as well as binary indicator of zero yield
Beta	Calculated quarterly from a rolling 60-month regression of stock excess (over Treasury bill) returns on S&P 500 excess returns, with a Vasicek Bayesian adjustment
Co-skewness	Calculated quarterly on a rolling 60-month basis as: $$\frac{\sum (R_i - \overline{R}_i)(R_m - \overline{R}_m)^2}{\sum (R_m - \overline{R}_m)^3}$$ where R_i is stock excess (over Treasury bill) return, R_m is the S&P 500 excess return, and $\overline{R}_i$ and $\overline{R}_m$ are rolling 60-month arithmetic averages
Sigma	Calculated as the standard error of estimate, or dispersion of error terms, from the beta regression
Small size	The negative of the natural log of market capitalization
Earnings torpedo	The change from the latest earnings per share last reported to next year's consensus estimate, divided by stock price
Earnings controversy	The standard deviation of next year's analysts' earnings estimates, divided by stock price
Neglect	The negative of the natural log of one plus the number of security analysts following each stock

Continued

TABLE 3–1

Concluded

Attribute	Definition
Low price	The negative of the natural log of stock price
Relative strength	The intercept, or alpha, from the rolling 60-month beta regression
Residual reversal	Measured separately for each of the two most recently completed months as the residuals from the beta regression
Tax-loss measures	Proprietary models of potential short- and long-term tax-loss-selling pressure for each stock
Trends in analysts' earnings estimates	Measured separately for each of the three most recently completed months as the change in the next fiscal year's consensus estimate, divided by stock price
Earnings surprise	Measured separately for each of the three most recently completed months as the difference between the announced earnings and the consensus estimate on that date, divided by stock price

(GLS) regression for the universe, which averaged 1183 of the largest-capitalization stocks.[27] The GLS weights, updated quarterly, were the squared reciprocal of each stock's residual risk. Each stock's weight was limited to a maximum of 10 times and a minimum of one-tenth the average GLS weight. The use of GLS regression produces greater estimation accuracy than ordinary least squares.

We normalized each independent variable (including DDM expected return in the ex post analysis only) by subtracting its capitalization-weighted average and dividing by its cross-sectional standard deviation. Outliers were truncated. The normalization procedure provided coefficients, or attributions of return, that are scaled consistently across measures. Each coefficient represents the marginal return to a stock with an exposure of 1 cross-sectional standard deviation to that measure. We refer to this as *one unit of exposure*. In addition to these normalized measures, some regressions include a zero-yield indicator in the form of a binary dummy variable and 38 binary industry variables to control for industry comovements.

Stability of Equity Attributes

Would the quarterly time frame we utilized bias our conclusions? On one hand, longer time frames hamper measures that are short-lived. The information content of variables such as earnings surprise may become stale quickly. On the other hand, characteristics such as book/price are relatively stable. We examined the relative stability of the various equity attributes to determine whether quarterly DDM expected return was sufficiently timely.

We calculated the correlation of each equity attribute between beginning-of-quarter and end-of-quarter exposures across stocks. Our stability measure for each attribute was an average of these quarterly correlations. Book/price and P/E turned out to be rather stable, with average correlations of 0.94 and 0.87, respectively. DDM expected return was less stable, with an average correlation of 0.66, and the more transient effects exhibited much less stability. For instance, the average correlation was 0.29 for earnings surprises and 0.15 for trends in analysts' earnings estimates.[28]

What are the implications for testing the DDM in a quarterly framework? DDM expected return is substantially more stable than transient measures but somewhat less stable than measures such as book/price. It should be noted that attribute exposures were updated quarterly; intraquarter correlations for 1 and 2 months apart would be even higher for all measures, including DDM expected return. But even a monthly framework could be criticized as being inferior to a daily one. Moreover, a quarterly analysis would definitely handicap short-lived measures such as earnings surprise. We believe our conclusions regarding the DDM are robust to shorter time frames.

EXPECTED RETURNS

We examined the relation of DDM expected security return to various predetermined equity characteristics. First, we considered naïve, or univariate, attributions of DDM expected return. These naïve attributions enable us to verify intuitive notions of association such as that between low P/E and DDM. We then analyzed pure, or multivariate, attributions of DDM expected return. Because multivariate regression disentangles the effects of one attribute from those of others, it provides for a proper attribution of DDM expected return and reveals the true relations between equity characteristics and DDM attractiveness.

Table 3-2 presents summary statistics for the ex ante cross-sectional regressions over the period from June 1982 to June 1987. Each quarter's regression coefficients can be interpreted as the expected return to the equity attributes, as implied by the DDM. Quarterly average regression coefficients, in both naïve and pure form, and associated t-statistics are displayed for the various attributes.

The t-statistic measures whether the average of expected returns differs significantly from zero. Another measure of the relation between equity attributes and DDM expected return is the frequency of cross-sectional significance. On average, an attribute may not be associated with an expected return significantly different from zero, but it may nonetheless be tied cross-sectionally to DDM expected return. To show cross-sectional explanatory power, we display a count of the number of quarters in which the attribute had a t-statistic greater than 2 in absolute value. This should occur by chance alone about 5 percent of the time, or in 1 out of 20 quarters.

T A B L E 3-2

Quarterly Average Expected Returns to Attributes

Attribute	Naïve			Pure		
	Average Expected Return	t-Statistic	Number of Quarters |t| > 2	Average Expected Return	t-Statistic	Number of Quarters |t| > 2
Low P/E	1.67	4.1**	16	1.11	5.5**	8
Book/price	0.92	8.2**	18	-0.22	-3.9**	0
Cashflow/price	0.51	2.1*	13	0.08	0.6	3
Sales/price	0.80	10.6**	17	0.53	9.6**	14
Yield	0.53	3.6**	15	1.66	17.7**	20
Zero yield	-0.10	-0.8	2	1.08	7.9**	11
Beta	0.52	3.1**	18	0.65	17.9**	16
Co-skewness	-0.09	-0.3	15	-0.23	-3.7**	1
Sigma	0.74	2.3*	14	0.50	7.3**	3
Small size	0.22	2.9**	6	-0.24	-5.2**	7
Earnings torpedo	0.43	2.0*	13	0.60	3.6**	13
Earnings controversy	0.22	0.9	7	-0.19	-1.5	2
Neglect	0.14	1.6	6	-0.05	-1.1	0
Low price	0.79	11.8**	17	0.67	11.1**	16
Relative strength	-0.45	-1.9*	15	0.10	1.6	2
Residual reversal (−1)	-1.04	-4.0**	17	-0.66	-13.8**	18
Residual reversal (−2)	-0.36	-1.9*	16	-0.25	-3.7**	11
Short-term tax-loss	1.51	6.1**	18	0.43	2.8*	5
Long-term tax-loss	0.09	0.3	11	-0.10	-1.3	1
Trend in estimates (−1)	0.02	0.2	6	0.19	1.9*	4
Trend in estimates (−2)	0.00	0.0	7	0.18	1.7*	6
Trend in estimates (−3)	0.24	1.9*	4	0.15	1.9*	2
Earnings surprise (−1)	-0.12	-0.2	1†	-0.09	-0.3	0†
Earnings surprise (−2)	0.04	0.1	3†	-0.06	-0.4	0†
Earnings surprise (−3)	-0.24	-1.7	2†	-0.09	-0.9	2†

* Significant at the 10 percent level.

** Significant at the 1 percent level.

† Data for the earnings surprise measures were available for the last 13 quarters. All other measures are for 20 quarters.

Naïve Expected Returns

In naïve form, all the simple financial ratios—P/E, book/price, cashflow/price, sales/price, and yield—have significant positive expected return attributions, ranging between 51 and 167 basis points for one unit of exposure. These expected payoffs are significant at the 1 percent level, except for cashflow/price, which is significant at the 10 percent level. Also, the number of times the financial ratios have a cross-sectional t-statistic greater than 2 in absolute value ranges from 13 to 18, which is much higher than would occur by chance alone.

We noted earlier that, under appropriate simplifying assumptions, the DDM reduces to simple financial ratios. Now we have found empirical evidence of an intimate relation between such ratios and DDM expected return.[29] This evidence supports the hypothesis that these ratios are mere proxies for value (a notion tested directly in a later section).

The beta and sigma attributes are also tied positively and significantly to DDM expected return. These relations are consistent with an expected reward for bearing risk. The average expected return to earnings torpedo, too, is significantly positive. Because DDM expected return is derived from analysts' earnings estimates, which tend to be overly optimistic for high-growth stocks, this relationship is not surprising.[30]

Significant associations between DDM expected return and price-based attributes may arise from changes in stock price that are unrelated to changes in value.[31] Price movements consistent with changes in value leave DDM expected return unaffected, hence induce no correlation with other attributes. Price movements unrelated to value, however, affect DDM expected return as well as price-based attributes, thereby inducing a correlation. For instance, a decline in price raises a stock's position on the low-price scale. If unassociated with a change in value, the price decline also raises its DDM expected return.[32] Price-based attributes include the simple financial ratios, but even more directly price-related are measures such as residual-return reversal and potential short-term tax-loss-selling. These measures are significantly related to DDM expected return.

Pure Expected Returns

Expected return attributions in pure form are sometimes consistent with those in naïve form. For instance, the expected naïve payoff to low P/E is 1.67 percent, with a t-statistic of 4.1, while the expected pure payoff is 1.11 percent with a t-statistic of 5.5. The expected pure return is less than the naïve return, indicating that the latter proxies for related effects such as yield. Despite the lower magnitude of the pure return, its larger t-statistic attests to the greater consistency of its association with DDM expected returns [Jacobs and Levy (1988c)].

Among the simple financial ratios, the cashflow/price attribution disappears in pure form. Sales/price remains significant at the 1 percent level, while yield becomes larger and more significant, with a t-statistic of 17.7. Expected return to book/price flips sign, becoming negatively related to DDM expected return. Naïve returns to book/price apparently proxy for positively correlated pure attributes such as yield. When these relationships are properly controlled, higher book/price is associated with lower DDM expected return.

Pure expected return to zero yield is notably different from its naïve counterpart. The pure expected payoff is 1.08 percent, with a t-statistic of 7.9. Controlling for the common features of zero-yielding stocks, such as their below-average size, allows a positive association between zero yield and DDM expected return to emerge. Expected return to small size flips sign and is negative in pure form.

The positive beta and sigma relationships with DDM expected return are even stronger, statistically, in pure form, while co-skewness emerges as significant and negative. Residual-return reversal becomes even more significant, while potential short-term tax-loss-selling weakens.

Trends in analysts' earnings estimates emerge significantly positive at the 10 percent level. This correlation might arise because of revisions in estimates that have not yet been fully reflected in stock prices. Such an upward revision in the consensus estimate would render a stock more attractive on a DDM basis.

Some measures, such as neglect and earnings surprise, are uncorrelated with DDM expected returns. These measures are associated, however, with anomalous returns [see Jacobs and Levy

(1988c)]. Calendar-related anomalies also appear unrelated to the DDM. It is improbable, for instance, that value varies in a fashion consistent with the day-of-the-week effect.[33] The DDM does not provide the whole story on returns.

We analyzed the time pattern of the association between DDM expected returns and pure returns to each attribute. Some relationships were quite stable. For example, the expected return to yield was positive and significant in all 20 quarters. Not surprisingly, weaker relationships were less stable. For instance, trends in analysts' estimates were positively related to DDM expected return in 14 quarters.

We derived the expected pure return to each attribute in a "bottom-up" fashion from individual security DDM expected returns. Such estimates may be useful in assessing the relative attractiveness of various sectors of the market [see Rudd and Clasing (1982)]. Alternatively, macroeconomic drivers can be used in a "top-down" fashion to forecast attribute, or sector, returns [see Jacobs and Levy (1988c)].

The average quarterly R-squared, or percentage of variation in cross-sectional return explained by our attributes, is 28 percent. Thus, a DDM strategy cannot be replicated with attributes alone. But if some attributes produce anomalous returns, a DDM strategy will not fully exploit them.

ACTUAL RETURNS

We tested the potency of the DDM by examining the determinants of actual return over the 5-year period from June 1982 to June 1987. First, we assessed the DDM's power by regressing actual, or ex post, stock return on DDM expected return. Then we examined the relative power of DDM and P/E by including both measures in a bivariate regression. We made this direct comparison because of the widespread use of P/E by practitioners.[34] Next, we pitted DDM against the simple financial ratios related to valuation modeling. Lastly, we carried our analysis to its logical conclusion by considering DDM simultaneously with 25 other attributes, as well as 38 industry classifications.

The four panels of Table 3-3 present summary statistics for the ex post cross-sectional regressions. The returns displayed represent an

T A B L E   3–3

Quarterly Average Actual Returns to Attributes

	Attribute	Average Actual Return	t-Statistic	Number of Quarters |t| > 2
Panel A	DDM	0.21	1.1	8
Panel B	DDM	0.15	0.7	10
	Low P/E	1.53	1.2	17
Panel C	DDM	0.06	0.3	9
	Low P/E	0.92	0.5	10
	Book/price	0.01	0.0	12
	Cashflow/price	0.18	0.2	9
	Sales/price	0.96	4.1**	7
	Yield	−0.51	−0.9	15
Panel D	DDM	0.23	1.4	6
	Low P/E	−0.22	−0.3	5
	Book/price	0.51	1.6	5
	Cashflow/price	0.61	1.6	4
	Sales/price	0.80	5.4**	7
	Yield	−0.33	−1.0	4
	Zero yield	−0.13	−0.4	2
	Beta	−0.18	−0.9	5
	Co-skewness	0.14	0.7	1
	Sigma	−0.99	−2.5*	9
	Small size	0.05	0.2	6
	Earnings torpedo	−0.33	−1.2	5
	Earnings controversy	0.19	0.5	2
	Neglect	0.50	2.0*	7
	Low price	0.08	0.3	8
	Relative strength	0.92	2.2*	12
	Residual reversal (−1)	−1.69	−8.1**	15
	Residual reversal (−2)	−0.37	−2.0*	8
	Short-term tax-loss	−0.83	−2.5*	5
	Long-term tax-loss	−0.17	−0.6	3
	Trend in estimates (−1)	1.11	4.5**	7
	Trend in estimates (−2)	0.52	2.2*	1
	Trend in estimates (−3)	0.38	1.4	2
	Earnings surprise (−1)	0.98	1.7	2†
	Earnings surprise (−2)	1.11	2.6*	1†
	Earnings surprise (−3)	0.74	2.4*	2†

* Significant at the 10 percent level.

** Significant at the 1 percent level.

† Data for the earnings surprise measures were available for the last 13 quarters. All other measures are for 20 quarters.

average of the quarterly cross-sectional regression coefficients. The t-statistics measure whether the average actual payoff differs significantly from zero. Also shown is a count of the number of quarters in which the attribute had a t-statistic greater than 2 in absolute value.

Power of the DDM

As Panel A shows, a one-unit-of-exposure bet on DDM expected return would have provided a quarterly average payoff of 21 basis points, exclusive of transaction costs, over the 5-year period. This average payoff has a t-statistic of 1.1, and thus is not significantly different from zero. The impotence of DDM should be viewed in context, however; this particular period was one of the worst performance stretches for the DDM in the last 20 years.[35]

While DDM had little predictive power, it was tied cross-sectionally to actual stock returns. DDM had a t-statistic with an absolute value exceeding 2 in 8 of the 20 quarterly regressions. The lack of significant average returns over this period, however, underscores the fact that DDM predictions were at times perverse. That is, DDM expected return was sometimes negatively correlated with actual returns.

Panel B shows the results of pitting DDM against low P/E.[36] The quarterly average payoff to DDM declines to 15 basis points. The average payoff to low P/E is larger—1.53 percent—but not statistically significant. Low P/E is significant in 17 of the quarterly cross-sectional regressions, while DDM is significant in only 10 quarters. If low P/E were a mere proxy for DDM, it would be subsumed by DDM. This is not the case; rather, DDM appears partially subsumed by low P/E.

Panel C displays results from the simultaneous analysis of DDM and the simple financial ratios. The average quarterly payoff to DDM drops to 6 basis points. The highest payoffs are 92 basis points to low P/E and 96 to sales/price. The payoff to sales/price is statistically significant at the 1 percent level, while the other payoffs are insignificant.

Power of Equity Attributes

Panel D displays results from the full multivariate regression. While DDM remains insignificant, many equity attributes provide statistically significant abnormal performance. These include sales/price,

T A B L E   3–4

Summary

	Average Adjusted R^2 (%)
Panel A: DDM	0.37
Panel B: DDM and P/E	3.38
Panel C: DDM and simple financial ratios	8.94
Panel D: DDM and all equity attributes	43.93

neglect, relative strength, residual return reversal, trends in analysts' earnings estimates, and earnings surprise.[37] Once again, the DDM does not subsume equity attributes.

The conjecture that the predictive power of equity characteristics arises solely from their proxying for value is wrong. To the contrary, equity attributes emerge important in their own right. In fact, many attributes were better predictors of subsequent return than the DDM.

Moreover, DDM expected return is nothing more than an additional equity attribute. Our test of the DDM's predictive power can be interpreted as a semistrong-form test of market efficiency. Because all inputs to the model are publicly available, this measure is no different from other predetermined attributes, such as P/E, from the perspective of market efficiency.

Table 3-4 summarizes the additional investment insight provided by equity attributes by showing the average quarterly R-squared, adjusted for degrees of freedom, for each set of ex post regressions. Clearly, the full model has substantially more explanatory power than the DDM alone. Stock returns are driven by much more than just value considerations.

Our previous article [Jacobs and Levy (1988c)] showed that returns to many equity attributes appear forecastable. This leads us next to examine the predictability of returns to the DDM.

FORECASTING DDM RETURNS

Figure 3-1 plots cumulative ex post returns to DDM in both naïve and pure form. The naïve returns arise from a constant bet of one unit of exposure on DDM, letting the chips fall where they may with

FIGURE 3-1

Cumulative Return to DDM

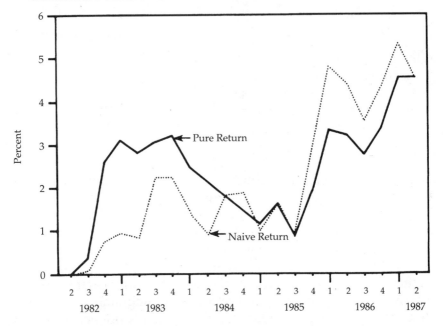

regard to unintentional bets on other attributes. The pure strategy places the same intensity of bet on DDM, but simultaneously neutralizes bets on all other attributes. That is, the pure strategy maintains equity characteristics, such as yield and industry exposures, identical to those of the market.

The similarity in the payoff patterns of the two strategies is not coincidental, because naïve returns equal pure returns plus noise from unintentional side bets. Below, we focus on the pure returns. The payoff to DDM appears unstable, which leads us to investigate its predictability.

First, we considered a time-series analysis of the pure returns, as we previously found such an approach to be useful.[38] However, no significant patterns were found.

We then examined correlations between the time series of pure returns to the DDM and pure returns to the simple financial ratios. All relationships were insignificantly different from zero, except for the correlation between pure returns to DDM and pure returns to yield. This correlation was –0.55, with a t-statistic of –3.3, significant at the 1 percent level. The fact that the payoff patterns of the simple financial ratios are not positively correlated with the DDM reinforces the notion that these ratios are not mere proxies for value. Moreover, the negative relationship with returns to the yield attribute suggests that the DDM may be "aggressive" in nature, as our previous work showed yield to be "defensive" [see Jacobs and Levy (1988c)].

We regressed quarterly pure returns to the DDM attribute on S&P 500 excess returns (over Treasury bills) for the 5-year period. We found the following relationship:

DDM pure return = –0.12 + 0.08 market excess return.

The DDM's positive market responsiveness of 0.08 has a t-statistic of 5.2, which is highly significant. For each additional 1 percent of positive (negative) quarterly market excess return, a one-unit-of-exposure bet on the DDM provides 8 more (fewer) basis points of return over this period. Contrary to conventional wisdom, the value attribute appears to detract from performance in bear markets.

Furthermore, the intercept of the DDM regression is negative (with a t-statistic of –1.0). On a market-adjusted basis, the DDM was detrimental to returns over this period. Positive returns to DDM accumulated only because this was a bull market period.

The DDM's dependency on market climate may arise from variations in investors' willingness to be far-sighted. Because the DDM discounts an infinite stream of future dividends, it is a forward-looking measure. When the market is rising, investors are more optimistic and extend their horizons; they are more willing to rely on DDM expectations. When the market is falling, they are less willing to trust DDM expectations and place greater emphasis on more tangible attributes such as current yield.

In theory, prices are value-based and immune to mood swings. In practice, we find investor psychology to be paramount.

CONCLUSION

Market efficiency, investor rationality, and value-based pricing are major tenets of conventional investment theory. All three of these presumptions are suspect.

We have demonstrated that equity characteristics are not mere proxies for value. The explanatory power of other equity attributes dwarfs that of the DDM. Furthermore, the DDM appears to be just another equity attribute and, like some attributes, may be amenable to prediction.

In an inefficient market driven by investor psychology, investment opportunities are bountiful. Blind adherence to value models is suboptimal, and a heavy dose of empiricism is warranted. As Noble laureate Herbert Simon (1987) has asserted (p. 39), the emerging laws of economic behavior "have much more the complexity of molecular biology than the simplicity of classical mechanics. As a consequence, they call for a very high ratio of empirical investigation to theory building." In a similar vein, Paul Samuelson (1987) has stated (p. 6): "I prefer paradigms that combine plausible Newtonian theories with observed Baconian facts. But never would I refuse houseroom to a sturdy fact just because it is a bastard without a name and a parental model."

ENDNOTES

The authors thank The Dais Group; Interactive Data Corporation; Institutional Brokers Estimate System (I/B/E/S); and Standard & Poor's Compustat for data and systems support.

1. For cross-sectional effects, see Jacobs and Levy (1988c). For a briefer treatment, see Jacobs and Levy (1988b). This evidence is more compelling than previous market anomaly research because it documents multiple independent rejections of efficiency. For calendar effects, see Jacobs and Levy (1988a and 1989).

2. This valuation formula is sometimes referred to as the Gordon-Shapiro model. It is developed in the context of a dynamic growth model in Gordon and Shapiro (1956).

3. Sorenson and Williamson (1985) find, however, improved predictive power for successively more complete security valuation models— including P/E, constant-growth DDM (Gordon-Shapiro), two-stage DDM, and three-stage DDM.

4. Estep (1985) argues that such attributes are incomplete estimators of expected return, in that they ignore important parts of the full valuation equation. Estep (1987b) asserts that returns to attributes

such as price/book are not anomalous, but rather evidence that PB is somewhat correlated with true value. The existence of returns to PB "does not mean, however, that PB is a 'factor' that 'generates' returns; in fact, when the true relation of PB to return is seen, it is clear that construing PB as a factor is not appropriate" (p. 42). Finally, Estep (1987a) concludes (p. 6) that "the success enjoyed by these naïve models [such as PB] comes in spite of, rather than because of, the level of understanding of their users."

5. For instance, the banking and tobacco industries have been attractive in recent years. Either the discount rates used do not adequately reflect the risks of third-world default and product liability suits or, alternatively, market prices reflect more than value characteristics.

6. The effectiveness of the DDM may be improved upon by incorporating timing and macroeconomic measures. At the individual stock level, see Arnott and Copeland (1985). They find value-oriented approaches to have unstable effectiveness over time and identify a statistically significant increase in DDM effectiveness in the first quarter of each year (perhaps related to the January effect), a significant first-order autocorrelation (or persistence), as well as a negative correlation between DDM effectiveness and inflation. At the aggregate market level, see Arnott and VonGermeten (1983). These methods depart from targeting value alone and are suggestive of pricing that is not solely value-based.

7. See Einhorn and Shangkuan (1984) for evidence on the usefulness of DDM for asset allocation. The recent growth of portfolio insurance strategies has led to more frequent and more significant departures of the market from value considerations. With insured assets recently as high as $68 billion, the insurers' trading rule of buying as the market rises and selling as it falls has increased market volatility. DDM strategies tend to follow the opposite trading rule. As market volatility increases, insured strategies become more costly and DDM strategies more profitable. See Jacobs (1987).

8. The S&P 500 returned 35.9 percent, versus –10.8 percent for long-term Treasury bonds.

9. See Sharpe (1985), pp. 68–69, for an articulation of this view and Verrecchia (1979) for a theoretical analysis.

10. Shiller does not totally dismiss rational expectations and the usefulness of fundamentals. Shiller (1987) states (pp. 318–319): "I think the truth may well be that financial prices can be successfully modeled as reflecting proper anticipations of those future

movements in dividends that can be predicted plus a term reflecting the anticipation of fashions or fads among investors."

11. The excess volatility argument remains controversial. For a summary of the debate, see Camerer and Weigelt (1986). Shiller (1987), pp. 320–321, discusses departures from value, rather than excess volatility, as evidence of fads.

12. See Niederhoffer (1971) on world news; Arrow (1982), Shiller (1984), and DeBondt (1985) on financial news; and Renshaw (1984) on panics. [O'Hanlon and Ward (1986) contend that Renshaw's rules fail out-of-sample tests.] Other markets may also overreact [Frankel and Meese (1987)].

13. Chan (1988) claims that DeBondt and Thaler's reversal effect is explained by changing risk: Stocks suffering price declines become riskier, and this heightened risk explains their subsequent outperformance. However, DeBondt and Thaler (1987) demonstrate that losers subsequently have higher betas in up markets and lower betas in down markets, and thus reject the changing-risk explanation. Fama and French (1987b) advance two possible explanations for the price reversals—market inefficiency and changing risk premiums.

14. French and Roll (1986) find that a significant portion of market volatility is due to mispricing. DeLong et al. (1987) maintain that noise traders cause prices to deviate so far from fair value as to create serious consequences for society as a whole.

15. Black, quoted in Bernstein (1987a), p. 56. Shefrin and Statman (1987) ascribe the persistence of noise trading to errors in cognition.

16. Akerlof and Yellen (1985) demonstrate that small amounts of irrationality can have large economic effects. See references to experimental markets in Plott (1987) and Hausch, Ziemba, and Rubinstein (1981).

17. For a theoretical elaboration, see Russell and Thaler (1985).

18. DeLong et al. (1987) demonstrate that irrational traders can earn higher returns because they bear the large amount of risk that they induce, and this risk scares off more rational investors.

19. For a theoretical model, see Aiyagari (1988).

20. Furthermore, Jacobs (1986) shows a simple financial measure to be superior to present value in predicting stock returns to changes in depreciation accounting methods having real economic impacts.

21. For neglect, see Arbell, Carvell, and Strebel (1983); for sigma, see Levy (1978); and for earnings controversy, see Arnott (1983).

22. On low P/E, see Shiller (1984). For a practitioner's viewpoint, see Dreman (1982).

23. On splits, see Ohlson and Penman (1985); on earnings, see DeBondt and Thaler (1987); on events, see Renshaw (1984), Howe (1986), and Brown and Harlow (1988).

24. This bias is also consistent with Prospect Theory's base-rate fallacy.

25. For an extensive discussion of these attributes and our methodology, see Jacobs and Levy (1988c).

26. For a description of the three-stage DDM, see Sharpe (1985), Chapter 14.

27. The universe each quarter was a subset of the 1500 largest-capitalization stocks for which all the necessary data were available to calculate DDM expected returns. The sample size ranged from a low of 1035 to a high of 1337.

28. The correlation, significant at the 1 percent level, between the unanticipated component of consecutive earnings announcements indicates that surprises tend to repeat. This may be due to the behavior of analysts, if they do not fully incorporate all relevant information in forming their earnings expectations. This persistence of earnings surprise is consistent with Jones, Rendleman, and Latane (1984). Rendleman, Jones, and Latane (1986) propose that most of the postannouncement stock response to an earnings surprise may actually be a preannouncement adjustment to next quarter's surprise.

29. See Michaud and Davis (1982) and Bethke and Boyd (1983) for earlier documentation on growth, P/E, and yield.

30. For discussion of this analyst bias, see Elton, Gruber, and Gultekin (1984). Michaud and Davis (1982) document a negative correlation of DDM expected return with long-term growth. Our earnings torpedo measure is not comparable because it looks ahead only 1 fiscal year.

31. Note that we lagged price 1 month to avoid bid/ask and pricing error problems for most measures, as discussed in Jacobs and Levy (1988c). DDM and residual-return reversal are notable exceptions.

32. Alternatively, a relationship could be spuriously induced by a price change near quarter-end consistent with a value change that has not yet been reflected in the DDM model. This may occur because of lags in updating consensus earnings databases for revisions in analysts' estimates [Jacobs and Levy (1988c)].

33. For an extensive discussion of calendar-based anomalies, see Jacobs and Levy (1988a) and Ferson, Foerster, and Keim (1987).

34. *Pensions & Investment Age* (November 10, 1986, p. 92) reported that 29.3 percent of all institutional managers identified low P/E as an integral part of their style.

35. See R. Jones (1987), p. 34, for a 20-year perspective. Jones' results are generally consistent with ours regarding the efficacy of the DDM. Moreover, Michaud and Davis (1982) find that even during the period 1973–1980, when the DDM provided significant economic rewards, it was still not statistically significant.

36. A skeptic might assert that our results may be affected by look-ahead bias. While DDM expected returns were collected in real time, P/E and other measures were determined retroactively. To avoid look-ahead bias, we lagged announced earnings 3 months, consistent with Banz and Breen (1986). We also reran the regressions in Panel B utilizing a P/E attribute based on expected, rather than historical, earnings. These earnings estimates were also used as inputs to the DDM, so that any potential advantage was eliminated. The results were almost identical to those in Panel B. The DDM average coefficient was 0.11 with t-statistic 0.44, and the low-P/E average coefficient was 0.88 with t-statistic 0.90.

37. Note that industry attributions are not shown in Panel D. For the time period studied, the returns to equity attributes are generally consistent with our earlier paper. However, the adoption of a quarterly, rather than a monthly, time frame does lead to some differences. First, the January effect is obscured. Second, transient measures such as residual reversal are less significant. Third, the 3-month-ago earnings surprise measure is more significant. This arises from a data artifact relating to the uneven distribution of firms across fiscal reporting months.

38. See Jacobs and Levy (1988c) for an autocorrelation analysis of all 25 non-DDM measures. Arnott and Copeland (1985) report significant first-order autocorrelation of naïve returns to the DDM. We find first-order autocorrelation insignificantly negative for naïve returns and insignificantly positive for pure returns. Also, both series exhibit the first-quarter seasonality reported by Arnott and Copeland.

REFERENCES

Aiyagari, S. 1988. "Economic fluctuations without shocks to fundamentals; or, does the stock market dance to its own music?" *Federal Reserve Bank of Minneapolis Quarterly Review* 12 (1): 8–24.

Akerlof, G. and J. Yellen. 1985. "Can small deviations from rationality make significant differences to economic equilibria?" *American Economic Review* 75 (4): 708–720.

Arbel, A., S. Carvell, and P. Strebel. 1983. "Giraffes, institutions and neglected firms." *Financial Analysts Journal* 39 (3): 57–62.

Arnott, R. 1983. "What hath MPT wrought: Which risks reap rewards?" *Journal of Portfolio Management* 10 (1): 5–11.

———. 1985. "The use and misuse of consensus earnings." *Journal of Portfolio Management* 11 (3): 18–27.

Arnott, R. and W. Copeland. 1985. "The business cycle and security selection." *Financial Analysts Journal* 41 (2): 26–32.

Arnott, R. and J. VonGermeten. 1983. "Systematic asset allocation." *Financial Analysts Journal* 39 (6): 31–38.

Arrow, K. 1982. "Risk perception in psychology and economics." *Economic Inquiry* 20 (1): 1–9.

Banz, R. and W. Breen. 1986. "Sample-dependent results using accounting and market data: Some evidence." *Journal of Finance* 41 (4): 779–793.

Bernstein, P. 1987a. "Liquidity, stock markets, and market makers." *Financial Management* 16 (2): 54–62.

———. 1987b. "The ill-behaved e's." *Journal of Portfolio Management* 13 (4): 1.

Bethke, W. and S. Boyd. 1983. "Should dividend discount models be yield tilted?" *Journal of Portfolio Management* 9 (3): 23–27.

Black, F. 1986. "Noise." *Journal of Finance* 41 (3): 529–543.

Brown, K. and W. Harlow. 1988. "Market overreaction: Magnitude and intensity." *Journal of Portfolio Management* 14 (2): 6–13.

Camerer, C. and K. Weigelt. 1986. "Rational price bubbles in asset markets: A review of theory and evidence." Working Paper #371, Salomon Brothers Center, New York University, New York, March. [See "Bubbles and fads in asset prices: A review of theory and evidence." *Journal of Economic Surveys* 3 (1): 3–41.]

Chan, K. 1988. "On the contrarian investment strategy." *Journal of Business* 61 (2): 147–163.

DeBondt, W. 1985. "Does the stock market react to new information?" Ph.D. dissertation, Cornell University, Ithaca, New York.

DeBondt, W. and R. Thaler. 1985. "Does the stock market overreact?" *Journal of Finance* 40 (3): 793–805.

——— and ———. 1987. "Further evidence on investor overreaction and stock market seasonality." *Journal of Finance* 42 (3): 557–581.

DeLong, B., et al. 1987. "The economic consequences of noise traders." Working Paper #218, Center for Research in Security Prices, University of Chicago, Chicago, September. [Subsequently published as "Noise trader risk in financial markets." *Journal of Political Economy* 98 (4): 703–738.]

Donnelly, B. 1985. "The dividend model comes into its own." *Institutional Investor*, March, pp. 77–82.

Dreman, D. 1982. *The New Contrarian Investment Strategy*. New York: Random House.

Einhorn, S. and P. Shangkuan. 1984. "Using the dividend discount model for asset allocation." *Financial Analysts Journal* 40 (3): 30–32.

Elton, E., M. Gruber, and M. Gultekin. 1979. "Capital market efficiency and expectational data." Working Paper, New York University, New York, May.

———, ———, and ———. 1984. "Professional expectations: Accuracy and diagnosis of errors." *Journal of Financial and Quantitative Analysis* 19 (4): 351–364.

Estep, T. 1985. "A new method for valuing common stocks." *Financial Analysts Journal* 41 (6): 26–33.

———. 1987a. "Manager style and the sources of equity returns." *Journal of Portfolio Management* 13 (2): 4–10.

———. 1987b. "Security analysis and stock selection: Turning financial information into return forecasts." *Financial Analysts Journal* 43 (4): 34–43.

Fama, E. 1976. *Foundations of Finance*. New York: Basic Books.

Fama, E. and K. French. 1987a. "Dividend yields and expected stock returns." Working Paper #215, Center for Research in Security Prices, University of Chicago, Chicago, July. [Published in *Journal of Financial Economics* 22 (1): 3–26.]

——— and ———. 1987b. "Permanent and temporary components of stock prices." Working Paper #178, Center for Research in Security Prices, University of Chicago, Chicago, February. [Published in *Journal of Political Economy* 96 (2): 246–273.]

Ferson, W., S. Foerster, and D. Keim. 1987. "Tests of asset pricing models with changing expectations." Working Paper, Stanford University, Stanford, California, November. [Subsequently published as "General tests of latent variable models and mean-variance spanning." *Journal of Finance* 48 (1): 131–156.]

Frankel, J. and R. Meese. 1987. "Are exchange rates excessively variable?" Working Paper #2249, National Bureau of Economic Research, Boston, May.

French, K. and R. Roll. 1986. "Stock return variances: The arrival of information and the reaction of traders." *Journal of Financial Economics* 17 (1): 5–26.

Friedman, B. 1984. Discussion: Stock prices and social dynamics. *Brookings Papers on Economic Activity* 15 (2): 407–508.

Gordon, M. and E. Shapiro. 1956. "Capital equipment analysis: The required rate of profit." *Management Science* 3 (October): 102–110.

Hausch, D., W. Ziemba, and M. Rubinstein. 1981. "Efficiency of the market for racetrack betting." *Management Science* 27: 1435–1452.

Hogarth, R. and M. Reder, eds. 1987. *Rational Choice: The Contrast Between Economics and Psychology*. Chicago: University of Chicago Press.

Howe, J. 1986. "Evidence on stock market overreaction." *Financial Analysts Journal* 42 (4): 74–77.

Jacobs, B. 1986. "Depreciation: Accounting, taxes, and capital market equilibrium." Ph.D. dissertation, Wharton School, University of Pennsylvania, Philadelphia.

———. 1987. "Portfolio insurance: It's prone to failure." *Pensions & Investment Age,* November 16, pp. 3, 79.

Jacobs, B. and K. Levy. 1988a. "Calendar anomalies: Abnormal returns at calendar turning points." *Financial Analysts Journal* 44 (6): 28–39.

——— and ———. 1988*b*. "Disentangling equity return regularities." In *Equity Markets and Valuation Methods.* Charlottesville, Virginia: Institute of Chartered Financial Analysts.

——— and ———. 1988*c*. "Disentangling equity return regularities: New insights and investment opportunities." *Financial Analysts Journal* 44 (3): 18–43.

——— and ———. 1989. "Trading tactics in an inefficient market." In *A Complete Guide to Securities Transactions: Controlling Costs and Enhancing Performance,* W. Wagner, ed. New York: John Wiley.

Jones, C., R. Rendleman, and H. Latane. 1984. "Stock returns and SUEs during the 1970's." *Journal of Portfolio Management* 10 (2): 18–22.

Jones, R. 1987. "Goldman Sachs stock selection." Goldman Sachs, New York, 2d quarter.

Kahneman, D. and A. Tversky. 1979. "Prospect Theory: An analysis of decision under risk." *Econometrica* 47 (2): 263–291.

Keynes, J. M. 1936. *The General Theory of Employment, Interest, and Money* (reprint). New York: Harcourt Brace, 1964.

Lanstein, R. 1987. "Using regression analysis to value stocks." Paper presented at the Institute for International Research Conference on Stock Valuation Methods, New York, May 20.

Levy, H. 1978. "Equilibrium in an imperfect market: A constraint on the number of securities in the portfolio." *American Economic Review* 68 (4): 643–658.

Merton, R. 1987. "A simple model of capital market equilibrium with incomplete information." *Journal of Finance* 42 (3): 483–510.

Michaud, R. and P. Davis. 1982. "Valuation model bias and the scale structure of dividend discount returns." *Journal of Finance* 37 (2): 563–573.

Miller, E. 1986. "Explaining the January small firm effect." Working Paper, University of New Orleans, New Orleans, November. [Published in *Quarterly Journal of Business and Economics* 29 (3): 36–55.]

Miller, M. and F. Modigliani. 1961. "Dividend policy, growth, and the valuation of shares." *Journal of Business* 34 (4): 411–433.

Modigliani, F. and R. Cohn. 1979. "Inflation, rational valuation and the market." *Financial Analysts Journal* 35 (2): 24–44.

Niederhoffer, V. 1971. "The analysis of world events and stock prices." *Journal of Business* 44 (2): 193–219.

O'Brien, J. 1987. "Testing for transient elements in stock prices." Working Paper, Board of Governors of the Federal Reserve System, Washington, D.C., September.

O'Hanlon, J. and C. Ward. 1986. "How to lose at winning strategies." *Journal of Portfolio Management* 12 (3): 20–23.

Ohlson, J. and S. Penman. 1985. "Volatility increases subsequent to stock splits: An empirical aberration." *Journal of Financial Economics* 14 (2): 251–266.

Penman, S. 1987. "The distribution of earnings news over time and seasonalities in aggregate stock returns." *Journal of Financial Economics* 18 (2): 199–228.

Plott, C. 1987. "Rational choice in experimental markets." In *Rational Choice: The Contrast between Economics and Psychology,* R. Hogarth and M. Reder, eds. Chicago: University of Chicago Press.

Poterba, J. and L. Summers. 1987. "Mean reversion in stock prices: Evidence and implications." Working Paper, Harvard University, Cambridge, Massachusetts. [Published in *Journal of Financial Economics* 22 (1): 27–60.]

Rendleman, R., C. Jones, and H. Latane. 1986. "Further insight into the S.U.E. anomaly: Size and serial correlation effects." Working Paper, University of North Carolina at Chapel Hill, April. [Published in *Financial Review* 22 (1): 131–144.]

Renshaw, E. 1984. "Stock market panics: A test of the efficient market hypothesis." *Financial Analysts Journal* 40 (3): 48–51.

Rosenberg, B. and V. Marathe. 1975. "The prediction of investment risk: Systematic and residual risk." In *Proceedings of the Seminar on the Analysis of Security Prices, November 1975.* Chicago: University of Chicago Press, pp. 35–225.

——— and ———. 1976. "Common factors in security returns: Microeconomic determinants and macroeconomic correlates." In *Proceedings of the Seminar on the Analysis of Security Prices, May 1976.* Chicago: University of Chicago Press, pp. 61–115.

Rudd, A. and H. Clasing. 1982. *Modern Portfolio Theory: The Principles of Investment Management.* Homewood, Illinois: Dow Jones-Irwin.

Russell, T. and R. Thaler. 1985. "The relevance of quasi-rationality in competitive markets." *American Economic Review* 75 (5): 1071–1082.

Samuelson, P. 1987. "Paradise lost and refound: The Harvard ABC barometers." *Journal of Portfolio Management* 13 (3): 4–9.

Sharpe, W. 1985. *Investments.* 3d ed. Englewood Cliffs, New Jersey: Prentice Hall.

Shefrin, H. and M. Statman. 1984. "Explaining investor preference for cash dividends." *Journal of Financial Economics* 13 (18): 253–282.

——— and ———. 1985. "The disposition to sell winners too early and ride losers too long: Theory and evidence." *Journal of Finance* 40 (3): 777–790.

——— and ———. 1987. "A behavioral finance solution to the noise trading puzzle." Working Paper, Santa Clara University, Santa Clara, California, December.

Shiller, R. 1981. "Do stock prices move too much to be justified by subsequent changes in dividends?" *American Economic Review* 71 (3): 421–436.

———. 1984. "Stock prices and social dynamics." *Brookings Papers on Economic Activity* 15 (2): 457–498.

———. 1987. "Comments." In *Rational Choice: The Contrast Between Economics and Psychology,* R. Hogarth and M. Reder, eds. Chicago: University of Chicago Press.

Simon, H. 1987. "Rationality in psychology and economics." In *Rational Choice: The Contrast Between Economics and Psychology,* R. Hogarth and M. Reder, eds. Chicago: University of Chicago Press.

Sorensen, E. and D. Williamson. 1985. "Some evidence on the value of dividend discount models." *Financial Analysts Journal* 41 (6): 60–69.

Summers, L. 1986. "Does the stock market rationally reflect fundamental values?" *Journal of Finance* 41 (3): 591–600.

Treynor, J. 1987. "Market efficiency and the bean jar experiment." *Financial Analysts Journal* 43 (3): 50–53.

Verrecchia, R. 1979. "On the theory of market information efficiency." *Journal of Accounting and Economics* 1 (1): 77–90.

Williams, J. 1938. *The Theory of Investment Value.* Cambridge: Cambridge University Press.

Zacks, L. 1979. "EPS forecasts–accuracy is not enough." *Financial Analysts Journal* 35 (2): 53–55.

Calendar Anomalies

Abnormal Returns at Calendar Turning Points[*]

The January effect and other time regularities.

Calendar anomalies have long been part of market folklore [Merrill (1966), Hirsch (1968–1987), and Fosback (1976)]. Studies of the day-of-the-week, holiday, and January effects first began to appear in the 1930s [Fields (1931, 1934) and Wachtel (1942)]. And although academics have only recently begun seriously to examine these return patterns, they have found them to withstand close scrutiny.

Calendar regularities generally occur at cusps in time—the turn of the year, the month, the week, the day. They often have significant economic impact. For instance, the "Blue Monday" effect was so strong during the Great Depression that the entire market crash took place over weekends, from Saturday's close to Monday's close. The stock market actually rose on average every other day of the week.

Calendar anomalies are often related to other return effects. For instance, some calendar anomalies are more potent for small- than for large-capitalization stocks. While analysis of cross-sectional effects requires fundamental databases—a relatively recent innovation—the study of calendar anomalies requires only time-dated records of market indexes. Hence calendar anomalies can be tracked historically for much longer periods than effects requiring fundamental data.

---

[*] Originally published in *Financial Analysts Journal* 44 (6): 28–39.

The availability of a century of data brings enormous statistical power for testing calendar effects, but it also increases the likelihood of data mining. If enough patterns are tested, some will appear significant merely by chance. In exploring calendar anomalies, therefore, significance levels must be properly adjusted for the number of hypotheses examined, out-of-sample tests should be encouraged, and only plausible hypotheses considered [Lakonishok and Smidt (1987)].

Calendar regularities appear to be even more aberrant than cross-sectional return effects. A skeptic, for instance, might assert that low-P/E stocks provide outperformance simply because of their greater riskiness; this argument can be deflected, but it requires potentially controversial assumptions about risk modeling [Jacobs and Levy (1988b)].

Others might claim that the low-P/E characteristic merely proxies for value [although this argument can also be rebutted; see Jacobs and Levy (1988c)]. Risk or value considerations appear insufficient to explain calendar anomalies such as the day-of-the-week effect.

Because calendar anomalies appear relatively easy to exploit, their continued existence seems inexplicable. To arbitrage the P/E effect, for example, investors would have to increase their demand for low-P/E stocks; psychological considerations may inhibit investors from doing so [Jacobs and Levy (1988b)]. But to arbitrage the time-of-day effect, investors merely have to schedule discretionary trades at a more advantageous time of day.

Calendar anomalies are difficult to exploit as a stand-alone strategy because of transaction cost considerations. For instance, full capture of the day-of-the-week effect would require 100 percent turnover per week. Calendar return patterns can, however, be of benefit in timing a preconceived trade. While cross-sectional return effects, such as low P/E, might be useful to portfolio managers in selecting stocks, calendar anomalies may be of greater interest to traders.[1]

THE JANUARY EFFECT

The turn of the year is a special time for the stock market. Most individuals have calendar tax years, and many firms close their books at this time. The turn of the year represents a clean slate for government, business, and consumer budgeting, as well as for purposes such as investment manager performance evaluation. Additionally, investors' cashflows may be jolted by bonuses, pension contributions, and holiday liquidity needs.

Stocks exhibit both higher returns and higher risk premiums in January [Rozeff and Kinney (1976)]. These results have been corroborated in many foreign markets [Gultekin and Gultekin (1983)]. But the higher returns accrue primarily to smaller stocks. January does not appear to be an exceptional month for larger-capitalization issues.[2]

January seasonals have been noted in returns to a variety of stock characteristics, including size, yield, and neglect [Keim (1983 and 1985) and Arbel (1985)]. Returns to small size, for example, occur at the turn of the year—specifically, on the last trading day in December and the first four trading days in January [Keim (1983) and Roll (1983b)]. The magnitude of this effect can be substantial. Over these five trading days from 1970 to 1981, small stocks provided an average return of 16.4 percent, compared with 1.9 percent for large stocks [Lakonishok and Smidt (1986a)].[3]

It is vital to disentangle interrelated effects in attributing returns to stock characteristics in order to identify properly underlying sources of return. Disentangled return attributions are referred to as "pure" returns, because they are purified of other related effects. After "purification," two effects emerge strongest in January. One is a return rebound for stocks with embedded tax losses, especially those with long-term losses. The other is an abnormal return to the yield characteristic, with both zero-yielding and high-yielding stocks experiencing the largest returns.

Other January seasonals appear to be mere proxies for these two effects. In fact, *pure* returns to smaller size (after controlling for other factors) exhibit no January seasonal at all. There is also evidence of January selling pressure for stocks with long-term gains, apparently due to the deferral of gain recognition until the new year.[4]

Rationales

The most commonly cited reason for the January return seasonal is tax-loss-selling rebound [Givoly and Ovadia (1983)]. That is, taxable investors dump losers in December for tax purposes, and the subsequent abatement of selling pressure in January explains the higher returns. The tax-loss explanation has been found to be consistent with returns in many foreign equity markets and for other asset classes, such as corporate bonds [Gultekin and Gultekin (1983) and Chang and Pinegar (1986)].[5]

But the tax-loss hypothesis does not seem fully satisfactory. First, there is little evidence that selling pressure near year end is strong enough to account for the rebound.[6] Second, it is not clear why rational investors would await the new year to reinvest, although temporary "parking" of proceeds in cash could account for the observed seasonality [Ritter (1987)]. Third, it seems suboptimal for investors to wait until year end to transact. Until the Tax Reform Act of 1986, short-term losses sheltered more income from taxes than long-term losses. It would thus have been preferable to establish tax losses before an asset's holding period became long term [Constantinides (1984)]. Also, the tax-loss theory would predict a larger rebound for stocks having short-term losses, yet the January rebound is stronger for stocks with long-term losses [Chan (1986) and Jacobs and Levy (1988b)]. Fourth, market returns prior to the imposition of the U.S. income tax, and returns in a few foreign countries, appear inconsistent with the tax-loss explanation.[7] In any case, sophisticated investors should anticipate predictable price patterns and arbitrage them away.

Tax-loss-selling pressure might be expected to be stronger in down-market years, when losses are more prevalent. Also, higher taxable incomes or higher tax rates may strengthen tax-loss-taking. Current evidence of such relationships is rather weak.[8]

Another rationale for the January effect is year-end "window-dressing" [Bildersee and Kahn (1987)]. In this view, some portfolio managers dump embarrassing stocks at year end to avoid their appearance on the annual report. Similar stocks are repurchased in the new year, resulting in the January effect. This argument also begs the question of countervailing arbitrage.

A January risk seasonal might explain the higher returns at the turn of the year. In fact, beta (systematic risk) and residual risk for small firms rise in January [Rogalski and Tinic (1986)]. According to the Capital Asset Pricing Model, only systematic risk earns compensation. While the January increase in beta for small firms is approximately 30 percent, it is insufficient to explain the January return seasonal.

Moreover, risk appears to be priced *only* in the month of January. In all other months, there is no significant relation between risk and return, whether risk is measured in a CAPM or APT framework, or even without appealing to any particular asset pricing model.[9] This remains a mystery. Foreign evidence on the point is mixed. In some countries, risk and return patterns do not coincide, belying the risk explanation for return seasonality [Corhay, Hawawini, and Michel (1987)].

Alternatively, the January return seasonal may be compensation for bearing informational risk [Arbel (1985)]. The seasonal may stem from the reduction of uncertainty associated with the dissemination of information after the close of the fiscal year, especially for small, neglected firms. But informational risk is not resolved precipitously at the turn of the year. Furthermore, a study of firms with non-December fiscal years presents stronger evidence [Chari, Jagannathan, and Ofer (1986)]. Such companies do not experience a return seasonal at the turn of their fiscal year, as informational risk is resolved, but rather at calendar year end. Thus informational risk appears to be an inadequate explanation of the January seasonal.

Cashflow patterns at the turn of the year may produce the return seasonal. Annual bonuses and holiday gifts might be invested in the stock market, along with year-end pension plan contributions. Also, savings spent on holiday consumption may, in part, be replenished. In Japan, where bonuses are paid semiannually, equities exhibit seasonals in January and June [Kato and Schallheim (1985)]. Once again, this predictable return regularity could be arbitraged.

Novel cognitive psychological approaches, including Prospect Theory and Procedural Rationality, offer substantial insight into market behavior.[10] Once we entertain the notions that investors are loath to admit mistakes, tend to "frame" decisions, have finite mental capacity, and generally behave in rather human ways, seemingly irrational market behavior is demystified. For instance, Prospect Theory is consistent with the predilection of investors to defer tax trading until year end and the finding that long-term tax-loss selling is stronger than short-term. These behaviors arise from the use of

FIGURE 4–1

The Turn-of-the-Month Effect (Average Daily Returns)

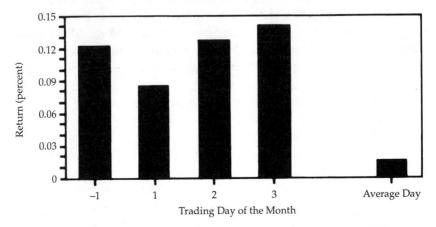

Source: Data from J. Lakonishok and S. Smidt, "Are seasonal anomalies real? A ninety-year perspective." Johnson Working Paper #87-07, Cornell University, Ithaca, New York, May 1987.

year-end tax planning as a justification for admitting mistakes and from the tendency to ride losers too long. Procedural Rationality also offers clues into behavioral causes for January anomalies such as the abnormal performance of both zero- and high-yielding stocks.

THE TURN-OF-THE-MONTH EFFECT

Recent academic studies demonstrate anomalous returns at the turn of each month, vindicating the claims of practitioners [Ariel (1987) and Lakonishok and Smidt (1987)]. While not as dramatic as the January effect, this anomaly is substantial. In fact, turn-of-the-month returns have alone accounted fully for the positive returns generated by the stock market.

Figure 4-1 plots average returns to the Dow Jones industrial average for trading days near month end for the period 1897 to 1986. Returns are high for each trading day from the last day in the previous month (denoted as day –1) to the third trading day in the current month. These four trading days averaged 0.118 percent, versus 0.015 percent for all trading days. While this anomaly has existed for almost a century, it has weakened somewhat in the most recent decade. It has, however, been documented in periods both before and after those in which it was first identified; this out-of-sample evidence rebuts allegations of data mining.

Might the turn-of-the-month effect merely proxy for other anomalies? Studies have rejected January, day-of-the-week, holiday, tax-loss-selling, and size effects as underlying causes [see, for example, Ariel (1987)].[11] Methodological deficiencies seem an unlikely explanation, as various studies have controlled for dividends, pricing errors, and outliers. Also, risk, as measured by standard deviation of market returns, is no higher at the turn of the month.

Some practitioners have suggested month-end portfolio rebalancing as a possible explanation; investors may reinvest accumulated cash dividends at this time. A more convincing rationale is based on higher month-end cashflows such as salaries. An interest-rate seasonal to Treasury bills maturing at the turn of the month has been attributed to investor cashflow considerations [Ogden (1987)]. Increased demand for equities at month end might produce the observed return regularity.

The timing of earnings announcements may provide additional insight. While companies often disclose good news voluntarily, the publication of bad news is often suppressed until the next mandatory quarterly report [McNichols (1987)]. Moreover, good earnings reports tend to be released faster than bad ones. Some observers have suggested that the positive returns around the first of each month reflect a clustering of positive earnings announcements [Penman (1987)]. But while good earnings news is predominant in the first half of the month, it is not concentrated in the first few days, when the return seasonality occurs. Also, excluding earnings report months from the sample diminishes the effect, but does not eliminate it [Ariel (1987)]. The absence of countervailing arbitrage remains a puzzle.

THE DAY-OF-THE-WEEK EFFECT

Stock returns are intimately tied to the day of the week. The market has a tendency to end each week on a strong note and to decline on Mondays. This pattern is deeply ingrained in folk wisdom, as evidenced by the recent book *Don't Sell Stocks on Monday* [Hirsch

F I G U R E   4–2

The Day-of-the Week Effect (Average Daily Returns)

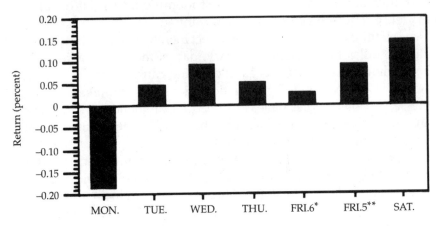

* Fri. 6 = Friday in a 6-day trading week.

** Fri. 5 = Friday in a 5-day trading week.

Source: Data from D. Keim and R. Stambaugh, "A further investigation of the weekend effect in stock returns," *Journal of Finance* 39 (3), 1984, pp. 819–837.

(1986)]. It is often referred to as the "weekend" or "Blue Monday" effect.

Figure 4-2 illustrates average daily returns of the S&P composite for each day of the week from 1928 to 1982. Monday is the only down day, and is significantly different statistically from all other days. The last trading day of the week—Friday in 5-day weeks and Saturday in 6-day weeks—has a substantial positive average return.

The economic magnitude of the effect is not trivial. For an equity portfolio with a cashflow of $100,000 per week, for example, switching the sale day from Monday to the previous Friday might earn an additional $14,700 per annum [Harris (1986c)].

As with the turn-of-the-month effect, researchers have recently verified the existence of this anomaly in both earlier and later periods than previously studied [Lakonishok and Smidt (1987)]. The robustness of the day-of-the-week effect across time periods attests to its stability and defuses any data-mining criticism.

Day-of-the-week patterns also exist in other U.S. markets. Because stock option and stock index futures prices are anchored by the underlying spot market, a day-of-the-week effect for these derivative securities would not be surprising. Such effects have been found in both markets, even though low transaction costs in the futures market facilitate arbitrage of this effect.[12] The U.S. Treasury bill and bond markets also display a weekly pattern similar to that of the equity markets. Most notably, Monday returns are negative, and more negative for longer-maturity instruments [Flannery and Protopapadakis (1988)].

A day-of-the-week effect is also present in many foreign equity markets, again with weeks ending strong and opening down, and in foreign exchange rates, which do not offset the local currency equity return patterns from the perspective of a U.S. investor.[13] A pattern remarkably similar to the day-of-the-week effect has even been identified for orange juice futures [Roll (1983a)]. We must thus be cautious in evaluating potential explanations that rely on institutional features peculiar to the U.S. stock market such as settlement procedures, specialist behavior, or dividend patterns.

The day-of-the-week effect is related to other anomalies. The weekly pattern is stronger for smaller-capitalization stocks. In fact, 63 percent of the small-size effect occurs on Fridays [Keim (1987)].[14] There are conflicting findings on the day-of-the-week effect in the month of January.[15] Interactions of day-of-the-week with holiday and time-of-day regularities are discussed later.

Rationales

Measurement error has often been suggested as a cause of the observed pattern, especially because the effect appears stronger for smaller-capitalization stocks. But this possibility has been rejected by many researchers.[16] For example, an upward bias in Friday closing prices can be dismissed as an explanation because the correlation between Friday and Monday returns is positive and the highest of any pair of days. Also, a Monday decline is even more likely than usual after a Friday decline. Explanations involving specialists, such as the frequency of closing at bid versus ask prices, have also been rejected by studies utilizing only over-the-counter bids and by others using markets with different structural characteristics [Keim and Stambaugh (1984)].

Attempts have been made to test various value-based explanations for the day-of-the-week effect. The obvious hypotheses that returns accrue during trading time or during clock time are easily rejected [French (1980)].[17] One study found the day-of-the-week effect to be subsumed by options expiration, unexpected inflation, and earnings surprise events [Whitford and Reilly (1985)]. But options, money supply announcements, and other explanatory measures utilized did not exist early in this century. Moreover, the 1 year examined in this study—1978—was perverse, in that Mondays were on average up and Fridays were down.

Others have proposed trade settlement rules as a partial explanation for stock value fluctuations across days of the week [Lakonishok and Levi (1982 and 1985) and Dyl and Martin (1985)]. While this rationale has theoretical appeal, the day-of-the-week effect predates the 1968 advent of current settlement procedures. The anomaly also exists in foreign countries where settlement procedures alone would predict different weekly return patterns. Furthermore, the effect has been stronger during periods of lower interest rates when, according to this theory, it should have been weaker [Keim and Stambaugh (1984)]. Finally, the large magnitude of the effect clearly swamps an interest-based, or even a dividend-based, explanation.

Similar arguments apply to explanations based on inventory adjustments. Short-sellers might, for peace of mind, cover positions prior to the weekend, and short again on Monday mornings. Specialists might close trading on Fridays at ask prices. Investors might be more inclined to throw in the towel after a weekend of introspection.[18] One problem with such rationales is that they seem insufficient to account for the ubiquitous nature of the anomaly. Day-of-the-week effects are evident over the entire century for which we have data, in spite of changing trading mechanics, short-sale regulations, methods of investment management, and even modes of communication. Furthermore, the anomaly is present in foreign equity markets, as well as other asset classes.

Risk considerations also seem inadequate as an explanation of the day-of-the-week effect. It is difficult to conceive of any market risk factor that could have varied so systematically over the past century as to produce the observed return regularity. The standard deviation of Monday returns is the highest of all days, but only slightly above average. If risk determined daily returns, Monday would be an above-average day.

Explanations rooted in human nature show promise. For example, in experimental market games conducted by psychologists, an effect similar to the day-of-the-week has been observed around trading halts [Coursey and Dyl (1986)]. The day-of-the-week effect has recently been related to the human tendency to announce good news quickly and defer bad news. The pattern of earnings and other announcements over the week may actually drive the observed return effect [Penman (1987)]. We indicated earlier that the entire market decline of the Great Depression occurred, on average, over weekends. Not coincidentally, most bad news, such as bank closings, was released after the Saturday close to allow the market to "absorb the shock" over the weekend. As a more recent example, the 1987 string of insider trading indictments was generally announced after the market close on Friday.[19]

THE HOLIDAY EFFECT

The unusually good performance of stocks prior to market holidays was first documented over the 1901 to 1932 period and has since become an article of faith among many practitioners. Recent academic studies confirm the existence of the holiday effect.

Figure 4-3 plots the average return for the day prior to each of the 8 market holidays for the period 1963 to 1982. The average preholiday return of 0.365 percent dwarfs the average regular-day return of 0.026 percent. In fact, 35 percent of the entire market advance over this period occurred on just the 8 preholiday trading days each year.

Another study examining both earlier and later periods confirmed the existence of the holiday anomaly [Lakonishok and Smidt (1987)]. This study also identified a holiday-related phenomenon occurring from December 24 to 31 each year. Not only Christmas and New Year's Eve, but also the days between the holidays exhibit exceptional returns. In fact, the average cumulative return for just these 8 calendar days is a remarkable 1.6 percent. This year-end rally was identified in the Dow and may reflect window dressing in

F I G U R E   4-3

The Holiday Effect (Average Preholiday Returns)

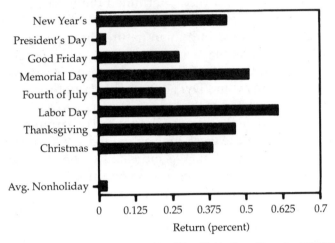

Source: Data from R. Ariel, "High stock returns before holidays," Sloan Working Paper, Massachusetts Institute of Technology, Cambridge, 1984.

Blue Chip issues toward year end. In any case, the dollar magnitude of this year-end, large-capitalization stock rally is several times the magnitude of the more well-known January small-size effect.

The holiday anomaly appears fairly stable over time. In the most recent decade, however, preholiday returns have not been exceptional. Nevertheless, the effect does not appear to be a statistical artifact. For instance, it is not driven by outliers, as 75 percent of preholiday days are up, versus only 54 percent of all trading days [Ariel (1984)].

The settlement process, discussed as a potential explanation for the day-of-the-week effect, has complex implications for fluctuations in value around holidays [Lakonishok and Levi (1982)]. For example, this theory predicts a high Thursday return preceding a Friday holiday, which is what occurs. But it predicts a lower-than-average Friday return preceding a Monday holiday, and this is not consistent with empirical results. Moreover, the magnitude of any value changes occurring because of settlement procedures is much too small to account for the holiday effect.

Abnormal preholiday returns are not attributable to increased risk. In fact, the standard deviation of preholiday returns—0.609—is less than the nonholiday volatility of 0.783 percent [Ariel (1984)].

Another perspective is afforded by holidays not associated with market closings, like St. Patrick's Day or Rosh Hashanah. Such days do not experience abnormal returns.[20] The absence of anomalous returns may be due to the lack of a trading break or to a lower level of festivity than that associated with major market holidays.

In a class by itself—almost considered the antithesis of a holiday by the superstitious—is Friday the 13th. Studies examining this day have had conflicting results. Over the 1940 to 1984 period, the Dow was up as frequently on Friday the 13th as on a regular Friday [Hirsch (1986), p. 38]. For the 1962 to 1985 period, however, the return for the CRSP index was significantly negative on this day [Kolb and Rodriguez (1987)]. There are several ways of reconciling these findings. Possibly the market has become more superstitious in recent years. Perhaps the large-capitalization Dow stocks are less susceptible to irrationality than smaller stocks. Also, the up-versus-down-day measure utilized in the first study may be less appropriate than percentage returns. If stocks suffer on Friday the 13th, market psychology would appear to be the likely culprit.

Holiday effects interact with other anomalies. The holiday effect appears to be stronger for smaller stocks [Rogalski (1984)]. It also swamps the day-of-the-week effect. Monday returns preceding a Tuesday holiday are on average positive [Lakonishok and Smidt (1987)]. After controlling for the holiday effect, the best day of the week shifts from Friday to Wednesday [Ariel (1984)]. The high frequency of holidays falling on Saturday, Sunday, or Monday benefits the previous Friday's return.

One potential hypothesis is that preholiday returns represent another manifestation of return abnormalities around trading halts such as weekends. There are important differences, however. While Mondays are, on average, down, the day after a holiday does not exhibit unusual returns [French (1980)]. Also, the holiday effect is two to five times the strength of the last-trading-day-of-the-week effect, which suggests that more than a simple trading halt is the cause [Lakonishok and Smidt (1987)].

Another possibility is that holiday euphoria leads to short-covering and general buying pressure. But there is little evidence of a market correction as holiday spirits subsequently subside. While no fully satisfactory explanation of the holiday effect has yet surfaced, psychological reasons appear to be the most promising.

THE TIME-OF-DAY EFFECT

Stock returns exhibit intraday, as well as interday, patterns. The advent of real-time pricing databases has only recently allowed academic scrutiny of these effects.

Figure 4-4 plots cumulative returns, at 15-minute intervals throughout each trading day of the week, for a recent 14-month period on the NYSE. Tuesday through Friday exhibit similar patterns: Prices rise for approximately the first 45 minutes, the bulk of the trading day is flat, and another rally takes place in the last 15 min-

FIGURE 4–4

The Time-of-Day Effect

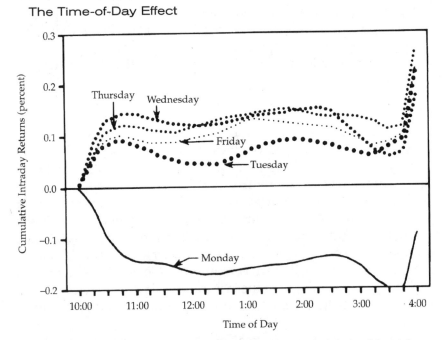

Source: Data from L. Harris, "A transaction data study of weekly and intradaily patterns in stock returns," *Journal of Financial Economics* (16), 1986, pp. 99–177.

utes of the day. The strong opening is roughly attributable to the first three trades of the day in each stock, while the strong close is due primarily to the last trade. On Monday, in contrast, prices during the first 45 minutes of trading are down sharply, while the rest of the day resembles the other days of the week.

The time-of-day anomaly has been fairly stable in recent decades, except that the "weekend effect" component has been moving up in time. Prior to 1968, the weekend effect took place all through the trading day on Monday, with every hour's return being negative. Since 1974, the effect has shifted forward in time to the weekend, with only the first 2 hours of Monday's trading being down in price [Smirlock and Starks (1986)].[21] This day-of-week/time-of-day interaction is also related to the size effect. Most of the weekend decline occurs prior to Monday's open for large-capitalization stocks, but continues into Monday morning for smaller stocks [Harris (1986b)]. Also, the closing-price anomaly has been found to be robust across days of the week but stronger at the turn of the month [Harris (1986a)].

One study analyzed the close-of-day anomaly in great detail [Harris (1986a)]. It found the average return of the last trade to equal 0.05 percent, or 0.6 cent per share. The return was higher, however, the closer the final trade to the close of business. Final trades occurring after 3:55 p.m. averaged a 0.12 percent return, or 1.75 cents per share.

The closing-price anomaly is unrelated to whether a stock has listed options or is traded on a regional exchange beyond the NYSE closing time. Results are not due to data errors, because there is little evidence of return reversals at the following open. The effect is robust over time and not attributable to outliers.

Do fundamental values rise at the open and close, causing the observed return pattern? Unanticipated good news toward the close might not be fully reflected in prices until the next morning, particularly if specialists dampen the rise in order to maintain orderly markets [Harris (1986a)]. Of course, this would not explain Monday morning negative returns. And what might account for a rush of good news just before the close? While stocks that trade right at the close experience the largest day-end effect, those that do not trade near the close do not catch up by morning. This seems to rule out the possibility that marketwide good news accounts for the day-end return anomaly.

There is a relation between risk and intraday returns. The unusually high opening and closing returns are more variable than returns during the rest of the day [Wood, McInish, and Ord (1985)].[22] Theories have been proposed that may account for the observed pattern in riskiness.[23] If investors are averse to volatility, they would require higher expected returns at the open and close. But the risk increase is insufficient to explain the magnitude of the observed return effect. Furthermore, Monday morning negative returns run counter to this hypothesis.

The open differs from the balance of the day in some important respects. Opening prices are determined by a market call, unlike the continuous market-making process the rest of the day. Also, orders at the open are heavily influenced by foreign investors. While opening returns exhibit greater dispersion, are less normally distributed, and more negatively autocorrelated than other returns, it remains unclear why any of these differences would result in the morning return anomaly [Amihud and Mendelson (1987)].

Closing prices are also special. They are utilized for valuing portfolios, for performance evaluation, as strike prices for program trades, and for settling options and futures contracts at expiration. They are the prices reported in the press and stored in databases. For all these reasons, closing prices might be likely candidates for manipulation, possibly causing the day-end return anomaly. However, volume for day-end trades is not abnormally small, as would be the case if someone were painting the tape [Harris (1986a)].

Those who must purchase a stock on a given day might conceivably rush to beat the closing bell, thus placing upward pressure on prices. But the converse should hold for sellers. As the day-end price effect is stronger at the turn of the month, window dressing might play a role. Also, about half the effect is attributable to changes in the frequency of trades at bid versus ask prices near the close, but the cause of this distributional shift remains unknown [Harris (1986a)].

As with the holiday and day-of-the-week effects, the day-end return anomaly may relate to the impending trading halt. As psychological experiments have demonstrated, there may be a behavioral predisposition to bid up prices prior to the close.

CONCLUSION

The existence of abnormal returns at calendar turning points is indisputable. Moreover, these effects are not implausible. A return regularity occurring at an arbitrary time on an arbitrary day might justifiably be regarded with suspicion. But calendar anomalies occur at cusps in time. These turning points have little economic significance, but they apparently evoke special investor behavior. Psychology appears to offer the most promising explanations for this behavior.

While cross-sectional return effects should be of interest to portfolio managers, calendar effects may be of greater interest to traders. Both classes of anomalies have important implications for market efficiency.

ENDNOTES

1. For portfolio management implications of cross-sectional return effects, see Jacobs and Levy (1988a). For trading implications of calendar anomalies, see Jacobs and Levy (1989).
2. Consider the absence of a January seasonal in the Dow Jones industrial average, noted by Lakonishok and Smidt (1987).
3. Results cited are for largest and smallest deciles of listed stocks. While large in percentage terms, however, the January effect is less substantial in dollar terms because of the illiquidity of small stocks.
4. See Jacobs and Levy (1988a and 1988b) for a complete discussion of January interrelationships.
5. Gultekin and Gultekin (1983) find higher returns coincident with the turn of the tax year in 13 countries, with the exception of Australia.
6. There is no documentation of downward price pressure on losers at year end comparable in magnitude to their subsequent January bounceback. While Lakonishok and Smidt (1986b) show evidence of tax-motivated trading in December and January, they find other trading motives more important.
7. Jones, Pearce, and Wilson (1987) find no difference in the January effect pre- and postincome tax. For foreign evidence, see Brown, et al. (1983) and Tinic, Barone-Adesi, and West (1987).
8. While Jacobs and Levy (1988b) found a January tax-loss rebound effect in each year of their sample, the weakest effects occurred in

1981 and 1986, after substantial stock market advances. However, if there are fewer individual stocks offering losses, there may be more tax-loss-selling pressure on each one.

9. See Tinic and West (1984) for CAPM, Gultekin and Gultekin (1987) for APT, and Chang and Pinegar (1988) for more general findings.

10. On Prospect Theory and January, see Shefrin and Statman (1985) and Ferris, Haugen, and Makhija (1988). On Procedural Rationality and January, see Miller (1986).

11. However, Ariel reports that when small-capitalization stocks perform poorly, it is generally in the last half of the month.

12. For options, see Peterson (1988). For futures, Cornell (1985) found no anomaly; however, Dyl and Maberly (1986) located an error in Cornell's data set. Phillips-Patrick and Schneeweis (1988) provide additional evidence.

13. Jaffe and Westerfield (1985) find patterns in the United Kingdom, Canada, Japan, and Australia similar to those in the United States. However, in Japan and Australia, both Monday and Tuesday are down, not only because of time-zone differences with the United States. Mixed evidence from other European countries is reported in Hawawini (1984). On exchange rates, see Jaffe and Westerfield (1985).

14. However, Miller (1988) argues that intraweek patterns in returns to size are unrelated to the long-run size effect.

15. Rogalski (1984) demonstrates that the January effect dominates the day-of-the-week effect (that is, Mondays are up on average in January) because of the good performance of small-capitalization stocks, especially during the first 5 trading days in January. Smirlock and Starks (1986) concur. However, Keim (1987) reports that the day-of-the-week effect is not different in January after controlling for the higher overall market return in that month. Although Mondays may be up in January, they lag other days, especially Fridays.

16. See Cross (1973), Gibbons and Hess (1981), Keim and Stambaugh (1984), Jaffe and Westerfield (1985), Harris (1986b), and Smirlock and Starks (1986).

17. The trading-time hypothesis posits that returns are equal each trading day. Clock time posits that Monday returns should be three times as high as other trading days, because of the weekend.

18. Miller (1988) suggests that individual investors buy stocks uniformly over weekdays, at their brokers' urging, but often make sell decisions over weekends.

19. "Federal prosecutors have made several of their most important moves in the [insider trading] scandal late on Friday afternoons, when the market is finished with business and investors can mull the situation over during the weekend" ("Dow Off 8.68," *New York Times*, March 14, 1987).

20. While Hirsch (1986) reports that St. Patrick's Day is up more frequently than a normal day (p. 121), the percentage return is not abnormal (p. 122).

21. This nonstationarity resolves previously conflicting evidence on the exact timing of the weekend drop.

22. A strong contemporaneous relation between intraday returns and trading volume is documented in Jain and Joh (1988).

23. For example, Admati and Pfleiderer (1987) develop a theory incorporating informational and liquidity trading that is consistent with the observed pattern of volatility.

REFERENCES

Admati, A. and P. Pfleiderer. 1987. "A theory of intraday trading patterns." Working Paper #927R, Stanford University, Stanford, California, August. [Published in *Review of Financial Studies* 1 (1): 3–40.]

Amihud, Y. and H. Mendelson. 1987. "Trading mechanisms and stock returns: An empirical investigation." *Journal of Finance* 42 (3): 533–555.

Arbel, A. 1985. "Generic stocks: An old product in a new package." *Journal of Portfolio Management* 11 (4): 4–13.

Ariel, R. 1984. "High stock returns before holidays." Working Paper, Sloan School, Massachusetts Institute of Technology, Cambridge.

———. 1987. "A monthly effect in stock returns." *Journal of Financial Economics* 18 (1): 161–174.

Bildersee, J. and N. Kahn. 1987. "A preliminary test of the presence of window dressing: Evidence from institutional stock trading." *Journal of Accounting, Auditing and Finance* 2 (3): 329–365.

Brown, P., et al. 1983. "Stock return seasonalities and the tax-loss selling hypothesis: Analysis of the arguments and Australian evidence." *Journal of Financial Economics* 12 (1): 105–127.

Chan, K. 1986. "Can tax-loss selling explain the January seasonal in stock returns?" *Journal of Finance* 41 (5): 1115–1128.

Chang, E. and M. Pinegar. 1986. "Return seasonality and tax-loss selling in the market for long-term government and corporate bonds." *Journal of Financial Economics* 17 (2): 391–415.

——— and ———. 1988. "A fundamental study of the seasonal risk-return relationship: A note." *Journal of Finance* 43 (4): 1035–1039.

Chari, V., R. Jagannathan, and A. Ofer. 1986. "Fiscal year end and the January effect." Working Paper #20, Kellogg Graduate School of Management, Northwestern University, Evanston, Illinois, July.

Constantinides, G. 1984. "Optimal stock trading with personal taxes: Implications for prices and the abnormal January returns." *Journal of Financial Economics* 13 (1): 65–89.

Corhay, A., G. Hawawini, and P. Michel. 1987. "Seasonality in the risk-return relationship: Some international evidence." *Journal of Finance* 42 (1): 49–68.

Cornell, B. 1985. "The weekly pattern in stock returns: Cash versus futures: A note." *Journal of Finance* 40 (2): 583–588.

Coursey, D. and E. Dyl. 1986. "Price effects of trading interruptions in an experimental market." Working Paper, University of Wyoming, Laramie. [See "Price limits, trading suspensions, and the adjustment of prices to new information." *Review of Futures Markets* 9 (2): 342–360.]

Cross, F. 1973. "The behavior of stock prices on Fridays and Mondays." *Financial Analysts Journal* 29 (6): 67–69.

Dyl, E. and E. Maberly. 1986. "The weekly pattern in stock index futures: A further note." *Journal of Finance* 41 (5): 1149–1152.

Dyl, E. and S. Martin. 1985. "Weekend effects on stock returns: A comment." *Journal of Finance* 40 (1): 347–349.

Ferris, S., R. Haugen, and A. Makhija. 1988. "Predicting contemporary volume with historic volume at differential price levels." *Journal of Finance* 43 (3): 677–699.

Fields, M. 1931. "Stock prices: A problem in verification." *Journal of Business* 4.

———. 1934. "Security prices and stock exchange holidays in relation to short selling." *Journal of Business* 7: 328–338.

Flannery, M. and A. Protopapadakis. 1988. "From T-bills to common stocks: Investigating the generality of intra-week return seasonality." *Journal of Finance* 43 (2): 431–450.

Fosback, N. 1976. *Stock Market Logic.* Fort Lauderdale, Florida: Institute for Econometric Research.

French, K. 1980. "Stock returns and the weekend effect." *Journal of Financial Economics* 8 (1): 55–69

Gibbons, M. and P. Hess. 1981. "Day of the week effect and asset returns." *Journal of Business* 54 (4): 579–596.

Givoly, D. and A. Ovadia. 1983. "Year-end tax-induced sales and stock market seasonality." *Journal of Finance* 38 (1): 171–185.

Gultekin, M. and B. Gultekin. 1983. "Stock market seasonality: The case of stock returns." *Journal of Financial Economics* 12 (3): 379–402.

——— and ———. 1987. "Stock return anomalies and the tests of the APT." *Journal of Finance* 42 (5): 1213–1224.

Harris, L. 1986a. "A day-end transaction price anomaly." Working Paper, University of Southern California, Los Angeles, October. [Published in *Journal of Financial and Quantitative Analysis* 24 (1): 29–46.]

———. 1986b. "A transaction data study of weekly and intradaily patterns in stock returns." *Journal of Financial Economics* 16 (1): 99–117.

———. 1986c. "How to profit from intradaily stock returns." *Journal of Portfolio Management* 12 (2): 61–64.

Hawawini, G. 1984. "European equity markets: Price behavior and efficiency." Monograph #4/5, Salomon Brothers Center, New York University, New York.

Hirsch, Y. 1968–1987. *The Stock Trader's Almanac.* Old Tappan, New Jersey: The Hirsch Organization.

———. 1986. *Don't Sell Stocks on Monday.* New York: Facts on File.

Jacobs, B. and K. Levy. 1988a. "Disentangling equity return regularities." In *Equity Markets and Valuation Methods.* Charlottesville, Virginia: Institute of Chartered Financial Analysts.

——— and ———. 1988b. "Disentangling equity return regularities: New insights and investment opportunities." *Financial Analysts Journal* 44 (3): 18–44.

——— and ———. 1988c. "On the value of 'value.'" *Financial Analysts Journal* 44 (4): 47–62.

——— and ———. 1989. "Trading tactics in an inefficient market." In *A Complete Guide to Securities Transactions: Controlling Costs and Enhancing Performance,* W. Wagner, ed. New York: John Wiley.

Jaffe, J. and R. Westerfield. 1985. "The week-end effect in common stock returns: The international evidence." *Journal of Finance* 40 (2): 433–454.

Jain, P. and G. Joh. 1988. "The dependence between hourly prices and trading volumes." *Journal of Financial and Quantitative Analysis* 23 (3): 269–284.

Jones, C., D. Pearce, and J. Wilson. 1987. "Can tax-loss selling explain the January effect? A note." *Journal of Finance* 42 (2): 453–561.

Kato, K. and J. Schallheim. 1985. "Seasonal and size anomalies in the Japanese stock market." *Journal of Financial and Quantitative Analysis* 20 (2): 243–260.

Keim, D. 1983. "Size-related anomalies and stock return seasonality: Further empirical evidence." *Journal of Financial Economics* 12 (1): 13–32.

———. 1985. "Dividend yields and stock returns: Implications of abnormal January returns." *Journal of Financial Economics* 14 (3): 473–489.

———. 1987. "Daily returns and size-related premiums: One more time." *Journal of Portfolio Management* 13 (2): 41–47.

Keim, D. and R. Stambaugh. 1984. "A further investigation of the weekend effect in stock returns." *Journal of Finance* 39 (3): 819–837.

Kolb, R. and R. Rodriguez. 1987. "Friday the thirteenth: 'Part VII'—a note." *Journal of Finance* 42 (5): 1385–1387.

Lakonishok, J. and M. Levi. 1982. "Weekend effects on stock returns: A note." *Journal of Finance* 37 (2): 883–889.

——— and ———. 1985. "Weekend effects on stock returns: A reply." *Journal of Finance* 40 (1): 351–352.

Lakonishok, J. and S. Smidt. 1986a. "Trading bargains in small firms at year-end." *Journal of Portfolio Management* 12 (3): 24–29.

——— and ———. 1986b. "Volume in winners and losers: Taxation and other motives for stock trading." *Journal of Finance* 41 (4): 951–974.

——— and ———. 1987. "Are seasonal anomalies real? A ninety year perspective." Working Paper #87-07, Johnson School, Cornell University, Ithaca, New York, May. [Published in *Review of Financial Studies* 1 (4): 403–425.]

McNichols, M. 1987. "A comparison of the skewness of stock return distributions at earnings announcement and non-announcement periods." Working Paper #953, Stanford University, Stanford, California, June. [Published in *Journal of Accounting and Economics* 10 (3): 239–273.]

Merrill, A. 1966. *Behavior of Prices on Wall Street*. Chappaqua, New York: Analysis Press.

Miller, E. 1986. "Explaining the January small firm effect." Working Paper, University of New Orleans, New Orleans, November. [Published in *Quarterly Journal of Business and Economics* 29 (3): 36–55.]

———. 1988. "Why a weekend effect?" *Journal of Portfolio Management* 14 (4): 43–49.

Ogden, J. 1987. "The end of the month as a preferred habitat: A test of operational efficiency in the money market." *Journal of Financial and Quantitative Analysis* 22 (3): 329–343.

Penman, S. 1987. "The distribution of earnings news over time and seasonalities in aggregate stock returns." *Journal of Financial Economics* 18 (2): 199–228.

Peterson, D. 1988. "A transaction data study of day-of-the-week and intraday patterns in option returns." Working Paper, Florida State University, Tallahassee, September. [Published in *Journal of Financial Research* 13 (2): 117–132.]

Phillips-Patrick, F. and T. Schneeweis. 1988. "The 'weekend effect' for stock indexes and stock index futures: Dividend and interest rate effects." *Journal of Futures Markets* 8(1): 115–122.

Ritter, J. 1987. "The buying and selling behavior of individual investors at the turn of the year." Working Paper, University of Michigan, Ann Arbor, July. [Published in *Journal of Finance* 43 (3): 701–717.]

Rogalski, R. 1984. "New findings regarding day-of-the-week returns over trading and non-trading periods: A note." *Journal of Finance* 39 (5): 1603–1614.

Rogalski, R. and S. Tinic. 1986. "The January size effect: Anomaly or risk mismeasurement?" *Financial Analysts Journal* 42 (6): 63–70.

Roll, R. 1983a. "Orange juice and weather." Working Paper #10-83, University of California at Los Angeles, November. [Published in *American Economic Review* 74 (5): 861–880.]

———. 1983b. "Vas is das? The turn of the year effect and the return premia of small firms." *Journal of Portfolio Management* 9 (2): 18–28.

Rozeff, M. and W. Kinney. 1976. "Capital market seasonality: The case of stock returns." *Journal of Financial Economics* 3 (4): 379–402.

Shefrin, H. and M. Statman. 1985. "The disposition to sell winners too early and ride losers too long: Theory and evidence." *Journal of Finance* 40 (3): 777–790.

Smirlock, M. and L. Starks. 1986. "Day-of-the-week and intraday effects in stock returns." *Journal of Financial Economics* 17 (1): 197–210.

Tinic, S., G. Barone-Adesi, and R. West. 1987. "Seasonality in Canadian stock prices: A test of the 'tax-loss selling' hypothesis." *Journal of Financial and Quantitative Analysis* 22 (1): 51–63.

Tinic, S. and R. West. 1984. "Risk and return: January vs. the rest of the year." *Journal of Financial Economics* 13 (4): 561–574.

Wachtel, S. 1942. "Certain observations in seasonal movements in stock prices." *Journal of Business* 15 (July): 184–193.

Whitford, D. and F. Reilly. 1985. "What makes stock prices move?" *Journal of Portfolio Management* 11 (2): 23–30.

Wood, R., T. McInish, and K. Ord. 1985. "An investigation of transactions data for NYSE stocks." *Journal of Finance* 40 (3): 723–739.

Forecasting the Size Effect[*]

Returns to small-cap stocks are driven by macroeconomic forces.

Some equity return regularities, such as the return reversal effect, produce persistent payoffs; they represent anomalous pockets of market inefficiency. Others, such as the size effect, are predictable only in a broader macroeconomic framework; that is, they are "empirical return regularities" driven by macroeconomic forces [see Jacobs and Levy (1988*b*)].

This article provides an in-depth look at the small-firm effect. We review the controversy surrounding this return effect and examine various methods for forecasting the size effect. Our findings indicate that macroeconomic "drivers" are essential in predicting returns to size.

THE SIZE EFFECT

Gordon showed in 1962 that common stock returns are inversely related to a firm's size. Banz (1981) later found that, over the 40 years ending in 1975, smaller firms on the New York Stock Exchange (NYSE) had higher average returns than larger firms, when returns were adjusted for risk using the Capital Asset Pricing Model (CAPM). Surprisingly, the strength of the relation between risk-adjusted average return and size was comparable in magnitude to

---

[*] Originally published in *Financial Analysts Journal* 45 (3): 38–54.

that between average return and systematic risk as measured by beta [see also Schwert (1983)].

Reinganum (1981a, 1981b, 1983a) examined the small-firm effect across a broader universe including both NYSE and American Stock Exchange (Amex) firms. He found superior risk-adjusted returns for small firms over the years 1963 to 1977. Brown, Kleidon, and Marsh (1983) discerned that average risk-adjusted returns were linearly related to the logarithm of firm size. Moreover, they found the magnitude and sign of the relation between return and size to be unstable. Over the 1969 to 1973 period, larger companies outperformed, while smaller companies fared better over the 1974 to 1979 period.

Does the size effect simply reflect transaction costs? Is it risk mismeasurement or the product of deficiencies in asset pricing models? Is it a proxy for other return effects? We review the evidence in the next section.

Size and Transaction Costs

Blume and Stambaugh (1983) found that studies using daily returns tended to overstate the small-firm effect because of the bid/ask effect. Reinganum (1981b), for example, had compounded arithmetic average daily returns to estimate the size effect. This procedure replicates a portfolio strategy of daily rebalancing to equally weighted positions; stocks closing at the bid are generally purchased and those closing at the ask are sold in order to reestablish equal weights. But assuming that purchases can be made at the bid and sales at the ask artificially inflates returns. This overstatement is greater for smaller firms, because they generally have lower prices, hence larger relative bid/ask spreads. Using 1-year holding-period returns, Blume and Stambaugh found the size effect to be only half the magnitude of the effect estimated by Reinganum; furthermore, on average, the size effect was confined to 1 month—January [see also Roll (1983a)].

Stoll and Whaley (1983) assessed the impact of transaction costs on the Banz (1981) and Reinganum (1981b) results, which were based on gross return. They examined NYSE securities and found the size effect eliminated for a 3-month horizon, after controlling for the higher bid/ask spreads and brokerage commissions on small stocks. For holding periods of 1 year, abnormal returns were positive, but only weakly significant.

Schultz (1983) extended the analysis to Amex stocks. Using this broader universe, he found that smaller stocks exhibited significant risk-adjusted returns after transaction costs, even over short holding periods. Schultz also noted that transaction costs cannot explain the periodic sign reversal found by Brown, Kleidon, and Marsh (1983) or the abnormal January behavior of smaller firms.

Amihud and Mendelson (1986a and 1986b) hypothesized that investors demand compensation for illiquidity, and that the size effect proxies for an illiquidity premium. They employed the bid/ask spread as a measure of market thinness. This spread is inversely correlated with attributes that reflect liquidity, such as trading volume, number of shareholders, number of dealers making a market, and degree of price continuity. They found that returns, both gross and net of trading costs, were an increasing function of the bid/ask spread; the effect of firm size was negligible after controlling for liquidity.

Chiang and Venkatesh (1988) maintained that the higher spread for small firms is not due to illiquidity, but results rather from the higher proportion of "insiders" trading these stocks. The presence of such informed traders leads dealers to raise the spread, which in turn causes ordinary investors to require a higher expected return on small stocks.

Size and Risk Measurement

Roll (1981a) proposed that a bias in beta estimates leads to an overstatement of the small-firm effect. Because small stocks trade less frequently than large stocks, their risk as estimated from daily returns understates their actual risk. Roll estimated the impact of nonsynchronous trading on beta by using Dimson's (1979) aggregated coefficients method. (Dimson betas are formed by regressing security returns on lagged, contemporaneous, and leading market returns, then summing the three slope coefficients.) The use of Dimson betas moderated the observed small-firm effect, but Reinganum (1982) found it insufficient to explain the full magnitude of the effect.

Handa, Kothari, and Wasley (1987) showed that even the betas of small-stock portfolios estimated from monthly returns will be downward biased. For all but the smallest companies, estimated betas approach their true values when quarterly returns are used. To minimize the beta measurement bias for the smallest firms, return intervals as long as 1 year are needed. Using quarterly returns to estimate beta, Handa et al. found the small-firm effect to be insignificant.

Roll (1977, 1980, and 1981b) demonstrated that performance mismeasurement arises when the selected surrogate market portfolio, or benchmark, is not ex ante mean-variance efficient. Banz (1981) and Reinganum (1981b) have acknowledged that their findings could be due to benchmark error. But Banz used several different surrogates for the market portfolio and found the small-firm effect to be robust in every case. Booth and Smith (1985) have concluded that the small-firm effect cannot be explained by measurement error caused by benchmark error or nonsynchronous trading. Using an errors-in-variables method, they demonstrated that the small-firm effect is robust over the feasible range of true coefficients.

Mounting evidence supports the proposition that risk, hence expected return, varies over time.[1] Ferson, Kandel, and Stambaugh (1987) examined the weekly returns on 10 portfolios of NYSE and Amex securities ranked by firm size over the 1963 to 1982 period. They found a single-premium, time-varying risk model capable of explaining the return differences across size-ranked portfolios.

Chan and Chen (1988a) used firm size in a novel fashion as an "instrument" to model changing risk premiums. In the original size studies, stock betas were estimated from 5 years of monthly return data. This is a common choice for beta estimation, representing a compromise between a period long enough to ensure statistical accuracy and short enough to ensure stationarity. If daily or weekly data are used to obtain a greater number of observations, nonsynchronous trading becomes an issue; as the length of the estimation period is increased, the stationarity of the data becomes questionable.

To overcome these problems, Chan and Chen formed portfolios based on size rankings and allowed the composition of these portfolios to change over time. They asserted that such portfolios maintain their risk characteristics over long spans of time. These size-ranked portfolios were used to estimate portfolio betas and to test if a size effect exists after controlling for beta. Estimating beta from over 30 years of return data, Chan and Chen found that the small-firm effect is subsumed.

Several studies have asked whether the size effect, or other market anomalies, can be accounted for by Ross' (1976) Arbitrage Pricing Theory (APT). Reinganum (1981c), controlling for APT risk using factor modeling, concluded that the size effect is not explained. Lehmann and Modest (1988) also found APT incapable of explaining the small-firm effect, even after adjusting for the January size seasonal and infrequent trading. Connor and Korajczyk (1988) found that APT appears to explain the January size seasonal but does not explain the size effect in other months. However, Chen (1983) reported that size has no power to explain return in an APT framework.

Size and Risk Premiums

Barry and Brown (1984, 1985, and 1986) have proposed that differential information across securities may account for the size effect. That is, there is more risk involved in estimating the valuation parameters for small firms, because there is less information available on small firms than on large ones. As a measure of information availability, Barry and Brown used the period of time a firm had been listed on an exchange. Analyzing beta, size, and period of listing, as well as the interactions between these variables, they found a period-of-listing effect present for NYSE firms over the 1926 to 1980 period. Unlike the firm-size effect, the period-of-listing effect had no January seasonal. Also, Barry and Brown found the interaction between size and period of listing to be more significant than the size effect itself.

Merton (1987) developed a model of capital market equilibrium with incomplete information, where each investor has information about only some of the available securities.[2] This appears to be a sensible assumption even for institutional investors, because their "closely followed" lists are often quite small compared with the universe of all listed securities. In Merton's model, the information available is the same for all stocks; that is, parameter estimation risk does not differ across securities. However, information about a particular stock is not available to all investors but only to some.

Under these assumptions, Merton proved that expected returns will be higher, the smaller a stock's investor base, the larger firm-specific variances, and the larger firm size. The positive association between expected return and large firm size appears contrary to the empirical evidence. But Merton compared small and large firms having identical investor bases and firm-specific variances. Smaller firms tend to have less investor recognition and larger specific variances than larger firms; Merton's finding is thus not necessarily inconsistent with the observed higher returns on smaller firms.

Barry and Brown's empirical evidence is consistent with Merton's theory to the extent that period of listing is positively associated with investor recognition. Arbel, Carvell, and Strebel's (1983) findings on neglected stocks (stocks not well followed by analysts and institutional investors) also support Merton.[3] Stratifying firms by risk, size, and degree of institutional ownership, they found higher returns associated with less institutional following, even after controlling for firm size. They also concluded that the small-firm effect is subsumed by the neglect factor.

Shefrin and Statman (1987) have conjectured that the size anomaly proxies for a "responsibility" effect. That is, advocacy of lower-quality stocks carries a higher degree of personal responsibility than advocacy of more reputable stocks. While no one ever second-guesses a recommendation to buy conventional names like IBM, recommending less well-known stocks carries greater potential for regret. Low-reputation stocks should thus provide higher expected returns than high-reputation stocks. Shefrin and Statman also suggested that the period-of-listing, neglected-firm, and low-P/E anomalies proxy for this responsibility effect.

Size and Other Cross-Sectional Effects

The small-firm effect may proxy for effects associated with other equity characteristics such as low P/E. In 1977, Basu, using the CAPM to adjust for risk, demonstrated that low-P/E stocks on the NYSE provided higher average risk-adjusted returns than high-P/E stocks. Reinganum (1981b) studied the low-P/E and size effects jointly to determine whether these anomalies are related. A two-way classification of NYSE and Amex firms by company size and P/E ratios revealed the size effect to subsume the P/E effect. That is, after controlling for company size, there was no remaining P/E effect, while the size effect existed even after controlling for P/E. However, Reinganum did not adjust for risk.

Basu (1983) examined NYSE firms over the 1963 to 1980 period; using a randomized design and adjusting for risk, he reached conclusions contrary to those of Reinganum. He found the P/E effect significant even after controlling for company size, but the size effect subsumed after controlling for differences in risk and P/E. The strength of the P/E effect appeared to vary inversely with firm size (stronger for smaller companies), however, so that an interaction may exist.

Cook and Rozeff (1984) reexamined the size-P/E controversy using an analysis of variance method. They reported that size does not subsume P/E, nor does P/E subsume size; rather, size and P/E are independent effects. They did not find an interaction between size and P/E, as claimed by Basu. Furthermore, they replicated Basu's method and found their results unaltered, thus concluding that Basu's findings must be specific to his sample.

Banz and Breen (1986) focused on the effect of database biases on the size-P/E connection. They examined two separate databases—one bias-free and the other bias-prone—over the 8 years from 1974 to 1981. The bias-free database was collected in real time from sequential Compustat tapes. The bias-prone database was represented by a current version of Compustat.

The Compustat database suffers from ex post selection bias, including survivorship bias (merged, bankrupt, and liquidated companies are absent) and retrospective inclusion bias (newly included firms are entered with their prior histories). It also suffers from look-ahead bias. The historical earnings reported for a given year end, for example, are not actually available until the following year. This bias tends to place companies that experience positive earnings surprises in low-P/E portfolios, and companies that experience negative earnings surprises in high-P/E portfolios. This tendency could magnify or even create a low-P/E effect.

Using the current Compustat database, Banz and Breen found evidence of statistically significant, independent P/E and size effects. Using the bias-free database, they found that the incremental returns accruing to low P/E were insignificant, while the size effect remained.

The small-firm effect may proxy for effects such as neglect, low price, or high volatility. Jacobs and Levy (1988b) fully "disentangled" the return effects associated with 25 different equity attributes, including firm size, in order to distinguish between "Naïve" and "pure" return effects.[4]

Naïve returns to the size effect were calculated using monthly cross-sectional regressions of security returns on a normalized size attribute. Such univariate regressions navïely measure the return effects associated with only one attribute at a time; no effort is made to control for related effects. In contrast, pure returns to the size attribute were calculated with monthly cross-sectional regressions of security returns on multiple attributes simultaneously. These multivariate regressions measure all effects jointly, thus purifying each effect so that it is independent of other effects.

Jacobs and Levy (1988b) measured pure returns to size and other effects for a bias-free universe of the 1500 largest-capitalization stocks over the 108-month period from January 1978 to December 1986. Noting the return effect to be linear in the logarithm of size, they used the logarithm of market capitalization as their measure of firm size. They found pure returns to size statistically significant, after controlling for all other attributes. They also found small size, low P/E, and neglect to be independent.

Size and Calendar Effects

The size effect appears to have significant interactions with calendar effects.[5] For example, the size effect has been related to the day-of-the-week effect. Among many researchers who have documented a stronger size effect on Fridays, Keim (1987) found that 63 percent of the size effect occurs on that day.[6]

In 1976, Rozeff and Kinney showed that the stock market exhibits higher returns in the month of January. Keim (1983) later showed this January return seasonal to be related to the size effect. Analyzing NYSE and Amex firms over the years 1963 to 1979, he found that one-half of the size effect occurs, on average, in January; moreover, one-quarter of the effect occurs during the first 5 trading days of the year.

Seasonalities in risk, in the release of information, and in insider trading activity have been proposed to explain the January size effect. Rogalski and Tinic (1986) found that both the systematic and nonsystematic risks of small stocks rise in January, but not by enough to account for the observed return pattern. Arbel (1985) cited year-end release of accounting information as a potential explanation of a neglect-driven size seasonal in January. But Chari, Jagannathan, and Ofer (1986) found no excess return at fiscal year end for companies that do not have a December year end, casting doubt on the informational hypothesis. Seyhun (1988) found that small-firm insiders adjust their positions around year end, but that insider trading activity does not explain the January size seasonal.

Roll (1983b) and Reinganum (1983b) have examined year-end tax-loss-selling as a possible explanation for the small-firm January seasonal. This research was motivated by Branch (1977) and Dyl (1977), who had earlier reported evidence of tax-loss-selling consistent with the observed January effect. The tax hypothesis maintains that investors establish losses to shelter taxable income prior to the new year. Once the year-end selling pressure abates around the turn of the year, prices rebound.

Roll regressed securities' turn-of-the-year returns on their returns over the preceding year and found a significant negative relationship. Those securities experiencing negative returns in the preceding year were more likely to be subject to tax-loss-selling and to bounce back early in the new year. Roll conjectured that the effect was largest for small firms because they are more likely candidates for tax-loss-selling, given their higher volatility and lower relative representation in tax-exempt institutional portfolios. Also, the higher transaction costs for smaller firms inhibit arbitrage of the January seasonal.

Reinganum constructed a measure of potential tax-loss-selling by using the loss suffered from the high price in the previous period, classified for tax purposes as short term. While he found the size seasonal early in January consistent with tax-loss-selling, the entire January size effect could not be fully explained. Inconsistent with the tax-loss hypothesis was the finding that last year's winners outperformed in January.

Several studies provide an international perspective on the January-size connection. Brown et al. (1983) examined stock returns in Australia, where the tax year ends June 30. They found that market returns exhibit July and also January seasonals; they also found a year-round size effect, but no size seasonals. They interpreted these results as inconsistent with the tax-loss hypothesis. However, Gultekin and Gultekin (1983) found seasonality in market returns consistent with a tax explanation in 13 countries (not including Australia).

Tinic, Barone-Adesi, and West (1987) have reported that, while taxes are not the sole explanation for the January size effect in Canada, the 1972 imposition of a capital gains tax did affect the behavior of returns. Also consistent with the tax-loss-selling hypothesis, Schultz (1985) found no evidence of a U.S. January seasonal prior to the levy of personal income taxes in 1917. But Jones, Pearce, and Wilson (1987) analyzed U.S. stock market returns extending back to 1871 and found evidence of a January seasonal prior to the advent of the income tax code.

Constantinides's (1984) model of optimal tax trading implies that there should be no relation between the January seasonal and rational tax trading; the optimal time to recognize losses should be just prior to their becoming long-term, not year end. Chan (1986) has noted that there is little reason to realize a long-term loss near year end, presumably at depressed prices. Employing two measures of potential short-term and long-term tax-loss-selling, he found the January seasonal to be as strongly related to long-term as to short-term losses. Chan concluded that the January seasonal is not explained by optimal tax trading.

Jacobs and Levy (1988b) examined the January size seasonal after controlling for potential short-term and long-term tax-loss-selling pressure, as well as the return effects associated with 22 other equity attributes. While they corroborated the existence of a January size seasonal for returns measured in naïve form, they found it fully dissipated in pure form. This evidence is consistent with the size seasonal being a mere proxy for tax-related selling.

Furthermore, Jacobs and Levy found the long-term tax-loss measure to have a rebound about twice the magnitude of the short-term measure. While this result is inconsistent with rational tax-trading strategies, it may be explained by investor psychology. Shefrin and Statman (1985) have noted that investors tend to ride losers too long in an effort to break even. Thus, tax-loss-selling is stronger for stocks suffering long-term losses.

FIGURE 5-1

Cumulative Return to Small Size

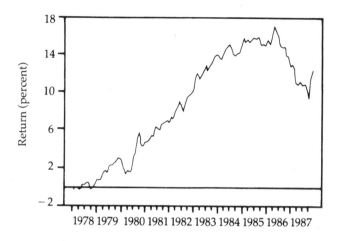

MODELING THE SIZE EFFECT

Figure 5-1 graphs cumulative pure returns to size, as measured by Jacobs and Levy (1988*b*).[7] In the following paragraphs, we develop some models for forecasting these returns. First, however, we discuss the criteria we used to assess the accuracy of alternative forecasting methods.

A commonly used measure in portfolio management is the *information coefficient* (IC), defined as the correlation between forecast and actual returns. One drawback of the IC as a forecast evaluation tool is its independence of both origin and scale. The measured correlation between forecast and actual returns is unaffected by adding a constant to each forecast or multiplying each forecast by a positive constant. But while IC is invariant to these transformations, the forecast errors—the difference between forecast and actual returns—clearly are not. Thus, the IC cannot differentiate between a perfectly accurate set of forecasts and an alternative set that consistently overestimates by 50 percent.

The criteria we use assess the accuracy of alternative forecasting methods more directly than the IC. They are defined in the appendix at the end of this chapter. The first criterion is *mean error* (ME), which is a simple average of forecast errors. If the ME is positive (negative), the model tends to underestimate (overestimate) actual returns. The ME is likely to be small, because positive and negative errors tend to offset each other. The *mean absolute error* (MAE), which is a simple average of the absolute value of forecast errors, avoids this problem. The MAE is an appropriate criterion if the cost of erring is proportionate to the size of the forecast error.

Root-mean-squared error (RMSE) is the square root of a simple average of squared forecast errors. The RMSE is consistent with a squared loss function, where the pain of erring grows with the square of the forecast error. Simply stated, the RMSE counts a larger error more heavily than a collection of smaller errors having similar aggregate magnitude. The RMSE is larger than the MAE unless all errors are of the same size, in which case the two measures are identical.

The three criteria reviewed thus far are all absolute measures. They do not facilitate comparisons across different variables or across different time periods. Relative measures can be constructed on the basis of percentage error. Still more useful is a criterion that measures gains in accuracy compared with a naïve benchmark forecast. The Theil U statistic compares the RMSE of the forecast model with that of a naïve forecast using last period's actual return [see Theil (1966)]. This naïve benchmark forecast explicitly assumes no change in the next period.

A Theil U less than (in excess of) one indicates that the forecast method is better (worse) than a naïve forecast. A Theil U of less than one should be interpreted with caution, however, because a no-change forecast may be a bad benchmark. For example, the level of the Consumer Price Index (CPI) generally rises over time; a forecast of the CPI will thus be more accurate if it adds a trend component, rather than just assuming that last period's level will continue unchanged. In this instance, a no-change benchmark is a poor one, and a Theil U of less than one is relatively easy to achieve.

We apply these forecast accuracy criteria "out of sample." That is, our models are estimated over a portion of the historical time series and their forecast accuracies tested over a more recent "holdout" sample. This is fundamentally different from "in-sample" fitting. For example, regression analysis locates the line of best fit to historical data. In ordinary least-squares (OLS) regression, squared errors are minimized. The focus is on "goodness-of-fit" measures such as R, the correlation coefficient between actual and fitted values, or, more commonly, R-squared, the proportion of the variance in the variable of interest explained by the regression.

But obtaining a good fit to historical data does not necessarily imply a good forecast model. In fact, a perfect fit can be obtained by using a polynomial of sufficiently high order. A polynomial of degree $n - 1$, for example, can be specified to pass through any n data points. The resulting model will match the data exactly, but it will tell us nothing about the process generating the data. Such a model has little or no forecasting power, even though the fit is perfect.

Out-of-sample tests, by contrast, focus on the predictive ability of a model. Rather than fitting a historical series, the goal is to improve the model's predictive ability. A particularly useful out-of-sample measure is a t-statistic on the economic insight provided by the model forecasts.

We use these criteria to compare the forecast models discussed in the following sections.

Simple Extrapolation Techniques

A simple extrapolation technique may use averages or moving averages to forecast. Such an approach is generally regarded as "deterministic," because it ignores the underlying randomness in the series. As a result, expected forecast accuracy cannot be measured. Nevertheless, these simple approaches sometimes work well.

We looked at a simple average of past observations. This approach assumes that the process generating the data is in equilibrium around a constant value—the underlying mean. The process is subject to random error, or "noise," which causes the observed returns to be scattered about the mean.

First, we calculated the average monthly pure return to size over the base period January 1978 to December 1981, and then used this average value as the return forecast for January 1982. In each successive month, the average return was updated by adding one additional observation, and the revised average became the return forecast for the next month. The last forecast month was December 1987. Table 5-1 gives statistics on the accuracy of forecasts for the next 1 to 6 months.

The simple average tended to overestimate actual returns slightly, as indicated by the MEs, which averaged –0.09 percent

TABLE 5-1

Forecast Statistics

Forecast Step	ME (%)	MAE (%)	RMSE (%)	THEIL U	t
			Constant Model		
1	-0.08	0.43	0.55	0.74	1.3
2	-0.08	0.43	0.56	0.73	1.3
3	-0.09	0.43	0.56	0.78	1.2
4	-0.08	0.43	0.56	0.77	1.2
5	-0.09	0.43	0.56	0.87	1.1
6	-0.10	0.44	0.57	0.80	0.9
			Exponential Smoothing Model		
1	0.07	0.45	0.55	0.74	0.8
2	0.07	0.45	0.56	0.73	0.9
3	0.07	0.45	0.56	0.78	1.3
4	0.07	0.45	0.56	0.77	1.6
5	0.06	0.45	0.56	0.87	1.8*
6	0.05	0.45	0.56	0.79	0.7
			Vector Time-Series Model		
1	-0.18	0.51	0.67	0.90	0.5
2	0.00	0.48	0.63	0.83	1.0
3	0.02	0.56	0.69	0.96	-1.1
4	0.89	0.96	1.15	1.58	-0.3
5	1.16	1.22	1.42	2.20	0.0
6	0.41	0.58	0.77	1.09	0.6
			Bayesian Model		
1	-0.08	0.41	0.53	0.71	3.1*
2	-0.06	0.42	0.54	0.71	3.0*
3	-0.07	0.42	0.54	0.76	2.8*
4	-0.07	0.41	0.55	0.76	2.5*
5	-0.09	0.41	0.56	0.86	2.3*
6	-0.10	0.42	0.57	0.80	2.0*

*Significant at the 5 percent level.

across forecast steps. The MAEs ranged from 0.43 to 0.44 percent, while the RMSEs ranged from 0.55 to 0.57 percent. The "goodness" of these absolute statistics can be assessed only by comparison with other forecast models.

The Theil U's indicate that the RMSE ranged from 73 to 87 percent of the RMSE associated with the naïve benchmark, which was simply last month's return. Thus, a simple historical average provided a much better return forecast than a no-change benchmark. The Theil values associated with the simple average became our standard for comparing the forecasting models.

Simple averaging equally weights all observations; with exponential smoothing, weights decay in an exponential manner, so that recent observations are weighted more heavily than older ones [see Gardner (1985)]. The rate of decay is determined by a parameter that ranges from zero to one. A parameter close to one places most of the weight on recent observations, while a parameter close to zero distributes the weight more evenly across all observations. While exponential smoothing adapts faster than simple averaging to recent changes, it will necessarily trail any trend in the data.

The second panel of Table 5-1 displays forecast statistics for exponential smoothing based on a parameter of 0.3. The results are generally similar to those for the constant process. The biggest difference is that the MEs are on average slightly positive, indicating a tendency to underestimate actual returns. Also, the MAEs are somewhat higher. (The forecast statistics obtained from an array of decay parameter settings were similar.)

Time-Series Techniques

The objective of time-series analysis is to identify and model patterns in the historical data. This assumes that a time series is generated by a "stochastic," or random, process which can be described and replicated by a model. Time-series approaches include autoregressive models, which depend on a weighted sum of past values, and moving-average models, which depend on a weighted sum of past errors. Some stochastic processes exhibit both autoregressive and moving-average characteristics, and can be modeled with mixed autoregressive/moving-average processes.[8]

Autocorrelations are used to measure the "memory" in the time series—that is, whether past values can predict future values.[9] Morgan and Morgan (1987) studied autocorrelation patterns in the returns of small-firm portfolios and found positive autocorrelation of monthly returns, 6 and 12 months apart, which was not specific to January. Lo and MacKinley (1988) found positive autocorrelation for weekly and monthly returns, independent of the effects of infrequent trading. Levis (1988) found significant autocorrelation of quarterly returns on the London Stock Exchange.[10] But these autocorrelation patterns are for naïve returns to size, hence may incorporate related return effects.

Figure 5-2, a correlogram, shows the autocorrelation pattern for pure returns to small size. The corridor defined by the dotted lines represents a 95 percent confidence band [see Barlett (1946) and Box and Jenkins (1976)]. Because all the autocorrelation coefficients lie within this confidence band, none is statistically significant at the 5 percent level.

The hypothesis that all the autocorrelations jointly are insignificant can be tested using the Portmanteau Q statistic [see Ljung and Box (1978) and Box and Pierce (1970)]. The Q statistic is not significantly different from zero. Pure returns to small size, at least over this time period, are indistinguishable from "white noise." That is,

FIGURE   5-2

Autocorrelations of Return

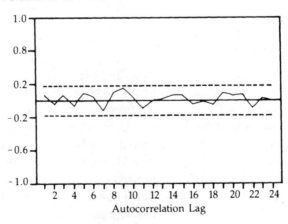

Autocorrelation Lag

the time series of returns does not differ from that of a random variable independently distributed across time.[11]

Transfer Functions

The analysis of any single series excludes information that may be contained in related series. Regression analysis allows one to ascertain cause-and-effect relations between one or more independent variables and the dependent variable being forecast. Regression methods are causal, or explanatory, in nature.[12]

Transfer functions blend time-series analysis with explanatory variables [see Box and Jenkins (1976), Chapters 10 and 11]. The dependent variable being forecast is related to a weighted sum of lagged values of itself, current and lagged values of one or more independent variables, and an error term. The error term is modeled with time-series techniques. Potentially useful explanatory variables may be chosen on the basis of economic theory, but the precise form the relationship takes will depend on the data, including the autocorrelation function of each series and contemporaneous and lagged cross-correlations between series.

The transfer-function approach has been applied to forecasting stock market returns, using the Composite Index of Leading Indicators as an explanatory variable [see Umstead (1977)]. Levis (1988) used transfer functions to examine the relation between the size effect in the United Kingdom and institutional trading patterns. He found the size effect on the London Stock Exchange unrelated to institutional acquisitions or dispositions. On the contrary, he found institutional trading follows, rather than leads, market behavior.

Transfer functions can only model one-way causality. Consider, for example, a time series, Y, to be forecast, and a related series, X. Information contained in time series X may be useful for forecasting series Y. X is said to "cause" Y if using past values of X, in addition to past values of Y, and yields a more accurate prediction of Y than past values of Y alone [see Granger (1969)].

This is a useful concept, which lends itself to statistical testing, but it does not necessarily correspond to the commonsense meaning of causality. Causality between time series can run in both directions: X can cause Y, and Y can cause X. In this instance, X and Y cause each other. This is referred to as "feedback." When series exhibit feedback, transfer-function modeling is not appropriate; vector time-series models should be considered.

Vector Time-Series Models

Vector time-series approaches model a group, or vector, of related variables [see Quenouille (1957)]. In vector autoregression (VAR), each variable is regressed on its own historical values as well as on past values of other explanatory variables. Such joint modeling of time series permits an understanding of the dynamic relationships among the series: Series may be contemporaneously related, some may lead others, or there may be feedback present. By incorporating the information contained in the multiple time series, the accuracy of forecasts can be improved.

The differential returns to smaller firms may derive from their greater sensitivity to certain pervasive, economywide factors. Chan, Chen, and Hsieh (1985) found, for example, that the return differential between corporate and government bonds explains much of the cross-sectional variation in return to firm size. Small firms fluctuate more with the business cycle than large firms. Their greater sensitivity to economic conditions arises from their more marginal nature.

Chan and Chen (1988b) found that small firms have often operated inefficiently, have recently decreased in size, have higher financial leverage, and have less access to external financing than larger firms.[13] Consistent with their higher risk, small firms tend to perform well when the default spread is narrowing and risk aversion is abating. The greater sensitivity of smaller firms to default spreads is a risk for which investors may demand compensation.

The perspective of Chan, Chen, and Hsieh derives from equilibrium pricing theory. Our perspective is quite different. We want to know whether differential returns to smaller firms are forecastable. Rather than examining contemporaneous pricing relationships, we want to predict future returns by employing macroeconomic drivers in a time-series framework.

We constructed a monthly VAR model of the size effect using the following set of economic measures as explanatory variables: (1) low-quality (BAA) corporate bond rate, (2) long-term (10-year) Treasury bond rate, (3) Treasury bill (90-day) rate, (4) S&P 500 total return, (5) Industrial Production Index (logarithmic), and (6) Consumer Price Index (logarithmic).[14] These macro drivers were chosen because of their importance in security valuation. (Of course, considerations other than value may be helpful in modeling the size effect.[15])

We used three autoregressive, or lag, terms for each of the six macroeconomic variables.[16] The model was first estimated over a base period from January 1978 to December 1981, then revised monthly through the end of 1987 using a Kalman filter update [see Kalman (1960) and Kalman and Bucy (1961)]. The third panel of Table 5-1 displays the forecast statistics.

A glance at the statistics reveals this model to be inferior to the constant model. The MEs, MAEs, and RMSEs are substantially larger, and the differences become especially pronounced at forecast steps four, five, and six. The Theil U exceeds 1 for the last three forecast steps, indicating that the forecasts are less accurate than no-change forecasts. The *t*-statistics are insignificant and sometimes negative.

The poor forecasting power of the model results from its overparameterization—a typical problem with VAR models. While VAR models have the virtue of allowing the data to "speak for themselves," there are rarely enough historical data available to allow the modeling of more than a few related series, because the number of coefficients to be estimated grows with the square of the number of variables. As a consequence, an unrestricted VAR model tends to become overparameterized; that is, it lacks sufficient data relative to the number of coefficients to be estimated.

Because it has a large number of coefficients available to explain a small number of observations, a VAR model can explain historical data well. But it is likely to "overfit" the data. That is, it will fit not only systematic, or stable, relationships, but also random, or merely circumstantial, ones. The latter are of no use in forecasting and may be misleading. Thus, while the model provides a good in-sample fit, it is likely to forecast poorly.[17]

Some improvement in forecasting ability may be gained by aiming for a more parsimonious, or simpler, representation of the return-generating process. This can be done by introducing moving-average (MA) terms, which should improve the efficiency of the parameter estimation process without assuming away important interactions among the variables. The disadvantage of introducing MA terms is that the identification of the order of the moving-average and autoregressive lag lengths is difficult, particularly in multivariate applications. Moreover, such vector autoregressive/moving-average (VARMA) models cannot cope with as many explanatory variables as we consider here.[18]

There are two traditional ways of reducing the dimensionality of vector models. One is simply to use univariate time-series methods. While this approach dramatically reduces dimensionality by excluding all cross effects, it is severely restrictive because interactions among variables are assumed to be nonexistent. The other approach is structural modeling, which relies on restrictions suggested by economic theory. In fact, there is no evidence to date that VARMA modeling can perform as well as commercially available structural models of the economy [see Litterman (1986)].

Structural Macroeconomic Models

The overparameterization of vector models has traditionally been resolved by incorporating economic theory. Such "econometric" models include only those variables and lags suggested by theory. As a result, the models require substantially fewer variables and lags than an unrestricted VAR.[19]

Econometric models are referred to as structural models because they explicitly incorporate theories about economic structure. There are, needless to say, many conflicting schools of economic thought. Although each theory undoubtedly contains some elements of truth, none is fully descriptive of reality. Thus, while structural models may avoid the overfitting problem of VAR, they also incorporate rigid beliefs, some of which may be unfounded. Furthermore, because theory forces the exclusion of a large number of variables at the outset, these variables never have the opportunity to refute the theory, no matter how strong the evidence of the data.

Structural models use prior beliefs based on economic theory to impose restrictions, but these restrictions are often too severe. As a result, the modeler's confidence in the theory may be overstated.[20] Unrestricted VAR models, by contrast, may understate the modeler's knowledge, because the data alone determine the values of the coefficients. An alternative approach is to represent statistically the modeler's uncertainty regarding the merits of alternative theories and to allow the data to revise the theory. Bayesian methods are designed to accommodate such uncertainty.[21]

Bayesian Vector Time-Series Models

Many economic measures are difficult to predict, but their behavior can often be approximated by a random walk. A random walk model for interest rates assumes it is equally likely that rates will rise or fall. A random walk forecast of next month's rate would simply be this month's rate of interest.

There are many ways to specify prior beliefs about the coefficients of a forecast model. One Bayesian specification imposes a random walk prior on the coefficients of a VAR model. This results in a powerful forecasting tool that provides a viable alternative to structural econometric modeling. In fact, it has been demonstrated that this approach "can produce economic forecasts that are at least competitive with the best forecasts commercially available" [Litterman (1986), p. 35].[22] Further, there is evidence that these methods can forecast economic turning points [see Litterman (1986), p. 33, and Kling (1987)].

The difficulty of predicting stock returns is no secret. But stock prices, like other economic data, can be approximated by a random walk. As early as 1900, Bachelier articulated a theory of random walks in security prices. A random walk model implies that successive price changes are independent draws from the same probability distribution. That is, the series of price changes has no memory and appears unpredictable. Using a random walk prior to model security returns is thus eminently sensible.[23]

We modeled the size effect using a Bayesian random walk prior and the same six macroeconomic drivers discussed earlier. The top part of Figure 5-3 displays cumulative returns to small size for the period January 1982 to December 1987. The lower part displays out-of-sample return forecasts for 1 month ahead. The forecasts for small stocks were positive during the early years; they gradually declined and turned negative during the last 2 years, implying that small stocks were expected to underperform large stocks.

The last panel of Table 5-1 displays forecast statistics for the Bayesian model. The MAEs, RMSEs, and Theil U's are substantially better than those of the unrestricted VAR. These statistics also show an improvement over the constant model. For instance, the Theil U for 1-month forecasts is 0.71 for the Bayesian model and 0.74 for the constant model, a relative improvement of about 5 percent. The margin of improvement declines with the forecast horizon. Similar

F I G U R E   5-3

Forecasting Returns to Small Size

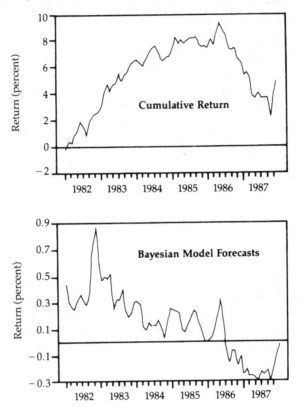

results hold for the MAE and RMSE. The *t*-statistics are significant for all six forecast steps, and decline gradually from 3.1 at step 1 to 2.0 at step 6. It is highly unlikely that the economic insight associated with this approach occurred as a result of chance.

We used an "impulse" analysis to estimate the impact of each macro driver on forecast returns. To consider the effect of an unexpected increase in the corporate bond rate on forecast returns to size, for example, we defined the magnitude of the rate increase to be 1 standard deviation, or one unit, of historical BAA interest rate volatility and applied this one-unit BAA rate "shock" to the model.[24]

Figure 5-4 graphs the forecast return response of small size to one-unit shocks in each of the six macro drivers. A shock in the BAA

FIGURE 5-4

Forecast Response of Small Size to Macroeconomic Shocks

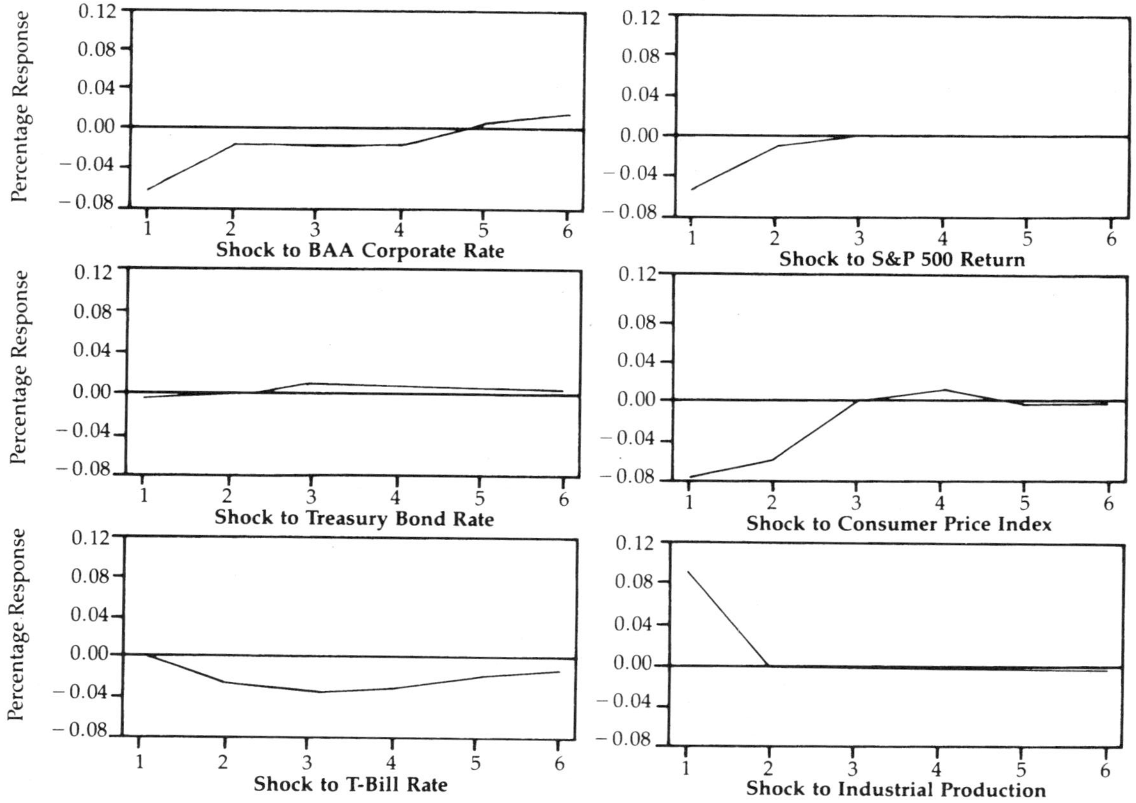

rate produces forecast changes of about –6 basis points 1 month ahead, –2 basis points 2, 3, and 4 months ahead, and +1 basis point 5 and 6 months ahead. The response to a shock in long government rates is negligible. The response to a Treasury bill shock is negative, ranging between 0 and –4 basis points. The response to a shock in the S&P 500 is –5 basis points 1 month ahead and negligible thereafter. A shock in the inflation rate lowers the forecast return by 8 basis points 1 month ahead and 6 basis points 2 months out. A shock in industrial production raises the forecast return by 9 basis points 1 month ahead.

The negative impact on returns to small size of an unexpected increase in BAA corporate interest rates and the positive impact of an unexpected increase in industrial production are consistent with the fragility of smaller firms. The negative response to an unexpectedly positive S&P 500 return, however, suggests that more is at work than risk considerations alone. The negative response to an increase in Treasury bill rates is consistent with the greater capital constraints on smaller firms. Also, smaller stocks fare less well during periods of unexpected inflation.

APPENDIX

The following criteria were used to assess the accuracy of the various forecasting methods:

mean error (ME), defined as $\left[\sum_{i=1}^{n}(A_t - F_t) \right] / n$;

mean absolute error (MAE), defined as $\left[\sum_{t=1}^{n} |A_t - F_t| \right] / n$;

root-mean-squared error (RMSE), defined as $\sqrt{\left[\sum_{t=1}^{n}(A_t - F_t)^2 \right] / n}$;

and Theil U, defined as $\dfrac{\sqrt{\left[\sum_{t=0}^{n-1}(A_{t+1} - F_{t+1})^2 \right] / n}}{\sqrt{\left[\sum_{t=0}^{n-1}(A_{t+1} - A_t)^2 \right] / n}}$

in which A_t equals the actual value at time t, F_t equals the forecast value for time t, and n equals the number of observations.

ENDNOTES

1. Rozeff (1984), Keim and Stambaugh (1986), and Fama and French (1988a and 1988b).

2. For some empirical results, see Amihud and Mendelson (1988) and Gilmer and Swanson (1988).

3. See also Arbel (1985) and Carvell and Strebel (1987).

4. See Table I in Jacobs and Levy (1988b) for references to earlier studies. The 25 measures used were low P/E, small size, yield, zero yield, neglect, low price, book/price, sales/price, cash/price, sigma, beta, co-skewness, controversy, three measures of trends in analysts' earnings estimates, three measures of earnings surprise, earnings torpedo, relative strength, two measures of return reversal, and two measures of potential tax-loss-selling. Also, 38 industry measures were utilized to purify returns further.

5. For a synthesis of the calendar literature, see Jacobs and Levy (1988a).

6. See Gibbons and Hess (1981), Keim and Stambaugh (1984), Harris (1986), and Keim (1987). However, Miller (1988) argues that intraweek patterns in returns to size are unrelated to the long-run size effect.

7. The payoffs shown are for an exposure of 1 cross-sectional standard deviation to the small-size attribute. For details, see Jacobs and Levy (1988b). The results from that article have been extended through the end of 1987.

8. The current observation in an autoregressive (AR) process of order p is generated by a weighted average of p lagged observations. Similarly, the current observation in a moving-average (MA) process of order q is generated by a weighted average of q lagged errors. Methods for identifying and fitting time-series models are provided in Box and Jenkins (1976).

9. The autocorrelation function is used to determine the order of the stochastic process. It provides a measure of the correlation between sequential data points. The nth-order autocorrelation is defined as the covariance between each observation and that of n periods earlier, divided by the variance of the process.

10. While these studies find short-term autocorrelation patterns, Grant (1984) documents long-term cycles in the daily returns of small-firm portfolios, and Fama and French (1988b) find strong negative serial correlation for long-horizon returns of duration 3 to 5 years, especially for smaller firms.

11. Further confirming evidence is provided by various criteria that determine the order of a stochastic process. Akaike's (1969) AIC criterion determines the order of autoregressive processes. The Hannan-Rissanen (1982, 1983) criterion determines the order of autoregressive/moving-average (ARMA) processes. Both indicate that this return series cannot be successfully modeled as an ARMA process. Significant autocorrelation patterns exist for pure returns to some other equity attributes. See Jacobs and Levy (1988b).

12. Makridakis, Wheelwright, and McGee (1983) observe (p. 18): "Unlike explanatory forecasting, time-series forecasting treats the system as a black box and makes no attempt to discover the factors affecting its behavior."

13. Chan and Chen (1988b) form two mimicking portfolios—one of firms in distress, as measured by reductions in dividend payments, and another of highly leveraged smaller firms. They find smaller firms have higher sensitivities to the mimicking portfolios than do larger firms, even after controlling for firm size.

14. Similar variables were used by Chan, Chen, and Hsieh (1985) to investigate links with the size effect, by Chen, Roll, and Ross (1986) to investigate links with stock returns, and by Fama and French (1987) to investigate links with stock and bond returns. These studies transform the variables; for instance, default spread measures are formed from the difference between yields, or returns, on low-quality corporate and government bonds. The default spread, and other spreads, are implicitly incorporated in our approach as differences between the independent variables.

15. Jacobs and Levy have demonstrated, for example, that value considerations alone are insufficient to explain security pricing. For instance, the effectiveness of the dividend discount model is dependent on market psychology [see Jacobs and Levy (1988c)]. And Japanese investments in U.S. stocks, which are generally concentrated in larger companies, are influenced by the dollar/yen exchange rate. For expository purposes, however, we limited our investigation to the six valuation variables.

16. Although standard VAR models use a uniform lag length for all variables, Hsiao (1981) has proposed a stopping-point criterion for choosing the optimal lag length for each variable in each equation.

17. For a critique of the usefulness of VAR models for understanding macroeconomic relationships, see Runkle (1987). VAR modeling for small-scale applications was first proposed by Sims (1980).

18. As the number of variables increases, VARMA models face what Jenkins and Alavi (1981) call the "curse of higher dimensionality." Granger and Newbold (1986) assert (p. 257) that:

> even if we had any confidence in our ability to identify a VARMA model relating say seven or eight time series, the full parameterization would involve a huge number of unknown parameters. Not only is model estimation extremely expensive in this case, it is also rather foolhardy, since though such a nonparsimonious structure may fit an observed data set well, it is likely to prove very disappointing when extrapolated forward for forecasting purposes.

19. Zellner and Palm (1974) show that any structural econometric model may be viewed as a restricted vector time-series model.

20. Sims (1980) argues that "existing large models contain too many incredible restrictions" and concludes that "the style in which their builders construct claims for a connection between these [structural] models and reality . . . is inappropriate, to the point at which claims for identification in these cannot be taken seriously." Also, Granger (1981) has asserted that "a 'moderate'-size econometric model of 400 or so equations is beyond the scope of current macroeconomic theory. The theory is hardly capable of specifying all of these equations in any kind of detail."

21. Bayes' theorem is the basis for combining "prior" beliefs with sample information to form a "posterior" distribution [Bayes (1763) and Zellner (1971)].

22. For a discussion of the merits of Bayesian VAR modeling, see Litterman (1987) and McNees (1986). For an elaboration on the technique, see Doan, Litterman, and Sims (1984). Antecedents in the literature include ridge regression, smoothness priors, and Stein-James shrinkage estimators. For applications in finance, see Martin (1978), Shiller (1973), and Jacobs and Levy (1988b), p. 32.

23. While short-run stock returns are approximated well by a random walk, there is evidence of a mean-reversion tendency for longer-run returns [Fama and French (1988b)].

24. The shocks are also referred to as "innovations," because they represent surprises not predicted from past data. They are constructed to be orthogonal by taking into account contemporaneous correlations with the other macroeconomic variables.

REFERENCES

Akaike, H. 1969. "Fitting autoregressive models for prediction." *Annals of the Institute of Statistics and Mathematics* 21: 243–247.

Amihud, Y. and H. Mendelson. 1986a. "Asset pricing and the bid-ask spread." *Journal of Financial Economics* 17 (2): 223–249.

────── and ──────. 1986b. "Liquidity and stock returns." *Financial Analysts Journal* 42 (3): 43–48.

────── and ──────. 1988. "The effects of beta, bid-ask spread, residual risk and size on stock returns." Working Paper, New York University, New York. [Published in *Journal of Finance* 44 (2): 479–486.]

Arbel, A. 1985. "Generic stocks: An old product in a new package." *Journal of Portfolio Management* 11 (4): 4–13.

Arbel, A., S. Carvell, and P. Strebel. 1983. "Giraffes, institutions and neglected firms." *Financial Analysts Journal* 39 (3): 57–62.

Bachelier, L. 1900. *Theorie de la speculation*. Paris: Cauthier-Villars.

Banz, R. 1981. "The relationship between return and market value of common stocks." *Journal of Financial Economics* 9 (1): 3–18.

Banz, R. and W. Breen. 1986. "Sample-dependent results using accounting and market data: Some evidence." *Journal of Finance* 41 (4): 779–793.

Barry, C. and S. Brown. 1984. "Differential information and the small firm effect." *Journal of Financial Economics* 13 (2): 283–294.

────── and ──────. 1985. "Differential information and security market equilibrium." *Journal of Financial and Quantitative Analysis* 20 (4): 407–422.

────── and ──────. 1986. "Limited information as a source of risk." *Journal of Portfolio Management* 12 (2): 66–72.

Bartlett, M. 1946. "On the theoretical specification of sampling properties of autocorrelated time series." *Journal of the Royal Statistical Society, serial B8* 27: 27–41.

Basu, S. 1977. "Investment performance of common stocks in relation to their price-earnings ratios: A test of the Efficient Market Hypothesis." *Journal of Finance* 32 (2): 663–682.

──────. 1983. "The relationship between earnings yield, market value and return for NYSE common stocks: Further evidence." *Journal of Financial Economics* 12 (1): 129–156.

Bayes, T. 1763. "Essay towards solving a problem in the doctrine of chances." *Philosophical Transactions of the Royal Society* 53: 370–418. Reprinted in *Biometrika* 45 (1958): 293–315.

Blume, M. and R. Stambaugh. 1983. "Biases in computed returns: An application to the size effect." *Journal of Financial Economics* 12 (3): 387–404.

Booth, J. and R. Smith. 1985. "The application of errors-in-variables methodology to capital market research: Evidence on the small-firm effect." *Journal of Financial and Quantitative Analysis* 20 (4): 501–515.

Box, G. and G. Jenkins. 1976. *Time Series Analysis: Forecasting and Control*. Rev. ed. San Francisco: Holden-Day.

Box, G. and D. Pierce. 1970. "Distribution of residual autocorrelations in autoregressive integrated moving average time series models." *Journal of the American Statistical Association* 65 (332): 1509–1526.

Branch, B. 1977. "A tax loss trading rule." *Journal of Business* 50 (2): 198–207.

Brown, P., et al. 1983. "Stock return seasonalities and the tax-loss selling hypothesis: Analysis of the arguments and Australian evidence." *Journal of Financial Economics* 12 (1): 105–127.

Brown, P., A. Kleidon, and T. Marsh. 1983. "New evidence on the nature of size-related anomalies in stock prices." *Journal of Financial Economics* 12 (1): 33–56.

Carvell, S. and P. Strebel. 1987. "Is there a neglected firm effect?" *Journal of Business Finance and Accounting* 14 (2): 279–290.

Chan, K. 1986. "Can tax-loss selling explain the January seasonal in stock returns?" *Journal of Finance* 41 (5): 1115–1128.

Chan, K. and N. Chen. 1988a. "An unconditional asset pricing test and the role of firm size as an instrumental variable for risk." *Journal of Finance* 43 (2): 303–326.

——— and ———. 1988b. "Business cycles and the returns of small and large firms." Working Paper #229, University of Chicago, Chicago, January. [Subsequently published as "Structural and return characteristics of small and large firms." *Journal of Finance* 46 (4): 1467–1484.]

Chan, K., N. Chen, and D. Hsieh. 1985. "An exploratory investigation of the firm size effect." *Journal of Financial Economics* 14 (3): 451–471.

Chari, V., R. Jagannathan, and A. Ofer. 1986. "Fiscal year end and the January effect." Working Paper #20, Kellogg Graduate School of Management, Northwestern University, Evanston, Illinois, July.

Chen, N. 1983. "Some empirical tests of the theory of arbitrage pricing." *Journal of Finance* 38 (5): 1393–1414.

Chen, N., R. Roll, and S. Ross. 1986. "Economic forces and the stock market." *Journal of Business* 59 (3): 383–403.

Chiang, R. and P. Venkatesh. 1988. "Insider holdings and perceptions of information asymmetry: A note." *Journal of Finance* 43 (4): 1041–1048.

Connor, G. and R. Korajczyk. 1988. "Risk and return in an equilibrium APT: Application of a new test methodology." *Journal of Financial Economics* 21 (2): 255–290.

Constantinides, G. 1984. "Optimal stock trading with personal taxes: Implications for prices and the abnormal January returns." *Journal of Financial Economics* 13 (1): 65–89.

Cook, T. and M. Rozeff. 1984. "Size and earnings/price ratio anomalies: One effect or two?" *Journal of Financial and Quantitative Analysis* 19 (4): 449–466.

Dimson, E. 1979. "Risk measurement when shares are subject to infrequent trading." *Journal of Financial Economics* 7 (2): 197–226.

Doan, T., R. Litterman, and C. Sims. 1984. "Forecasting and conditional projection using realistic prior distributions." *Econometric Review* 3 (1): 1–144.

Dyl, E. 1977. "Capital gains taxation and year-end stock market behavior." *Journal of Finance* 32 (1): 165–175.

Fama, E. and K. French. 1987. "Forecasting returns on corporate bonds and common stocks." Working Paper #220, University of Chicago, Chicago, December. [Subsequently published as "Business conditions and expected returns on stocks and bonds." *Journal of Financial Economics* 25 (1): 23–50.]

―――― and ――――. 1988a. "Dividend yields and expected stock returns." *Journal of Financial Economics* 22 (1): 3–26.

―――― and ――――. 1988b. "Permanent and temporary components of stock prices." *Journal of Political Economy* 96 (2): 246–273.

Ferson, W., S. Kandel, and R. Stambaugh. 1987. "Tests of asset pricing with time-varying expected risk premiums and market betas." *Journal of Finance* 42 (2): 201–220.

Gardner, E. 1985. "Exponential smoothing: The state of the art." *Journal of Forecasting* 4 (1): 1–38.

Gibbons, M. and P. Hess. 1981. "Day of the week effects and asset returns." *Journal of Business* 54 (4): 579–596.

Gilmer, R. and H. Swanson. 1988. "An empirical test of Merton's incomplete information model." Working Paper, Mississippi State University, Mississippi State, September.

Gordon, M. 1962. *The Investment, Financing and Valuation of the Corporation.* Homewood, Illinois: Richard D. Irwin.

Granger, C. 1969. "Investigating causal relations by econometric models and cross-spectral methods." *Econometrica* 37 (3): 424–438.

――――. 1981. "The comparison of time series and econometric forecasting strategies." In *Large-Scale Macroeconomic Forecasting,* J. Kmenta and J. Ramsey, eds. Amsterdam: North-Holland Publishing.

Granger, C. and P. Newbold. 1986. *Forecasting Economic Time Series.* 2d ed. Orlando: Academic Press.

Grant, J. 1984. "Long-term dependence in small firm returns." Working Paper #84-10, Boston College, Boston, March.

Gultekin, M. and B. Gultekin. 1983. "Stock market seasonality: International evidence." *Journal of Financial Economics* 12 (4): 469–481.

Handa, P., S. Kothari, and C. Wasley. 1987. "Bias in estimation of systematic risk and its implications for tests of the CAPM." Working Paper #404, New York University, New York, January. [See "The relation between the return interval and betas: Implications for the size effect." *Journal of Financial Economics* 23 (1): 79–100.]

Hannan, E. and J. Rissanen. 1982. "Recursive estimation of mixed autoregressive-moving average order." *Biometrika* 69: 81–94.

―――― and ――――. 1983. "Correction." *Biometrika* 70: 303.

Harris, L. 1986. "A transaction data study of weekly and intradaily patterns in stock returns." *Journal of Financial Economics* 16 (1): 99–117.

Hsiao, C. 1981. "Autoregressive modelling and money-income causality detection." *Journal of Monetary Economics* 7: 85–106.

Jacobs, B. and K. Levy. 1988a. "Calendar anomalies: Abnormal returns at calendar turning points." *Financial Analysts Journal* 44 (6): 28–39.

——— and ———. 1988b. "Disentangling equity return regularities: New insights and investment opportunities." *Financial Analysts Journal* 44 (3): 18–43.

——— and ———. 1988c. "On the value of 'value.'" *Financial Analysts Journal* 44 (4): 47–62.

Jenkins, G. and A. Alavi. 1981. "Some aspects of modelling and forecasting multivariate time series." *Journal of Time Series Analysis* 2: 1–47.

Jones, C., D. Pearce, and J. Wilson. 1987. "Can tax-loss selling explain the January effect? A note." *Journal of Finance* 42 (2): 453–561.

Kalman, R. 1960. "A new approach to linear filtering and prediction problems." *Journal of Basic Engineering* (March): 35–44.

Kalman, R. and R. Bucy. 1961. "New results in linear filtering and prediction theory." *Journal of Basic Engineering* (March): 95–107.

Keim, D. 1983. "Size-related anomalies and stock return seasonality: Further empirical evidence." *Journal of Financial Economics* 12 (1): 13–32.

———. 1987. "Daily returns and size-related premiums: One more time." *Journal of Portfolio Management* 13 (2): 41–47.

Keim, D. and R. Stambaugh. 1984. "A further investigation of the weekend effect in stock returns." *Journal of Finance* 39 (3): 165–168.

——— and ———. 1986. "Predicting returns in the stock and bond markets." *Journal of Financial Economics* 17 (2): 357–390.

Kling, J. 1987. "Predicting the turning points of business and economic time series." *Journal of Business* 60 (2): 201–238.

Lehmann, B. and D. Modest. 1988. "The empirical foundations of the Arbitrage Pricing Theory." *Journal of Financial Economics* 21 (2): 243–254.

Levis, M. 1988. "Size related anomalies and trading activity of UK institutional investors." In *Stock Market Anomalies*, E. Dimson, ed. Cambridge: Cambridge University Press.

Litterman, R. 1986. "Forecasting with Bayesian vector autoregression—five years of experience." *Journal of Business and Economic Statistics* 4 (1): 25–38.

———. 1987. "A statistical approach to economic forecasting." *Journal of Business and Economic Statistics* 5 (1): 1–4.

Ljung, G. and G. Box. 1978. "On a measure of lack of fit in time series models." *Biometrika* 65: 297–303.

Lo, A. and C. MacKinlay. 1988. "Stock market prices do not follow random walks: Evidence from a simple specification test." *Review of Financial Studies* 1 (1): 41–66.

Makridakis, S., S. Wheelwright, and V. McGee. 1983. *Forecasting Methods and Applications*. 2d ed. New York: John Wiley.

Martin, C. 1978. "Ridge regression estimates of the ex post risk-return trade-off on common stocks." *Review of Business and Economic Research* (Spring).

McNees, S. 1986. "Forecasting accuracy of alternative techniques: A comparison of U.S. macroeconomic forecasts." *Journal of Business and Economic Statistics* 4 (1): 5–15.

Merton, R. 1987. "A simple model of capital market equilibrium with incomplete information." *Journal of Finance* 42 (3): 483–510.

Miller, E. 1988. "Why a weekend effect?" *Journal of Portfolio Management* 14 (4): 43–49.

Morgan, A. and I. Morgan. 1987. "Measurement of abnormal returns from small firms." *Journal of Business and Economic Statistics* 5 (1): 121–129.

Quenouille, M. 1957. *The Analysis of Multiple Time-Series*. London: Griffon.

Reinganum, M. 1981*a*. "Abnormal returns in small firm portfolios." *Financial Analysts Journal* 37 (2): 52–56.

———. 1981*b*. "Misspecification of capital asset pricing: Empirical anomalies based on earnings' yields and market values." *Journal of Financial Economics* 9 (1): 19–46.

———. 1981*c*. "The Arbitrage Pricing Theory: Some empirical results." *Journal of Finance* 36 (2): 313–321.

———. 1982. "A direct test of Roll's conjecture on the firm size effect." *Journal of Finance* 37 (1): 27–35.

———. 1983*a*. "Portfolio strategies based on market capitalization." *Journal of Portfolio Management* 9 (2): 29–36.

———. 1983*b*. "The anomalous stock market behavior of small firms in January: Empirical tests for tax-loss selling effects." *Journal of Financial Economics* 12 (1): 89–104.

Rogalski, R. and S. Tinic. 1986. "The January size effect: Anomaly or risk mismeasurement?" *Financial Analysts Journal* 42 (6): 63–70.

Roll, R. 1977. "A critique of the asset pricing theory's tests, Part I: On past and potential testability of the theory." *Journal of Financial Economics* 4 (2): 129–176.

———. 1980. "Performance evaluation and benchmark errors I." *Journal of Portfolio Management* 6 (4): 5–12.

———. 1981*a*. "A possible explanation of the small firm effect." *Journal of Finance* 36 (4): 371–386.

———. 1981*b*. "Performance evaluation and benchmark errors II." *Journal of Portfolio Management* 7 (1): 17–22.

———. 1983*a*. "On computing mean returns and the small firm premium." *Journal of Financial Economics* 12 (3): 371–386.

———. 1983*b*. "Vas is das? The turn of the year effect and the return premia of small firms." *Journal of Portfolio Management* 9 (2): 18–28.

Ross, S. 1976. "The arbitrage theory of capital asset pricing." *Journal of Economic Theory* 13 (3): 341–360.

Rozeff, M. 1984. "Dividend yields are equity risk premiums." *Journal of Portfolio Management* 11 (1): 68–75.

Rozeff, M. and W. Kinney. 1976. "Capital market seasonality: The case of stock returns." *Journal of Financial Economics* 3 (4): 379–402.

Runkle, D. 1987. "Vector autoregressions and reality." *Journal of Business and Economic Statistics* 5 (4): 437–442.

Schultz, P. 1983. "Transaction costs and the small firm effect: A comment." *Journal of Financial Economics* 12 (1): 81–88.

———. 1985. "Personal income taxes and the January effect: Small firm stock returns before the War Revenue Act of 1917: A note." *Journal of Finance* 40 (1): 333–343.

Schwert, G. 1983. "Size and stock returns, and other empirical regularities." *Journal of Financial Economics* 12 (1): 3–12.

Seyhun, H. 1988. "The January effect and aggregate insider trading." *Journal of Finance* 43 (1): 129–142.

Shefrin, H. and M. Statman. 1985. "The disposition to sell winners too early and ride losers too long: Theory and evidence." *Journal of Finance* 40 (3): 777–790.

——— and ———. 1987. "A behavioral finance solution to the noise trading puzzle." Working Paper, University of Santa Clara, Santa Clara, California, December.

Shiller, R. 1973. "A distributed lag estimator derived from smoothness priors." *Econometrica* 41 (4): 775–788.

Sims, C. 1980. "Macroeconomics and reality." *Econometrica* 48 (1): 1–48.

Stoll, H. and R. Whaley. 1983. "Transaction costs and the small firm effect." *Journal of Financial Economics* 12 (1): 57–79.

Theil, H. 1966. *Applied Economic Forecasting.* Amsterdam: North-Holland Publishing.

Tinic, S., G. Barone-Adesi, and R. West. 1987. "Seasonality in Canadian stock prices: A test of the 'tax-loss selling' hypothesis." *Journal of Financial and Quantitative Analysis* 22 (1): 51–63.

Umstead, D. 1977. "Forecasting stock market prices." *Journal of Finance* 32 (2): 427–441.

Zellner, A. 1971. *An Introduction to Bayesian Analysis in Econometrics.* New York: John Wiley.

Zellner, A. and F. Palm. 1974. "Time series analysis and simultaneous equation econometric models." *Journal of Econometrics* 2 (1): 17–54.

Earnings Estimates, Predictor Specification, and Measurement Error[*]

The right choice of data and model can improve performance.

Securities researchers today are able to draw upon a wider array of data from a broader universe of companies and a more extensive time horizon than ever before. This new wealth of information offers new ways to fine-tune and improve investment decision making—but it also offers greater leeway for error. While the right choice of data can enhance investment performance, the wrong choice may introduce measurement error that detracts from performance.

This article explores some of the crucial decisions that arise when expectational data are used to construct explanatory variables for predicting returns. We show how these decisions can lead to measurement error when variables are misspecified, and how treatment of incomplete data sets can affect empirical analyses. We focus on expectational earnings data and their use in constructing earnings predictors for portfolio screening and for quantitative modeling (forecast E/P and earnings trend, in particular). The findings are generalizable to a wide range of data, predictors, and investment approaches.

We begin with a brief exploratory analysis of the issues that arise in predictor specification. We then present some evidence on how predictor specification can affect the results of screening and

---

* Originally published in *Journal of Investing* 6 (4): 29–46. Mitchell C. Krask, Financial Econometrician at Jacobs Levy Equity Management, also contributed to this article.

modeling processes. The findings suggest that the importance of the specification problem varies, depending upon the predictor and the use to which it is being put.

We also discuss some issues that further complicate the specification problem. When data are unavailable, one must decide whether to exclude from the analysis stocks lacking the desired data or to fill in the gaps using substitute data. We suggest a method that can be used to arrive at the best available data set when observations are missing. Further, we examine whether the importance of predictor specification varies, not only across predictors, but also across different types of stocks. As an illustration, we stratify stocks by extent of analyst coverage.

PREDICTOR SPECIFICATION AND MEASUREMENT ERROR

In screening stocks for portfolio selection or in modeling stock behavior, one typically considers a number of variables as potential predictors of return. These include forecast E/P, forecast earnings trend (changes in estimates), earnings surprise, forecast earnings controversy (dispersion of earnings estimates), growth rates in expected earnings, measures related to analyst coverage or neglect, and analyst participation rates in earnings changes (number of revisions). Beyond the problem of selecting the variable or set of variables that will provide the best estimate of future return, one faces the problem of selecting the data that will provide the best estimate of the variable.[1]

Consider *forecast E/P*. It is typically defined as the mean earnings forecast divided by stock price. But which "mean" does this mean? A mean based on all available estimates, that is, the consensus mean? Or a mean based on some but not all available estimates? Which estimates should such a subset include? Should inclusion be based upon timeliness? If so, how does one measure timeliness? On the basis of some fixed horizon—say, a 6-week "flash" estimate using only those estimates revised over the last 6 weeks? Or should one include all the latest estimates available for a given sample of stocks, whenever they were made?[2]

Nor is the mean the only possible measure of the central tendency of analyst forecasts. Other candidates are the median, the trimmed mean, or the midpoint between the high and low estimates. All of these will provide an estimate that can be used to calculate forecast E/P.[3]

Expectational data may also cover many different fiscal periods. Expected earnings, for example, are often provided not only for the current fiscal year (that is, fiscal year 1), but also for the following year and the year after that. Expectational estimates are also provided for quarterly earnings and for a long-term (5-year) growth rate. Should one use expectations for fiscal year 1 only? Or should information from other periods be used as well? If so, should one construct a separate predictor for each fiscal period, or combine periods, using a composite indicator?

Different choices of expectational earnings can lead to different estimates of E/P for the same company. That is to say, the various possible specifications of the predictor will produce a distribution of E/P estimates. Some estimates may be different enough to result in different relative valuations for the same company.[4] Predictive power may also differ across alternative specifications.

Use of less than the best available data set can reduce the accuracy of a given predictor, leading to measurement error. A predictor based upon a particular specification may be inferior because the data are less available, less timely, or more error-prone than alternative specifications. A mean based on consensus earnings data, for example, may be less accurate than a mean based on earnings revisions made in the past 4 weeks, because the consensus data are likely to include stale estimates. If this is the case, then the use of consensus data to construct forecast E/P when more timely analysts' revisions are available will result in measurement error.

Measurement error can, in turn, affect the empirical analyses associated with quantitative modeling. In a simple linear regression, for example, measurement error in the forecast E/P will bias the estimated positive relationship between forecast E/P and subsequent return downward. In general, the greater a predictor's measurement error, the greater the bias toward zero. Intuitively, measurement error dilutes the information content associated with a given predictor. (See the appendix to this chapter.)

In real life, it is difficult to know which specification is best. Furthermore, the best specification may differ both over time and across different types of stocks. In other words, the degrees of measurement error associated with alternative specifications may change over time with changes in the economy, the industry, or the firm, or with changes in data technology. At a given time, they may also differ across industries or sectors or market capitalizations. Predictor specification may also be sensitive to the investment horizon, with the specification best suited to predicting monthly returns not optimal for a daily or quarterly horizon. Finally, the best specification may depend on the investment strategy, and on related criteria such as portfolio turnover and risk.

Given the complexities involved in choosing among alternative predictor specifications, it may be wise to question whether attempts to improve specification are worth the effort required. Just how important is predictor specification? Is it more important for some predictors than others? For some investment approaches than others?

We consider these questions in the context of two predictors—forecast E/P and forecast earnings trend—for two alternative specifications—consensus versus flash data—two investment approaches—portfolio screening and return modeling—and two investment universes—one of 30 and the other of 3000 stocks.

Alternative Specifications of E/P and Earnings Trend for Screening

Table 6-1 presents the 30 Dow Jones industrial stocks as of December 1996, together with their prices and fiscal year 1 consensus and flash earnings estimates. These data are used to calculate two alternative specifications of forecast E/P for each stock. The table provides the calculated values and each stock's ranking by each specification.

The last four columns of Table 6-1 can be used to compare the consensus forecast E/P (fiscal year 1 consensus earnings mean divided by price) with the flash forecast E/P (fiscal year 1 6-week flash earnings mean divided by price). There is little difference between the two specifications. The two sets of E/P values are highly correlated, with a Pearson correlation of 0.9990 and a Spearman rank correlation of 0.9996.[5]

As Table 6-1 shows, the two E/P specifications result in identical rankings except in the case of two stocks—Philip Morris and Sears Roebuck. Sears is ranked ninth by the consensus fore-

TABLE 6-1

Consensus versus Flash Forecast E/P for 30-Stock Universe

Ticker	Company	Number of FY1 Consensus Estimates	Number of FY1 Flash Estimates	Consensus FY1 Mean, December 1996	Flash FY1 Mean, December 1996	Price, December 1996	Consensus FY1 E/P	Flash FY1 E/P	Rank Consensus FY1 E/P	Rank Flash FY1 E/P
AA	Aluminum Company of America	22	2	3.59	3.80	60.88	0.0590	0.0624	14	14
ALD	Allied Signal	19	3	3.60	3.62	68.25	0.0527	0.0530	18.5	18.5
AXP	American Express	18	4	3.57	3.60	53.63	0.0666	0.0671	11	11
BA	Boeing	25	9	2.96	2.94	101.50	0.0292	0.0290	28	28
BS	Bethlehem Steel	15	4	0.32	0.29	9.00	0.0356	0.0322	27	27
CAT	Caterpillar Tractor	28	4	6.92	6.94	74.25	0.0932	0.0935	3	3
CHV	Chevron	31	15	4.03	4.04	64.13	0.0628	0.0630	13	13
DD	DuPont	23	7	6.61	6.66	93.00	0.0711	0.0716	7	7
DIS	Walt Disney	34	20	2.66	2.65	71.50	0.0372	0.0371	26	26
EK	Eastman Kodak	19	3	4.43	4.41	79.63	0.0556	0.0554	15	15
GE	General Electric	24	1	4.39	4.40	99.25	0.0442	0.0443	23	23
GM	General Motors	25	16	5.75	5.65	54.50	0.1055	0.1037	1	1
GT	Goodyear Tire & Rubber	14	6	4.37	4.35	49.50	0.0883	0.0879	5	5
IBM	IBM	23	6	11.01	11.09	158.63	0.0694	0.0699	8	8
IP	International Paper	23	9	1.53	1.48	39.63	0.0386	0.0373	25	25
JPM	J.P. Morgan	24	3	7.47	7.35	96.88	0.0771	0.0759	6	6
KO	Coca-Cola	26	2	1.40	1.40	48.38	0.0289	0.0289	29	29
MCD	McDonald's	33	9	2.22	2.22	45.50	0.0488	0.0488	20	20
MMM	Minnesota Mining & Manufacturing	19	4	3.61	3.61	81.13	0.0445	0.0445	22	22
MO	Philip Morris	24	3	7.66	7.70	111.63	0.0686	0.0690	10	9

Continued

TABLE 6-1

Concluded

Ticker	Company	Number of FY1 Consensus Estimates	Number of FY1 Flash Estimates	Consensus FY1 Mean, December 1996	Flash FY1 Mean, December 1996	Price, December 1996	Consensus FY1 E/P	Flash FY1 E/P	Rank Consensus FY1 E/P	Rank Flash FY1 E/P
MRK	Merck	37	16	3.17	3.18	76.88	0.0412	0.0414	24	24
PG	Procter & Gamble	24	3	4.81	4.81	104.13	0.0462	0.0462	21	21
S	Sears Roebuck	33	11	3.06	3.06	44.38	0.0689	0.0689	9	10
T	AT&T	34	6	3.48	3.48	38.81	0.0897	0.0897	4	4
TX	Texaco	26	12	6.30	6.33	97.63	0.0645	0.0648	12	12
UK	Union Carbide	16	16	3.86	3.86	39.00	0.0990	0.0990	2	2
UTX	United Technologies	19	3	3.39	3.41	64.38	0.0527	0.0530	18.5	18.5
WX	Westinghouse	11	5	-0.05	-0.08	17.88	-0.0028	-0.0045	30	30
XON	Exxon	35	14	5.35	5.38	97.25	0.0550	0.0553	16	16
Z	Woolworth	9	6	1.17	1.17	22.00	0.0532	0.0532	17	17

cast E/P but tenth by the flash forecast E/P, whereas Philip Morris is ranked tenth by consensus forecast E/P but ninth by flash forecast E/P.

The similarities in rankings by the two E/P specifications lead to similarities in portfolio composition. For the top five, bottom five, top 10, and bottom 10 stock portfolios constructed on the basis of E/P, compositions would be the same whether E/P were specified with consensus earnings data or flash earnings data. These results suggest that the precise specification of E/P may matter little, at least in terms of screening a small universe of stocks for potential portfolio inclusion.

To extend the analysis, we consider the same E/P specifications applied to a larger universe of stocks and over a longer time period. Results for a 3000-stock universe are similar to those for the 30-stock universe.[6] In particular, the consensus and flash forecast E/Ps are highly correlated, with a Pearson correlation of 0.9863 and a Spearman rank correlation of 0.9921.

Furthermore, portfolio compositions across the two specifications, although not identical, as is the case with the 30-stock universe, are quite close. The top 100, 300, and 500 portfolios selected from consensus and flash E/P forecasts have 90, 282, and 479 stocks in common, respectively, while the bottom 100, 300, and 500 portfolios constructed from the alternative specifications have 96, 288, and 478 stocks in common.

The similarities between the alternative specifications of E/P also hold over a longer time frame—from April 1990 through December 1996. Over this period, Pearson correlations between the two specifications range from 0.8500 to 0.9975; Spearman rank correlations are even higher, ranging from 0.9725 to 0.9950. The proportions of stocks common to portfolios selected by the alternative specifications remain similar to those found for the 3000-stock universe in December 1996.[7]

What holds true for E/P, however, may not hold true for other predictors. Table 6-2 shows alternative specifications of earnings trend for fiscal year 1, defined as follows:

$$\text{Consensus trend} = \frac{\substack{\text{currrent consensus mean} \\ -1\,\text{month ago consensus mean}}}{\text{price}} \qquad (6.1)$$

TABLE 6-2

Consensus versus Flash Forecast Trend for 30-Stock Universe*

Ticker	Company	Number of FY1 Consensus Estimates	Number of FY1 Flash Estimates	Consensus FY1 Mean, December 1996	Consensus FY1 Mean, November 1996	Flash FY1 Mean, December 1996	Flash FY1 Mean, November 1996	Price, December 1996	Consensus FY1 Trend	Flash FY1 Trend	Rank Consensus FY1 Trend	Rank Flash FY1 Trend
AA	Aluminum Company of America	22	2	3.59	3.64	3.80	3.46	60.88	-0.000821	0.005585	25	1
ALD	Allied Signal	19	3	3.60	3.60	3.62	3.62	68.25	0.000000	0.000000	18	15
AXP	American Express	18	4	3.57	3.55	3.60	3.60	53.63	0.000373	0.000000	5	15
BA	Boeing	25	9	2.96	2.96	2.94	3.05	101.50	0.000000	-0.001084	18	26
BS	Bethlehem Steel	15	4	0.32	0.36	0.29	0.31	9.00	-0.004444	-0.002222	28	27
CAT	Caterpillar Tractor	28	4	6.92	6.90	6.94	6.92	74.25	0.000269	0.000269	6	6
CHV	Chevron	31	15	4.03	3.96	4.04	4.01	64.13	0.001092	0.000468	2	3
DD	DuPont	23	7	6.61	6.59	6.66	6.65	93.00	0.000215	0.000108	9	11
DIS	Walt Disney	34	20	2.66	2.65	2.65	2.65	71.50	0.000140	-0.000000	11	15
EK	Eastman Kodak	19	3	4.43	4.42	4.41	4.44	79.63	0.000126	-0.000377	13	21
GE	General Electric	24	1	4.39	4.39	4.40	4.41	99.25	0.000000	-0.000101	18	19
GM	General Motors	25	16	5.75	6.08	5.65	6.10	54.50	-0.006055	-0.008257	29	29
GT	Goodyear Tire & Rubber	14	6	4.37	4.38	4.35	4.38	49.50	-0.000202	-0.000606	23	24
IBM	IBM	23	6	11.01	11.02	11.09	10.98	158.63	-0.000063	0.000693	22	2
IP	International Paper	23	9	1.53	1.57	1.48	1.57	39.63	-0.001009	-0.002271	26	28
JPM	J.P. Morgan	24	3	7.47	7.46	7.35	7.42	96.88	0.000103	-0.000723	14	25

Continued

TABLE 6-2

Concluded

Ticker	Company	Number of FY1 Consensus Estimates	Number of FY1 Flash Estimates	Consensus FY1 Mean, December 1996	Consensus FY1 Mean, November 1996	Flash FY1 Mean, December 1996	Flash FY1 Mean, November 1996	Price, December 1996	Consensus FY1 Trend	Flash FY1 Trend	Rank Consensus FY1 Trend	Rank Flash FY1 Trend
KO	Coca-Cola	26	2	1.40	1.39	1.40	1.40	48.38	0.000207	0.000000	10	15
MCD	McDonald's	33	9	2.22	2.23	2.22	2.22	45.50	-0.000220	0.000000	24	15
MMM	Minnesota Mining & Manufacturing	19	4	3.61	3.61	3.61	3.60	81.13	0.000000	0.000123	18	10
MO	Philip Morris	24	3	7.66	7.66	7.70	7.68	111.63	0.000000	0.000179	18	9
MRK	Merck	37	16	3.17	3.16	3.18	3.16	76.88	0.000130	0.000260	12	7
PG	Procter & Gamble	24	3	4.81	4.81	4.81	4.81	104.13	0.000000	0.000000	18	15
S	Sears Roebuck	33	11	3.06	3.05	3.06	3.07	44.38	0.000225	-0.000225	8	20
T	AT&T	34	6	3.48	3.47	3.48	3.48	38.81	0.000258	0.000000	7	15
TX	Texaco	26	12	6.30	6.22	6.33	6.31	97.63	0.000819	0.000205	3	8
UK	Union Carbide	16	16	3.86	4.19	3.86	4.19	39.00	-0.008462	-0.008462	30	30
UTX	United Technologies	19	3	3.39	3.39	3.41	3.39	64.38	0.000000	0.000311	18	4
WX	Westinghouse	11	5	-0.05	-0.02	-0.08	-0.07	17.88	-0.001678	-0.000559	27	23
XON	Exxon	35	14	5.35	5.31	5.38	5.35	97.25	0.000411	0.000308	4	5
Z	Woolworth	9	6	1.17	1.09	1.17	1.18	22.00	0.003636	-0.000455	1	22

*Note: Walt Disney had a fiscal year change; thus, we use FY2 mean data for November 1996 in trend calculations.

$$\text{Flash trend} = \frac{\begin{array}{c}\text{current 6 - week flash mean}\\ -1\,\text{month ago 6 - week flash mean}\end{array}}{\text{price}} \qquad (6.2)$$

Table 6-2 provides the calculation of these predictors and rankings for each stock in the 30-stock universe.

Unlike the forecast E/P specifications, the alternative specifications of earnings trend do not lead to a similarity of results. In fact, for a number of companies, the forecast trends differ not only in magnitude but also in direction. Sears, for example, has an increasing earnings trend based on consensus data, but a decreasing trend based on 6-week flash data. Aluminum Company of America has a decreasing consensus trend but an increasing flash trend.

The differences between the two specifications are reflected in their correlations. The Pearson correlation of 0.7688 and Spearman rank correlation of only 0.4270 are much lower than the correlations between the E/P specifications. The differences are also reflected in the two trend specifications' rankings of the 30 stocks. These have substantial implications for stock selection and portfolio composition.

As Table 6-3 shows, although the bottom five portfolios selected by the two trend specifications hold four stocks in common, the top five portfolios hold only two of the same stocks. Only four stocks are common to both top 10 portfolios, while seven are common to the bottom 10 portfolios. In fact, three stocks in the top five portfolio based on the flash specification, including its top-ranked stock, Aluminum Company of America, are placed in the bottom 10 portfolio ranked by consensus data. Conversely, Woolworth, the top-rated stock on the basis of consensus data, is ranked twenty-second on the basis of flash data. Over time, such dissimilarities between rankings by alternative specifications affect portfolio composition and lead to differences in performance.[8]

Similar results hold when the earnings trend specifications are applied to the larger 3000-stock universe over the longer April 1990 through December 1996 period. The correlations between the 6-week flash trend and the consensus trend are much lower than the correlations observed for the forecast E/P specifications, ranging from 0.450 to 0.750 for the Spearman rank and 0.200 to 0.950 for the Pearson. The proportions of stocks common to various-sized portfolios constructed on the basis of the two trend specifications are also lower, on the order

T A B L E   6–3

Consensus versus Flash Trend Portfolios

Consensus Trend		Flash Trend
	Top Five Stocks	
Z		AA
CHV		IBM
TX		CHV
XON		UTX
AXP		XON
	Bottom Five Stocks	
UK		UK
GM		GM
BS		IP
WX		BS
IP		BA
	Top 10 Stocks	
Z		AA
CHV		IBM
TX		CHV
XON		UTX
AXP		XON
CAT		CAT
T		MRK
S		TX
DD		MO
KO		MMM
	Bottom 10 Stocks	
UK		UK
GM		GM
BS		IP
WX		BS
IP		BA
AA		JPM
MCD		GT
GT		WX
IBM		Z
7 tied for tenth		EK

of 70 percent for the top 100, 300, and 500 stock portfolios and 67 percent for the bottom 100, 300, and 500 stock portfolios.

These findings suggest that, in screening, the precise specification of the E/P predictor (at least as between 6-week flash and consensus data) may not have much effect on portfolio results, especially when the investment universe consists of well-known, widely followed stocks. For forecast earnings trend, however, different specifications of the predictor may lead to very different portfolios and very different investment results.

Alternative Specifications of E/P and Trend for Modeling Returns

Does the relationship between stock returns and their possible predictors depend on the specification of the predictors? To examine this, we fit the model:

$$
\begin{aligned}
\text{Return} = a &+ b \text{ (consensus predictor)} \\
&+ c \text{ (flash – consensus predictor)} \\
&+ d \text{ (controversy)} \\
&+ e \text{ (neglect)}
\end{aligned} \tag{6.3}
$$

Here "return" is the excess return for the subsequent month (relative to the Treasury bill rate). The "consensus" and "flash predictors" used are based on fiscal year 1 earnings estimates. *Controversy* is defined as the standard deviation of fiscal year 1 earnings estimates, where the estimates are based on flash data if available or otherwise on consensus data. *Neglect* is defined as

$$-\log (1 + \text{number of fiscal year 1 analysts})$$

Controversy and neglect are included to control for some important expectational-related return effects.[9]

We estimate two separate models—one for the forecast E/P predictor and the other for the forecast earnings trend predictor—using the 3000-stock universe and monthly data from April 1990 through December 1996.[10] The analysis includes only those stocks for which at least consensus data are available. All explanatory variables are standardized with winsorization set at ± 5 standard deviations from the mean in order to truncate outliers. Methods of estimation include equal-weighted least-squares regression and monotone regression.[11]

If the inclusion of flash data has explanatory power beyond that provided by consensus data, the coefficient c in Eq. (6.3) will be significantly different from zero. This would indicate that the relationship between returns and predictors based upon flash data differs from that between returns and predictors based on consensus data. Furthermore, a positive and significant coefficient would suggest that companies with a positive flash-consensus differential would be expected to have higher excess returns, on average, than companies with a flash mean below the consensus mean.

Such a finding would imply not only that the relationship between returns and predictor is sensitive to specification, but also that the relationship between returns and flash data is stronger than the relationship between returns and consensus data. A priori, one might expect this to be the case, since flash data are more timely, and hence likely have higher information content than consensus data.

Tables 6-4 and 6-5 present the results from the estimated models. The evidence in Table 6-4 pertaining to forecast E/P suggests that the return-predictor relationship is sensitive to specification. With least-squares estimation, the coefficient c for the flash-consensus differential is positive, with a p value of less than 0.0001.[12]

This suggests that the incremental effect of flash data is highly significant, and that one may expect differences between the flash and consensus forecast E/Ps for a given company to lead to differences in return. Other things equal, those companies with flash forecast E/Ps higher than their consensus E/Ps will tend to enjoy higher returns than those companies with flash E/Ps lower than their consensus E/Ps. The regression estimate of 0.2210 for the flash-consensus forecast E/P differential suggests that, with a 1 standard deviation increase in the differential, average excess return can be expected to increase by around 22 basis points, other things being equal.

Our results suggest that the use of consensus E/P can capture the positive relationship between returns and forecast E/P. Other things equal, average excess return increases by around 34 basis points with a 1 standard deviation increase in exposure to forecast E/P. But the use of flash E/P can lead to even higher returns. The other predictors included in the model—controversy and neglect—

T A B L E   6–4

Incremental Effect of the Flash Forecast E/P–Regression Results
for 3000-Stock Universe–April 1990 to December 1996

	Consensus Forecast E/P	Incremental Flash Forecast E/P	Controversy	Neglect
Least-Squares Regression				
Mean	0.3353	0.2210	−0.0448	−0.1540
Standard error mean	0.1009	0.0428	0.0924	0.0962
t-statistic	3.3230	5.1618	−0.4845	−1.6006
p value	0.0014	0.0000	0.6294	0.1134
Monotone Rank Regression				
Mean	0.0412	0.0235	−0.0155	−0.0258
Standard error mean	0.0090	0.0040	0.0068	0.0091
t-statistic	4.5710	5.8112	−2.2622	−2.8224

T A B L E   6–5

Incremental Effect of the Flash Forecast Trend–Regression
Results for 3000-Stock Universe–April 1990 to December 1996

	Consensus Trend	Incremental Flash Trend	Controversy	Neglect
Least-Squares Regression				
Mean	0.3859	0.0134	−0.1289	−0.1704
Standard error mean	0.0606	0.0341	0.0872	0.1001
t-statistic	6.3696	0.3922	−1.4785	−1.7025
p value	0.0000	0.6960	0.1432	0.0925
Monotone Rank Regression				
Mean	0.0456	0.0031	−0.0115	−0.0284
Standard error mean	0.0062	0.0022	0.0065	0.0094
t-statistic	7.4019	1.4320	−1.7692	−3.0297
p value	0.0000	0.1560	0.0807	0.0033

have p values of 0.6294 and 0.1134, respectively, indicating that both predictors are not significantly different from zero, even at the 10 percent level.

The results from the monotone regression in Table 6-4 are somewhat different from those of the least-squares regression, however.[13] All the predictors are significant at the 5 percent level. That is, all predictors are monotonically related to return, with consensus forecast E/P and the incremental flash forecast E/P positively related to returns, and controversy and neglect inversely related.

The average estimates from the monotone regressions may be interpreted as the marginal effect on stock return rank of an increase in the rank of each predictor, other things equal. While least-squares coefficients represent the partial estimated return between standardized predictors and subsequent monthly returns, monotone regression coefficients estimate the relationship in terms of rank. Thus, over the period of study, an increase of 100 in the rank for the consensus E/P predictor is associated with an increase in return rank of 4.12. Similarly, an increase of 100 in the incremental flash forecast E/P rank is associated with an increase of 2.35 in the return rank.

Table 6-5 reports the results from estimating the model using the earnings trend predictor rather than the E/P predictor. Here the evidence for an incremental effect from the use of flash data is much less conclusive. With least-squares regression, the estimated incremental effect is positive, but very small, with an average value of 0.0134; that is, on average, excess return increases by only about 1 basis point with a 1 standard deviation increase in the flash-consensus trend differential. The p value of 0.6960 also indicates that the incremental effect is not significant; one can conclude that the relationship between earnings trend and stock returns, at least over this period, does not differ between a quantitative model using consensus data and one using 6-week flash data.

Clearly, the most significant predictor in the least-squares estimation is the fiscal year 1 consensus earnings trend. This predictor is positive and highly significant, with a p value of less than 0.0001. Other things equal, our results suggest that, for every 1 standard deviation increase in consensus earnings trend, excess return increases by about 39 basis points.

The incremental flash effect is somewhat stronger in the monotone regression model, although still statistically insignificant. The consensus earnings trend predictor remains highly significant. As with the E/P predictor, however, the monotone regression gives stronger support than the least-squares regression for significant relationships between returns and the controversy and neglect predictors. Neglect is significant at the 1 percent level, while controversy is significant at the 10 percent level.

The results from modeling stock returns using E/P and trend predictors provide evidence that the return-predictor relationship can be sensitive to predictor specification. Companies with flash E/Ps higher than their consensus E/Ps experience higher excess returns than companies having flash E/Ps lower than their consensus E/Ps. Specification of the earnings trend predictor, at least when the choice is between the two specifications considered here, does not seem to matter, however.[14]

The results also demonstrate that, while the general conclusions reached about consensus forecast E/P and trend and incremental flash effects are largely the same across different methods of estimation, the significance of controversy and neglect are sensitive to the estimation procedure employed. Unlike the least-squares regressions, the monotone regressions provide support for significant inverse relationships between these predictors and subsequent return. That is, companies whose expected earnings estimates are more dispersed, and those with less analyst coverage, tended in this period to have lower excess returns.[15]

To summarize, specification of earnings predictor variables appears to matter, in the sense that alternative specifications of the same predictor can result in quite different investment decisions. Specification is not of the same importance to all predictors, however, nor to all types of analyses or estimation procedures. In particular, when we use the forecast E/P predictor to screen stocks for portfolio selection, it gives roughly equivalent results whether specified with consensus or flash data. The forecast trend predictor, however, can yield substantially different portfolios when specified with consensus rather than flash data.

In contrast, when we use the forecast E/P predictor to model returns, its relationship to subsequent returns differs markedly, depending on whether the predictor is constructed with consensus or with flash data. This holds true whether the relationship is estimated with least-squares or monotone regression. Specification of the trend predictor is relatively less crucial in modeling returns, especially when limited to the two specifications analyzed here.[16]

PREDICTOR SPECIFICATION WITH MISSING VALUES

Besides having to choose among alternative specifications of a given predictor, one may face the problem of how to deal with missing data values. In the case of a universe of large-capitalization, widely followed stocks, this problem may not arise. For example, both consensus and flash data are available for all 30 of the Dow Jones industrials in Tables 6-1 and 6-2. For a broader universe of stocks and a greater number of predictor specifications, however, all information may not be available for every stock.

Figure 6-1 illustrates that the availability of flash earnings data may be limited, especially in the case of companies covered by only a few analysts. For the great majority of companies covered by nine or more analysts (over 90 percent), both consensus and flash data are available. As the number of analysts covering a stock declines, however, the percentage of companies with both consensus and flash data declines.[17]

What does one do when data are unavailable? One possible solution is to exclude companies with missing observations from the analysis. This could result, however, in a substantially reduced sample of companies for parameter estimation, especially if the model includes several variables with missing observations for different companies. In this situation, it may be worthwhile to consider other options.

One alternative is to impute estimated values to missing observations. One could, for example, assign some average value (for example, the sector or industry average), or use the values from a comparable company or group of companies for which the data are available. In choosing among alternative treatments for missing values, the aim should be to arrive at the best possible estimates. The poorer the estimates, the greater the measurement error and the resulting bias in regression coefficients.

To get some idea of the impact on estimated returns of the treatment of missing observations, we examine the relationship between a 6-week trend predictor and subsequent 1-month returns, using all stocks in the 3000-stock universe for which consensus data are avail-

F I G U R E 6–1

Analyst Coverage and Flash Data Availability—3000-Stock
Universe—April 1990 to December 1996

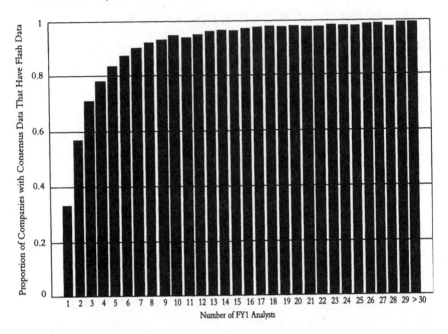

able over the April 1990 through December 1996 period. We calculate
flash predictors, using two methods of substituting for flash data
when the data are unavailable or of questionable integrity.[18]

The first method uses the company's consensus data as a proxy
for flash data. The second method uses the universe average flash
data. (The data are standardized, as before, with winsorization set
at ± 5 standard deviations from the mean.)

Use of consensus data when flash data are not available may
result in less measurement error than use of the universe flash
mean. One might expect to find a stronger relationship between returns and the first method of specification than between returns and
the second method. Figure 6-2 illustrates the differences between
the two methods, according to equal-weighted least-squares regressions run over the period from April 1990 through December 1996.

Treatment of Missing Flash Trend Observations Affects Return*

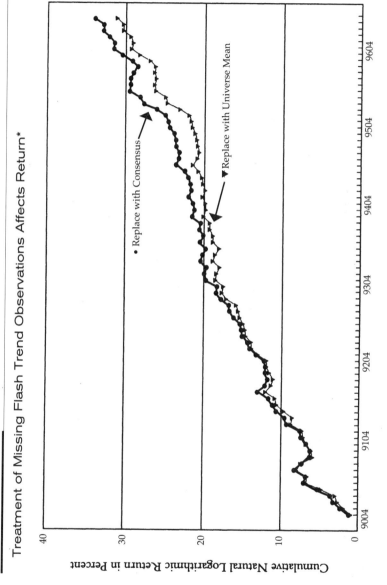

Cumulative Natural Logarithmic Return in Percent

•Simple least squares regression of one-month returns on fiscal year 1 forecast trend.

*Simple least-squares regression of 1-month returns on fiscal year 1 forecast trend.

Cumulative return under method 1 (flash/consensus data) is greater than cumulative return under method 2 (flash/universe average data), and the differential in favor of method 1 tends to grow over time. Under method 1, cumulative return grows to nearly 34 percent over the period, compared with 30.5 percent under method 2.[19] This finding is consistent with the notion that treatment of missing values via method 2 entails more measurement error than treatment via method 1. Method 2, in other words, ignores useful data that method 1 incorporates. As a result, the return-trend relationship is biased downward when trend is specified according to method 2.

To help ensure inclusion of the best estimates in computing predictors, one can employ a stepwise process that relies on the best data available for a given company at a given time. On the basis of theory, empirical evidence, experience with data, intuition, or other relevant considerations, one first determines the preferred ranking of all available data items. Specification of predictors then relies on this sequence.

For example, if the most recent estimate is believed to be the most accurate, followed by the 6-week flash mean, the consensus mean, the industry mean, and the universe mean, the value for a given predictor for each company would be calculated on the basis of this sequence, according to data availability. As data availability will vary across different companies, computed predictor values will be based upon different data items. But they will constitute the most accurate specifications available for each company at a given time.

PREDICTOR SPECIFICATION AND ANALYST COVERAGE

The issues that arise in earnings predictor specification become more complex as the number of analysts covering a stock increases. Consider a company followed by only one analyst: The consensus mean, the flash mean, and the most recent estimate collapse to the same value, and choice of predictor specification becomes a trivial issue. For companies with more than one analyst, however, the consensus mean will likely differ from the flash mean and the most recent estimate. As a result, different specifications will result in different predictor values. One is then faced with the problem of choosing among different specifications, or calculating the grand mean and dispersion across a number of specifications (and even here, one would need to determine whether all possible specifications are included).

Analyst coverage may also affect specification choice because it affects data availability. Figure 6-1, for example, shows that the availability of 6-week flash data declines noticeably as the number of analysts falls below nine. The greater availability of data items for more widely followed companies opens the door to greater choice in predictor specification. There is some evidence to suggest, however, that predictor specification may be relatively less critical for widely followed companies. Figures 6-3 and 6-4 illustrate why this may be the case.

Figure 6-3 shows the standard deviations of the differences between fiscal year 1 flash E/P and consensus E/P predictor values for the 3000-stock universe over the April 1990 to December 1996 period, stratified by the number of analysts following each stock. Figure 6-4 provides the standard deviations for the differences between fiscal year 1 flash and consensus trend predictor values, stratified by number of analysts. For both E/P and trend predictors, the difference between flash and consensus specifications declines noticeably as the number of analysts increases.

The decreased difference between the alternative specifications as analyst following increases reflects two factors. First, the number of analysts following a company tends to increase as the company's stock price increases; relatively higher prices in the denominators of the predictors for widely followed stocks tend to dilute the difference across earnings estimators in the numerators. Second, the range in the differences between 6-week flash means and consensus means narrows as analyst coverage increases.[20]

The implication is that the valuation of stocks with less analyst coverage may be more sensitive to predictor specification than the valuation of widely followed stocks. This is confirmed by an examination of differences in the rank orderings of the stocks, stratified by the number of analysts, between the two alternative E/P specifications.

For stocks followed by two to four analysts, rank order may change by as much as ±1000, depending upon predictor specification. For stocks followed by 20 or more analysts, rank order changes tend to be much smaller, on the order of ±100.

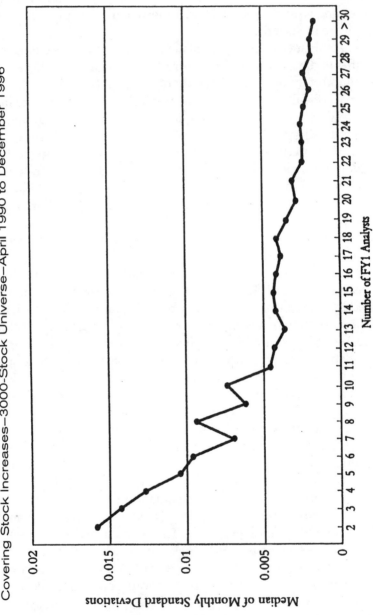

FIGURE 6-3

Difference Between Flash and Consensus Forecast E/P Declines as Number of Analysts Covering Stock Increases–3000-Stock Universe–April 1990 to December 1996

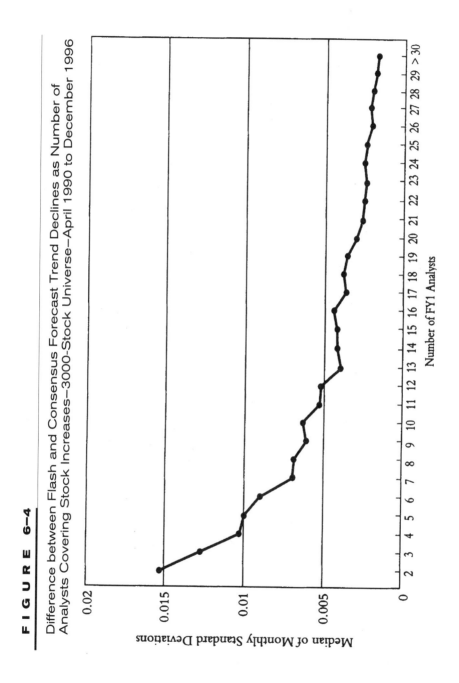

F I G U R E 6–4

Difference between Flash and Consensus Forecast Trend Declines as Number of Analysts Covering Stock Increases–3000-Stock Universe–April 1990 to December 1996

The Return-Predictor Relationship and Analyst Coverage

There are several reasons to believe that the relationship between an expectational predictor and returns is distributed differentially across a universe of stocks by the degree of analyst coverage. For one, investors may differentiate between widely followed and less widely followed companies when considering expectational earnings data. The more analysts covering a given stock, the greater may be their tendency to "herd," that is, to tailor their earnings estimates so that they are in line with those of other analysts.

If such herding tendencies exist, then differences in estimates may tend to be small, and changes in earnings forecasts, rather than signaling an informative change in expected earnings distributions, may be more a reflection of analyst repositionings within the distribution of earnings estimates. In this case, investors may perceive earnings forecasts for widely followed companies as less meaningful than earnings forecasts for companies with a smaller analyst following, and the return-predictor relationship may be stronger for the latter group than for the former.

There may, of course, be other reasons why the predictor-return relationship differs across companies with varying levels of analyst coverage. More widely followed companies, for example, may be priced more efficiently to begin with, or they may be less risky. Alternatively, the finding of such differences could reflect model or predictor misspecification.

To examine whether such distributed effects are present in our 3000-stock universe, we fit a model over the period from April 1990 through December 1996:[21]

$$
\begin{aligned}
\text{Return} = a &+ b \, (\text{predictor}) \\
&+ c \, (\text{distributed predictor for large coverage stocks}) \\
&+ d \, (\text{distributed predictor for small coverage stocks}) \\
&+ e \, (\text{controversy}) \\
&+ f \, (\text{neglect})
\end{aligned} \tag{6.4}
$$

Here "return" is excess return in the subsequent month. Predictors are calculated using consensus data for fiscal year 1. "Controversy" and "neglect" are as defined previously.

The "distributed predictor for large coverage stocks" is the marginal E/P or trend effect for companies having more than 10 fiscal year 1 analysts. The "distributed predictor for small coverage stocks" is the marginal E/P or trend for companies having from one to four fiscal year 1 analysts.

The coefficient b represents the estimated predictor effect for companies covered by 5 to 10 analysts. The estimated predictor effect for companies with more than 10 analysts is computed by adding the coefficient c (the distributed effect for large coverage companies) to coefficient b. The predictor effect for companies with one to four analysts is computed by adding b and d (the distributed effect for small coverage companies). Thus, c and d represent marginal effects relative to the base case group of companies followed by 5 to 10 analysts. In addition, the t values for c and d indicate whether the marginal effects are significantly different from the base case.

The breakpoints for analyst coverage are chosen because they split the universe of stocks approximately into thirds. They also consistently partition the universe into thirds over the entire period of study, so modification of breakpoints over time was not necessary. Other models were examined, including one based on an interaction effect between the number of analysts and earnings trend. The results are consistent with those reported for the model based upon partition into thirds.

If the distribution of the forecast predictors differs across the three stock groups, we would expect to see c and d coefficients significantly different from zero. In particular, if investors tend to view expectational data for widely followed stocks as less meaningful than the data for less widely followed stocks, we would expect the coefficient c to be negative and significant.

Table 6-6 reports the least-squares and monotone rank regression results for the fiscal year 1 consensus trend predictor. The evidence here, with either estimation procedure, suggests that the relationship between trend and subsequent monthly returns is distributed differentially, depending on the level of analyst coverage. Specifically, the relationship is weaker (that is, less positive) for stocks with more than 10 analysts than it is for stocks with 5 to 10 analysts.

The least-squares regression shows that, for those companies followed by 5 to 10 analysts, a 1 standard deviation increase in the trend predictor is associated with an increase in return of about 44 basis points. This value is highly significant, with a p value of zero.[22]

TABLE 6-6

Effects of Forecast Trend by Number of Analysts—Regression Results Using Consensus Data for 3000-Stock Universe—April 1990 to December 1996

	Overall Trend	Distributed Trend Effect (>10 Analysts)	Distributed Trend Effect (One to Four Analysts)	Controversy	Neglect
		Distributed Least-Squares Regression			
Mean	0.4438	-0.2423	-0.0340	-0.1396	-0.1741
Standard error mean	0.0990	0.1086	0.0863	0.0847	0.0997
t-statistic	4.4821	-2.2316	-0.3939	-1.6480	-1.7459
p value	0.0000	0.0284	0.6947	0.1033	0.0847
		Distributed Monotone Regression			
Mean	0.0513	-0.0203	-0.0011	-0.0144	-0.0359
Standard error mean	0.0070	0.0068	0.0042	0.0062	0.0093
t-statistic	7.2833	-2.9687	-0.2710	-2.3217	-3.8634
p value	0.0000	0.0039	0.7871	0.0228	0.0002

For companies followed by one to four analysts, a 1 standard deviation increase in the trend predictor is associated with a slightly smaller increase in return—around 41 basis points (0.4438–0.0340)—but the level of significance is such that we may conclude that the trend-return relationship does not differ between stocks followed by one to four analysts and those followed by 5 to 10 analysts. For companies followed by more than 10 analysts, however, a 1 standard deviation increase in the trend predictor results in a return increase of about 20 basis points (0.4438–0.2423)—significantly less than the increase observed for the other groups.

As in the previous least-squares regression, we find that the controversy and neglect predictors are inversely related to subsequent returns, but only marginally (with p values near or slightly below 0.10).

The monotone regression results in Table 6-6 also indicate a significantly different and less positive trend-return relationship for widely followed stocks. The estimated effect for these companies is significantly smaller than the effects for the small-coverage and medium-coverage groups; furthermore, the monotone regression assigns even higher significance to the difference than the least-squares regression does, with a p value of 0.0039. Again, the trend effect does not appear to differ significantly between stocks with 5 to 10 analysts covering them and stocks with 1 to 4 analysts.

Once again, the monotone regression gives stronger support than the least-squares regression for the controversy and neglect predictors. Both have p values well below 0.05, suggesting a significant inverse monotonic relationship between these predictors and subsequent returns.[23]

Table 6-7 reports the least-squares and monotone regression results for forecast E/P. The evidence here is somewhat mixed.

The least-squares estimation yields no strong evidence of a significant distributed effect. The monotone regression, however, indicates a significant (p value of 0.0241) distributed effect of –0.0106 for widely followed stocks. The E/P-return relationship for this group is significantly less positive than the E/P-return relationship for the medium-coverage group. The distributed effect for the small-coverage group remains insignificant. And, once again, the mono-

T A B L E 6-7

Effects of Forecast E/P by Number of Analysts–Regression Results Using Consensus Data for 3000-Stock Universe–April 1990 to December 1996

	Overall Trend	Distributed E/P Effect (>10 Analysts)	Distributed E/P Effect (One to Four Analysts)	Controversy	Neglect
Distributed Least-Squares Regression					
Mean	0.3720	-0.1191	-0.0157	-0.1231	-0.1573
Standard error mean	0.1457	0.1091	0.1024	0.0947	0.0961
t-statistic	2.5540	-1.0917	-0.1535	-1.2995	-1.6365
p value	0.0126	0.2782	0.8784	0.1975	0.1057
Distributed Monotone Regression					
Mean	0.0446	-0.0106	-0.0001	-0.0209	-0.0285
Standard error mean	0.0098	0.0046	0.0051	0.0071	0.0090
t-statistic	4.5619	-2.2996	-0.0254	-2.9603	-3.1791
p value	0.0000	0.0241	0.9798	0.0040	0.0021

tone regression results in a finding of significance for the controversy and neglect predictors, with increases in either associated with decreases in subsequent return.

The overall results are thus unclear. Distributed effects appear to exist for the trend predictor specified with consensus data, regardless of the estimation procedure. For the E/P predictor, however, distributed effects show up only in monotone estimation. Given that the least-squares estimators may be more sensitive to leverage points and outliers, one may want to place more reliance on the monotone results.[24]

Might one find distributed effects across other possible E/P and trend specifications? Across other expectational earnings predictors—say, forecast growth rates or earnings surprise? Might inclusion in the return model of different explanatory variables affect the results? Are distributed effects robust across other statistical paradigms? Do they appear in other investment strategies with different investment horizons? These are all important questions in the search for return opportunities.

SUMMARY

Our examination of predictor specification indicates that specification can play an important role in model building. When a number of alternative specifications are possible, different specifications of the same predictor may not result in the same portfolio compositions or be related to stock returns in the same way. The choice of expectational data with which to specify a given predictor (including the selection of data to fill in gaps in data availability) thus has the potential to introduce noise and measurement error into investment decision making.

The importance of specification choice may vary depending upon the predictor, the investment strategy, the estimation procedure used, and the number of analysts following a stock. In general, however, decisions regarding predictor specification have the potential to influence the results of empirical analyses. This is true not only for research based upon traditional methods of statistical analysis, but also for new-wave techniques such as genetic algorithms and neural nets, which also require the specification of predictors or inputs. Finally, although we have focused on expectational earnings data for individual firms, our findings also have relevance for predictors based upon fundamental and technical data, as well as aggregate data for industries, sectors, and the overall market.

APPENDIX

The Effect of Measurement Error on Regression Coefficients

Theoretically, the effect of measurement error on the estimated coefficient in the simple linear regression model may be seen as follows. Suppose the appropriate model is

$$\text{Return} = a + b \text{ (flash predictor)} + e.$$

Instead, however, we use the following model:

$$\text{Return} = a + b \text{ (consensus predictor)} + e$$

with consensus predictor = flash predictor + u. That is, the consensus predictor is an imperfect proxy for the appropriate flash predictor.

Linear regression calculates the coefficient as

$$\hat{b} = \frac{\text{covariance (return, consensus predictor)}}{\text{variance(consensus predictor)}}$$

or

$$\hat{b} = \frac{\text{covariance (return, flash predictor} + u}{\text{variance(flash predictor} + u)}$$

or

$$\hat{b} = \frac{\text{covariance } [a + b(\text{flash predictor}) + e, \text{flash predictor} + u}{\text{variance(flash predictor} + u)}$$

or

$$\hat{b} = \frac{b \times \text{variance(flash predictor)}}{\text{variance(flash predictor)} + \text{variance } (u)}$$

assuming that the measurement error, u, and residual model error, e, are independent and that measurement error is not a function of the flash predictor.

Alternatively, one can write the preceding equation as:

$$\hat{b} = \frac{b}{1 + [\text{variance}(u)/\text{variance (flash predictor)}]}.$$

This suggests that the estimated coefficient, $\hat{b}$, has a bias toward zero that depends upon the variance in the measurement error relative to the variance in the flash predictor. Other things equal, the greater the variance in the measurement error, the more biased the estimate of $\hat{b}$. Why? Because the consensus provides a more noisy estimate of flash earnings as measurement error increases.

For models with more than one explanatory variable, the effect of measurement error becomes a bit more complex. It will depend on, among other things, the number of predictors with measurement error, the correlations between predictors, the correlations between measurement errors, and the signs of the regression coefficients. For the special case where predictors are not correlated and not related to measurement errors, and measurement errors across predictors are independent, the regression coefficients will be biased toward zero. As predictors become more highly correlated, however, any bias will depend on the signs of the regression coefficients and the variance of the measurement errors relative to the variance of the predictors, other things equal.[25]

ENDNOTES

The authors thank Judith Kimball for her editorial assistance.

1. One can choose from a variety of data vendors as well. For this study we use Institutional Brokers Estimates System (IBES) data.

2. There are a variety of options regarding the estimates to include as well as their weights. A dynamic weighting strategy, for example, would weight more recent estimates more heavily than older estimates.

3. Trimmed means remove a proportion of the most extreme observations from a data set and compute the mean of the remaining observations. This procedure reduces the influence of outliers.

4. The different possible estimates represent proxies for a company's earnings. For any given company, one would like to use the proxies providing the best estimate of current and future earnings. Changes in technology and in the way analysts update estimates may also influence the estimates selected.

5. The Pearson correlation estimates the linear association between the actual values of the predictors. The Spearman rank correlation measures the association between the ranks, not the actual values. Because variables may be monotonically related, but in a highly nonlinear way, the Spearman rank can capture information the Pearson cannot.

6. The 3000-stock universe consists of the approximately 3000 most liquid U.S. stocks having IBES coverage.

7. We find larger differences in the tails of the rankings, especially for the most highly ranked companies. The companies with the greatest differences tended to have limited analyst following.

8. The effects of these differences may also depend on investment strategy. For example, a long-only manager using flash data would hold Aluminum Company of America and not Woolworth, while a long-only manager using consensus data would hold Woolworth and not Aluminum. If the two were long-short managers, however, one would hold Aluminum long and Woolworth short, while the other held Woolworth long and Aluminum short.

9. See Jacobs and Levy (1988) for a discussion of the benefits of disentangling related effects.

10. The universe is updated regularly in order to reflect changes over the period of study. Eighty-one monthly cross-sectional regressions are run for each model. Parameter estimates for each month are unrestricted and allowed to vary from month to month.

11. Monotone regression is based upon ranks. See Conover (1980) and Iman and Conover (1979). We also ran robust regressions based on an iterative weighting procedure. Both Huber (1964 and 1981) and Beaton-Tukey (1974) bi-weights are used. In general, these procedures reduce the influence of outliers on regression estimates. The results from these procedures are not presented here because they did not affect the conclusions of our analysis. For a more general discussion of alternative robust regression methods, see Rousseeuw and Leroy (1987).

12. The p value is the smallest level of significance for which the null hypothesis can be rejected. Reporting the p value gives others the opportunity to determine how sensitive a hypothesis test is to

changes in the significance level. For example, two test statistics, one with a p value of 0.045 and another with a p value of 0.0001, are both significant at the 5 percent level, but the conclusions based upon the former would be much more sensitive to changes in the level of significance.

13. Monotone regression uses the ranks of both the dependent and explanatory variables. The inverse rank transform may be used to determine actual values for predictors stated in terms of ranks. In essence, monotone rank regression is to linear regression as Spearman rank correlation is to Pearson correlation.

14. We also undertook tests with specifications using shorter than 6-week flash horizons, which show significant incremental effects (and differences in portfolio composition) between flash and consensus specifications.

15. One might expect firms about which there is more controversy to have lower returns, in the absence of short-selling, because the wider range of earnings forecasts tends to lead to higher prices and lower subsequent returns. With regard to neglect, however, one might expect to find, a priori, a positive rather than a negative relationship (that is, a small-firm effect). Over the period of study, however, large-cap stocks tended to outperform small-cap stocks. As analyst coverage is positively correlated with market capitalization, it is likely that our neglect predictor is capturing this return differential between large- and small-cap stocks.

16. The finding of a significant incremental flash effect for E/P may seem surprising, given the high correlation between the two specifications. Results from a semiparametric model (relaxing the linearity assumption for the consensus and incremental flash effects) suggest that the return to the flash predictor is significantly higher in the positive tail, other things equal.

17. The proportion of individual analysts revising forecasts appears to be independent of the level of coverage. This is true for stocks covered by one or numerous analysts. On average, each analyst tends to revise his or her estimates about one-third of the time.

18. Data were run through a set of integrity checks. If data looked questionable, for whatever reason, they were not used.

19. Both trend predictors are positive and significant. We tested for an incremental effect of the difference between consensus and flash universe average controlling for the availability of flash data, and found statistical significance at the 1 percent level in both least-squares and monotone regressions.

20. Note that this phenomenon is not due to analysts making more frequent revisions for well-followed stocks.

21. One might be concerned about possible collinearity and its impact on estimator precision for the neglect (analyst coverage) and the distributed effects predictors. We examined the degree of collinearity present in our models using the singular value decomposition and condition indexes proposed by Belsley, Kuh, and Welsch (1980). In general, we find no evidence to suggest that collinearity is seriously degrading our estimates. Nor do we find that collinearity is changing (increasing) over time.

22. A significance level of less than 0.05 percent would be needed not to reject the null hypothesis that the trend predictor, on average, is not significantly different from zero. This is one-twentieth the level set for conservative tests (where the significance level is set at 1 percent). Thus, there is strong evidence suggesting that trend and returns are directly related.

23. As earlier regression results show, these predictors tend to be negative but highly insignificant in the least-squares estimation. They appear to be monotonically related to returns but not linearly related on the basis of the raw data. A primary reason for this finding is the existence of influential leverage points for these two predictors in the least-squares model. Leverage points exert undue influence on unbounded influence estimators, such as least squares, and hence have a significant effect on regression coefficients. Use of robust regression procedures, such as least median squares or robust regression with Beaton-Tukey bi-weights, reduces the influence of such observations on regression coefficients. Application of these procedures to our data results in findings similar to those for the monotone regression.

24. Use of other robust methods also results in contradictory findings regarding the significance of distributed effects in the E/P model, however. The iterative Beaton-Tukey procedure, for example, finds no distributed effects, while L1 (least absolute value) regression finds a significant negative distributed effect for large-coverage stocks. Interestingly, the distributed-effects E/P model is the only one where alternative estimation procedures give conflicting results; in all other cases, the results from the alternative robust estimation procedures are consistent with those from monotone rank regressions.

25. See Maddala (1977), Levi (1973), and Theil (1961, 1971).

REFERENCES

Beaton, A. W. and J. W. Tukey. 1974. "The fitting of power series, meaning polynomials, illustrated on band-spectroscopic data." *Technometrics* (May).

Belsley, D. A., E. Kuh, and R. E. Welsch. 1980. *Regression Diagnostics: Identifying Influential Data and Sources of Collinearity.* New York: John Wiley.

Conover, W. J. 1980. *Practical Nonparametric Statistics.* New York: John Wiley.

Huber, P. J. 1964. "Robust estimation of a location parameter." *Annals of Mathematical Statistics* (March).

————. 1981. *Robust Statistics.* New York: John Wiley.

Iman, R. L. and W. J. Conover. 1979. "The use of the rank transform in regression." *Technometrics* (November).

Jacobs, B. I. and K. N. Levy. 1988. "Disentangling equity return regularities: New insights and investment opportunities." *Financial Analysts Journal* 44 (3): 18–44.

Levi, M. D. 1973. "Errors in the variables bias in the presence of correctly measured variables." *Econometrics* 41 (5): 985–986.

Maddala, G. S. 1977. *Econometrics.* New York: McGraw-Hill.

Rousseeuw, P. J. and A. M. Leroy. 1987. *Robust Regression and Outlier Detection.* New York: John Wiley.

Theil, H. 1961. *Economic Forecasts and Policy.* 2d ed. Amsterdam: North-Holland.

————. 1971. *Principles of Econometrics.* New York: John Wiley.

Managing Portfolios

The chapters in Part 1 focused on disentangling the complex inter-relationships between stock prices and the forces that affect them. The chapters in Part 2 look at how the insights gained from this process of disentangling can be translated into investment performance.

As noted, our philosophy at Jacobs Levy Equity Management is that stock returns are driven by a combination of factors, ranging from stock-specific fundamentals, such as earnings announcements and return on equity, to behavioral elements, such as investor over-reaction and herding, to economic conditions, such as interest rates and inflation. Our security selection process considers a wide range of variables designed to capture economic and psychological effects, as well as company-specific information and events.

The sheer breadth of variables considered, as well as the depth of variable definition, help to capture the complexity of market pricing. But we also note that the effects of these variables can differ across different types of stock. It is thus important that the stock selection process include breadth in terms of the coverage of stocks, as well as the variables, considered. For this reason, our approach to stock selection is in some ways 180 degrees removed from the approach taken by traditional active equity managers.

Traditional active managers have tended to mine distinct subsets of the overall equity market. Value managers, for example, have concentrated on finding stocks selling at prices perceived to be low relative to the company's assets or earnings. Growth managers have sought stocks with above-average earnings growth not fully reflected in price. Small-capitalization managers have looked for opportunity in stocks that have been overlooked by most investors. The establishment of benchmark indexes based on growth, value, and small-cap segments of the market has encouraged this type of claims-staking.

While such style preferences and other forces act to segment the equity market, however, other forces act to integrate it. After all, some managers select their portfolios from the broad universe of stocks, and others may focus on a particular type of stock given current economic conditions, but are poised to change their focus should underlying conditions change. The capital of these investors flows across style segments, integrating the overall market.

Most importantly, all stocks can be defined by the same fundamental parameters—by market capitalization, price/earnings ratio, dividend discount model ranking, and so on. All stocks can be found at some level on the continuum of values for each parameter. Furthermore, their positions are not static; an out-of-favor growth stock may slip into value territory or a small-cap company may grow into the large-cap range. Arbitrage works toward market integration. If too many investors want low P/E, for example, low-P/E stocks will be bid up to higher P/E levels. Some investors will sell them and buy other stocks deserving of higher P/Es.

The tenuous balance between integration and segmentation is one aspect of the market's complexity. We find that this dimension of complexity is best captured by viewing the broadest possible range of stocks through a wide-angle analytical lens. This does not mean that we ignore the very real differences in price behavior that distinguish particular market subsets, or that we cannot choose to focus on a particular subset. It simply means that the model used for analyzing individual stocks incorporates all the information available from a broad universe of stocks.

This approach offers a coherent framework for analysis that may be lacking in more segment-oriented approaches. Consider, for example, a firm that runs one model on its total universe of, say, 3000 stocks and then runs a different, segment-specific model on a 500-stock subset of large-cap value stocks. What if the total-universe model predicts GM will outperform Ford, while the value model shows the opposite? Should the investor start the day with multiple estimates of a single stock's alpha? A broad, unified approach avoids this investment conundrum.

It is also poised to take advantage of more information than a narrower view of the market might provide. The effects of inflation on value stocks, for example, may have repercussions for growth stocks; after all, the two segments represent opposite ends of the same P/E continuum. But the interrelationships between individual stocks and between stock subsets become clear only when viewed from the perspective of the whole.

A wide-angle approach that considers all the stocks in the universe—value and growth stocks, large- and small-cap stocks—benefits from all the information to be gleaned from a wide and diverse range of stock price behavior. It is not only poised to take advantage of more profit opportunities than a more narrowly focused approach affords, but its results, based as they are on a more heterogeneous set of variables, are likely to be more robust.

A broad, unified approach, combined with the power of a security selection system based on an appropriate multivariate analysis of a large number of variables, allows for numerous insights into profit opportunities and improves the goodness of those insights. More insights, and better insights, translate into superior performance. The translation process, from insights into performance, involves portfolio construction. As we noted in the Introduction to Part 1, combining securities in portfolios that preserve excess returns without adding undue risk constitutes the second basic task of investment management.

With respect to portfolio construction, quantitative management has a major advantage over traditional qualitative investment processes: The numerical estimates for expected returns and risks that emerge from a quantitative stock selection system are eminently suitable for portfolio construction via portfolio optimization. Optimization employs quantitative methods to combine securities into portfolios that offer the maximum expected returns for given levels of risk, while eliminating unintended risk exposures.

Most often in quantitative management, portfolio construction is designed to deliver performance relative to a chosen benchmark, although, as we will see later, this goal may be relaxed for certain portfolios. The benchmark may be a broad market index such as the Wilshire 5000, a large-capitalization index such as the S&P 500, a small-capitalization index such as the Russell 2000, or a growth or value style index. Whatever the specific benchmark chosen, optimization aims to provide a portfolio that has a level of systematic risk similar to the benchmark's risk and to ensure that the portfolio incurs no more incremental, or residual, risk than is warranted by the portfolio's expected excess return.

We find that this task is enhanced by the use of an optimizer that is customized to include exactly the same dimensions found relevant by the stock selection model. A commercially available optimizer applied in a one-size-fits-all manner is likely to result in mismatches between model insights and portfolio exposures, hence may detract from portfolio return and/or add to portfolio risk. Risk reduction using a commercial optimizer, for example, will reduce the portfolio's exposures only along the dimensions the optimizer recognizes, which are unlikely to be fully congruent with dimensions of the selection model. As a result, the portfolio is likely to wind up less exposed to those variables common to both the model and the optimizer and more exposed to those variables recognized by the model, but not the optimizer.

Imagine a manager who seeks low-P/E stocks that analysts are recommending for purchase, but who uses a commercial optimizer that incorporates a P/E factor but not analyst recommendations. The resulting portfolio will likely have a lower exposure to low P/E than the model would deem optimal and a higher exposure to analyst buy recommendations. Optimization using all relevant variables ensures a portfolio whose risk and return opportunities are balanced in accordance with the selection model's insights. Furthermore, the use of more numerous variables allows portfolio risk to be more finely tuned.

Portfolio implementation involves trading. As we noted in Part 1, estimates of the expected returns to insights from the stock selection model must be combined with estimates of trading costs in order to arrive at realistic returns net of trading costs. The use of electronic trading venues can help to reduce trading costs and thereby enhance portfolio returns.

Electronic trading generally involves lower commissions and less market impact. And, of course, an automated trading system can take account of more factors, including market conditions and the urgency of a particular trade, than any trader can be expected to bear in mind. Trading costs may be further reduced because of the real-time monitoring available with electronic venues. Real-time monitoring of each stock's opportunity costs, for example, can highlight when a trader should turn to traditional trading channels in order to obtain immediacy of execution.

Because the quantitative investment process, both stock selection and portfolio construction, is computer-based, it is quite adaptable to electronic trading. Hands-on oversight of the trading process is nevertheless vital. Ongoing analysis of corporate news, for example, can ensure that trades are not blindsided by breaking news not yet reflected in the selection model.

Another ongoing task for the manager is performance attribution. This involves monitoring each portfolio to determine how its actual performance is, or is not, meeting expectations—basically, what's working, and what isn't. As with portfolio optimization, it is important that performance attribution consider all the sources of return identified by the selection model, and incorporated in the portfolio construction process. If we have designed a portfolio with exposure to low P/E and positive analyst recommendations, for example, we want to know how each of these factors has paid off; we will be less interested in the returns that a commercial system might ascribe to variables that weren't a part of the selection process.

A performance evaluation process based on the selection model serves as a check on model reliability. Has actual performance validated the model insights incorporated in the portfolio? Have some insights become less profitable over time? A feedback loop between the evaluation and the research/modeling processes can help ensure that the model retains robustness over time.

The chapters in this section focus primarily on the portfolio construction aspect of the investment process. "Engineering Portfolios: A Unified Approach," the lead article in a Special Technology Issue of the *Journal of Investing* (Winter 1995), outlines the benefits of a unified stock selection model that affords breadth of inquiry as well as depth of analysis. One benefit of such a model is the flexibility it allows the manager to engineer portfolios for a variety of client needs.

"The Law of One Alpha," from the Summer 1995 issue of the *Journal of Portfolio Management*, investigates one of the conundrums of investment management that arises when stock selection and portfolio construction take a fragmented rather than a holistic approach to the equity market.

The lead article in the Spring 1996 issue of the *Journal of Portfolio Management*, "Residual Risk: How Much Is Too Much?" considers the impacts of investor risk tolerance and manager skill on portfolio selection. It demonstrates that portfolios that artificially constrain risk can end up sacrificing return needlessly.

"High-Definition Style Rotation" (*Journal of Investing*, Fall 1996) examines a portfolio construction approach that is not tied to an underlying market benchmark, but is designed rather to exploit model insights into how payoffs to variables change over different market and economic environments. This chapter looks back to Part 1, in emphasizing the return-enhancement potential of disentangling equity returns, and anticipates Part 3, in providing an example of a portfolio that is engineered along other than strict benchmark lines.

Engineering Portfolios

A Unified Approach[*]

A "holistic" approach permits both breadth and depth.

Common stock managers, whether by design or default, have tended to work particular market niches. Value managers, using disciplines such as P/E screening, concentrate on detecting earnings that can be bought cheaply. Growth managers seek companies with above-average growth prospects that are not fully reflected in current prices. Small-cap managers search out stocks that are off the beaten path and may offer opportunities for both value and growth investing.

Investment consultants have reinforced these tendencies. Faced with clients' desires to evaluate prospective managers, consultants found the ready-made style subsets a useful typology by which to group and compare managers. This has encouraged the development of "style" indexes to benchmark manager performance.

Investment clients can now pick and choose from a menu that serves up the equity universe in a number of ways. Some would argue that this places the ultimate responsibility for decision making exactly where it belongs—with clients. If clients believe growth, or small-cap, or value stocks will outperform the overall market, they can choose to overweight that subset. Alternatively, risk-averse clients can diversify across different styles to reduce the volatility of overall equity returns.

---

[*] Originally published in the *Journal of Investing* 4 (4): 8–14.

There is, nevertheless, an equally strong argument for an approach to equity investing that is 180 degrees removed from this kind of specialization. It begins with the largest feasible equity universe and the largest number of factors that may impact equity price. It searches for inefficiencies that can provide profit opportunities, regardless of industry, sector, or style. At the same time, it recognizes and takes advantage of systematic differences in stock price behavior across different types of stock and over time.

The goal is a unified model of a complex market, one that offers a detailed map of the investment terrain [see, for example, Jacobs and Levy (1989b)]. By enhancing the strength of investment insights as well as increasing the number of investment opportunities, such an approach provides a solid base from which to engineer any number of specific strategies.

IS THE MARKET SEGMENTED OR UNIFIED?

We live in an age of specialization; everyone from research scientists to assembly line workers seems to specialize to one degree or another. In many cases, specialization may optimize application of talent, maximizing the potential for reward. As Henry Ford discerned, it can also save time and money by streamlining the work effort.

Investment analysts have long recognized that stocks that share certain characteristics (industry affiliation, say, or market capitalization) tend to have similar price responses to given economic factors [see, for example, Farrell (1975)]. Does it make sense for analysts—quantitative analysts in particular—to specialize their research efforts along the lines of these stock groupings?

The advantages of this type of specialization are perhaps most obvious in the case of fundamental investors who undertake very detailed company analyses. Fundamental research may become positively ungainly in the absence of some kind of focusing lens.

Quantitative analysts, too, often feel most comfortable in traditional market niches, finding or adapting valuation models for the very same stock groupings followed by fundamental analysts. And research has shown that different quantitative models may be more or less successful when applied to specific types of stock [see, for example, Jones (1990)]. Thus, dividend discount model measures have performed better for utilities than for transportation, finance, and health sectors, whereas momentum measures such as earnings estimate revisions have done best in identifying attractive growth companies.

This type of specialization can present some theoretical and practical problems, however. In particular, does a focus on specific stock groupings reflect a market that is truly segmented?

It is certainly true that investors differ in terms of their return requirements, their risk tolerances, their investment horizons, and in many other respects. To the extent that these differences are relatively static, and to the extent they become the basis for differences between the price behaviors of stocks in different industry and style groupings, the equity market could become virtually segmented along industry/style lines.

But all stocks can be defined by the same parameters—by market capitalization, by price/earnings ratio, by a dividend discount model ranking, and so on. All stocks can be found at some level on the continuum of values for each parameter. Thus, growth and value stocks can be seen to inhabit the opposite ends of the continuums of P/E and dividend yield, and small- and large-cap stocks the opposite ends of the continuum of firm size.

By the same token, changes in the values of the parameters for any individual stock can change that stock's position on the continuum. An out-of-favor growth stock may slip into value territory, while a small-cap company may grow into the large-cap range.

Furthermore, while the values of these parameters vary across stocks of different styles and industries, and different investors favor certain values above others—low P/E over high, for example—arbitrage tends to counterbalance too pronounced a predilection on the part of investors for any one set of values. In equilibrium, all stocks must be owned; if too many investors want low P/E, low-P/E stocks will be bid up to higher P/E levels; some investors will step in to sell them, and buy stocks deserving of higher P/Es. Arbitrage works toward a single, integrated market subject to a single pricing mechanism.

To the extent the market is integrated, a quantitative approach to valuation that models each industry or style grouping separately, as if it were a universe unto itself, is not the best approach: It is bound to ignore pertinent pricing information. A better approach would be to consider all the stocks in the universe, in order to glean the greatest amount of information possible. At the same time, one doesn't want to ignore the fact that the equity universe is characterized by subsets of stocks that behave similarly to one another and differently from the stocks in other subsets.

A complex equity market, one that is neither completely integrated nor discretely segmented, calls for a valuation approach that considers the largest possible universe of stocks, while taking into account the differences between subsets that are captured by specific style models. In addition to a coherent evaluation framework, such an approach offers two major advantages over specific subset models.

First, it is likely to provide more robust results. Because a model based on extensive and heterogeneous data better controls for multicollinearity in the independent variables, its parameter estimates are more efficient. Second, because of its range and depth of coverage, it is poised to take advantage of more profit opportunities than a more narrowly defined subset model proffers.

A UNIFIED MODEL

The unified approach starts with a blank slate, having no built-in biases regarding any particular group or groups of stocks. It searches the widest possible universe for insights that may offer profitable investment opportunities. Rather than focusing on one or a few attributes—a DDM derivation of value, say, or stock P/E level, or firm size—the unified model is multidimensional. It includes the largest number of pertinent variables possible. In addition to a company's industry affiliations, the model may look, for example, at price/earnings and price/cashflow, size and neglect, beta and idiosyncratic risk, return reversal and momentum.

Single-factor models of these variables offer only a naïve indication of their relationships to price behavior. Such models cannot tell us how much of any detected correlation between P/E and price changes, for example, actually reflects variables such as firm size and/or industry affiliation, which are not included in the model. Simultaneous modeling of all these variables across companies can disentangle the "pure" return to each [Jacobs and Levy (1988)]. It will show whether there is any abnormal return to P/E, after variables such as firm size and DDM value have been controlled for.

The size of the universe and the number of attributes encompassed by the unified model are matched by its depth of inquiry into the behavior of pure returns across different types of stocks. Researchers have noted, for example, that small-cap stocks have outperformed large-cap stocks in some periods. They have attributed the outperformance to various factors, including a low-P/E effect, book/price ratio, earnings surprise, lack of coverage by analysts, and tax-related calendar effects. A clear picture of the small-firm effect emerges only when we model all these factors, and other potential candidates, jointly, across the universe of stocks. Doing so allows us to disentangle the effects and to determine which are most significant for the returns of small stocks, and which might be most significant for large-stock returns.

Of particular interest is whether the relationships between stock prices and particular attributes are linear or nonlinear. Does price change by a constant increment with a unit change in, say, earnings revisions? Or do positive revisions have a greater or lesser effect on price than negative revisions? Do these relationships change over time? That is, are some price responses stronger in some market environments than others? Are some linear in up markets but nonlinear in down markets, or vice versa?

The aim in examining the behavior of price-attribute relationships across stock groups and over time is, of course, return prediction. Pure returns to equity attributes are more predictable than naïve returns, because they are not contaminated by incidental factors. Naïve returns to low P/E, for example, exhibit considerable volatility because of the effects of oil price shocks on utilities, which constitute a substantial portion of the low-P/E subset. Pure returns to P/E do not conflate this spurious effect with the low-P/E effect [see Jacobs and Levy (1989*b*)].

Pure attribute returns, combined with multivariate time-series analyses that take explicit account of macroeconomic drivers such as inflation, interest rates, and exchange rates, can help in predicting how stock prices will vary over time as market and economic conditions change. The pure return to small size, for instance, can be expected to decline with increasing inflation and interest rates and rise with industrial production [Jacobs and Levy (1989*a*)].

A COMMON EVALUATION FRAMEWORK

Use of a unified model ensures that all the stocks within the firm's investment universe share a common evaluation framework. This may not be the case with a "family" of subset portfolios, even if they are managed by the same firm. Consider, for example, a firm that manages a diversified core portfolio and several "style" portfolios. Suppose the firm runs a model on its total universe of, say, 3000 stocks. It then runs the same or a different model on a 500-stock subset of large-cap value stocks.

The expected returns that derive from running the model on the entire 3000-stock universe will differ from those returns the firm gets from running the model on the smaller subset, either because the model coefficients are bound to differ between the large universe and the smaller subset or because the models differ. What if the model run on the broad universe shows GM outperforming Ford, while the model run on the large-cap value subset shows the reverse? [See also Jacobs and Levy (1995*c*.)]

The firm could ensure consistency by using separate models for each universe subset—growth, value, small-cap—and linking the results via a single, overarching model that relates all the subsets. But, in an integrated market, the pricing of securities in one subset may contain information relevant to the security prices in other subsets. An economist attempting to forecast labor market conditions in the northeastern United States would undoubtedly consider economic expansion in the southeastern states. Similarly, the effects of inflation on value stocks might have repercussions for growth stocks, as the two groups represent opposite ends of the same P/E continuum.

An approach that merely "connects the dots" of various style portfolios is not efficient in terms of making use of all available information. The unified approach, by contrast, considers the whole picture—the interrelationships of numerous variables across a wide cross section of stocks and over a range of market environments. Its insights emerge from an in-depth examination of a market universe in which value and growth, large-cap and small-cap, and everything in between interact and evolve in complex ways.

PORTFOLIO CONSTRUCTION AND EVALUATION

Before a unified model's results can be implemented, they must be tested. The aim of testing is to find out how robust the results are, both for the whole universe of stocks and for each style subset within that universe.

Does the power of the model's insights differ across different subsets, as subset industry and sector concentrations, idiosyncratic risks, and the relative impacts of economic and fundamental factors differ? Simulations also should be carried out to determine if insights offer real-world profit opportunities: Are perceived profit opportunities too ephemeral, or too small to survive such frictions as trading costs?

To optimize implementation of the model's insights, the portfolio construction process should consider all the dimensions found relevant by the unified valuation model. Failure to do so can lead to imbalances in the portfolio's factor exposures.

Consider, as an example, a commercially available portfolio optimizer that recognizes only a subset of the factors in the unified model. Risk reduction using such an optimizer will reduce the portfolio's factor exposures, but only along the dimensions the optimizer recognizes. As a result, the portfolio is likely to wind up more exposed to those factors recognized by the model—but not the optimizer—and less exposed to those factors common to both the model and the optimizer.

Optimization that uses all relevant factors from the unified model ensures a portfolio whose risk and return opportunities are balanced in accordance with the model's insights. Furthermore, use of the more numerous model factors allows portfolio risk to be more finely tuned.

Any performance measurement process should similarly consider all the factors found relevant by the unified model and used in the portfolio's construction. A measurement process that is congruent with the unified model's return-generating dimensions is likely to provide more insightful direction than a commercial performance attribution system applied in a "one-size-fits-all" manner. A performance measurement process tailored to the unified model functions as a monitor of the model's reliability, while the addition of a feedback loop to the research/modeling process can help ensure that the model retains robustness over time.

ENGINEERING "BENCHMARK" STRATEGIES

Given its range and depth of coverage, a unified model can provide a firm with substantial flexibility to engineer portfolios to meet a variety of client risk/return preferences. And a portfolio construction process that includes the same multidimensional variables that the unified model uses to forecast returns can offer substantial control over the portfolios' risk/return profiles.

Suppose a client desires a style-specific return. This could be a return that tracks a published value, growth, or small-stock index, or even a return related to a customized index—one focusing on, say, high-yield stocks or stocks within a limited capitalization range. As we have noted previously, the unified model "purifies" returns to many style-related attributes; hence expected returns to any one attribute are not influenced by illusory effects. As we also note, the model predictions can be expected to be more robust and consistent than the predictions derived from more limited style-specific models. The result: Portfolios that will behave like, while offering value-added with respect to, passive style benchmarks.

Over time, different style subsets offer different payoffs as economic conditions change. A portfolio of value stocks is thus unlikely to outperform the broad market, or a portfolio of growth stocks, on a consistent basis over time. An investment strategy devoted to one style is bound to experience significant variability relative to broad market averages.

Clients in search of a smoother return path can, as we noted at the outset of this chapter, diversify their assets across a variety of different style portfolios. But there are likely to be gaps between the aggregate of a client's portfolios and the client's target benchmark. A manager can take advantage of the range of the unified approach to construct completeness funds designed to fill such gaps.

Alternatively, risk-averse clients can choose to hold a "core" portfolio, one representative of the overall market, including all style subsets. The unified approach can be used to engineer core portfolios that have systematic risk and other attributes similar to a capitalization-weighted benchmark such as the S&P 500, the Russell 1000, or the Wilshire 5000. Given the model's insights, these portfolios can be designed to deliver value-added relative to the passive market benchmark, at any given level of residual risk relative to the market.

Furthermore, given the large universe of stocks covered by the unified model, the manager can fairly readily accommodate special client constraints, if necessary. If an endowment fund does not want to hold any alcohol, tobacco, or defense stocks, for example, the manager should be able to find "sin-free" substitutes that offer equivalent risks with little return give-up.

ADDED FLEXIBILITY

The advantages of the unified approach are perhaps most fully exploited by strategies that are not constrained to deliver returns that are representative of a style or a broad market index. A style rotation strategy, for example, seeks out profit opportunities as they arise, rotating the portfolio aggressively among various universe subsets as defined by stock attributes [see Jacobs and Levy (1995a)]. Portfolio weights and changes in those weights are determined not by some benchmark index, but by the insights of the unified model. Such a strategy takes advantage of the entire universe of stocks covered and the entire range of insights uncovered by the model, and offers potentially high returns at commensurate risk levels.

Allowing short sales as an adjunct to an active strategy can enhance implementation of and increase the opportunities to profit from the insights of a unified model. Say the model indicates a high likelihood of underperformance by the steel industry. The manager has more latitude to underweight steel with shorting than if the only option were *not to hold* steel companies.

Or consider the investment opportunities that may arise with earnings surprises. With a preponderance of security analysts focused on identifying purchase candidates, the price effects of positive earnings surprises may be arbitraged away very quickly. The effects of negative surprises may be more long-lasting, as sales are limited to investors who already hold the affected security and to those investors willing and able to sell short. A portfolio that is allowed to sell short can benefit by taking advantage of negative earnings surprises, and will also profit more from shorts than longs when the model detects such nonlinearities in price response.

In general, shorting allows the manager to pursue potential mispricings without constraint, by going long underpriced stocks and selling short overpriced stocks. To the extent that overpricing is of a greater magnitude or more prevalent than underpricing, shorting offers enhanced profit potential vis-à-vis a long-only strategy. But shorting can also be used to reduce portfolio risk.

For example, we have noted that low-P/E stocks are influenced by a variety of factors, which can add unwanted risk. The manager in pursuit of "pure" portfolio exposure to low P/E can better neutralize these other factors by taking offsetting long and short positions.

Complete realization of the return enhancement and risk reduction possibilities of shorting involves using long positions to collateralize an equal dollar position in shorts. By investing approximately equal dollar amounts long in stocks expected to outperform and short in stocks expected to underperform, given the stocks' characteristics and expectations for the market and the economy, the manager can construct a long-short portfolio that is virtually immunized against risk from broad market movements [see Jacobs and Levy (1993)].

Such a market-neutral strategy reflects neither the risk nor the return of the overall equity market. What it does offer is an active return, and residual risk, from the spread between the securities held long and sold short (as well as interest on the short-sales proceeds, which will approximate the risk-free rate).

This active return will likely benefit from the strategy's added flexibility to underweight via shorting, and also from the freeing up of capital to take active long positions. Being market-neutral, the portfolio is not constrained to hold a stock merely in order to reflect a market exposure; every dollar invested long (or sold short) either reduces risk or establishes an active position. Furthermore, every position long or short represents an active exposure; this is not true of index-constrained long-only portfolios, in which only the percentage of a stock position that represents an overweight (or underweight) relative to the benchmark is active [see Jacobs and Levy (1995b)].

An investor can take advantage of the flexibility of the long-short structure, while adding back a risk/return dimension representative of an equity market benchmark, by purchasing stock index futures equal in amount to the capital underlying the long-short strategy. The resulting portfolio with futures overlay adds the long-short spread to the equity market's performance. In effect, long-short construction frees a portfolio from asset-class constraint, allowing the investor to separate the security selection decision from the asset allocation decision.

ECONOMIES

A unified approach may offer economies not available to a client utilizing separate managers for various strategies. The client's management and monitoring costs, for example, are likely to be lower under a single, unified manager. Furthermore, a unified approach is better able to minimize incidental costs, such as may arise if lack of coordination among managers leads to portfolio overlaps and gaps in coverage. It may also be better poised to take advantage of opportunities to arbitrage between different styles via style rotation.

Long-short strategies are especially suited to management under one roof. In particular, single-manager coordination of the long and short positions enhances profit potential and risk control compared with using separate long and short managers. Furthermore, because the stocks held long can be used to collateralize the short positions, the client's investment capital can be effectively doubled.

All these advantages do not come without some costs. Any firm that offers multiple strategies, unified or not, must address implementation issues such as liquidity constraints and allocation of trades across various strategies. Construction of a multidimensional, dynamic model entails, in addition, a great deal of research effort. The more complex the model is, the more time-consuming will be the testing required to ensure its robustness.

The wide-screen entertainment center with high-definition resolution and stereo sound has substantial development costs, more than the standard color television. But it's also going to provide a bigger, better, more lifelike picture. To the extent that a unified model's complexity, better reflecting the range and depth of the market, captures the complexities of security pricing, the rewards it offers are worth the effort.

The magnitude of the rewards to active investment management depends upon the strength (predictive accuracy) of the underlying insights and their number. Both better insights and more numerous insights provide additional profitability. Moreover, their impact on portfolio profitability is multiplicative [see Grinold and Kahn (1995)]. Widening the range and deepening the focus of the investment research effort can significantly enhance investment performance.

ENDNOTE

The authors gratefully acknowledge the helpful comments of Dennis Trittin and thank Judy Kimball for her editorial assistance.

REFERENCES

Farrell, James L., Jr. 1975. "Homogeneous stock groupings." *Financial Analysts Journal* 31 (3): 50–61.

Grinold, Richard C. and Ronald N. Kahn. 1995. *Active portfolio management: Quantitative theory and applications.* Chicago: Probus, pp. 117–135.

Jacobs, Bruce I. and Kenneth N. Levy. 1988. "Disentangling equity return regularities: New insights and investment opportunities." *Financial Analysts Journal* 44 (3): 18–43.

—— and ——. 1989a. "Forecasting the size effect." *Financial Analysts Journal* 45 (3): 38–54.

—— and ——. 1989b. "The complexity of the stock market." *Journal of Portfolio Management* 16 (1): 19–27.

—— and ——. 1993. "Long/short equity investing." *Journal of Portfolio Management* 20 (1): 52–63.

—— and ——. 1995a. "High-definition style rotation." Working Paper, Jacobs Levy Equity Management. [Published in *Journal of Investing* 5 (3).]

—— and ——. 1995b. "Market-neutral equity strategy limits risk." *Pension Management*, June.

—— and ——. 1995c. "The law of one alpha." *Journal of Portfolio Management* 21 (4): 78–79.

Jones, Robert C. 1990. "Designing factor models for different types of stock: What's good for the goose ain't always good for the gander." *Financial Analysts Journal* 46 (2): 25–30.

The Law of One Alpha[*]

As there is one price, there is only one mispricing.

Arbitrage ensures that there is only one price for a single financial instrument at any one time. If a share of Apple Computer is trading at $40 in New York, it can't trade at $45 in Chicago.

But it is estimates of *mis*pricing that make a market. Investors have different horizons, different cashflow needs, different economic outlooks, and different approaches to valuation. Their expectations for any given stock are likely to differ accordingly.

Should what holds true for investors in general also hold true for a single investment firm? In particular, for quantitative firms, where "discipline" connotes a philosophy as well as an investment approach, does it make sense to have multiple expectations for the same stock? Yet multiple expectations may be the result when a single firm applies a variety of models to its investment portfolios.

Consider a firm that manages a "core" portfolio whose selection universe is coterminous with some broad market index such as the Russell 1000 and a "value" portfolio whose selection universe comprises 500 stocks within that broader universe. The firm presumably has a single expectation (or a single range of expectations) for each stock in the broad, core universe. Should it have a second set of expectations for the 500 stocks that form the value subset of that universe?

---

[*] Originally published in the *Journal of Portfolio Management* 21 (4): 78–79.

If the firm uses one model for selecting the core portfolio and a different model—a specialized "value" model—for selecting the value portfolio, it is virtually guaranteed to come up with two different expectations for each of the 500 value stocks—one expectation from the core model and one from the value model. Even if it uses the same model, but applies it separately, first to the core universe and then to the value subset, the expected returns will differ between the two universes, because the model coefficients are bound to differ between the broad universe and the smaller subset. What if the model run on the broad universe shows GM outperforming Ford, while the model run on the value subset shows the reverse?

The firm could ensure consistency by using separate models for each subset of its selection universe—growth, value, small-cap, whatever—and then, for the core portfolio, linking the results via a single, overarching model that relates all the subsets. This would work if the market were constituted of discrete groups of stocks that are totally uncorrelated with each other. Growth stocks do behave differently from value stocks, as small-cap stocks behave differently from large-cap stocks. But do style groupings constitute distinct market segments, each subject to its own distinct pricing mechanism?

We think it unlikely. Consider an out-of-favor growth stock that slips into the value category, or a small-cap company that matures into the large-cap group. Does such a transition signify a qualitative change in the underlying company? Should its stock now be subject to a different pricing mechanism?

All stocks share similar characteristics, or attributes; all may be categorized by market capitalization, by price/earnings ratio, by a dividend discount model notion of value, or any number of variables. It is the magnitudes of these characteristics, rather than their nature, that differ across stocks and may differ markedly across stocks of different styles and industries. To the extent these differences affect the sensitivities of stocks to economic and market forces and their attractiveness to investors, stock returns can and will differ.

Value stocks and growth stocks do not represent two distinct market segments, but the extremes on continuums of P/E, dividend yield, and other attributes.[1] Investors who favor certain levels of these attributes—low P/E or high yield, for example—will find stocks at these levels attractive and other stocks unattractive. Imbalances—say, too pronounced a predilection on the part of investors for either growth or value—will lead to self-correcting arbitrage. This arbitrage makes for a single, integrated market subject to a single pricing mechanism.

Modeling each style grouping separately, as if it were a universe unto itself, is not the best approach if the market is integrated. This is because each subset model is bound to ignore information contained in the other subsets. The behavior of growth stocks, for example, may have a lot to say about the behavior of value stocks, the two groups anchoring opposite ends of the P/E continuum. Totally independent subset models are not optimal because they do not utilize all available information.

The opposite tack—modeling the broadest possible selection universe, and using the results to construct a variety of portfolios—is much the better approach [see Jacobs and Levy (1995)]. Because it is based on a large, diverse cross section of stocks and stock characteristics, this approach can take advantage of all available pricing information. (It also reduces multicollinearity in the model variables and leads to more robust parameter estimates.)

The return-attribute relationships indicated by the model are thus more stable, hence more predictable, than those that may be garnered from a model focusing on a narrower subset of stocks that exhibit less diverse behavior. And, importantly, this approach ensures a consistent view of every security's potential: Each stock will have one and only one expected alpha.

At the end of the day, there is only one true mispricing: A given stock's price will have changed by a given amount relative to its price at the start. It hardly makes sense to begin the investment selection process with an approach that allows for the possibility of multiple mispricings for a given stock over a given horizon.

ENDNOTE

The authors thank Judy Kimball for her editorial assistance.

1. Warren Buffett, the quintessential value investor, also views growth and value investing as "joined at the hip" (*The Wall Street Journal*, February 15, 1995, p. A3).

REFERENCE

Jacobs, B. I. and K. N. Levy. 1995. "Engineering portfolios: A unified approach." *Journal of Investing* 4 (4): 8–14.

Residual Risk

How Much Is Too Much?*

Artificial limits on a portfolio's residual risk can lead to suboptimal behavior on the part of investors and managers.

In portfolio management, excess return measures the difference between the portfolio's returns and those of an underlying benchmark, and residual risk measures the volatility of those excess returns. An investor who is averse to incurring residual risk relative to a benchmark is not risk-averse in the same sense that an investor who shies away from stocks in favor of bonds and cash is risk-averse. The latter investor does not want to incur the riskiness associated with stock returns. The former investor may be willing to incur the risk associated with stocks, or at least those stocks represented by the benchmark, but is more or less averse to incurring the additional risks that are associated with security selection.

For such an investor, gains and losses that come from holding the benchmark are not a matter for concern, but gains and losses relative to the benchmark are of some importance. As Clarke, Krase, and Statman (1994) put it (p. 19):

> Gains and losses that come with holding the benchmark portfolio are an "act of God." Gains and losses that come with deviation from the benchmark portfolio are an "act of man." Choice involves responsibility, and responsibility brings the pain of regret when the choice turns out badly.

* Originally published in the *Journal of Portfolio Management* 22 (3): 10–16.

This investor is regret-averse, rather than risk-averse in the traditional sense.

Clarke et al. explain the difference by an analogy to a lottery participant who has bet on the same numbers for some time but is now considering a new set of numbers. The odds of either set of numbers winning are the same. But the lottery participant would feel extreme regret if he or she were to change numbers and the old numbers won; choice of a new set of numbers entails a high risk of regret.

Some investors, like lottery participants, wish to hold only the number represented by a given equity index. These investors are willing to accept the risks associated with holding the equity index, in exchange for receiving equity returns, but are so regret-averse that they are unwilling to incur any additional risks. These investors are likely to hold passive, indexed portfolios.

Other investors, however, may be willing to incur the residual risks associated with active security selection in exchange for expected excess returns. How much residual risk should they incur? The answer will depend upon the investor's aversion to residual risk and the portfolio manager's skill. The values of these parameters can be estimated, but the task is frequently simplified by placing simple constraints on portfolio residual risk levels.

Consultants and managers often categorize portfolios into specific ranges of residual risk. For example, "enhanced passive" or "index-plus" portfolios (which account for about $100 billion of institutional assets) are typically bounded by residual risks relative to a benchmark of between 0.30 and 2.00 percent [Schramm (1995), p. 3]. Their expected excess returns are generally between 0.15 and 1.00 percent. The next tier of residual risk portfolios, those having residual risk levels over 2 percent, are classified as "core" strategies.

A constraint, such as a 2 percent limit on residual risk, in effect brings down a curtain, beyond which lie excess returns and residual risks unavailable to the investor. Does this make sense? Shouldn't the investor be aware of what lies beyond the curtain, if only to understand what is being given up?

BEYOND THE CURTAIN

A framework developed by Grinold and Kahn (1995), pp. 91–99, can provide some guidance for understanding what lies beyond the 2 percent curtain. Development of a complete picture depends crucially upon the notion of the information ratio as a measure of the portfolio manager's skill. The *information ratio*, IR, is the maximum ratio of annualized excess return, α, to annualized residual risk, ω, the manager can obtain:[1]

$$IR = \frac{\alpha}{\omega} \tag{9.1}$$

The IR is assumed to be constant over all risk levels (that is, excess return will increase proportionally with residual risk).[2] A good manager might have an IR of 0.5, while an exceptional manager might have an IR of 1.0.

For any given level of residual risk, ω, the objective is to maximize investor utility, U, defined as portfolio excess return less the disutility of portfolio residual risk:

$$U = \alpha - (\lambda \omega^2) \tag{9.2}$$

Investor utility increases with increases in portfolio excess return. Increases in portfolio residual risk, however, reduce investor utility by a factor, λ, that reflects the investor's aversion to residual risk (regret aversion).

Substituting from Eq. (9.1), investor utility can be expressed in terms of residual risk, investor regret aversion, and manager IR:

$$U = (\omega \times IR) - (\lambda \times \omega^2) \tag{9.3}$$

Utility will increase with an increase in IR and decrease with increases in the investor's level of residual risk aversion. The optimal level of aggressiveness or residual risk, ω^*, for a portfolio will also increase with IR and decrease with aversion to residual risk:[3]

$$\omega^* = \frac{IR}{2\lambda}. \tag{9.4}$$

Figure 9-1 illustrates some of the trade-offs involving residual risk, excess return, investor aversion to risk, and manager skill. The two lines ascending from the zero-residual-risk, zero-excess-return origin (the underlying benchmark) represent various possible combinations of excess return and residual risk that could be offered by two managers.[4] The first manager has an IR of 1.0; the portfolios on this frontier offer excess returns equal to their residual risks. The second manager has an IR of 0.5; the

F I G U R E   9–1

Investor Risk Aversion and Manager Skill

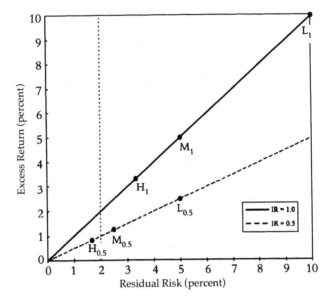

portfolios on this frontier offer excess returns half the magnitude of their residual risks.

The points H, M, and L on the efficient frontiers illustrate the optimal portfolios for investors with three levels of aversion to residual risk—0.15 (high), 0.10 (medium), and 0.05 (low). We can place some numbers on these points, using Eq. (9.4). Given a manager with an IR of 1.0, the optimal portfolios for investors with high, medium, and low aversions to residual risk, H_1, M_1, and L_1, will have residual risk levels of 3.33, 5.00, and 10.00 percent, respectively. Given a manager with an IR of 0.5, the optimal portfolios, $H_{0.5}$, $M_{0.5}$, and $L_{0.5}$, will have residual risk levels of, respectively, 1.67, 2.50, and 5.00 percent.

Note that, along both frontiers, higher levels of residual risk are associated with higher expected excess returns. Furthermore, the optimal (for the assumed risk tolerances) portfolios of the higher-IR manager have both higher residual risks and higher expected excess returns than those of the lower-IR manager. Higher

F I G U R E   9–2

Sacrifice in Utility from Overestimating Investor Risk Aversion

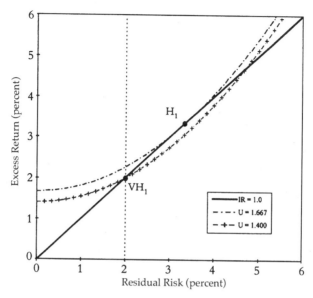

expected excess returns accrue to higher-residual-risk portfolios and to higher-IR managers.

The dotted vertical line in Figure 9-1 represents a 2 percent residual risk cutoff. Note that only one portfolio falls within this boundary—the portfolio corresponding to the high-regret-aversion investor with the IR = 0.5 manager. The medium- and low-regret-aversion portfolios on the IR = 0.5 frontier and all three portfolios on the IR = 1.0 frontier have residual risks above 2 percent. These portfolios would be unavailable to the investor with a 2 percent residual risk constraint.

In Figure 9-2, point VH_1 on the IR = 1.0 frontier represents a portfolio with a residual risk level of 2 percent. According to Eq. (9.4), this portfolio will be optimal for an investor with a regret aversion level of 0.25—a very high level of aversion to residual risk. Point H_1 represents the optimal portfolio for the investor with a high-regret aversion level of 0.15 and a manager with an IR of 1.0. This portfolio is located at the point of tangency between the IR = 1.0

manager's efficient frontier and the utility curve for an investor with a regret aversion level of 0.15. All points on this curve are equally desirable for an investor with this level of regret aversion. The investor is thus indifferent between portfolio H_1 and a certain excess return of 1.667 percent (the certainty equivalent found at the curve's intersection with the vertical axis).

The investor with residual risk aversion of 0.15 who opts for portfolio VH_1 because of a 2 percent constraint on residual risk will suffer a loss in utility. This loss can be calculated, using Eq. (9.3), as the difference between the utility of portfolio H_1 (1.667 percent) and the utility of portfolio VH_1 (1.400 percent), assuming the investor's residual risk aversion is actually 0.15 and the manager's IR is 1.0. The magnitude of this sacrifice—0.267 percentage point—is the distance between the utility curve passing through point H_1 and the curve passing through point VH_1. It corresponds to a certainty-equivalent sacrifice of 0.267 percentage point.

As noted previously, the efficient frontier for an IR = 0.5 manager will be lower than that of an IR = 1.0 manager. Point $H_{0.5}$ in Figure 9-3 represents the optimal portfolio for an investor with regret aversion of 0.15 and a manager with an IR of 0.5. Point $H_{0.5}$, with residual risk of 1.67 percent, is well within the 2 percent curtain. It offers the best deal for the investor if there is no manager with a higher IR, who can offer more return at the investor's regret tolerance level. An investor who settles for portfolio $H_{0.5}$ when portfolio H_1 is available, however, will sacrifice 1.25 percentage points (1.667 − 0.417) in utility.

Of course, investing in portfolio H_1 means accepting a residual risk level above 2 percent. Does this imply that the investor constrained to a residual risk level of 2 percent or less should stick with portfolio $H_{0.5}$, even if a superior manager can be found? A better solution for the investor would be to dilute the residual risk of portfolio H_1 by investing some portion of funds in the underlying benchmark index.

Figure 9-4 shows that portfolio IH_1, evenly divided between a passive indexed portfolio and portfolio H_1 and having half the residual risk of portfolio H_1 alone, will lie directly above portfolio $H_{0.5}$ at the same risk level. Portfolio IH_1 is stochastically dominant to portfolio $H_{0.5}$; it offers higher expected excess return at the same level of residual risk. Its utility will be 1.250 percent. Compared

F I G U R E   9–3

Sacrifice in Utility from Using Less-Skillful Manager

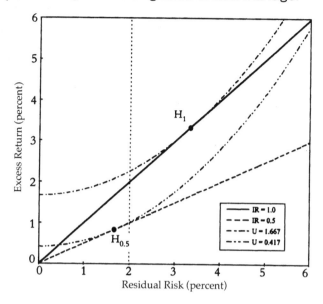

Residual Risk (percent)

with portfolio $H_{0.5}$, with utility of 0.417 percent, portfolio IH_1 offers the investor a gain in utility of 0.833 percentage point $(1.250 - 0.417)$.

However, as Figure 9-5 indicates, even portfolio IH_1 is suboptimal for the investor with 0.15 residual risk aversion and access to a manager with an IR of 1.0. This investor will maximize utility by holding the original portfolio H_1 (utility of 1.667 percent). Permitting portfolios beyond the 2 percent curtain, in this case H_1, provides a gain in utility of 0.417 percentage point $(1.667 - 1.250)$.

SOME IMPLICATIONS

We have raised the 2 percent curtain to view some of the opportunities that lie beyond it. Not surprisingly, the landscape beyond the curtain abides by the same laws as the landscape within: Greater excess return comes at a cost of greater residual risk. We have found that the slope of the ascent will depend upon the manager's skill, as measured by IR:

F I G U R E   9–4

Gain in Utility Available within the 2 Percent Curtain

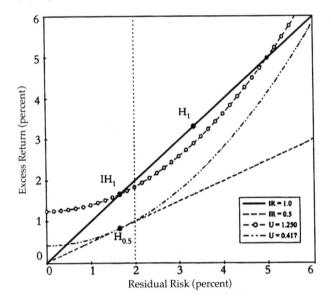

The higher the IR, the steeper the slope. On any given slope, the optimal portfolio for an investor will depend upon the investor's level of aversion to residual risk. The more regret-averse the investor, the closer to the origin the preferred portfolio will be.

The familiarity of the landscape beyond highlights the artificiality of the curtain itself. Imposition of a constraint such as the 2 percent limit on residual risk would seem to imply that either excess return (residual risk) drops (rises) precipitously at a given level of residual risk (2 percent in this case), or that some investors have discontinuous utility functions. These investors would be willing to incur residual risk up to 2 percent but unwilling even to consider portfolios with residual risks above 2 percent, whatever their expected returns. Neither of these assumptions seems reasonable.

In fact, imposition of constraints such as the 2 percent curtain may well encourage suboptimal behavior on the part of investors. Overemphasizing the portfolio's level of residual risk may, as in Figure 9-2, lead investors to sacrifice utility by overestimating their aver-

Gain in Utility Available beyond the 2 Percent Curtain

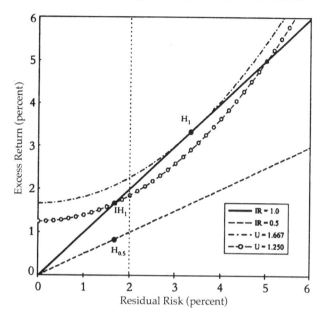

sion to residual risk. Or it may, as in Figure 9-3, lead them to prefer, in exchange for a low level of residual risk, a less skillful manager.

Constraints on residual risk may also encourage suboptimal behavior on the part of managers. As Grinold (1990) has pointed out (p. 239), there already exist business reasons for high-skill managers to underemploy their insights by taking less than the optimal level of risk:

> Aggressiveness creates a large element of business risk for the manager. Even the most effective active managers will experience significant runs of negative active return with high probability. If they are more aggressive than the other managers employed by the sponsor, they risk being . . . [last]. . . . Managers with high information ratios should, in general, be more aggressive. However, the high level of aggressiveness may threaten the success of the manager's business. This tension will probably result in less than optimal levels of aggressiveness among skillful managers.

Imposition of risk constraints is likely only to exacerbate this tendency.

This is not to say there are no valid reasons for holding enhanced passive portfolios with residual risk levels below 2 percent. As we have noted, even at an exceptional manager IR level of 1.0, all investors with residual risk aversions of 0.25 or higher should prefer portfolios with residual risks below 2 percent. Furthermore, as IRs decrease, optimal residual risk levels for all degrees of residual risk aversion shift downward. Thus, the lower the active manager's level of skill, the lower portfolio residual risk levels should be.

Investors should nevertheless be aware that accepting any arbitrary limit on residual risk may entail a significant sacrifice in utility. They can take two steps to guard against this eventuality. First, they should attempt to determine independently their levels of residual risk tolerance. Low levels of tolerance will lead naturally to portfolios with low residual risk levels; higher levels suggest that higher levels of residual risk, and higher expected excess returns, are more suitable.

Second, investors should actively search out high-IR managers. The higher the manager's IR, the greater the return that can be provided at any given level of risk or any given level of residual risk aversion.

ENDNOTES

The authors thank Judith Kimball for her editorial assistance.

1. The IR is identical to the Sharpe ratio when the latter is measured in terms of excess return and residual risk relative to the underlying benchmark. See Sharpe (1994).

2. The IR is a linear function of residual risk when short-selling is unrestricted and liquidity is unlimited. In practice, the IR slope will decline at high levels of residual risk.

3. Equation (9.4) is derived by setting the first derivative of U with respect to ω equal to zero.

4. The underlying benchmark can be thought of as a risk-free asset in this context, as it is riskless for the investor concerned only with excess return and residual risk.

REFERENCES

Clarke, Roger G., Scott Krase, and Meir Statman. 1994. "Tracking errors, regret, and tactical asset allocation." *Journal of Portfolio Management* 20 (3): 16–24.

Grinold, Richard C. 1990. "The fundamental law of active management." In *Managing Institutional Assets*, F. J. Fabozzi, ed. New York: Harper & Row, pp. 225–244.

Grinold, Richard C. and Ronald N. Kahn. 1995. *Active Portfolio Management: Quantitative Theory and Applications*. Chicago: Probus.

Schramm, Sabine. 1995. "Index managers get active." *Pensions & Investments*, October 16.

Sharpe, William F. 1994. "The Sharpe ratio." *Journal of Portfolio Management* 21 (1): 49–58.

High-Definition Style Rotation[*]

Distinguishing between subtle style attributes pays off.

According to William Sharpe (1992), p. 9:

> Those concerned with [style] distinctions have focused most of their research on long-run average return differences; that is, they have asked whether small stocks or value stocks "do better than they should" in the long run. Less attention has been paid to likely sources of short-run variability in returns among such groups.

While most active managers have focused on adding value via stock selection, research suggests that, for large, well-diversified multi-manager plans, stock selection adds little value [see, for example, Brinson, Singer, and Beebower (1991)]. Rather, as Brinson and his co-authors have documented, it is asset allocation that has the largest impact on investment fund returns. Over 90 percent of an average fund's total return variance can be traced to its investment policy, the long-term allocation of its investments across asset classes.

Consultants and funds have lately become more concerned with the allocation of investments *within* an asset category—in particular, equities. How much does an equity portfolio's allocation to different categories of equity—growth, value, large-cap, small-cap—contribute to its total return?

---

[*] Originally published in the *Journal of Investing* 5 (3): 14–23.

Recent studies suggest that a regression of portfolio returns on the returns to various equity style indexes can explain much of a portfolio's return. Thus, for 1985 to 1989, over 97 percent of the returns of a well-known "stock picker"—the Fidelity Magellan Fund—were mirrored by a passive fund invested in large-cap growth stocks (46 percent), medium-size stocks (31 percent), small stocks (19 percent), and European stocks (4 percent) [see Sharpe (1992), p. 13)].

A glance at Figures 10-1 and 10-2 gives some idea of the importance of style. Figure 10-1 shows the rolling 3-year return to the Frank Russell large-cap growth stock index minus the comparable return to the Russell large-cap value stock index. Figure 10-2 illustrates the rolling 3-year return to the small-cap index less the return to the large-cap index.[1] The figures indicate significant differential performance across styles.

For the 3 years ending in December 1991, for example, large-cap growth stocks returned 91 percent and large-cap value stocks 43 percent, for a return spread of almost 50 percentage points. Value stocks outperformed growth stocks by a similar spread over the 3-year period ending in mid-1985. Small-cap stocks outperformed large-cap stocks by about 45 percentage points in the 3-year period ending in the fourth quarter of 1993, while they underperformed large-cap stocks by about 42 percentage points for the 3 years ending in mid-1987.

The performance of style managers tends to reflect the differentials between style indexes. For the 3 years ending in the fourth quarter of 1991, for example, the median growth manager in the Frank Russell universe returned 57 percentage points more than the median value manager (104 versus 47 percent). And for the 3-year period ending in the fourth quarter of 1993, the median small-cap manager in the Frank Russell universe returned 48 percentage points more than the median large-cap manager (111 versus 63 percent).

These substantial return differentials suggest that style rotation—rotating portfolio investments across stocks of different styles as economic and market conditions change—offers an opportunity to enhance portfolio returns. We find, moreover, that style rotation based on finely drawn distinctions between style attributes offers return enhancement over style rotation carried out via passive style

Growth-Value Spread–Rolling 3-Year Returns–1979–1994

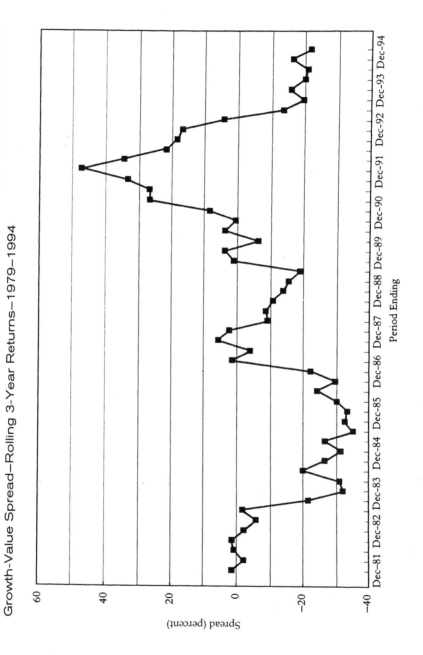

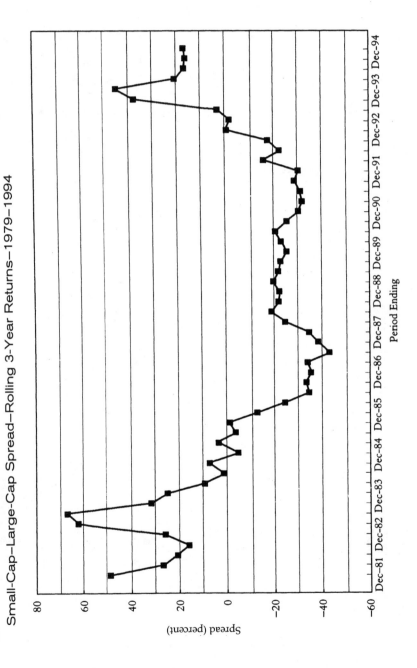

FIGURE 10-2

Small-Cap–Large-Cap Spread–Rolling 3-Year Returns–1979–1994

indexes. Clear and precise definitions of style (or high-definition style) facilitate more accurate style allocations, which can provide superior realized returns.

HIGH-DEFINITION STYLE

According to Sharpe (1992), p. 9:

> While the terms "value" and "growth" reflect common usage in the investment profession, they serve only as convenient names for stocks that tend to be similar in several respects. As is well known, across securities there is significant positive correlation among: book/price, earnings/price, low earnings growth, dividend yield, and low return on equity. Moreover, the industry compositions of the value and growth groups differ.

Definitions of style can be extremely simple. One example: Rank the securities in the investment universe by book-to-price ratio or earnings-to-price ratio, and divide in two. Stocks with above-average ratios are categorized as value stocks, and those with low ratios are categorized as growth stocks. Define small-cap stocks as the ninth and tenth deciles of market capitalization, or all stocks with capitalizations below a certain amount.

Simple solutions are not always the best, however; sometimes they are just simplistic. For one thing, what do you do with all the stocks that fall in the middle of these divisions? Will stocks with average P/Es or B/Ps perform like value stocks? Growth stocks? What about medium-capitalization companies? Are they large companies that are shrinking? Small companies that are growing?

Also, many different factors can be used to define style. Is growth potential best captured by historical growth? Sustainable growth? Analysts' growth estimates? Is B/P the best marker of potential value? What about dividend discount model (DDM) value? Or fundamentals such as earnings, cashflow, and sales?

Most style managers and many consultants now recognize the limitations of "single-screen" style definitions. Some consultants use probability weightings to assign stocks to various style categories. Others use multiple value/growth screens. An even more complex approach considers a large number of stock attributes and industry affiliations for a large and diverse universe of stocks. This approach permits more finely tuned style allocations, as well as greater flexibility in rotating the portfolio across stock attributes in pursuit of profit opportunities.

Value analysis, for example, may entail an examination of earnings, cashflow, sales, dividend discount value, and yield, among other attributes. Growth measurements to be considered include historical, expected, and sustainable growth, as well as the momentum and stability of earnings. And in addition to market capitalization as a size measure, one can use share price, volatility, analyst coverage, and other size-related attributes.

These factors are often closely correlated with each other. Consider the example of small-cap stocks. Small-cap stocks tend to have low P/Es; low P/E is correlated with high yield; both low P/E and high yield are correlated with dividend discount model estimations of value [see Jacobs and Levy (1989b)]. Furthermore, all these attributes may be correlated with a stock's industry affiliation. A simple low-P/E screen, for example, will often end up selecting a large number of bank and utility stocks. Such correlations can distort naïve attempts to relate returns to style attributes.

Consider Figure 10-3, which plots the cumulative excess returns (relative to a 3000-stock universe) to a 1 standard deviation exposure to three different size-related attributes over the period from January 1, 1978, through December 31, 1994. These results represent estimates from monthly univariate regressions; the "small cap" line thus represents the cumulative excess returns to a portfolio of stocks naïvely chosen on the basis of their size (small), with no attempt made to control other attributes.[2] An investment in such a portfolio made in January 1978 and rebalanced monthly would have returned (before transaction costs) about 23 percentage points more than the overall market by the end of December 1994.

Note that, in Figure 10-3, the returns to small-cap are closely correlated with the returns to the measure of analyst neglect. In general, returns to all three attributes—small-cap, neglect, and low price per share—tend to move together, if not in lockstep. This is confirmed by the first column of Table 10-1, which presents the correlation coefficients between the "naïve" returns to the three attributes. The correlations between the returns to small-cap and low price and neglect each exceed 0.80, while neglect and low price per share are correlated at 0.64.

FIGURE 10-3

Naïve Returns to Size-Related Attributes–1978–1994

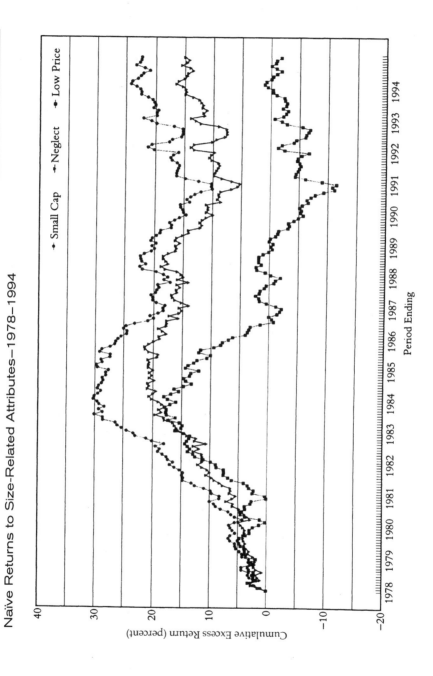

T A B L E   10–1

Correlations Between Monthly Returns to Size-Related
Attributes–1978–1994*

Attribute	Naïve	Pure
Small-cap/low price	0.80	−0.14
Small-cap/neglect	0.85	−0.22
Neglect/low price	0.64	−0.14

*A coefficient of 0.14 is significant at the 5 percent level.

Pure Style Returns

A different picture emerges when these size attributes are "disentangled" to derive "pure" returns to each attribute. This is done by using multivariate regression analysis, which allows one to examine the relationship between returns and a given stock attribute while controlling for the effects of other related factors. In this way, one can look at returns to a portfolio that is characterized by, say, its market capitalization (small) or by its price per share (low); in all other respects, the portfolio is marketlike, having average values of all other size-related attributes, as well as marketlike value and growth attributes and industry weightings.

Figure 10-4 plots the "purified," disentangled cumulative excess returns to each of the attributes shown in Figure 10-3 over the same period. Two results are immediately apparent. First, the attributes no longer appear to be so positively correlated. Figure 10-3 shows the naïve returns to small-cap and neglect to be virtually identical over a rather long horizon. The pure returns in Figure 10-4, however, show returns to small-cap behaving quite differently from returns to neglect.

This finding is supported by the pure correlation results in the last column of Table 10-1. The often large positive correlations of the naïve returns have disappeared—to be replaced by significant negative correlations. The naïve small-cap measure's 0.80 and 0.85 correlations with low price and neglect, for example, become −0.14 and −0.22 when one examines pure returns.

FIGURE 10-4

Pure Returns to Size-Related Attributes—1978–1994

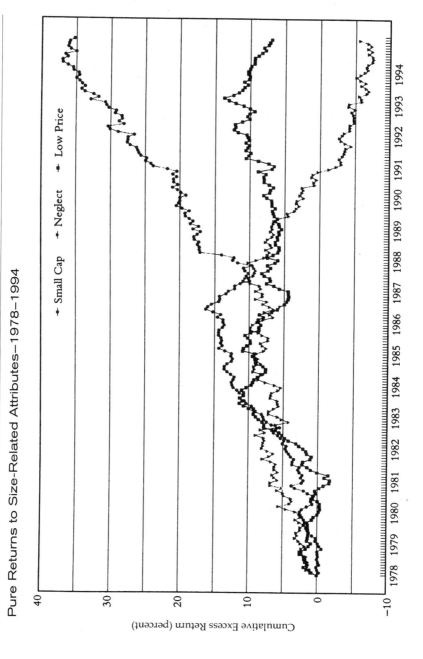

T A B L E   10–2

Percentage Standard Deviations of Monthly Returns to Size-
Related Attributes–1978–1994*.

Attribute	Naïve	Pure
Small-cap	0.85	0.58
Neglect	0.87	0.69
Low price	1.04	0.58

*All differences between naïve and pure return standard deviations are significant at the 1 percent level.

Second, the returns in Figure 10-4 display much less volatility than those in Figure 10-3. While the returns in Figure 10-3 plot a general up/down/up pattern (corresponding to eras favoring small-cap, large-cap, and then small-cap stocks), they show much month-to-month volatility within these trends. By contrast, the results in Figure 10-4 appear to be much smoother and more consistent.

The latter impression is verified by a look at Table 10-2, which presents monthly standard deviations for both naïve and pure returns to the size-related attributes. All the pure return series exhibit significantly less volatility.[3]

Implications

The use of pure returns rather than naïve returns to equity attributes can help investors avoid some investment pitfalls and can highlight more investment opportunities.

Value modeling, for example, often considers price/earnings ratios and dividend yields. The naïve returns to low P/E and to high yield suggest the two are highly correlated (0.47 correlation over the 1978 to 1994 period). The pure returns display little correlation, however (0.07). Similarly, the growth stock investor would do well to distinguish between historical and sustainable growth measures; the pure returns to these attributes are negatively correlated (–0.13), although their naïve returns are fairly highly correlated (0.56).

Investors may look to value stocks in unsettled or bearish markets. But what value attributes should they use? DDM value? Divi-

T A B L E 10–3

Market Sensitivities of Monthly Returns to Value-Related Attributes–1978–1994

Attribute	Naïve Sensitivity (*t*-Statistic)	Pure Sensitivity (t-Statistic)
DDM	0.06 (5.5)	0.04 (5.1)
B/P	–0.10 (–6.1)	–0.01 (–0.9)
Yield	–0.08 (–7.3)	–0.03 (–3.3)

dend yield? Book-to-price ratio? Table 10-3 shows the results of regressing both naïve and pure returns to several value-related attributes on market (S&P 500) returns over the 1978 to 1994 period.

The results suggest that DDM value is a poor indicator of a stock's ability to withstand a tide of receding market prices. The regression coefficient in the first column indicates that a portfolio with a 1 standard deviation exposure to DDM value will tend to underperform by 0.06 percent when the market falls by 1.00 percent (and to outperform by a similar magnitude when the market rises); the coefficient for pure returns gives a similar result. Whether their returns are measured in pure or naïve form, stocks with high DDM values tend to behave procyclically.

Book-to-price ratio appears to be a better indicator of defensiveness. It has a regression coefficient of –0.10 in naïve form. In pure form, however, B/P is virtually unaffected by market movements; it is neither aggressive nor defensive. Apparently, B/P as naïvely measured picks up the effects of truly defensive value-related attributes such as high yield.

The value investor in search of a defensive posture in uncertain market environments should consider moving toward high yield: The regression coefficients for both naïve and pure returns to high yield indicate significantly negative market sensitivities. Stocks with high yields may be expected to move in a direction opposite to that of the overall market.[4]

A comparison of Figures 10-3 and 10-4 highlights some examples of the investment opportunities that may be uncovered by using pure returns. In Figure 10-3, naïve returns to small-cap and neglect are highly correlated; it would seem that investing in a small-cap portfolio over the sample period would have provided results similar to an investment in a portfolio whose stocks are chosen on the basis of analyst neglect.

Figure 10-4 reveals some major differences that lie beneath the surface of naïve returns. Pure returns to small-cap have behaved differently from—in fact, largely opposite to—pure returns to neglect, especially since 1986. While by the end of the period an investment in the former would have earned about 35 percentage points in excess of the market return (before transaction costs), an equivalent investment in the latter would have lost about 5 percentage points relative to the market. A hypothetical portfolio designed to exploit pure returns to both attributes could have aimed for superior returns by selecting small-cap stocks with a higher-than-average analyst following (a negative exposure to analyst neglect).

Purified returns, because of their generally lower volatility, may also be more consistent, hence more predictable, than naïve returns. Consider the naïve returns to one value attribute—high book-to-price ratio. Most banks and electric utility companies have high B/Ps, so these industries constitute a significant portion of many value portfolios. The returns to such a portfolio will be buffeted by industry-related events such as oil embargoes, which may affect utilities although having no fundamental bearing on value stocks in general. Returns to a value portfolio based on naïve high B/P will, therefore, be less predictable than those to a value portfolio based on a pure B/P measure that controls for spurious related variables such as industry concentration.

This is evident from Figure 10-5, which plots pure and naïve returns to high B/P over the 1978 to 1994 sample period. The return patterns are similar but not identical. Note, in particular, the divergence of returns over the 12-month period beginning in March 1979. Naïve B/P slid 6 percentage points, while pure B/P was flat. Not coincidentally, the crisis at the Three Mile Island nuclear plant occurred on March 28, 1979. Relative to the market, electric utilities plunged 24 percentage points over the next 12 months, dragging down returns to the naïve B/P measure.

FIGURE 10-5

Returns to Book/Price—1978–1994

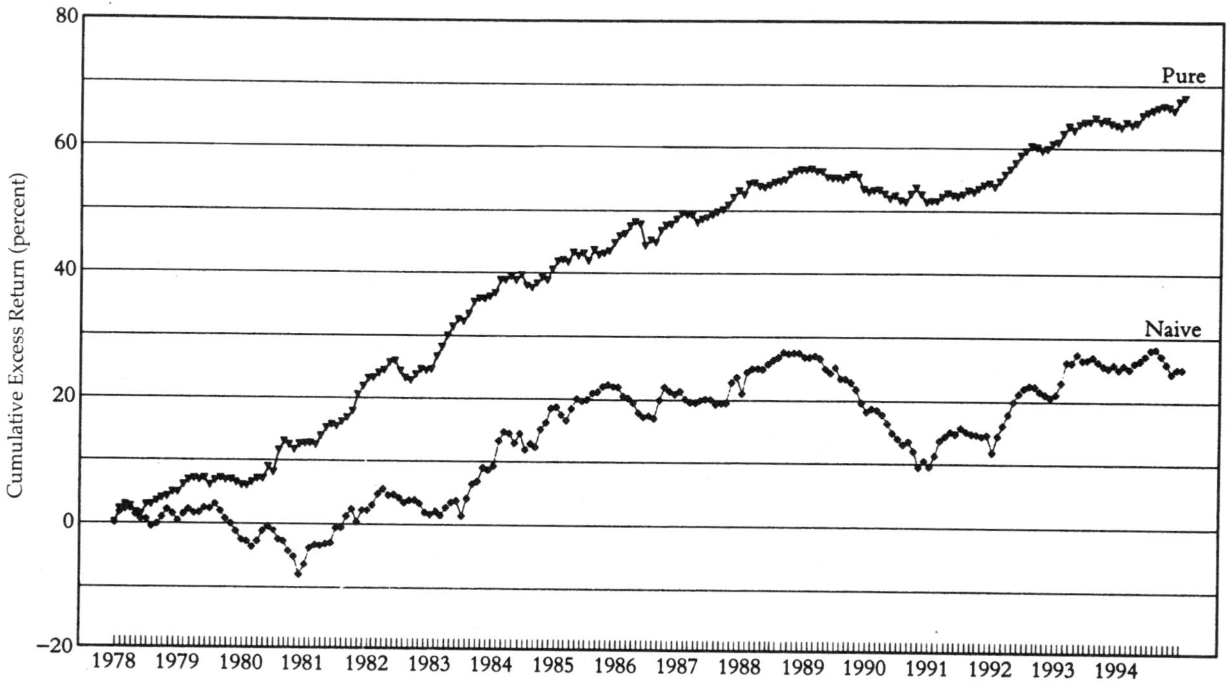

HIGH-DEFINITION MANAGEMENT

The behavior of the time series of pure attribute returns indicates that they are driven by a combination of economic fundamentals and the psychology of investors, the latter manifesting itself in such return anomalies as trend persistence and reversion to the mean [see Jacobs and Levy (1989b)]. That is, economic fundamentals, such as interest rates, industrial production, and inflation, can explain much, but by no means all, of systematic return variation. Psychology, including investors' tendencies to overreact, their desire to seek safety in numbers, and their selective memories, also plays a role in security pricing. What's more, the effects of different variables, fundamental and otherwise, vary across stocks with different attributes.

Figure 10-6 illustrates, as an example, the estimated effects of changes in various macroeconomic variables on the pure returns to small size (market capitalization). Pure returns to small size may be expected to be negative in the first 4 months following an unexpected increase in the BAA corporate rate and positive in the first month following an unexpected increase in industrial production. These responses are consistent with the capital constraints on small firms and their relatively greater fragility [see Jacobs and Levy (1989a)].

Such insights into the behavior of security prices can be used to forecast returns to pure attributes. These forecasts can, in turn, be used to manage a style-rotation strategy that seeks to capitalize on the variations in returns to different styles by rotating across stock attributes. Figure 10-7 "maps" the behavior of a portfolio based on such a strategy over the December 1984 to December 1994 period.[5]

The style allocations in Figure 10-7 are derived from BARRA's style analysis system, which is based on original work by Sharpe (1988). Style analysis typically regresses portfolio returns on returns to various style indexes, then allocates the portfolio's returns across styles according to the regression coefficients. A cross section created by drawing a line vertically through the chart represents the combination of style indexes that is best able to explain the portfolio's returns over the 3 years ending at that particular time.

For the 3 years ending in February 1985, for example, the portfolio was pretty much divided between medium- and small-capitalization value stocks, with a very minor allocation to medium-

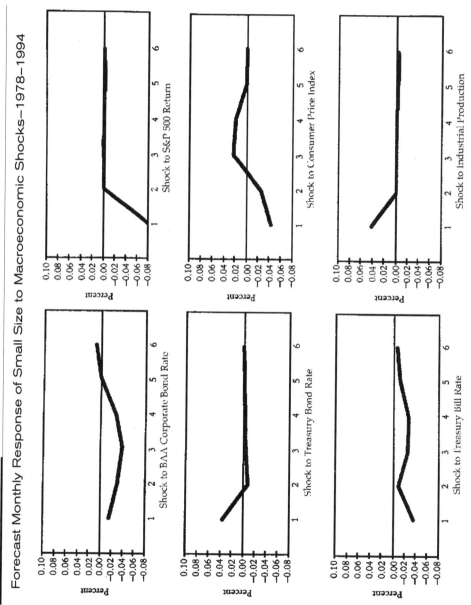

FIGURE 10-6

Forecast Monthly Response of Small Size to Macroeconomic Shocks–1978–1994

277

F I G U R E   10-7

Strategy Style Allocations for 3-Year Periods Ending
December 1984 to December 1994

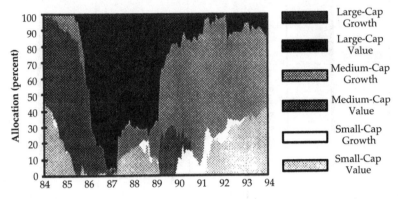

Data source: BARRA.

cap growth stocks. By December 1987, however, it was predominantly invested in large-cap growth stocks (67 percent), with about a 28 percent allocation to large-cap value and a minor (less than 5 percent) allocation to medium-cap value. By the end of the period illustrated, the portfolio's allocation had changed to include a preponderance of medium-cap growth stocks (about 44 percent), with significant exposures to small-cap value (38 percent) and large-cap value (15 percent), and less than 4 percent in small-cap growth.

Figure 10-8 displays the style rotation strategy's average allocations over the 1982 to 1994 period. Note that the strategy, over the whole period, displays no bias toward either growth or value; the allocations to each style total approximately 50 percent. The strategy did, however, overweight small- and medium-capitalization companies; large-, medium-, and small-cap allocations were 25, 51, and 24 percent, respectively. These allocations reflect the view that, over time, small companies are less efficiently priced than larger, more widely researched firms.

BENEFITS OF HIGH-DEFINITION STYLE

Figure 10-9 compares the actual performance of the style rotation portfolio with the performance of the market (as proxied by the

F I G U R E   10–8

Strategy's Average Style Allocations for 1982–1994 Period

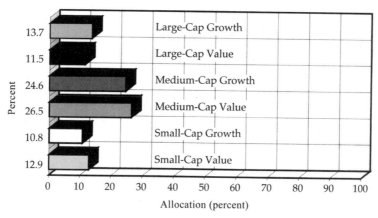

Data source: BARRA.

Russell 3000) over the 5-year period from January 1, 1990, through December 1994. Over this period, the strategy outperformed the market substantially.

Figure 10-9 also shows that the strategy outperformed a hypothetical index-based style rotation strategy. This hypothetical index-based portfolio provides a measure of the success of style rotation in general and of high-definition style rotation in particular. To construct this strategy, assets are allocated to Russell style indexes in accordance with the high-definition strategy's actual allocations at the beginning of each month.

Note that the *allocations* for this index-based style rotation strategy, being the same as the actual strategy allocations, reflect the same insights into pure attribute returns and market behavior. The investments themselves, however, are cruder than the actual strategy's to the extent that style indexes do not make the same fine distinctions between stock attributes.

Table 10-4 gives the annual returns, standard deviations, and Sharpe ratios for the two style rotation strategies and for the market.[6] The actual high-definition style rotation strategy outperformed the market by an annualized 5.45 percentage points (14.56 versus 9.11 percent). Its standard deviation of 16.68 percent, al-

FIGURE   10–9

Cumulative Returns to High-Definition Style Rotation–
1990–1994

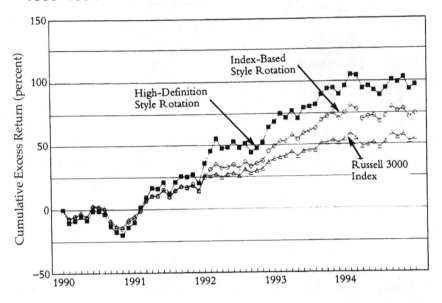

TABLE   10–4

Style Rotation Performance–1990–1994

Strategy	Annual Return (%)	Annual Standard Deviation (%)	Sharpe Ratio
High-definition style rotation	14.56	16.68	0.58
Index-based style rotation	11.78	12.82	0.54
Russell 3000 index	9.11	12.62	0.33

though substantially higher than that of the index-based style rotation strategy, or the market, was not so high as to outweigh the
gains in return from exploiting the nuances of high-definition style.
The Sharpe ratio of 0.58 compares favorably with the index-based
strategy's 0.54 and the market's 0.33.

The high-definition strategy's 5.45 percentage point return in excess of the market can be broken down into two components. One component reflects success in rotating across broad styles of stock and can be proxied by the 2.67 percentage point excess return of the index-based style rotation strategy. But rotation across broad styles accounts for slightly less than half of the high-definition strategy's outperformance. The strategy adds another 2.78 percentage points on top of the index-based rotational strategy's return.

Some might attribute this last degree of outperformance to stock selection, on the grounds that such return increments represent a manager's ability to select outperforming stocks within a particular style category. But the style rotation strategy makes no attempt at stock selection per se. What it does do (and over this period, at least, successfully) is to recognize the subtle distinctions of style that can add value. Exploiting the nuances within broad style definitions adds value relative to a strategy of rotating across traditional style indexes over time.

ENDNOTES

The authors thank Judith Kimball for her editorial assistance.

1. The large-cap growth stock index, the Russell 1000 Growth, and the large-cap value index, the Russell 1000 Value, roughly divide the market capitalization of the Russell 1000, the index representing the largest 1000 stocks in the Russell universe of 3000 stocks. The small-cap index consists of all stocks in the Russell 2000—the 2000 smallest stocks in the Russell 3000.

2. Data prior to January 1987 are based on a universe of 1500 securities. For a discussion of the methodology, see Jacobs and Levy (1988*a*).

3. The reductions in standard deviation also suggest that the use of multivariate regression has not introduced serious multicollinearity problems [see Kmenta (1971), pp. 380–391].

4. For an interpretation of why some value measures are procyclical and others countercyclical, see Jacobs and Levy (1988*b*).

5. Allocations are based on actual portfolio returns since January 1990 and on simulated returns prior to that date.

6. The *Sharpe ratio* is defined as the portfolio's return less the risk-free return, divided by the portfolio's standard deviation.

REFERENCES

Brinson, G. P., B. D. Singer, and G. L. Beebower. 1991. "Determinants of portfolio performance II: An update." *Financial Analysts Journal* 47 (3): 40–48.

Jacobs, B. I. and K. N. Levy. 1988*a*. "Disentangling equity return regularities: New insights and investment opportunities." *Financial Analysts Journal* 44 (3): 18–44.

———— and ————. 1988*b*. "On the value of 'value.'" *Financial Analysts Journal* 44 (4): 47–62.

———— and ————. 1989*a*. "Forecasting the size effect." *Financial Analysts Journal* 45 (3): 38–54.

———— and ————. 1989*b*. "The complexity of the stock market." *Journal of Portfolio Management* 16 (1): 19–27.

Kmenta, J. 1971. *Elements of Econometrics.* New York: Macmillan.

Sharpe, W. F. 1988. "Determining a fund's effective asset mix." *Investment Management Review*, November/December.

————. 1992. "Asset allocation: Management style and performance measurement." *Journal of Portfolio Management* 18 (2): 7–19.

Expanding Opportunities

Part 1 focused on security analysis in a complex market, and our method of disentangling return-predictor relationships in order to arrive at "pure" returns to numerous pricing attributes. Part 2 focused on the importance of taking a broad, unified approach to stock selection and on the proper implementation of analytical insights in the portfolio construction process. The chapters in Part 3 describe the construction of portfolios that take advantage of short selling and derivatives to expand investment opportunities and further enhance performance.

One of the major benefits of an investment approach that evaluates a broad universe of stocks is that it allows the manager to tailor portfolios to a wide variety of client needs. "Engineering Portfolios: A Unified Approach," in Part 2, discussed the construction of core portfolios tied to chosen benchmarks. As that chapter noted, it is also possible to engineer portfolios that are not tied to a specific capitalization-weighted benchmark. As in "High-Definition Style Rotation," for example, an insight-weighted strategy can be designed to take advantage of numerous precisely defined style attributes by shifting security weights in accordance with model insights as market and economic conditions evolve.

The ability to sell stocks short can benefit both security selection and portfolio construction. To begin with, it expands the list of implementable ideas from "winning" securities to both "winning" and "losing" securities. Portfolios that cannot sell short are restricted in their ability to incorporate insights about losing securities. For example, a long-only portfolio can sell a loser, if it happens to hold the stock, or it can refrain from buying a loser. But, in either case, the potential impact on portfolio return relative to benchmark is limited absolutely by the weight of the security in the benchmark.

Consider, for example, that the typical stock in a broad market index constitutes about 0.01 percent of that index's capitalization. Not holding the stock (or selling it from a portfolio) thus gives the portfolio a 0.01 percent underweighting in the stock, relative to the underlying benchmark index. This is unlikely to give the portfolio's return much of a boost over the underlying benchmark, even if the stock does end up performing poorly. Furthermore, it does not give the manager much leeway to distinguish between gradations of negative opinions; a stock about which the manager holds an extreme negative view is likely to have roughly the same underweight as a stock about which the manager holds only a mildly negative view.

Short-selling removes this constraint on underweighting. Significant portfolio underweights can be established as easily as portfolio overweights. The ability to short thus enhances the manager's ability to implement the insights gained from the analytical process.

The ability to short proves particularly attractive when overpriced stocks (potential candidates for short sale) are less efficiently priced than underpriced stocks (potential candidates for purchase). This may be the case in markets in which short-selling is not widespread. In such markets, prices tend to adjust to investor pessimism less efficiently than to investor optimism. Finding overpriced securities to sell short may prove a more rewarding endeavor than finding underpriced stocks to purchase.

Hedge funds and some investors have long recognized the potential benefits of shorting selected issues in certain market environments. Jacobs Levy Equity Management was among the first money managers to exploit the potentials of short-selling within the framework of disciplined, engineered equity management. Engineered long-short portfolios offer the benefits of shorting within the risk-controlled environment of quantitative portfolio construction.

Within this environment, short-selling can be used not only to enhance the implementation of insights from the stock selection process, but also to expand the profile of risk-return trade-offs available from the portfolio construction process. Through the use of short sales, for example, one can construct portfolios that balance equal dollar amounts and equal systematic risks long and short. The balanced long and short positions neutralize the portfolio's exposure to the underlying market. The portfolio incurs no systematic risk, nor does it earn the market return.

The long-short portfolio does earn the returns on the individual securities held long and sold short, and incurs the risks associated with the individual securities held long and sold short. Both the portfolio's overall risk and its overall return should benefit from the ability to sell short. The result is an improved trade-off between risk and return vis-à-vis a long-only portfolio.

As we have noted, a long-only portfolio's ability to underweight stocks is limited absolutely by the weights of the stocks in the underlying benchmark. Benchmark weights also constitute the starting point for determining the portfolio's residual risk (the risk that the portfolio's performance will diverge from that of the underlying benchmark). As departures from benchmark weights, whether over- or underweights, introduce residual risk, a long-only portfolio tends to converge toward the weights of the stocks in its underlying benchmark in order to control risk.

The need to converge toward benchmark weights necessarily limits the portfolio's potential for excess return, as returns in excess of the benchmark's accrue only to positions that are over- or underweighted relative to their weights in the benchmark. Consider, for example, a stock that constitutes 4 percent of the benchmark. If the portfolio likewise holds a 4 percent weight, the stock can contribute nothing to the portfolio's excess return; the portfolio weight of 4 percent is totally passive.

In a long-short portfolio in which securities' market sensitivities are balanced long and short, there is no benchmark risk, hence no need to converge to benchmark weights. This not only eliminates the constraint on security underweights, but frees up capital for investment in active positions. At the same time, the portfolio's risk, reflecting the security-specific risks of the constituent securities, can be controlled by offsetting the exposures of the securities held long and the exposures of the securities sold short.

An engineered long-short approach also offers added flexibility in asset allocation. With a market-neutral long-short portfolio such as the one discussed previously, portfolio risk and return are solely reflective of the individual stocks selected for inclusion; the return and risk of the market do not enter the picture. The portfolio can be "equitized" to capture market return and risk, however, by purchasing stock index futures. The equitized long-short portfolio will reflect the equity market's performance in addition to the performance of the long-short portfolio. Choice of other available derivatives can provide the long-short portfolio's return from security selection in combination with exposure to other asset classes.

Derivatives, including stock index futures, bond futures, and customized swaps, can be used in conjunction with long-short or long-only portfolios to "transport" the performance of specific managers to virtually any desired asset class. This is a relatively new area of investment engineering, but one that may revolutionize investing in much the same way that the growth in indexed and quantitative management has over the last few decades. The chapters in this last section provide a detailed look at these leading-edge ideas.

The first chapter, "Long/Short Equity Investing" (*Journal of Portfolio Management*, Fall 1993 and, in translation, *Security Analysts Journal of Japan*, March 1994) considers the basics of long-short portfolio construction and provides charts that illustrate the rewards. It also addresses some commonly voiced concerns, including the beliefs that shorting is "too risky" or even "un-American" and "bad for the economy." "20 Myths about Long-Short" (*Financial Analysts Journal*, September/October 1996) extends this discussion, drawing some vital distinctions between perceptions and realities and debunking some popular misconceptions about long-short.

"The Long and Short on Long-Short" (*Journal of Investing*, Spring 1997) covers the proper construction of market-neutral long-short portfolios, explains their benefits over long-only portfolios, and demonstrates how the investor can add back exposure to the equity market's return (and risk) via derivatives. In particular, this article emphasizes our findings on the importance of integrated portfolio construction. The real benefits of long-short arise from an integrated optimization that considers the candidates for purchase and the candidates for short sale simultaneously, and result in a single portfolio in which the contributions of the long positions and those of the short positions are inextricably linked.

"Long-Short Portfolio Management: An Integrated Approach" (*Journal of Portfolio Management*, Winter 1999), our latest article on long-short and winner of a *Journal of Portfolio Management* award for outstanding article, further develops our insights into the importance of portfolio integration. Here we extend the analysis from the integration of long and short positions within the portfolio to the integration of long and short positions together with desired benchmark holdings. Of special interest is the finding that imposing market neutrality with respect to an underlying benchmark is not necessarily optimal in terms of investment performance.

"Alpha Transport with Derivatives," which appeared in the special 25th Anniversary Issue of the *Journal of Portfolio Management* (May 1999), propels investment management into the space age, with derivatives providing the booster rockets. Using futures and swaps, one can separate the security selection decision from the asset allocation decision. The alpha from security selection, whether in a long-only or long-short context, can be transported to virtually any desired asset class. Alpha transport with derivatives has the potential to maximize both manager performance and investor returns.

CHAPTER 11

Long-Short Equity Investing*

Profit from both winners and losers.

The traditional focus of equity investing has been on finding stocks to buy long that offer opportunity for appreciation. Institutional investors have given little, if any, thought to incorporating short-selling into their equity strategies to capitalize on overvalued stocks. More recently, however, a growing number of investors have begun holding both long and short stock positions in their equity portfolios. Long-short equity investing presents many benefits and opportunities unavailable with traditional methods heretofore.

In our examination of the various aspects of long-short investing, we cover four topics: (1) the various ways in which long-short strategies can be implemented, (2) the theoretical and practical benefits afforded by long-short strategies, (3) the practical issues and concerns to which shorting gives rise, and (4) the positioning of long-short strategies in an overall investment program.

LONG-SHORT EQUITY STRATEGIES

Three ways of implementing long-short equity are the market-neutral, equitized, and hedge strategies. The *market-neutral* strategy holds longs and shorts in equal dollar balance at all times. This approach eliminates net equity market exposure, so the returns pro-

---

* Originally published in the *Journal of Portfolio Management* 20 (1): 52–63.

vided should not be affected by the market's direction. In effect, market risk is immunized. Profits are made from the performance spread between the names held long and the names sold short. These profits are in addition to the interest received on proceeds of the short sales.

The *equitized* strategy, in addition to holding stocks long and short in equal dollar balance, adds a permanent stock index futures overlay in an amount equal to the invested capital. Thus, the equitized portfolio has a full equity market exposure at all times. Once again, profits are made from the long-short spread in addition to the profits or losses resulting from the equity market's rise or fall.

The *hedge* strategy also holds stocks long and short in equal dollar balance but has a variable equity market exposure based on a market outlook. The variable exposure is achieved using stock index futures. Once again, profits are made from the long-short spread. These profits are in addition to the profits or losses attributable to the changing stock index futures position. This approach is similar to typical hedge fund management but is more structured. Hedge funds sell stocks short to hedge their long exposure partially and to benefit from declining stocks. This differs from investing the entire capital—both long and short—to benefit from the full long-short spread and obtaining the desired market exposure through stock index futures.

SOCIETAL ADVANTAGES OF SHORT-SELLING

There are advantages to security markets and society at large that arise from short-selling. Consider the view expressed by Hoffman (1935) over half a century ago (pp. 398–399):

> One of the most essential functions of organized markets is to reflect the composite opinion of all competent interests. To admit only opinion looking to higher prices is to provide a one-sided market. To bring together an open expression of both long and short opinion is to provide a two-sided market and . . . a better reflection of prevailing conditions will be shown in the price structure.

Moreover, according to Nobel laureate William F. Sharpe (1990), when shorts are precluded there results (p. 48) "a diminution in the efficiency with which risk can be allocated in an economy . . . [and] overall welfare may be lower."

EQUILIBRIUM MODELS, SHORT-SELLING, AND SECURITY PRICES

The leading equilibrium models, the Capital Asset Pricing Model (CAPM) and Arbitrage Pricing Theory (APT), both assume there are no restrictions to selling stock short. In the real world, however, several impediments to short-selling exist.

First, investors have less than full use of the cash proceeds of the short sales. Depending upon their clout with the broker, they may or may not receive an interest rebate on short sale proceeds. Beyond this, investors must also post cash or securities as collateral for the short positions.

Also, investors may not be able to short certain stocks, because the shares are not available for borrowing. The uptick rule, which prohibits shorting a stock when its price is falling, restricts the ability to sell short. Additionally, institutional investors have concerns about short-selling that have caused them to avoid it. We address these concerns later.

The impact of restricted shorting on market equilibrium depends on whether investors have uniform or divergent opinions about expected security returns. Four cases are shown in Figure 11-1. These cases differ according to whether short-selling is unrestricted or restricted and investor opinion uniform or diverse.

If all investors have a uniform opinion, they all hold the market portfolio of all assets. That is, each investor holds each asset in proportion to its outstanding market value; there is no short-selling. So restricting short-selling has no impact. In either case, the market portfolio is efficient, and the CAPM and APT hold.

If investors have diverse opinions and short-selling is unrestricted, the market portfolio is efficient, and the CAPM and APT hold. While investors hold unique portfolios, security prices are efficient because arbitrage is unimpeded, and security prices reflect the opinions of all investors. If short-selling is restricted, however, arbitrage is impeded and the opinion of pessimistic investors is not fully represented. As a consequence, the market portfolio is not efficient and the CAPM and APT do not hold. The real world resembles

F I G U R E   11–1

Impact of Divergence of Opinion and Restricted Shorting on Market Equilibrium

Investor Opinion

		Uniform	Diverse
Short-Selling	Unrestricted	Market Portfolio Efficient CAPM and APT Hold (No One Shorts)	Market Portfolio Efficient CAPM and APT Hold
	Restricted	Market Portfolio Efficient CAPM and APT Hold	Market Portfolio Not Efficient CAPM and APT Do Not Hold

this last case, because investor opinion is indeed diverse and short-selling is restricted.

Edward Miller (1987 and 1990) examines the impact of divergence of opinion and restricted shorting on security prices. He shows that restricted shorting leads to security overvaluation, because each stock's price is bid up by optimistic investors, while pessimists have difficulty shorting. As a consequence of this overvaluation, a shortfall arises between the returns anticipated by the optimistic investors and what they subsequently receive.

Further, a stock's overvaluation is greater, the more the divergence of opinion about it, because the most optimistic investors are even more extreme in their expectations. Hence, the wider the dispersion of opinion about a stock, the greater the overvaluation and eventual disappointment. An empirical measure of the divergence of opinion about a stock's prospects is the dispersion of security analysts' earnings estimates, often referred to as "earnings controversy." Jacobs and Levy (1988b) find that companies with higher earnings controversy experience lower subsequent returns, consistent with Miller's hypothesis.

Miller concludes that overvalued stocks are easier to find than undervalued stocks, and that investors should focus their efforts on avoiding holding overvalued stocks in their portfolios. He proposes replacing the standard notion of market efficiency with one of "bounded efficiency." In support of bounded efficiency, Jacobs and Levy (1988a, 1988b, and 1989) find substantial empirical evidence that the stock market is not fully efficient.

PRACTICAL BENEFITS OF LONG-SHORT INVESTING

Investors who are able to overcome short-selling restrictions and have the flexibility to invest both long and short can benefit from both winners and losers. For example, suppose you expect the Yankees to win their game and the Mets to lose theirs. If you wager on baseball, you would certainly not just bet on the Yankees to win. You would also "short" the Mets.

The same logic holds for stocks. Why bet on winners only? Why avail yourself of only half the opportunity? Profits can be earned from both winning and losing stocks simultaneously, earning the full performance spread.

Another benefit of long-short investing is that, potentially, shorts provide greater opportunities than longs. The search for undervalued stocks takes place in a crowded field because most traditional investors look only for undervalued stocks. Because of various short-selling impediments, relatively few investors search for overvalued stocks.

Also, security analysts issue far more buy than sell recommendations. Buy recommendations have much more commission-generating power than sells, because all customers are potential buyers, but only those customers having current holdings are potential sellers, and short-sellers are few in number.

Analysts may also be reluctant to express negative opinions. They need open lines of communication with company management, and in some cases management has cut them off and even threatened libel suits over negative opinions. Analysts have also been silenced by their own employers to protect their corporate finance business, especially their underwriting relationships. Some analysts have actually been fired for speaking too frankly.

FIGURE 11–2

Payoffs: Long Portfolio

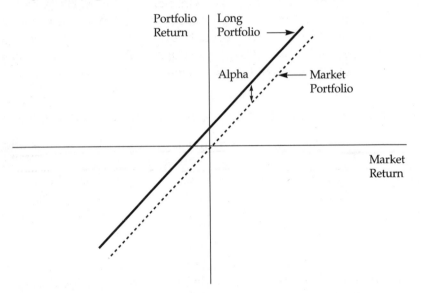

Shorting opportunities may also arise from management fraud, "window-dressing" negative information, or negligence, for which no parallel opportunity exists on the long side.

PORTFOLIO PAYOFF PATTERNS

Theoretical portfolio payoff patterns are illustrated in Figures 11-2 to 11-6 for separate long and short portfolios (the two building blocks of long-short portfolios), market-neutral portfolios, equitized portfolios with a permanent futures overlay, and hedge portfolios with a variable futures position.

In Figure 11-2, a long portfolio's return is graphed against the stock market's return. The market portfolio itself is shown as a 45-degree upward-sloped dashed line intersecting the origin. The long portfolio is parallel to the market portfolio line but higher by the assumed amount of value-added, or alpha.

A short portfolio's return is graphed in Figure 11-3. A baseline short market portfolio is a 45-degree downward-sloped dashed line

F I G U R E   11–3

Payoffs: Short Portfolio

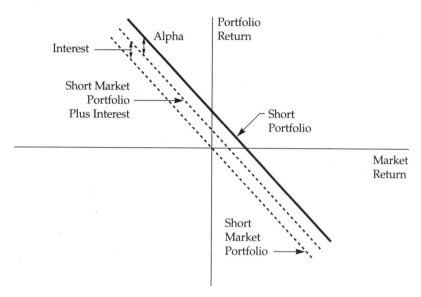

intersecting the origin. The short market portfolio plus interest is parallel to the baseline, but higher by the amount of interest assumed. The short portfolio is also parallel, but higher than the baseline by the sum of interest plus alpha.

A market-neutral portfolio's return, shown in Figure 11-4, is derived from the long and short portfolio payoff patterns shown in the previous figures. The market-neutral portfolio's payoff line is horizontal at a level above the origin by twice the level of alpha plus interest. The implicit assumption is that the full amount of capital is invested both long and short, so alpha is earned from both the long and short sides, providing a "double alpha."[1]

For an equitized portfolio (Figure 11-5), the market portfolio itself is shown as a 45-degree upward-sloped dashed line intersecting the origin. The equitized portfolio is parallel to the market portfolio line, but higher by twice alpha. Again, the implicit assumption is that the capital is invested both long and short, so alpha is earned from both the long and short sides.

F I G U R E   11–4

Payoffs: Market-Neutral Portfolio

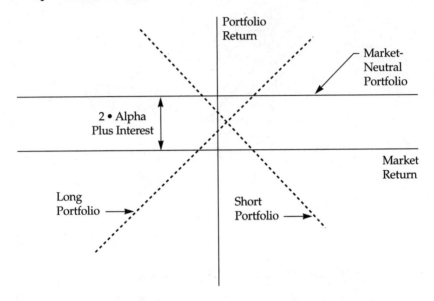

F I G U R E   11–5

Payoffs: Equitized Portfolio

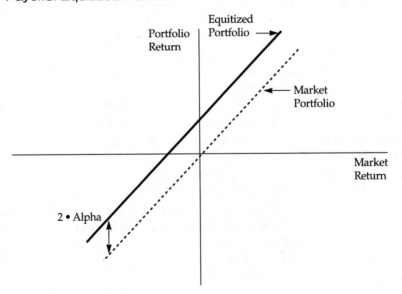

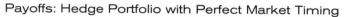

FIGURE 11–6

Payoffs: Hedge Portfolio with Perfect Market Timing

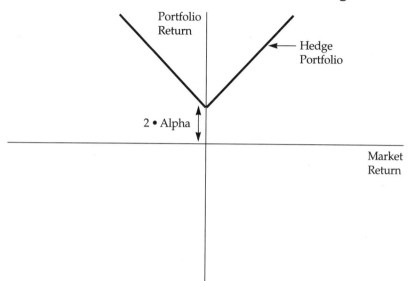

The hedge portfolio illustration (Figure 11-6) assumes perfect market timing. That is, a 100 percent long futures position is established when the market's return is positive, and a 100 percent short position is established when the market's return is negative. The hedge portfolio line is an upward-sloping 45-degree line in the northeast quadrant intersecting the vertical axis at a height of twice alpha, the mirror image of the line in the northwest quadrant. Again, capital is invested both long and short, so alpha is earned from both the long and short sides.

LONG-SHORT MECHANICS AND RETURNS[2]

Under Federal Reserve Board regulations, shorts must be housed in a margin account, which requires custody at a brokerage firm. Custodians are referred to as "prime brokers," because they clear all trades and arrange to borrow all stock, whatever brokerage firms execute the trades.

Typically, 90 percent of the capital is used to purchase attractive stocks and to sell short unattractive stocks. The securities purchased are delivered to the prime broker and serve as collateral for the shorts. The prime broker also arranges for the borrowing of the unattractive securities that the manager wants to sell short. These shares may come from the broker's inventory of shares held in street name or may be borrowed by the broker from a stock lender. The short sale of these securities results in cash proceeds, which are posted as collateral with the stock lender to provide security for the borrowed shares.

Once these transactions settle, the remaining 10 percent of capital is retained as a liquidity buffer at the prime broker to meet the daily marks to market on the short positions. This liquidity buffer is interest-earning.

The collateral posted with the stock lender is adjusted daily to reflect the changing value of the shorts. For example, if the shorts rise in price, the mark to market is negative, and the lending institution is provided additional capital to remain fully collateralized. If the shorts fall in price, the mark to market is positive, and the lending institution releases capital because it is overcollateralized. Also, the short-seller must reimburse the stock lender for any dividends paid on the securities borrowed.

The cash proceeds of the short sales, which have been posted as collateral with the securities lender, earn interest. The lender receives a small portion of this interest as a securities lending fee, the prime broker retains a portion to cover expenses and provide a profit, and the balance is earned by the investor. The actual split of interest is negotiable. Typically, the institutional short-seller receives interest at approximately a Treasury bill rate. This interest is referred to as "short rebate."

The market-neutral strategy's return depends solely on the performance spread between the long and short portfolios and the interest rate received. The return is independent of the market's direction. Because the market-neutral strategy produces approximately a Treasury bill rate of return when there is no performance spread between the longs and shorts, an appropriate benchmark for the strategy is the Treasury bill rate.

Figure 11-7 is a scatterplot of our live monthly market-neutral returns versus the monthly returns of the S&P 500 index. It can be

F I G U R E   11–7

Market-Neutral versus S&P 500 Monthly Returns—June
1990–December 1992

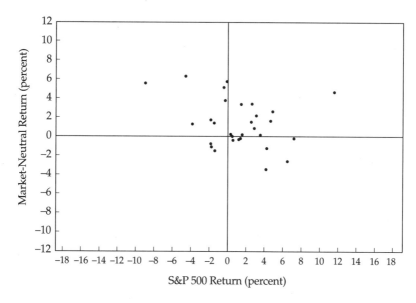

seen that this market-neutral strategy has lived up to its name, because its returns have been uncorrelated with the stock market.

The mechanics for the equitized strategy are identical to those
of market-neutral with the addition of a stock index futures overlay.
S&P 500 futures are purchased in an amount equal to the capital to
"equitize" the long-short portfolio. Buying futures requires the
posting of margin, usually in the form of Treasury bills. This reduces the liquidity buffer, but because the daily marks to market on
the long futures tend to offset the daily marks on the short portfolio,
the smaller buffer remains adequate.

S&P 500 futures contracts are priced so that they provide approximately the return of the S&P 500 index including dividends,
less the cost of carry at about a Treasury bill rate. The short rebate interest earned plus interest earned on the Treasury bill margin and liquidity buffer, in conjunction with the price change on the S&P 500
futures, should provide a return similar to that of the S&P 500 index.

FIGURE 11-8

Equitized versus S&P 500 Monthly Returns—June
1990–December 1992

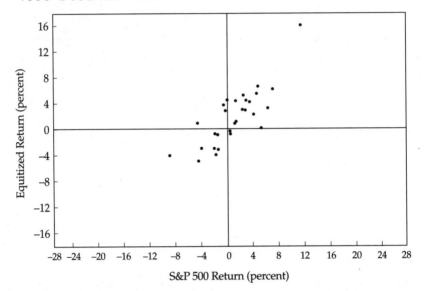

S&P 500 Return (percent)

The value-added is the same as that achieved in the market-neutral strategy, but the futures overlay "transports" the long-short spread to the S&P 500 benchmark. In the same way, bond futures can be used to transport the long-short value-added to a bond index, and so forth.

Because the equitized strategy produces approximately an S&P 500 return when there is no performance spread between the longs and shorts, an appropriate benchmark for the strategy is the S&P 500 index. Figure 11-8 is a scatterplot of our live monthly equitized returns versus the monthly returns of the S&P 500 index. As expected, the strategy's returns are highly correlated with the stock market.

THEORETICAL TRACKING ERROR

In addition to return considerations, it is instructive to consider the theoretical tracking error of long-short portfolios relative to their benchmarks. Assume the standard deviation of the long portfolio's alpha, or value-added, is 4 percent, and the short portfolio alpha's

What is SD of
Short portfolios?

standard deviation is also 4 percent. Consider two cases, which are dependent on the correlation between the long and short portfolios' values-added. First, assume the correlation is zero. In this case, the standard deviation of the market-neutral (or equitized) portfolio's value-added is the square root of 2 times 4 percent, or 5.7 percent.

Second, assume the correlation of the long and the short portfolios' values-added is 1. In this case, the standard deviation of the market-neutral (or equitized) portfolio's value-added is twice 4 percent, or 8 percent. It is a reasonable assumption that the correlation lies somewhere between zero and 1, in which case the tracking error standard deviation lies between 5.7 and 8 percent.

ADVANTAGES OF THE MARKET-NEUTRAL STRATEGY OVER LONG MANAGER PLUS SHORT MANAGER

Using a market-neutral strategy rather than separate long and short managers has several advantages. The market-neutral strategy co-ordinates the names held long and short to maximize profits while controlling risk. It avoids the situation where one manager is long a stock while the other manager is short the same stock, thereby wasting assets. It also precludes excessive risks arising, for example, when one manager is buying oil stocks while the other is shorting airlines, thereby magnifying the oil price risk.

A market-neutral strategy also enables the capital to work twice as hard as with separate long and short managers. Each dollar of capital is invested both long and short, with the longs collateralizing the shorts. With separate long and short managers and $1 of capital, each would have only 50 cents of capital to invest.

Also, a single manager fee structure is likely more economical than that for two managers. This is especially true in a performance fee setting. A market-neutral manager earns a performance fee only if the entire strategy adds value. With separate managers, if either is ahead, an incentive fee must be paid, even if the combined strategy is behind.

ADVANTAGES OF THE EQUITIZED STRATEGY OVER TRADITIONAL LONG EQUITY MANAGEMENT

The equitized strategy has several advantages over traditional long equity management. It can profit from both winners and losers. Why tear *The Wall Street Journal* in half, and focus solely on good

news stories? Bad news stories present potentially greater opportunity. Also, investment insights can be levered without any borrowing, resulting in a double alpha. Of course the key to good
performance is good insight.

The enhanced flexibility afforded by including longs and
shorts in a portfolio provides greater latitude to implement investment ideas. This flexibility makes it more likely that investment insights will produce profits, and more profits at that. Importantly,
overvalued companies and industries may be underweighted without the usual constraints associated with long equity management.

For example, the automobile industry today is 2 percent of the
capitalization weight of the S&P 500 index. A traditional long manager, bullish on automobiles, can overweight the industry as much
as desired but can underweight the industry by no more than 2 percent. By shorting when bearish, the manager can underweight companies and industries beyond the usual constraints present in long
equity management. The portfolio manager's flexibility to overweight and underweight becomes symmetric.

Managers investing long and short can focus solely on market
sectors in which the most significant misvaluations exist, ignoring
fairly priced sectors, without inducing any risk. For example, if all
health care stocks are fairly priced, there is no need to hold any long
or short, nor any potential benefit. In this way, assets are not
wasted, yet the full market exposure to health care stocks is obtained with the futures overlay.

A traditional long manager, however, would likely include
some fairly priced, or even overpriced, health care stocks in the
portfolio to avoid a substantial industry underweight. By holding
some stocks in the health care sector, the long manager reduces risk
versus the market benchmark, although there are no perceived
profit opportunities.

Also, managers investing long and short can target desired
bets and reduce incidental bets better than traditional long managers. For example, a traditional long manager emphasizing low-
price/earnings stocks will wind up with incidental bets on related
attributes, such as high dividend yield, and on low-P/E industries,
such as utilities. But in a long-short portfolio, related attributes and
industries can be neutralized more effectively, creating a "pure"
low-P/E bet without incidental biases.

IMPLEMENTATION OF LONG-SHORT STRATEGIES: QUANTITATIVE VERSUS JUDGMENTAL

Any active equity management style can be implemented in a long-short mode. To date, however, most long-short managers are quantitative rather than judgmental in their investment approach. Quantitative models generally can be applied to a large universe of stocks, providing the potential to identify a large long-short spread. Shorts naturally fall out of a quantitative process as the lowest-ranked stocks. Quantitative styles are amenable to simulation and backtesting, the results of which are helpful in both developing and marketing a novel investment approach. Also, most quantitative managers use structured portfolio construction methods, which are important to control risk taking in a long-short portfolio.

In contrast, judgmental approaches rely generally on in-depth company analyses, but of a limited universe of stocks, thereby limiting the range of opportunities and potentially reducing the performance spread. Also, traditional security analysts are generally not accustomed to recommending stocks to sell short. Judgmental analysis, however, should help detect fraud, negligence, and financial window dressing, which can provide exceptional short sale opportunities.

IMPLEMENTATION OF LONG-SHORT STRATEGIES: PORTFOLIO CONSTRUCTION ALTERNATIVES

Long-short managers use a few primary portfolio construction techniques to control risk. Simplest to implement is "pairs trading," which identifies mispriced pairs of stocks having returns likely to be highly correlated. For example, if Ford Motor Company and General Motors Corporation are identified as mispriced relative to each other, the underpriced stock can be bought and the overpriced one sold short.

Some managers neutralize industry exposures by investing the same percentage of capital both long and short within each industry. A few will even restrict their attention to a single industry that they know well. In this case, all stocks held long and sold short will be in the same industry. Others neutralize industries and common factors such as beta or average company size. Some managers coordinate long and short portfolio characteristics statistically in order to control risk taking, but are not necessarily characteristic- or industry-neutral, hence the term "statistical arbitrage."

PRACTICAL ISSUES AND CONCERNS

A long-short strategy gives rise to a variety of issues not encountered in traditional long management. We will discuss issues relating to shorting, trading, custody, legality, and morality.

Shorting Issues

Investors sometimes ask whether short-selling is an appropriate activity for those with long-term horizons. Dedicated short managers must fight an uphill battle because of the stock market's long-term upward trend. They are short the equity risk premium that the market provides for bearing equity risk. Market-neutral strategies, having no net exposure to the market, neither pay nor earn the equity risk premium. Equitized strategies are fully exposed to the market and earn the equity risk premium, similar to traditional long investing. Hedge strategies are opportunistic with respect to the equity risk premium. Thus, short-selling can be incorporated as part of a long-term equity program to meet differing investment objectives.

Another concern is that a rising market can force the covering of shorts as losses mount. Those who engage solely in short-selling, without offsetting long positions, can indeed find themselves forced to cover as the general market rises and their shorts go against them. In a long-short approach, however, as the market rises, the losses on the shorts are offset by gains on the longs.

Another common concern regards the unlimited liability of a short position. Although one cannot lose more than the original capital invested in a long position, the potential loss on a short position is, in theory, unlimited because the price of a stock can rise without bound. Long-short managers generally mitigate this risk by holding widely diversified portfolios—with many stocks and small positions in each—and by covering their shorts as position sizes increase.

Another often-asked question is whether the market can accommodate the growing volume of shorting. This is a question of market depth. The current market capitalization of the U.S. stock market is approximately $4.4 trillion. The current volume of short open interest is approximately $45 billion, or about 1 percent of the market capitalization of stocks held long. The amount of shorts outstanding remains small relative to the depth of the stock market.

Not all stocks can be borrowed easily, and brokers maintain a list of "hard-to-borrow" names. The lack of supply on these hard-to-borrow names is much less of an impediment for quantitative managers, because they can select from a broad universe of stocks and have the flexibility to substitute other stocks with similar characteristics. Hard-to-borrow names can pose a serious problem, however, for dedicated short-sellers. They often specialize in illiquid names and make concentrated bets, such as on fraud situations, for which no near-substitutes exist.

Shorting a name that is hard to borrow presents the risk of being forced to cover the short if the lender demands the return of the security. This can occur, for instance, if the lender simply decides to sell the security and so needs it back. If the prime broker cannot locate an alternative lender, the result is a "buy-in," or forced cover. Our experience has been that buy-ins are rare, especially for typical institutional quality stocks.

A "short squeeze" is a deliberate attempt by some investors to squeeze the short-seller by reducing the lendable supply of a stock while simultaneously pushing the stock's price higher through purchases. A successful short squeeze can force the short-seller to cover at inflated prices. This is more a concern for dedicated short-sellers than for long-short managers, because the latter generally have many small positions and focus on larger institutional names for which stock lending and share price are more difficult to manipulate.

Trading Issues

Managing long-short strategies entails some special trading considerations. For instance, Securities and Exchange Commission (SEC) Rule 10a-1 regarding short sales, adopted in 1938, requires that exchange-listed securities be sold short only on an uptick (higher price than the last trade) or a zero-plus tick (same price as the last trade, but higher than the last trade at a different price). We find that the uptick rule is less constraining for patient trading styles.

Also, managing two interrelated portfolios requires substantial care in execution and rebalancing to maintain long-short dollar balance. Controlling transaction costs is especially important because turnover runs about twice that of traditional long management. Some new electronic trading systems are especially conducive to long-short management, because they are inexpensive and allow simultaneous execution of large programs with dollar trading constraints to maintain long-short dollar balance.

Custody Issues

Federal Reserve regulations require short-selling in a margin account, necessitating custody at a prime broker. Since assets are custodied away from the master trust bank, safety and soundness issues must be addressed, and due diligence is required.

Also, while some master trustees can account for shorts and maintain a set of books, at this time others cannot. Even when a master trustee can account for shorts, some plan sponsors rely on a reconciliation of the prime broker's accounting records with the manager's to avoid paying the master trustee for a triplicate set of books.

Legal Issues

Long-short management gives rise to two fundamental legal issues. One is whether these strategies are prudent for ERISA plans, public employee retirement systems, endowments, and foundations. Several institutional investors have concluded that these strategies are prudent and risk-diversifying for the overall plan.

The other issue is whether shorting gives rise to unrelated business taxable income (UBTI). In 1988, the Internal Revenue Service issued a private letter ruling exempting long-short strategies used by one large institutional investor from UBTI.[3] In 1992, the IRS approved regulations specifically exempting swaps, where the tax issues are similar. The IRS has not commented any further, despite the growing use of long-short and hedge strategies by tax-exempt investors. Nonetheless, this is not a settled issue, and tax counsel should be consulted.

Morality Issues

The use of shorting raises moral issues for some investors. Although selling something that one does not own may appear to be immoral, this is common commercial practice. Farmers sell wheat before it is grown, and home builders sell houses before they are built.

Some fear that short-selling destabilizes security prices. While this might have been possible prior to the uptick rule and SEC oversight, today most agree that short-selling stabilizes prices by checking speculative bubbles, equilibrating day-to-day supply and demand, and increasing liquidity.

Others charge that short-selling depresses prices. During the collapse of the Dutch East India Company stock bubble in the year 1610, some claimed that short-selling hurt "widows and orphans." Because shorting allows countervailing negative opinion to balance positive opinion, however, prices better reflect the consensus opinion of all investors, thereby providing a better indication of value.

Short-sellers are often accused of rumor-mongering. While it is sometimes alleged that dedicated short-sellers spread unsubstantiated rumors about their target companies, long-short managers are not adversarial. They go long and short various stocks to exploit subtle mispricings, not because they want or expect a particular company to go bankrupt.

Some suggest short-selling is antimanagement or anti-American. But shorting actually promotes all-American values by checking management abuses and improving market efficiency and social welfare.

WHAT ASSET CLASS IS LONG-SHORT?

The long-short strategies can be categorized by asset class, using risk-reward comparisons, so that their fit in an overall investment program becomes apparent.

Figure 11-9 displays experienced risk, measured by annualized standard deviation, and annualized return for our market-neutral, equitized, and hedge strategies and their respective benchmarks from the inception of live performance in June 1990 through December 1992.

The market-neutral strategy added substantial value over Treasury bills, and its risk was between that of Treasury bills and the S&P

Risk-Return Comparisons—Long-Short Strategies versus
Benchmarks—June 1990–December 1992

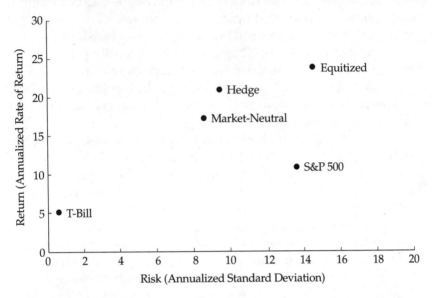

Note: Live hedge returns commence 10/91.

500. The equitized strategy added roughly the same value versus the
S&P 500 as the market-neutral strategy did versus Treasury bills. The
stock index futures overlay transported the long-short spread to the
stock market. The equitized strategy had about the same risk as the
S&P 500. The hedge strategy, in terms of risk and reward, was between the market-neutral and equitized strategies.

The market-neutral strategy has an absolute return objective,
because its returns are not correlated with those of the stock market.
It has about half the volatility of the market and is obviously riskier
than cash. We categorize market-neutral as an "alternative equity."

The equitized strategy has a relative return objective, because
its returns are highly correlated with those of the stock market.
While it has about the same volatility as the market, its tracking error will generally be higher than that of traditional long strategies.
We categorize equitized as "flexible equity," because it allows more
flexible portfolio management than traditional long investing.

The hedge strategy can arguably be assigned an absolute or a relative return objective, because its returns are somewhat correlated with the stock market. Its volatility is between that of the market-neutral and equitized strategies. We categorize hedge as an "alternative equity."

CONCLUDING REMARKS

The institutional acceptance of long-short strategies is increasing rapidly, as indicated in White (1991) and Williams (1991). Current estimates of long-short assets under management in U.S. equities range from $3 to $5 billion. Long-short strategies merit serious consideration as part of an overall investment program.

ENDNOTES

This article is based on a presentation at the Association for Investment Management and Research conference entitled "The CAPM Controversy: Policy and Strategy Implications for Investment Management," held in New York in March 1993.

1. In practice, the Federal Reserve Board's Regulation T margin requirements and the 10 percent cash reserve discussed in the mechanics section constrain the maximum alpha to a factor of 1.8 [see Jacobs and Levy (1993b)].
2. For a graphical depiction of long-short mechanics, see Jacobs and Levy (1993a).
3. IRS private letter ruling 8832052 to The Common Fund, May 18, 1988.

REFERENCES

Hoffman, G. Wright. 1935. "Short selling." In *The Security Markets*, A. L. Bernheim and M. G. Schneider, eds. New York: Twentieth Century Fund, Inc., pp. 356–401.

Jacobs, Bruce I. and Kenneth N. Levy. 1988a. "Calendar anomalies: Abnormal returns at calendar turning points." *Financial Analysts Journal* 44 (6): 28–39.

——— and ———. 1988b. "Disentangling equity return regularities: New insights and investment opportunities." *Financial Analysts Journal* 44 (3): 18–43.

——— and ———. 1989. "The complexity of the stock market." *Journal of Portfolio Management* 16 (1): 19–27.

——— and ———. 1993a. "A long-plus-short market neutral strategy." In *The CAPM Controversy: Policy and Strategy Implications for Investment Management*. Charlottesville, Virginia: Association for Investment Management and Research.

——— and ———. 1993b. "The generality of long-short equitized strategies: A correction." *Financial Analysts Journal* 49 (2): 22.

Miller, Edward M. 1987. "Bounded efficient markets: A new wrinkle to the EMH." *Journal of Portfolio Management* 13 (4): 4–13.

———. 1990. "Divergence of opinion, short selling, and the role of the marginal investor." In *Managing Institutional Assets*, F. J. Fabozzi, ed. New York: Harper & Row.

Sharpe, William F. 1990. "Capital asset prices with and without negative holdings." In *The Founders of Modern Finance: Their Prize-Winning Concepts and 1990 Nobel Lectures*. Charlottesville, Virginia: The Research Foundation of the Institute of Chartered Financial Analysts.

White, James A. 1991. "How Jacobs and Levy crunch stocks for buying and selling." *The Wall Street Journal*, March 20, p. C1.

Williams, Terry. 1991. "Market neutral funds gain fans." *Pensions & Investments*, September 16, p. 3.

20 Myths About Long-Short*

Distinguishing between fact and fiction.

Most institutional investors focus on the management of long port-folios and, in that context, the selection of "winning" securities. The short sale of securities has generally been confined to *alternative* invest-ing, including hedge funds and dedicated shorts, where the focus is on identifying "losing" securities. Combining long and short holdings of approximately equal value and systematic risk into a single portfolio in an institutional setting dates only to the late 1980s.

Although the mechanics and merits of long-short portfolio construction have since become the subject of lively debate, the pro-cedure still seems to elude the intuitive grasp of many investors.[1] Perhaps confusion arises because investors tend to view long-short through the lens of long-only or short-only management. Just as the wrong pair of glasses will distort one's vision of the world, using a long-only or short-only perspective has resulted in some misperceptions about the implementation and goals of long-short investing.

Long-short investing is fundamentally different from conven-tional investing in some important aspects. Conventional invest-ment perspectives on portfolio construction, risk and return, implementation costs, performance measurement, asset class allo-cation, and plan structure can thus result in a distorted image when

---

* Originally published in *Financial Analysts Journal* 52 (5): 81–85.

applied to long-short strategies. Readjusting those perspectives dispels some of the more common myths surrounding long-short investing.

Myth 1. A 100 percent short position against longs does not make as much sense as selling short only those stocks with negative expected returns.

Provided expected security returns are symmetrically distributed around the underlying market return, there will be as many unattractive securities for short sale as attractive undervalued securities for purchase. Balancing equal dollar amounts and equal market sensitivities, long and short, takes full advantage of this spread of returns. At the same time, it neutralizes underlying market return and risk (which can be added back, if desired, by purchasing stock index futures). The securities return on the basic long-short portfolio is reflective solely of the manager's skill at stock selection. In effect, long-short construction separates the security selection return from the underlying equity asset class return.

Myth 2. A long-short portfolio consists of two portfolios—one long and one short.

Although a long-short portfolio may be considered two portfolios from an accounting perspective, the proper construction process for a long-short portfolio requires integrated optimization of long and short positions together. Integrated optimization allows the portfolio the flexibility to use offsetting positions on long and short sides to enhance portfolio return and control risk. Selection of the securities to be held long is determined simultaneously with the selection of securities to be sold short. The result from an investment perspective is a single long-short portfolio. Neither the long nor the short position can be considered a separate portfolio because neither would be held in the absence of the other.

Myth 3. Long-short investing has no inherent advantage over long-only investing except to the extent that the correlation between the excess returns on the long and the short positions is less than 1.

A long-only portfolio manager can purchase securities on margin to obtain the financial leverage effects of a long-short strategy and can sell short stock index futures to establish return neutrality to underlying market movements. Furthermore, long-only and long-short managers both have the freedom to select names from the same universe of securities. The long-only portfolio, however, can control risk relative to the underlying index only by converging toward the weightings of the names in the index; underlying index weights are constraining. The long-short portfolio is emancipated from underlying index weights; sensitivity to the underlying index is neutralized via the offsetting long and short positions. Furthermore, the long-only portfolio's ability to underweight a security is limited by the security's weight in the index. With shorting, the long-short portfolio can underweight a security by as much as investment insight (and risk considerations) dictates. Lessening of constraints affords the long-short portfolio greater leeway in the pursuit of return and control of risk, which is the real advantage long-short offers over long-only investing. The diversification benefit of a less-than-1 correlation between long and short excess returns will be the sole benefit provided only when the long-short portfolio is constructed suboptimally as two index-constrained portfolios—one long and one short, each optimized to have the same index-relative residual risk and return as the long-only portfolio.[2] In this restrictive case, long-short investing offers no flexibility benefits over long-only.

Myth 4. The performance of a long-short portfolio can be measured as the excess return of the longs and the excess return of the shorts relative to an underlying market index.

Within the context of integrated optimization, long and short "alphas" are meaningless (as is their correlation) because neither the long nor the short position is determined with regard to the weightings in any particular index. Rather, the constituent securities of an integrated optimization represent a single portfolio, one that is not constrained by underlying index weights. The performance of this integrated long-short portfolio can be measured as the weighted return on the constituent securities—those held long and those sold short—or, in shorthand, as the spread between the long and short returns.

Myth 5. A long-short portfolio has no underlying index.

A long-short portfolio is constructed to be "neutral" to some selected market index. That index defines the securities' market sensitivities, without which market neutrality cannot be measured. An underlying index is thus necessary for long-short construction. As noted above, however, the index weights are not constraining.

Myth 6. Constraints on underweighting do not have a material effect on long-only portfolio results.

A security with a median market capitalization has a weighting of approximately 0.01 percent of the market's capitalization. The maximum active underweight of that security in a long-only portfolio is 0.01 percent, achieved by not holding any shares of the security. Placing a similar limit on the maximum active overweight would be equivalent to saying the long-only manager could hold, at most, a 0.02 percent position in the stock (a 0.01 percent overweighting) no matter how appetizing its expected return. Long-short portfolios have no such constraints on underweighting.

Myth 7. A long-short portfolio's advantage over the residual risk-return provided by a long-only portfolio relies on the existence of larger inefficiencies on the short side of the market.

If short selling is restricted, there are reasons to believe that shorting stocks can offer more opportunity than buying stocks. An advantage may arise because restrictions on short-selling do not permit investor pessimism to be fully represented in prices; pessimism thus cannot counterbalance investor optimism. If so, the shorts in a long-short portfolio may offer additional advantages beyond those related to the flexibility inherent in the long-short structure. Greater inefficiency on the short side, however, is not a necessary condition for long-short investing to offer benefits compared with the residual risk-return offered by long-only investing; these benefits stem from the enhanced flexibility of long-short investing.

Myth 8. Long-short is a separate asset class and should be treated as such in any asset allocation analysis.

Long-short is a portfolio construction technique. The resultant portfolio will belong to a conventional asset class. The long-short manager or client, however, enjoys some flexibility in deciding which asset class, because the long-short spread—the return from security selection—can be "transported" to various asset classes. When the long-short portfolio takes a market-neutral form, the long-short spread comes on top of a cash return (the interest received on the proceeds from the short sales). In this case, portfolio performance is appropriately measured as the manager's ability to enhance (at the cost of added risk) the cash return. Alternatively, the long-short manager can offer, or the client initiate, a position in stock index futures combined with a market-neutral portfolio. This equitized portfolio will offer the long-short spread from security selection on top of the equity market return from the futures position. In this case, portfolio performance is properly measured relative to the equity index underlying the futures. Any asset allocation analyses should thus treat a market-neutral long-short portfolio as cash and an equitized long-short portfolio as equity.

Myth 9. Overall market movements have no effect on long-short portfolios.

Although long-short construction eliminates the portfolio's exposure to market risk and return, market price movements will likely affect the values of long and short positions and may require trading activity. Consider, as an example, a $100 initial investment in a market-neutral long-short portfolio. The manager buys $90 worth of securities and sells short an equivalent amount; the proceeds of the short sales are posted with the securities' lenders. The manager seeks to retain in cash 10 percent of the capital ($10 at the outset, in this case) as a liquidity buffer to meet marks to market on the short positions. Now, assume the market rises and both longs and shorts rise 5 percent. The long positions are now worth $94.50, and the short positions are also worth $94.50. The overall portfolio has gained $4.50 on the longs and lost $4.50 on the shorts, so its net capital is still $100; it is still well above Regulation T minimum margin requirements. An additional $4.50, however, must be posted with the lenders of the securities sold short to collateralize fully the increased value of their shares. Paying $4.50 out of the liquidity buffer reduces it to $5.50. To restore the liquidity buffer to 10 percent of the $100 capital, the manager will need to sell $4.50 worth of long positions (and cover an equal amount of short positions). Thus, overall market movements may have implications for the implementation of long-short portfolios.

Myth 10. A market crash is the worst-case scenario.

As the previous example illustrates, market rallies can pose mechanical problems for long-short managers because of the effects of marks to market on portfolio cash positions (and, in extreme and unlikely circumstances, the potential for margin violations). A market crash, however, although it will likely result in a substantial loss on the long positions, will also likely result in a substantial gain on the short positions. Furthermore, marks to market on the shorts will be in the account's favor. Consider, for example, the effects on our $90/$90/$10 portfolio of a crash such as occurred on Black Monday in 1987, when the market fell by about 20 percent. Assuming the longs and shorts move in line, the value of the long positions will decline from $90 to $72, for a loss of $18, and the value of the short positions will also decline from $90 to $72 (but for a gain of $18). The securities' lenders are now overcollateralized and will transfer $18 to the long-short account, increasing the liquidity buffer to $28. A crash, in effect, creates liquidity for a long-short portfolio!

Myth 11. Long-short portfolios are infinitely riskier than long-only portfolios because losses on short positions are unlimited.

Whereas the risk to a long investment in a security is limited because the price of the security can go to zero but not below, the risk of a short position is theoretically unlimited because there is no bound on a rise in the security's price. The risk of a precipitous rise, or gap-up, in a security's price is a consideration, but it is one that is tempered in the context of a portfolio diversified across many securities. The prices of all the securities sold short are unlikely to rise dramatically at the same time with no offsetting increases in the prices of the securities held long. Furthermore, the trading imperatives of long-short management, which call for keeping dollar amounts of aggregate longs and aggregate shorts roughly equalized on an ongoing basis, will tend to limit short-side losses because shorts are covered as their prices rise; if a gap-up in the price of an individual security does not afford the opportunity to cover, the overall portfolio will still be protected as long as it is well diversified. So, the risk represented by the theoretically unbounded losses on short positions is considerably mitigated in practice.

Myth 12. Long-short portfolios must have more active risk than long-only portfolios because they take "more extreme" positions.

Because it is not constrained by index weights, a long-short portfolio may be able to take larger positions in securities with higher (and lower) expected returns compared with a long-only portfolio, which is constrained by index weights. The benefits of long-short construction, however, do not depend upon the manager's taking such positions. Integrated optimization will ensure that long-short selections are made with a view to maximizing expected return at the risk level at which the client feels most comfortable. Given the added flexibility a long-short portfolio affords in the implementation of investment insights, it should be able to improve upon the excess return of a long-only portfolio based on the same set of insights, whatever the risk level chosen.

Myth 13. Long-short risk must be greater than long-only residual risk because of the use of leverage.

Leverage does increase risk, but leverage is not a necessary part of long-short construction. The amount of leverage in a long-short portfolio is within the investor's control. The initial investment does not have to be leveraged by as much as two-to-one, as Federal Reserve Regulation T permits. Given an initial $100, for example, $50 can be invested long and $50 sold short; the amount at risk in securities is then identical to that of a $100 long-only investment, but the long-short portfolio retains the flexibility advantages of long-short construction. Furthermore, a long-only portfolio can also engage in leverage and to the same extent as a long-short portfolio. In this regard, however, long-short has a definite advantage over long-only because purchasing stock on margin gives rise to a tax liability for tax-exempt investors.

Myth 14. Long-short portfolios generate tax liabilities for tax-exempt investors.

A January 1995 Internal Revenue Service ruling has laid to rest concerns about the tax status of profits from short positions. It holds that borrowing stock to initiate short sales does not constitute debt financing. Any profit that results from closing a short position thus does not give rise to unrelated business taxable income.

Myth 15. Long-short trading activity is much higher than long-only.

The difference in levels of trading activity is largely a reflection of the long-short strategy's leverage, but the client can control the degree of leverage. Again, the client could choose to invest only half of a $100 initial investment, going long $50 and selling short $50, so securities trading is roughly equivalent to trading in a $100 long-only equity portfolio. Although changes in market levels can induce trading activity in long-short, as discussed previously, an equitized long-short implementation mitigates additional trading, because the daily marks to market on the futures can offset the marks to market on the shorts. For instance, in the preceding example, with a 5 percent market increase, a $100 stock futures position would have produced a $5 profit. In this case, no trading would be required, because the $5 profit on the futures position would more than offset the $4.50 of additional collateral that must be posted with the securities' lenders. Adding the remaining $0.50 to the liquidity buffer increases it to $10.50, or 10 percent of the new portfolio capital value of $105.

Myth 16. Long-short management costs are high relative to long-only.

If one considers management fees per dollar of securities positions, rather than per dollar of capital, there is not much difference between long-short and long-only fees. Furthermore, management fees per active dollar managed may be lower with long-short than with long-only management. Long-only portfolios contain an often substantial "hidden passive" element. Active long-only positions consist of only those portions of the portfolio that represent overweights or underweights relative to the market or other benchmark index; a large proportion of the portfolio may consist of index weights, which are essentially passive. To the extent that a long-only manager's fee is based on the total investment rather than just the active over- and underweightings, the long-only fee per active dollar managed may be much higher than that of a long-short manager.

Myth 17. The long-short portfolio does not receive use of the cash proceeds from the shares sold short.

What may be true for retail investors is not true for institutions. Today, institutional investors, although they do not have use of the cash proceeds from short sales, do receive a large portion of the interest on the cash. Although the prime broker and the securities' lenders extract a payment for securing and providing the shares, the cost is not inordinately large. Incurred as a haircut on the interest, the cost averages 25 to 30 basis points annually (more for harder-to-borrow shares). To this cost should be added any opportunity costs incurred because shares are not available for borrowing (or shares already shorted are called in by the lender and are not replaceable) or because uptick rules delay or prevent execution of short sales. (Uptick rules can be circumvented by use of principal packages or options, but the former are expensive and the latter are subject to limited availability and offer limited profit potential.) These incremental costs of long-short management can be, and often are, outweighed by the flexibility benefits offered by long-short construction.

Myth 18. Long-short portfolios are not prudent investments.

The responsible use of long-short investment strategies is consistent with the prudence and diversification requirements of

ERISA. As discussed previously, the risks related to both security selection and leverage can be controlled to be consistent with the investor's preferences. Moreover, long-short portfolios offer potential benefits compared with the residual risks and returns available from long-only portfolios.

Myth 19. Shorting is "un-American" and bad for the economy.

As Bill Sharpe noted in his 1990 Nobel laureate address, precluding short sales can result in "a diminution in the efficiency with which risk can be allocated in an economy. More fundamentally, overall welfare may be lower than it would be if the constraints on negative holdings could be reduced or removed."

Myth 20. Long-short investing complicates a plan's structure.

Long-short management, with the flexibility it offers to separate security selection from asset allocation, can actually simplify a plan's structure. Sponsors can take advantage of superior security selection skills (the long-short spread) while determining the plan's asset allocation mix independently. They can, for example, establish domestic or foreign equity or bond market exposures via the appropriate futures while deploying some funds in long-short strategies with the objective of achieving active returns from security selection.[3]

ENDNOTES

1. For some of the debate on the subject, see the proceedings of the recent Q Group conference on "Long/Short Strategies" (The Institute for Quantitative Research in Finance, Autumn 1995 Seminar), particularly the presentations by R. Michaud, B. Jacobs, and N. Dadachanji. See also Garcia and Gould (1992) and comments by Jacobs and Levy (1993) and Michaud (1993), together with comments from Arnott and Leinweber [and Michaud's reply (1994)] and from Jacobs and Levy (1995).

2. According to Michaud (1993), the ratio of excess return to residual risk of a long-short portfolio divided by that of a long-only portfolio will equal $\sqrt{2/(1+\rho)}$, where ρ is the correlation coefficient of the long and short excess returns of the long-short portfolio. According to this formula, the ratio of excess return to residual risk of the long-short portfolio improves upon that of the long-only if, and only if, ρ is less than 1. Michaud derives this formula by assuming, explicitly, that the excess returns on the long and short positions of the long-short

portfolio are identical, as are their residual risks, and implicitly, that the excess return on and the residual risk of the longs (and shorts) of the long-short portfolio are identical to the excess return on and the residual risk of a long-only portfolio. This implicit assumption permits neither the aggregate long nor the aggregate short positions of the long-short strategy to improve upon the risk-return trade-off of a long-only portfolio.

3. The authors thank Judy Kimball for her editorial assistance.

REFERENCES

Arnott, R. D. and D. J. Leinweber. 1994. "Long-short strategies reassessed." *Financial Analysts Journal* 50 (5): 76–80.

Garcia, C. B. and F. J. Gould. 1992. "The generality of long-short equitized strategies." *Financial Analysts Journal* 48 (5): 64–69.

Jacobs, B. I. and K. N. Levy. 1993. "The generality of long-short equitized strategies: A correction." *Financial Analysts Journal* 49 (2): 22.

——— and ———. 1995. "More on long-short strategies." *Financial Analysts Journal* 51 (2): 88–90.

Michaud, R. 1993. "Are long-short equity strategies superior?" *Financial Analysts Journal* 49 (6): 44–49.

CHAPTER 13

The Long and Short on Long-Short*

Constructing and trading long-short portfolios.

Long-short is an active portfolio construction discipline that balances long positions in high-expected-return securities and short positions in low-expected-return securities of approximately equal value and market sensitivity.[1] Because overall market moves are "canceled out" by the movements of the securities held long and sold short, the portfolio is "neutralized" or immunized against changes in the value of the underlying market; it has zero systematic, or beta, risk. The portfolio's performance will reflect the return and risk of security selection. If the selected securities perform as expected, the long-short positions will provide a positive return, whether the market rises or falls.

Long-short construction offers advantages over long-only, advantages that should translate into improved performance for long-short portfolios vis-à-vis long-only constructs. Long-short will be especially advantageous if, as many market observers believe, candidates for short sale are less efficiently priced than candidates for purchase. But the major benefits of long-short do not depend on such greater inefficiency on the short side.

In freeing the portfolio from the underlying market's systematic risk, long-short construction with integrated optimization also frees it from constraints typically imposed on long-only portfolio

---

* Originally published in the *Journal of Investing* 6 (1): 73–86.

management. For example, a long-short portfolio can take full advantage of insights on overpriced securities, because its ability to underweight a security is not constrained by the security's weight in the underlying market, as is long-only's. Furthermore, properly optimized long-short portfolios can use offsetting long and short positions to control portfolio residual risk; long-only portfolios must seek to control residual risk by balancing over and underweightings relative to the underlying market's weights.

Finally, long-short construction enables the investor to separate the return and risk of security selection from the return and risk of the equity market, because the return to a market-neutral portfolio is independent of the equity asset class underlying it. The investor can recapture the equity class return by purchasing stock index futures. The performance of the long-short-plus-futures, or "equitized," portfolio will reflect the underlying market's return and risk plus the return and risk of the long-short portfolio. Alternatively, the investor can purchase other derivatives, thus transporting the return from stock selection to other desired asset classes.

Compared with long-only portfolios, then, long-short portfolios offer enhanced flexibility not only in the control of risk and pursuit of return, but also in asset allocation. These benefits, of course, must be weighed against the costs of long-short. Long-short is often perceived as much costlier and riskier than long-only, but it is inherently neither. Long-short does experience some incremental costs relative to long-only; these include the trading costs incurred in meeting the demands of long-short balancing, margin requirements, and uptick rules, as well as the financial intermediation costs of borrowing shares to sell short. In general, these costs are not large and should not outweigh the flexibility benefits of long-short construction.

BUILDING A MARKET-NEUTRAL PORTFOLIO

Figure 13-1 illustrates the deployment of capital in a market-neutral implementation of long-short. It presupposes that the investor has already selected the securities to be held long and sold short. The stock evaluation and selection process may be traditional or quantitative, but the outcome should be some listing or ranking of "winners," or underpriced stocks expected to perform well, and "losers,"

F I G U R E   13–1

Market-Neutral Long-Short Deployment of Capital

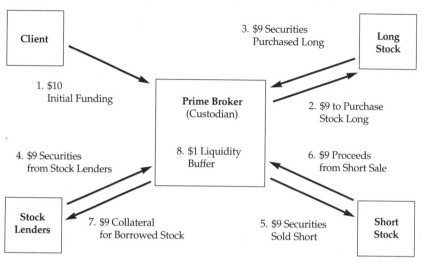

or overpriced stocks expected to perform poorly. The winners are to be considered for purchase and the losers for short sale.[2]

Federal Reserve Board regulations require that short positions be housed in a margin account at a brokerage firm; the broker will clear all trades and arrange to borrow the shares to be sold short. Figure 13-1 assumes the investor deposits $10 million with this custodial prime broker. Because Federal Reserve Board Regulation T requires at least 50 percent initial collateralization of margined positions, the investor could use this $10 million of capital to collateralize up to $20 million of securities positions—$10 million of longs and $10 million of shorts.[3]

In practice, however, the investor will retain some of the initial capital as a "liquidity buffer" to meet marks to market on the short positions. Figure 13-1 assumes the investor uses only $9 million of the initial $10 million to purchase the desired long positions, which are held at the prime broker. The broker arranges to borrow the $9 million in securities to be sold short. Upon their sale, the broker provides the $9 million in proceeds to the securities' lenders as collateral for the shares borrowed.[4]

The securities' lenders require full collateralization of the shares they lent. If those shares increase in value, the borrower (our long-short investor) will have to arrange payment to the lenders so collateral continues to match the value of the shares. If the borrowed shares fall in value, the money will flow in the opposite direction, with the lenders releasing funds to the investor's prime broker account. A liquidity buffer equal to 10 percent of the account's capital ($1 million at the outset of our example) is generally sufficient to meet these daily marks to market.[5]

In Figure 13-1, then, the long-short portfolio consists of $9 million in shares held long and $9 million in shares sold short. The portfolio's return will reflect the performances of these long and short positions.

It will also benefit from a cash return stemming from two sources. First, the account will earn interest on the cash held as a liquidity buffer, at approximately the prevailing short-term rate. Second, the $9 million in proceeds from the short sales, posted as collateral with the securities' lenders, will earn interest. The lenders will retain a small portion of this interest as a securities lending fee, and the prime broker will retain a portion to cover expenses and provide some profit; the investor's account will receive the rest.[6] Although the exact distribution is a matter for negotiation, we will assume the amount rebated to the investor (the "short rebate") approximates the short-term rate.[7]

Figure 13-2 illustrates the hypothetical one-period performance of the long-short portfolio, assuming bull market and bear market scenarios. The bull market scenario assumes the market (as proxied by the S&P 500) rises 30 percent over the period, while the long positions rise by 33 percent and the shorts by only 27 percent. The long positions are worth $11.97 million at the end of the period, for a gain of $2.97 million, and the shorts are worth $11.43 million, for a loss of $2.43 million.

The long-short portion of the portfolio has a net gain of $0.54 million. This amounts to 6 percent of the $9 million invested (equal to the spread between the long and short returns), or 5.4 percent of the initial $10 million.[8] In addition, the portfolio receives a short rebate of 5 percent of the short sale proceeds ($0.45 million) and 5 percent interest on the liquidity buffer (equal to $0.05 million), for a "cash" return of $0.5 million, or 5 percent of the initial $10 million.

Market-Neutral Long-Short Hypothetical Performance–Bull and Bear Markets

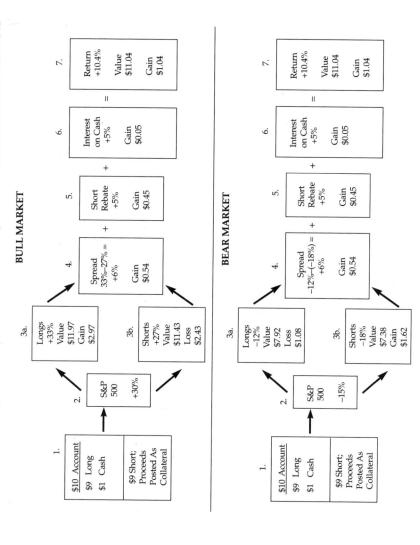

Overall, the portfolio increases in value from $10 to $11.04 million, for a net gain of $1.04 million and a 10.4 percent return.

The bear market scenario assumes the market falls by 15 percent, with the long positions falling by 12 percent and the short positions by 18 percent. This provides the same return spread as in the bull market scenario. The decline in value of the longs translates into a loss of $1.08 million, while the decline in value of the shorts translates into a gain of $1.62 million. The net gain for the long-short portfolio is, again, $0.54 million, exactly the same result as when the market rose by 30 percent. Cash returns are the same in both market environments, so overall portfolio results are the same.

The return to the basic market-neutral portfolio, then, consists of three components—the interest on the liquidity buffer, the rebate from the short sale proceeds, and the return spread between the aggregate long and aggregate short positions in the long-short portfolio. Because the aggregate long positions and the aggregate short positions are of approximately equal value and have equal sensitivity to the underlying market, those portions of their returns that reflect overall market movements (their returns to beta) cancel out. All that is left is the return spread. The return to the long-short portfolio is thus a true reflection of the success of the manager's stock selection skills.

A QUESTION OF EFFICIENCY

Figure 13-2 assumes symmetric market-relative returns for the long and short positions; that is, in both bull and bear market environments, the longs were assumed to outperform the market by 3 percent while the shorts were assumed to underperform by 3 percent. But there are reasons to believe that short sale candidates—the most overpriced stocks, which offer the lowest expected returns—may be more common or more mispriced than the underpriced stocks that constitute the candidates for purchase. In that case, one might expect higher excess returns from short positions than from long positions.

Stocks may be overpriced, and overpricing may continue over some nontrivial period, because investors tend toward overoptimism. Several theories and some evidence suggest that this may be the case. Bubbles and fads, for example, may cause investors to bid prices up beyond reasonable valuations [see, for example, Camerer (1989)]. Company practices may also encourage overpricing. Many companies, for example, are eager to publicize good news in a timely manner, but may delay releasing bad news or attempt to disguise it via window dressing (or, more rarely, commit actual fraud). Stock prices may thus reflect good news more quickly and unambiguously than bad news.

Overpricing may also exist because brokers and analysts favor buy over sell recommendations, and focus research efforts on purchase rather than sale candidates. Such bias may reflect an economic rationale: Buy recommendations may elicit more commissions, as all customers are potential purchasers, while commissions from sales will come primarily from customers who already own the stock. Bias may reflect political issues: Publishing negative opinions about a company may jeopardize investment banking relationships and even threaten analyst job security [Regan (1993)]. And it may reflect underlying analyses: Evidence suggests, for example, that brokers may produce overly optimistic earnings estimates, especially for firms with the least stable earnings histories [Huberts and Fuller (1995)].

Whatever its source, the greater the uncertainty about "true" value, the more overpricing is likely. This is because increasing uncertainty leads to increasing divergence of investor opinions. And those investors with the most optimistic opinions will become the buyers, setting security prices [see Miller (1990)]. Theoretically, of course, short-sellers should act to keep shares from becoming overpriced; if overly optimistic investors bid up share prices beyond what other investors consider reasonable, those investors should sell short, reducing upward pressure on prices. But short-selling is certainly not as unrestricted as buying long.

Share borrowability and uptick rules make short-selling more difficult than going long. Short-selling is also costlier, because investors do not receive full interest on the proceeds from short sales (and retail investors rarely receive any of the interest). Short-selling may also be legally or contractually restricted for some investors (such as mutual funds, which can take only limited short positions). Other investors may eschew it because they consider it too speculative or morally objectionable.

In fact, short sales have historically accounted for a very small percentage of shares outstanding; short interest on the NYSE has risen only slightly in recent years, from 0.25 percent at year-end 1980 to 1.32 percent at year-end 1995. And only a portion of this interest is motivated by security selection; most short sales are undertaken by dealers supplying liquidity or investors shorting for risk-hedging, tax-deferral, or arbitrage purposes.

In a market in which prices tend to reflect overoptimism on the part of investors and in which short-selling is restricted de facto and de jure, inefficiencies may be concentrated in overpriced stocks. Short sales of the most overpriced stocks may, therefore, offer higher positive returns than long purchases of underpriced stocks.

Nevertheless, the benefits of long-short are not dependent upon the existence of greater inefficiencies in overpriced than in underpriced stocks. Rather, they flow from the increased flexibility allowed by short-selling within the context of the long-short portfolio construction process.

BENEFITS OF LONG-SHORT

Long-short portfolio construction can offer real advantages over long-only construction in terms of both pursuit of return and control of risk. These benefits stem primarily from the enhanced implementation of investment insights afforded by the removal of index constraints in an integrated optimization of long-short portfolios.

Integrated optimization releases the long-short portfolio from the constraints imposed by an underlying index on the construction of long-only portfolios. Consider, for example, a long-only portfolio whose selection universe is a given market index, and whose performance is measured against that index. By holding every name in the index in proportion to its weight in the index, the portfolio will achieve a return, and a risk level, equivalent to the benchmark's. If it expects to achieve a return over and above that of the underlying market index (an excess return), it must be able to overweight, relative to their market index weights, securities that are expected to earn above-average returns, and underweight those expected to earn below-average returns.

Underweightings or overweightings relative to the underlying benchmark, necessary to produce excess return, also introduce benchmark-relative, or residual, risk. The more the portfolio departs from underlying benchmark weights, the greater the probability that its return will not match the return on the benchmark. Control of portfolio excess return and residual risk requires control of underweightings and overweightings relative to the benchmark. Benchmark weights thus have substantial influence on the portfolio's allocation of capital and can constrain the implementation of investment insights.

Consider a stock that constitutes 5 percent of the benchmark's weight. What if the investor expects the stock to offer an above-benchmark return? The investor will want to overweight the stock in the portfolio. Establishing an overweight, however, will require investing more than 5 percent of the portfolio's capital; a 1 percentage point overweight, for instance, requires a 6 percent portfolio position. Furthermore, as the overweighting represents a departure from the benchmark weight, it introduces residual risk. The portfolio's ability to take an active position in the stock will be constrained both by allocation requirements and by risk considerations.

Somewhat counterintuitively, the portfolio may also have to allocate capital to limit stock underweights. Say the investor wants to underweight a stock that is expected to provide a below-benchmark return. If the stock constitutes 5 percent of the underlying index, as in the preceding example, establishing a 1 percentage point portfolio underweight requires holding a 4 percent portfolio position in the security.

Of course, if the security represents a smaller-capitalization company, less capital is required to establish either an overweight or an underweight, but the portfolio's ability to underweight a small-capitalization company may be severely restricted. Consider, for example, a stock that makes up 0.1 percent of the index. The investor can establish a 1 percentage point overweight of this stock by holding a 1.1 percent portfolio position. Little capital is needed to establish an underweight; the maximum underweight the portfolio can attain is only 0.1 percent—achieved by not holding the stock at all. The latter constraint, however, may become binding if the investor thinks the stock will perform poorly and wants to underweight it significantly. The maximum attainable underweight for this stock is equivalent to saying that the portfolio cannot hold more than a 0.1 percent overweight in a stock that is expected to perform well.

More than a few discussions of long-short portfolios have assumed an identity between an index-constrained long-only portfolio and the long and short portions of a long-short portfolio. In this view, the aggregate longs and the aggregate shorts of long-short constitute two separate, index-constrained portfolios. By definition, neither can offer advantages over a long-only portfolio. Together, they may offer diversification benefits over long-only if the return on the long portfolio in excess of the market return and the excess return on the short portfolio are less than perfectly correlated.[9]

With integrated optimization, however, a long-short portfolio is not constrained by index weights. Once an underlying index has been used to determine the systematic risks of the candidate securities, its role in long-short construction is effectively over. The offsetting market sensitivities of the aggregate long and aggregate short positions eliminate market sensitivity and the need to consider index weightings in establishing security positions. The portfolio is not constrained to moving away from or toward market weights in order to pursue return or control risk. Rather, it can allocate its capital without regard to the securities' weights in the underlying market.

To establish a 1 percent "overweight" or "underweight," it merely has to allocate 1 percent of its capital long or allocate 1 percent of its capital short. And because it can short securities, the long-short portfolio can "underweight" a security by as much as investment insights (and risk considerations) dictate. Negative opinions can thus be more freely and fully reflected in long-short than in long-only.

Furthermore, in an integrated optimization, selection of the securities to be held long is determined simultaneously with selection of the securities to be sold short. The result is a single long-short portfolio, not one long portfolio and one short portfolio. Just as one cannot attribute the qualities of water, its wetness, say, to its hydrogen or oxygen components separately, one cannot reasonably dissect the performance of an integrated long-short strategy into one element attributable to long positions alone and another attributable to short positions alone. Only jointly do the long and short positions of long-short define the strategy. Long and short excess returns, or "alphas," are thus meaningless concepts.

Rather than being measurable as long and short performance in excess of an underlying benchmark, the performance of the equity portion of the long-short portfolio is measurable as the overall return on the long and short positions—or the spread between the longs and shorts—relative to their risk. Compared with the excess return–residual risk of long-only management, this performance should be enhanced by the elimination of index constraints, which allows the long-short portfolio increased flexibility to implement investment insights, both long and short.

EQUITIZING LONG-SHORT

The return enhancement afforded by long-short construction reflects the removal of the constraints an underlying index imposes on long-only portfolio construction. Of course, the basic, market-neutral long-short construction also eliminates exposure to the underlying index's risk—and its return. Market return, and risk, can be added back by purchasing stock index futures contracts in an amount equal to the invested capital.[10] The return to the resulting long-short-plus-futures, or equitized, portfolio will then reflect the market return (the change in the price of the futures contracts plus interest) plus the spread on the long-short portfolio. The equitized portfolio will retain the flexibility benefits of long-short construction, reflected in the long-short spread, while also participating in overall market movements.

Figure 13-3 illustrates the deployment of capital for equitized long-short portfolio construction. Note that the major difference between Figures 13-3 and 13-1, other than the addition of the $10 million of stock index futures, is the size of the liquidity buffer. As noted, the liquidity buffer serves to meet marks to market on the short positions; when short positions rise in price, the lenders of the securities sold short need more collateral from the investor's account. With an equitized long-short strategy, however, an increase in the price of the short positions induced by a rise in the overall market should be accompanied by an increase in the price of the futures contracts held long. The marks to market on the futures can offset the marks to market on the shorts.

A smaller liquidity buffer, therefore, suffices to ensure that short positions will be fully collateralized at all times. Most of the freed-up capital, however, is used to margin the futures position.[11] Thus, in Figure 13-3, as in Figure 13-1, $9 million of the initial $10 million investment is assumed available for purchase of securities.

Figure 13-4 illustrates the performance of the equitized long-short portfolio in bull and bear market scenarios, using the same as-

F I G U R E   13–3

Equitized Long-Short Deployment of Capital

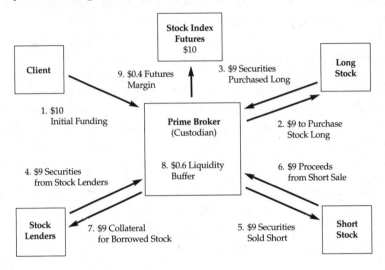

sumptions as Figure 13-2. Returns to the long-short portfolio are the same as in Figure 13-2. Cash returns are also the same, as the reduced interest from the smaller liquidity buffer is combined with the interest earned on the futures margin.

Total returns on the portfolios in Figures 13-2 and 13-4 differ markedly, however, and the entire difference is attributable to the performance of the overall market, which is reflected in the equitized but not the market-neutral portfolio. Because of its market exposure, the equitized portfolio does not behave the same in both bull and bear market scenarios; it is not market-neutral. Unlike the market-neutral portfolio, the equitized portfolio's overall return will be sensitive to market movements; it will also benefit fully, however, from the return spread on the long-short portfolio.

This result underlines one of the major benefits of long-short—the "transportability" of the return on the basic, market-neutral long-short portfolio. In essence, the return on the long-short portfolio represents a return to security selection alone, independent of the overall return to the equity market from which the securities are selected. This return, and all the benefits of long-short construction that it reflects, can be transported to other asset classes through the

FIGURE 13-4

Equitized Long-Short Hypothetical Performance–Bull and Bear Markets

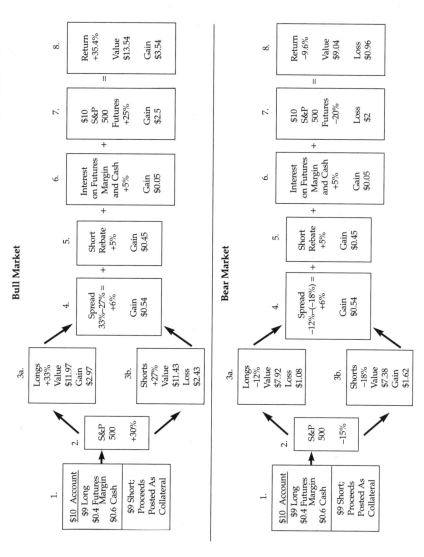

use of derivatives. The equitized long-short portfolio transports the return to the equity asset class, adding the security selection return (and its associated risk) to the equity market return (and its risk). Other derivatives (for bonds or foreign equity, for example) can be used to establish other asset class returns.

The transportability of the long-short spread has at least two implications for investment management. First, it offers the investor the benefits of being able to separate stock selection skills from asset allocation decisions. The talents of an equity manager particularly skilled in stock selection need no longer be confined to an equity market allocation. They can be transported to virtually any asset class with established derivative markets.

Second, it implies that the identity of a long-short portfolio is flexible. The basic market-neutral construction offers a return (and risk) from security selection on top of a cash return (represented by the short rebate); portfolio performance in this case is appropriately measured as the manager's ability to enhance a cash return (at the cost of added risk). When the long-short portfolio is equitized, however, the security selection return and risk from the long-short portfolio comes on top of an equity market return, and portfolio performance is properly measured relative to the equity index underlying the futures.

Furthermore, long-short is not in and of itself an asset class. Asset class analyses and optimizations should not treat long-short as a separate asset class but as a member of a conventional asset class—cash, equity, bonds—depending upon the long-short portfolio's particular implementation.

TRADING LONG-SHORT

The trading of long-short portfolios is more complicated than that of long-only. First, the values and market sensitivities of the aggregate long and aggregate short positions must be kept in balance on a real-time basis in order to ensure market neutrality. Second, the account must meet Federal Reserve, stock exchange, and individual broker initial and maintenance margin requirements. Third, marks to market on short (and, if present, futures) positions must be satisfied.

In order to ensure overall portfolio neutrality throughout a trading program, long and short trades may be speeded up or slowed down relative to their occurrence in a typical long-only portfolio. Because short sales are more problematic and more likely to experience delays that would lead to long-short imbalances, for example, some long-short managers start off with their short trades before beginning their long trading programs. Should imbalances occur, securities may have to be bought or sold long or sold short or covered until balance is restored. Derivatives may also be used to correct temporary imbalances.

At all times, at its establishment and throughout its life, a long-short portfolio is subject to margin requirements, as its short positions represent borrowed shares. As noted earlier, under Federal Reserve Board Regulation T, establishment of a short position requires at least 50 percent margin. Once established, short positions are subject to less stringent maintenance margins, set by the exchanges or individual brokers. New York Stock Exchange Rule 431, for example, requires collateral equal to 25 percent of the value of long positions held in a margin account, and 30 percent or more of the value of the short positions.[12] In the interests of self-protection, brokers usually require at least 30 percent collateralization of all positions in margin accounts.

An account that falls below maintenance margin requirements will have to decrease its securities exposure by covering shorts or selling longs or increase its capital by adding cash. An account that meets maintenance margin requirements but not the initial margin requirement is restricted in the sense that it can make no transactions that would cause further reduction in margin, such as shorting additional shares or withdrawing cash.

Tables 13-1 through 13-3 illustrate how maintenance of long-short balance, margin requirements, and marks to market can require portfolio trading. Table 13-1 shows the effects on a $10 million market-neutral (unequitized) portfolio when both long and short positions either fall in value by 50 percent or rise in value by 100 percent. At the outset, the long-short portfolio easily meets initial margin requirements, as long and short positions totaling $18 million ($9 million long plus $9 million short) are collateralized by $10 million in equity (the longs plus the cash in the liquidity buffer), for a margin of 55.6 percent.

A 50 percent decline in the values of the longs and shorts results in the securities' lenders being overcollateralized; they will

T A B L E 13–1

Market-Neutral Long-Short—Trading Required When Long and Short Positions Fall 50 Percent or Rise 100 Percent

	Initial Values, Fall or Rise	Return		Gain/Loss		Owe/Owed		New Values		Action		After-Action Values, Fall or Rise
		Fall	Rise	Fall	Rise	Fall	Rise	Fall	Rise	Fall	Rise	
Long	$9	−50%	+100%	−$4.5	+$9			$4.5	$18	Buy $4.5	Sell $9	$9
Short	$9	−50%	+100%	+$4.5	−$9	Owed $4.5 by lenders	Owe lenders $9	$4.5	$18	Sell short $4.5	Cover $9	$9
Cash	$1							$5.5	−$8			$1
Equity	$10							$10	$10			$10
Margin	55.6%							111.1%	27.8%			55.6%

have to transfer $4.5 million to the long-short account. The liquidity buffer will then be larger than needed. The investor can buy an additional $4.5 million in securities and sell short an additional $4.5 million, restoring the account to its initial values.

A 100 percent increase in the values of the longs and shorts results, by contrast, in the securities' lenders being undercollateralized; they hold only $9 million in cash proceeds from the initial short sales, but the securities they lent are now worth $18 million. The long-short account must transfer an additional $9 million to the securities' lenders. Taking this sum from the liquidity buffer, however, would result in a deficit of $8 million and leave the overall portfolio undermargined, by brokers' standards, at 27.8 percent. In order to meet the marks to market on the short positions and reestablish maintenance margin, the investor can sell $9 million worth of securities held long and cover $9 million worth of securities sold short. This will restore the portfolio to its initial starting values.[13]

Table 13-2 illustrates the advantages, in terms of trading activity, of equitizing a long-short strategy by purchasing a $10 million position in stock index futures, using $0.4 million of Treasury bills as margin; the initial liquidity buffer is $0.6 million. If, as assumed, the long and short positions as well as the futures position now double in value, the long-short account will owe the securities' lenders $9 million on the marks to market on the shorts, but it will also receive a $10 million positive mark to market on the futures. The securities' lenders can be paid out of this $10 million, with $1 million left over. However, the futures positions, worth double their initial value, are now undermargined by $0.4 million (assuming futures margin dollar requirements double or percentage margins stay the same). Purchasing an additional $0.4 million in Treasury bills will meet the futures margin and restore the initial long-short portfolio margin. No securities trades are required.

The behavior of the long, short, and futures values in Tables 13-1 and 13-2 is consistent with the effects of underlying market movements; that is, the equivalent systematic risks of the long and short positions would lead to equivalent value changes in the absence of residual, or nonsystematic risk, and the futures positions would be expected to perform in line with the market underlying the behavior of the long and short positions. We can thus infer that, even though the return on a basic long-short portfolio is neutral to

T A B L E 13–2

Equitized Long–Short–Trading Required When Securities, Long and Short, and Futures Rise 100 Percent

	Initial Values	Return	Gain/Loss	Owe/Owed	New Values	Action	After-Action Values
Long	$9	+100%	+$9		$18		$18
Short	$9	+100%	–$9	Owe lenders $9	$18		$18
Cash	$0. 6				$1.6		$1.2
Equity	$9.6				$19.6		$19.2
Margin	53.3%				54.4%		53.3%
Futures	$10 + $0.4 in Treasury bills	+100%	$10	Owed $10 on mark to market	$20 + $0.4 in Treasury bills	Buy $0.4 in Treasury bills	$20 + $0.8 in Treasury bills

overall market movements, market movements can have implications for the implementation of long-short strategies; in particular, they may necessitate trading activity.

In practice, of course, one is unlikely to experience market movements of the magnitudes illustrated. More likely market movements would lead to fewer violations of margin requirements and less trading. With a 5 percent market rise, for example, the initial long and short positions in Table 13-1 could be expected to increase to $9.45 million, calling for a payment of $0.45 million to the securities' lenders and a reduction in the liquidity buffer to $0.55 million. There would be no violation of margin (margin would be 52.9 percent), but restoring the liquidity buffer would require selling $0.45 million worth of long positions and covering $0.45 million worth of shorts. Market declines would be even less problematic. A market decline of 20 percent, in line with what occurred on Black Monday in 1987, would lead to a decline in the value of the long and short positions from $9 to $7.2 million and the liquidity buffer's receipt of $1.8 million from the securities' lenders.

Tables 13-1 and 13-2 assume that returns to the long and short positions are equal. If it performs as expected, however, the long-short portfolio will experience a positive spread between the returns on the securities held long and the returns on the securities sold short, whether the market rises or falls. Table 13-3 assumes a 2 percentage point return spread between the longs and the shorts: The long positions rise 4 percent and the shorts 2 percent. Although these movements lead to no margin violation, payment of the $0.18 million in additional collateral owed the securities' lenders reduces the liquidity buffer below 10 percent of equity; furthermore, long and short positions are no longer balanced. By selling $0.198 million in long positions and covering $0.018 million worth of shorts, the investor can restore the liquidity buffer to 10 percent and rebalance the portfolio. Differential returns on long and short positions, then, even if favorable to overall portfolio performance, can induce some trading activity.

EVALUATING LONG-SHORT

Long-short construction maximizes the implementation of potentially valuable investment insights via the elimination of index constraints. Long-short thus offers advantages over long-only. But it

T A B L E 13-3

Two Percentage Point Long-Short Spread

	Initial Values	Return	Gain/Loss	Owe/Owed	New Values	Action	After-Action Values
Long	$9	+4%	+$0.36		$9.36	Sell $0.198	$9.162
Short	$9	+2%	–$0.18	Owe lenders $0.18	$9.18	Cover $0.018	$9.162
Cash	$1				$0.82		$1.018
Equity	$10				$10.18		$10.18
Margin	55.6%				54.9%		55.6%

also involves complications not encountered by long-only management, many of which are related to the use of short-selling.

In choosing a prime broker to act as account custodian, the investor must employ due diligence to ensure the broker's capability and creditworthiness. The prime broker will clear all trades for the long-short portfolio; although the long-short investor can execute trades with other brokers, the prime broker usually assesses a "ticket charge" on such "away" trades to cover the costs of bookkeeping. The prime broker will also arrange to borrow stock for shorting. In this capacity, the prime broker must be advised of possible short sales in order to ensure that the shares are available.

The vast majority of shares are available for borrowing, but borrowability may be a problem for some shares, particularly those of small-capitalization companies. Harder-to-borrow shares may also pose problems even after they have been obtained for short sale. This is because shares sold short are subject to recall by the lender at any time. In most cases, the prime broker will be able to find alternative lenders for the securities subject to recall, but if these are not available, the long-short investor will be subject to "buy-ins" and have to cover the short positions.[14]

Long-short also incurs costs not encountered by long-only, again primarily because of shorting. The financial intermediation cost of borrowing shorts, which includes the costs associated with securing and providing lendable stocks, averages 25 to 30 basis points (although harder-to-borrow names will cost more). It is incurred as a "haircut" on the short rebate received from the interest earned on the short sale proceeds.

With equitized long-short, there may be mismatches between the short rebate, which is based on overnight rates, and the futures contracts, which are priced off an equivalent-maturity LIBOR. Such mismatches can usually be mitigated, however, by negotiating term deals with the prime broker.

Finally, short sales are subject to various uptick rules. SEC Rule 10a-1, for example, states that exchange-traded shares can be shorted only at a price that is higher than the last trade price ("uptick") or the same as the last trade price if that price is higher than the previous price ("zero-plus-tick"). Uptick rules vary across the different exchanges and proprietary trading systems.

Uptick rules can delay, or in some cases prevent, execution of short sales, resulting in opportunity costs. Tick tests can be circumvented, but doing so is expensive. For example, the long-short manager can submit a package of trades to a broker that guarantees their execution at the market's closing prices. Such "principal packages," which are crossed overseas outside U.S. market hours, avoid uptick rules as well as public disclosure of the trades. But brokers charge higher fees for principal packages.

As an alternative to short-selling, the long-short manager can sell deep-in-the-money call options, avoiding both uptick and borrowability problems. Options, however, are generally short-lived, often illiquid, and not available for all securities. In addition, an option seller's profit potential is limited to earning the option premium, no matter how far the underlying stock falls.

The cost of avoiding uptick rules may be greater than any opportunity costs incurred as a result of the rules. Such costs will, in any event, be greatest for strategies that depend on immediacy of execution. For patient traders, who supply rather than demand liquidity, uptick rules should generally not pose a serious problem.

Some other costs of long-short may seem as though they should be high relative to long-only and are often portrayed as such. For example, trading activity for a fully leveraged long-short strategy will be roughly double that for a comparable long-only strategy. This differential, however, is a function of long-short's leverage, and leverage is not a necessary component of long-short. Given an initial $10 million, the client can choose to invest $5 million long and sell $5 million short; trading activity for the resulting long-short portfolio will be roughly equivalent to that for a $10 million long-only portfolio. Although the exigencies of maintaining long-short balance and meeting collateralization requirements may force trading that would not be incurred by long-only, the magnitude of such incremental trading should not be large, given typical security price changes.

Furthermore, a long-only portfolio can engage in leverage to the same extent as long-short. Long-short has the advantage here, however, because purchasing stock on margin can give rise to a tax liability for tax-exempt investors. According to a January 1995 Internal Revenue Service ruling (IRS Ruling 95-8), borrowing stocks to initiate short sales does not constitute debt financing, so any profits realized when short sales are closed out do not give rise to unrelated business taxable income.

Management fees for a long-short portfolio will tend to be higher than those for a comparable long-only portfolio, but again only to the extent that leverage is employed in the former and not in the latter. If one considers management fees per dollar of securities positions, rather than per dollar of capital, there should not be much difference between long-short and long-only.

Furthermore, there can be a substantial "hidden passive" element in long-only portfolios. Only those portions of a long-only portfolio that represent overweights or underweights relative to the underlying market or other benchmark index are truly active; the remaining portion of the portfolio constitutes index weightings, which are essentially passive. To the extent the long-only manager's fee is based on total investments, rather than just the active investments, the fee per active dollar managed may be much higher for long-only than for long-short.

Finally, long-short is often portrayed as inherently riskier than long-only. This view in part reflects a concern for potentially unlimited losses on short positions. While it is true that the risk of a short position is theoretically unlimited because there is no bound on a rise in the price of the shorted security, this source of risk is considerably mitigated in practice. It is unlikely, for example, that the prices of all the securities sold short in a long-short portfolio will rise dramatically at the same time, with no offsetting increases in the prices of the securities held long. Also, the trading imperatives of long-short, which call for keeping dollar amounts of longs and shorts roughly equalized on an ongoing basis, will tend to limit short-side losses, because shorts are covered as their prices rise. And if a gap-up in the price of an individual security does not afford the opportunity to cover, the overall portfolio will still be protected, provided it is well diversified.

A long-short portfolio will incur more residual risk than a comparable long-only portfolio to the extent it engages in leverage and/or takes more active positions. A long-short portfolio that takes full advantage of the leverage available to it will have at risk roughly double the amount of assets invested compared with a long-only portfolio. And because it is not constrained by index weights, a long-short portfolio may take larger positions in securities with higher (and lower) expected returns compared with a long-only portfolio. But both the degree of leverage and the "activeness" of the long-short portfolio are within the control of the investor.

It is ultimately the investor who decides the long-short portfolio's level of residual risk. As noted previously, given an initial $10 million, the investor may choose to invest only $5 million long and sell $5 million short, in which case the amount at risk in securities will be identical to that of a $10 million long-only investment. And the investor will determine the activeness of the positions taken by selecting the desired level of portfolio residual risk. With integrated optimization, long-short selections will be made with a view to maximizing expected return at the desired level of risk; risk will not be incurred without the expectation of a commensurate return. Given the added flexibility it affords in the implementation of investment insights, long-short portfolio construction should be able to improve upon the excess returns available from long-only construction based on the same set of insights, whatever the risk level chosen.

In summary, although long-short is often perceived and portrayed as much costlier and much riskier than long-only, it is inherently neither. Much of the incremental cost and risk is either largely dependent on the amount of leverage employed (transaction costs, management fees, and risk) or controllable via optimization (security selection risk). Those costs and risks that are not—including the financial intermediation costs of borrowing shares to short; the trading costs incurred to meet long-short balancing, margin requirements, and uptick rules; and the risks of unlimited losses on short positions—do not invalidate the viability of long-short strategies.

Neither should some long-standing prejudices against short-selling. Selling short is not "bad for the economy" or "un-American," as some investors have maintained. In fact, no less a scholar than William Sharpe (1991) has noted, in his Nobel laureate address, that shorting can increase market efficiency and overall economic welfare by allowing for the full expression of negative as well as positive investment opinions.

Nor are long-short portfolios inherently "imprudent" in an ERISA sense. Appropriately constructed long-short portfolios, with long and short positions used to offset market risk and optimization used to control residual risk, are fully consistent with the prudence and diversification requirements of ERISA.

A meaningful evaluation of long-short calls for an objective balancing of the real costs against the real benefits. Those benefits may reflect greater inefficiencies on the short side of the market but are not dependent on them. The benefits arise from the added flexibility that long-short affords in control of risk and pursuit of return, via the elimination of index constraints, and in asset allocation, via the liberation of security selection return from the underlying equity class return.

Do the benefits outweigh the costs? The rewards to a long-short portfolio, like those to any active strategy, will depend ultimately upon the insights that underlie its security selections. Good insights will yield good results, whether to a long-short or long-only strategy. Long-short can enhance those results, however, by enhancing implementation of the insights.

ENDNOTES

The authors thank Judith Kimball for her editorial assistance.

1. Balancing equal dollar amounts long and short is often desired as a means to achieve market neutrality, and it is also the optimal investment posture under certain conditions. For simplicity, assuming the same constant correlation between all securities, long-short balance is optimal when the equation holds:

$$c \sum_{i=1}^{N} \frac{\mu_i}{\sigma_i^2} + d \sum_{i=1}^{N} \frac{\mu_i}{\sigma_i} = 0$$

where c and d are functions of the correlation, the number of securities, and the summation of the inverse of the σ_i s, and

μ_i = expected excess return of security i
σ_i^2 = variance of security i's excess return
N = number of securities

We thank Harry M. Markowitz for this insight.

Under the further, although somewhat restrictive, simplifying assumption that all securities have the same constant variance, the equation reduces to

$$\sum_{i=1}^{N} \mu_i = 0$$

Nonsymmetrical distributions of security excess returns can lead to the optimality of long equal to short dollar balances if the summation of the excess returns is zero. The simplest condition for equal dollar amounts is a symmetrical distribution of expected excess returns.

2. We do not mean to trivialize the importance of the selection process. The ability to discriminate between stocks that will perform well and stocks that will perform poorly is the ultimate arbiter of the success or failure of any active portfolio. But it is also beyond the scope of this article.

3. Regulation T would alternatively permit up to $20 million in total long positions (given the initial $10 million capital). The purchase of the additional $10 million long would require a margin loan, which has tax implications for tax-exempt investors (as discussed later).

4. Actually, the lenders of the securities sold short will require somewhat more than the proceeds from the short sale to collateralize their loan, in order to protect themselves in the eventuality that the short-seller cannot meet daily marks to market. In practice, the securities' lenders demand 102 percent of the value of the shares borrowed. The prime broker will arrange for this incremental collateral.

5. The liquidity buffer must also be available to reimburse securities' lenders for dividends on borrowed shares. If the liquidity buffer is inadequate to meet mark-to-market and dividend demands, the long-short manager may have to sell long positions for short settlement (receiving cash proceeds faster than the usual 3-day settlement period), an expensive proposition, or borrow funds from the broker, also an expensive option and one that may have tax consequences for tax-exempt investors.

6. Retail investors generally do not receive interest on the cash proceeds from short sales. Institutional investors generally do receive a substantial portion of the interest on the cash proceeds, but they do not technically have use of those proceeds. That is, they cannot decide where to invest the proceeds, nor do the proceeds serve as equity for determining the margin level of the investor's account at the prime broker.

7. While the liquidity buffer must be invested at short-term rates to ensure availability of funds, there is some room for negotiation in the investment of the short-sale proceeds. Typically overnight rates are pegged to Fed funds, LIBOR (London interbank offer rate), or broker call, but the funds may be committed for longer terms at higher rates. Investment for longer terms will subject the proceeds to

interest rate risk if the performance is linked to a floating rate, but it may reduce risk for an equitized long-short portfolio (for instance, if the maturity of the investment matches that of the stock index futures contracts used as an overlay on the portfolio).

8. The return spread of 6 percent is achieved in this example with a long return exceeding the market return by 3 percentage points and a short return falling shy of the market return by 3 percentage points. The market return is provided solely for illustration and is irrelevant to the return spread (as will become evident later, in the discussion of "integrated optimization"). Any pair of long and short returns where the longs outperform the shorts by 6 percent provides the same return spread, regardless of the market's return.

9. Such an argument is made by Michaud (1993), who assumes that (using his notation):

$$\alpha_L = \alpha_S$$

and

$$\omega_L = \omega_S$$

or the excess return and residual risk of the long positions in long-short equal the excess return and residual risk of the short positions. He also implicitly assumes that the excess returns and residual risks of the long and short positions equal the excess return and residual risk of an index-constrained long-only portfolio. That is:

$$\alpha_L = \alpha_S = \alpha_{\text{long-only}}$$

and

$$\omega_L = \omega_S = \omega_{\text{long-only}}$$

From these assumptions he concludes that

$$\Gamma_{LS} / \Gamma_L = \sqrt{2/(1+\rho)}$$

where Γ equals the ratio of portfolio excess return to portfolio residual risk. Thus, the long-short portfolio can offer no benefits over a long-only portfolio except to the extent that the correlation between the excess returns on its long and short positions, ρ, is less than 1. But such diversification benefits can be obtained by combining any assets that are less than fully correlated.

10. A consideration in equitizing a portfolio is the use of a tail hedge. See Kawaller and Koch (1988).

11. We assume a futures margin of 4 percent. The futures margin is currently set at $12,500 per contract, so the percentage margin will rise and fall with changes in the contract's value.

12. For shorted shares selling at $5.00 or more, collateral must equal the greater of $5.00 or 30 percent of share value, while for shorted shares selling at less than $5.00, collateral must equal the greater of $2.50 or share price.

13. Alternatively, the investor could deposit additional funds to meet the margin call.

14. One also occasionally hears about a "short squeeze," in which speculators buy up lendable stock to force a buy-in at elevated prices. This will be more of a problem for dedicated short-sellers who take concentrated positions in illiquid stocks than for a long-short investor holding small positions diversified across many stocks.

REFERENCES

Camerer, C. 1989. "Bubbles and fads in asset prices: A review of theory and evidence." *Journal of Economic Surveys* 3 (1): 3–41.

Huberts, L. C. and R. J. Fuller. 1995. "Predictability bias in the U.S. equity markets." *Financial Analysts Journal* 51 (2): 12–28.

Kawaller, I. G. and T. W. Koch. 1988. "Managing cash flow risk in stock index futures: The tail hedge." *Journal of Portfolio Management* 15 (1): 41–44.

Michaud, R. 1993. "Are long-short strategies superior?" *Financial Analysts Journal* 49 (6): 44–49.

Miller, E. M. 1990. "Divergence of opinion, short selling, and the role of the marginal investor." In *Managing Institutional Assets*, F. J. Fabozzi, ed. New York: Harper & Row, pp. 143–183.

Regan, P. J. 1993. "Analyst, analyze thyself." *Financial Analysts Journal* 49 (4): 10–12.

Sharpe, W. F. 1991. "Capital asset prices with and without negative holdings." In *The Founders of Modern Finance: Their Prize-Winning Concepts and 1990 Nobel Lectures*. Charlottesville, Virginia: Research Foundation of the Institute of Chartered Financial Analysts.

Long-Short Portfolio Management

An Integrated Approach[*]

The real benefits of long-short are released only by an integrated portfolio optimization.

Most investors focus on the management of long portfolios and the selection of "winning" securities. Yet the identification of winning securities ignores by definition a whole class of "losing" securities. The ability to sell short frees the investor to take advantage of the full array of securities and the full complement of investment insights by holding expected winners long and selling expected losers short.

A long-short portfolio, by expanding the scope of the investor's sphere of activity, can be expected to result in improved performance from active security selection vis-à-vis a long-only portfolio. But the benefits of long-short are, to a large extent, dependent on proper portfolio construction. Only an integrated optimization of long and short positions has the potential to maximize the value of investors' insights. The benefits that emerge from integrated optimization encompass not only freedom from the short-selling constraint but also freedom from the restrictions imposed by individual securities' benchmark weights.

Of course, these benefits do not come without some cost. Much of the incremental cost associated with a given long-short portfolio reflects the strategy's degree of leverage. Nevertheless, as we will

---

[*] Originally published in the *Journal of Portfolio Management* 26 (2): 23–32. David Starer, Senior Quantitative Analyst at Jacobs Levy Equity Management, also contributed to this article.

see, long-short is not necessarily much costlier or, indeed, much riskier than long-only.

Although most existing long-short portfolios are constructed to be neutral to systematic risk, we will see that neutrality is neither necessary nor, in most cases, optimal. Furthermore, we show that long-short portfolios do not constitute a separate asset class; they can, however, be constructed to include a desired exposure to the return (and risk) of virtually any existing asset class.

LONG-SHORT: BENEFITS AND COSTS

Consider a long-only investor who has an extremely negative view about a typical stock. The investor's ability to benefit from this insight is very limited. The most the investor can do is exclude the stock from the portfolio, in which case the portfolio will have about a 0.01 percent underweight in the stock, relative to the underlying market.[1] Those who do not consider this to be a material constraint should consider what its effect would be on the investor's ability to overweight a typical stock. It would mean the investor could hold no more than a 0.02 percent long position in the stock—a 0.01 percent overweight—no matter how attractive its expected return.

The ability to short, by increasing the investor's leeway to act on insights, has the potential to enhance returns from active security selection.[2] The scope of the improvement, however, will depend critically on the way the long-short portfolio is constructed. In particular, an integrated optimization that considers both long and short positions simultaneously not only frees the investor from the nonnegativity constraint imposed on long-only portfolios, but also frees the long-short portfolio from the restrictions imposed by securities' benchmark weights. To see this, it is useful to examine one obvious (if suboptimal) way of constructing a long-short portfolio.

Long-short portfolios are sometimes constructed by combining a long-only portfolio, perhaps a preexisting one, with a short-only portfolio. This results in a long-plus-short portfolio, not a true long-short portfolio. The long side of this portfolio is identical to a long-only portfolio; hence it offers no benefits in terms of incremental return or reduced risk.

In long-plus-short, the short side is statistically equivalent to the long side, hence to the long-only portfolio.[3] In effect:

$$\alpha_L = \alpha_S = \alpha_{LO}$$

$$\omega_L = \omega_S = \omega_{LO}$$

That is, the excess return or alpha, α, of the long side of the long-plus-short portfolio will equal the alpha of the short side, which will equal the alpha of the long-only portfolio. Furthermore, the residual risk of the long side of the long-plus-short portfolio, ω, will equal the residual risk of the short side, which will equal the residual risk of the long-only portfolio.

These equivalencies reflect the fact that all the portfolios, the long-only portfolio and the long and short components of the long-plus-short portfolio, are constructed relative to a benchmark index. Each portfolio is active in pursuing excess return relative to the underlying index only insofar as it holds securities in weights that depart from their index weights. The ability to pursue such excess returns may be limited by the need to control the portfolio's residual risk by maintaining portfolio weights that are close to index weights. Portfolio construction is index-constrained.

Consider, for example, an investor who does not have the ability to discriminate between good and bad oil stocks, or who believes that no oil stock will significantly outperform or underperform the underlying benchmark in the near future. In long-plus-short, this investor may have to hold some oil stocks in the long portfolio and short some oil stocks in the short portfolio, if only to control each portfolio's residual risk.

The ratio of the performance of the long-plus-short portfolio to that of the long-only portfolio can be expressed as follows:[4]

$$\frac{IR_{L+S}}{IR_{LO}} = \sqrt{\frac{2}{1+\rho_{L+S}}}$$

where IR is the information ratio, or the ratio of excess return to residual risk, α/ω, and ρ_{L+S} is the correlation between the alphas of the long and short sides of the long-plus-short portfolio.

In long-plus-short, the advantage offered by the flexibility to short is curtailed by the need to control risk by holding or shorting securities in indexlike weights. A long-plus-short portfolio thus offers a benefit over a long-only portfolio only if there is a less-than-1 correlation between the alphas of its long and short sides. In that case, the long-plus-short portfolio will enjoy greater diversification and reduced risk relative to a long-only portfolio. A long-only portfolio can derive a similar benefit by adding a less than fully correlated asset with comparable risk and return, however, so this is not a benefit unique to long-short.

The Real Benefits of Long-Short

The real benefits of long-short emerge only when the portfolio is conceived of and constructed as a single, integrated portfolio of long and short positions. In this framework, long-short is not a two-portfolio strategy. It is a one-portfolio strategy in which the long and short positions are determined jointly within an optimization that takes into account the expected returns of the individual securities, the standard deviations of those returns, and the correlations between them, as well as the investor's tolerance for risk.

Within an integrated optimization, there is no need to converge to securities' benchmark weights in order to control risk. Rather, offsetting long and short positions can be used to control portfolio risk. This allows the investor greater flexibility to take active positions.

Suppose, for example, that an investor's strongest insights are about oil stocks, some of which are expected to do especially well and some especially poorly. The investor does not have to restrict the portfolio's weightings of oil stocks to indexlike weights in order to control the portfolio's exposure to oil sector risk. The investor can allocate much of the portfolio to oil stocks, held long and sold short. The offsetting long and short positions control the portfolio's exposure to the oil factor.

Conversely, suppose the investor has no insights into oil stock behavior. Unlike the long-only and long-plus-short investors discussed previously, the long-short investor can totally exclude oil stocks from the portfolio. The exclusion of oil stocks does not increase portfolio risk, because the long-short portfolio's risk is independent of any security's benchmark weight. The flexibility afforded by the absence of the restrictions imposed by securities' benchmark weights enhances the long-short investor's ability to implement investment insights.

Costs: Perception versus Reality

Long-short construction maximizes the benefit obtained from potentially valuable investment insights by eliminating long-only's constraint on short-selling and the need to converge to securities' index weights in order to control portfolio risk. While long-short offers advantages over long-only, however, it also involves complications not encountered in long-only management. Many of these complications are related to the use of short-selling.

Costs Related to Shorting

To engage in short-selling, an investor must establish an account with a prime broker. The broker clears all trades for the long-short portfolio and arranges to borrow stock for shorting. For some shares, especially those of the smallest-capitalization companies, borrowability may be problematic. Even when such shares are available for borrowing, they may pose a problem for the short-seller if they are later called back by the stock lender. In that case, the broker may not be able to find replacement shares, and the long-short investor will be subject to a "buy-in" and have to cover the short positions.

The financial intermediation cost of borrowing, which includes the costs associated with securing and administering lendable stocks, averages 25 to 30 basis points and may be higher for harder-to-borrow names. This cost is incurred as a "haircut" on the short rebate received from the interest earned on the short sale proceeds.

Short-sellers may also incur trading opportunity costs because exchange rules delay or prevent short sales. Securities and Exchange Commission Rule 10a-1, for example, states that exchange-traded shares can be shorted only at a price that is higher than the last trade price (an uptick) or the same as the last trade price if that price was higher than the previous trade (zero-plus-tick).

Such tick tests can be circumvented by the use of "principal packages" (traded outside U.S. markets) or the sale of call options, but the costs involved may be higher than the costs exacted by the rules themselves. For a long-short strategy that engages in patient trading, where the plan is to sell short only after a price rise, the incremental impact of uptick rules will be minimal.

Trading Costs

Some other costs of long-short may seem as though they should be high relative to long-only and are often portrayed as such. For example, a long-short portfolio that takes full advantage of the leverage allowed by Federal Reserve Board Regulation T (two-to-one leverage) will engage in about twice as much trading activity as a comparable unlevered long-only strategy. The differential, however, is largely a function of the portfolio's leverage. Long-short management does not require leverage. Given capital of $10 million, for example, the investor can choose to invest $5 million long and sell $5 million short; trading activity for the resulting long-short portfolio will be roughly equivalent to that for a $10 million long-only portfolio.[5]

Aside from the trading related to the sheer size of the investment in long-short versus long-only, the mechanics of long-short management may require some incremental trading not encountered in long-only. As security prices change, for example, long and short positions may have to be adjusted in order to maintain the desired degree of portfolio leverage and to meet collateralization requirements (including margin requirements and marks to market on the shorts). When a long-short portfolio is equitized by a position in stock index futures contracts, the need for such trading is reduced because price changes in the long futures positions will tend to offset marks to market on the short stock positions. [For some examples, see Jacobs (1998).]

Management Fees

Management fees for a long-short portfolio may appear to be higher than those for a comparable long-only portfolio. Again, the differential is largely a reflection of the degree to which leverage is used in the former and not in the latter. If one considers management fees per dollar of securities positions, rather than per dollar of capital, there should not be much difference between long-short and long-only.

Furthermore, investors should consider the amount of active management provided per dollar of fees. As noted, long-only portfolios must be managed with an eye to the underlying benchmark, as departures from benchmark weights introduce residual risk. In general, long-only portfolios have a sizable "hidden passive" component; only their overweights and underweights relative to the benchmark are truly active. By contrast, virtually the entire long-short portfolio is active. In terms of management fees per active dollars, then, long-short may be substantially less costly than long-only. Furthermore, long-short management is almost always offered on a performance-fee basis.

Risk

Long-short is often portrayed as inherently riskier than long-only. In part, this view reflects a concern for potentially unlimited losses on short positions. Although it is true that the risk of a short position is theoretically unlimited because there is no bound on a rise in the price of the shorted security, this source of risk is considerably mitigated in practice. It is unlikely, for example, that the prices of all the securities sold short will rise dramatically at the same time, with no offsetting increases in the prices of the securities held long. And the investor can guard against precipitous rises in the prices of individual shorted stocks by holding small positions in a large number of stocks, both long and short.

In general, a long-short portfolio will incur more risk than a long-only portfolio to the extent that it engages in leverage and/or takes more active positions. A long-short portfolio that takes full advantage of the leverage available to it will have at risk roughly double the amount of assets invested in a comparable unlevered long-only strategy. And, because it does not have to converge to securities' benchmark weights in order to control risk, a long-short strategy may take larger positions in securities with higher (and lower) expected returns compared with an index-constrained long-only portfolio.

But both the portfolio's degree of leverage and its "activeness" are within the explicit control of the investor. Furthermore, proper optimization should ensure that incremental risks, and costs, are compensated by incremental returns.

THE OPTIMAL PORTFOLIO

Here we consider what proper optimization involves, and what the resulting long-short portfolio looks like. There are some surprises. In particular, a rigorous look at long-short optimality calls into question the goals of dollar- and beta-neutrality—common practices in traditional long-short management.

We use the utility function:[6]

$$U = r_p = \frac{1}{2}\sigma_p^2 / \tau \qquad (14.1)$$

where r_p is the expected return of the portfolio over the investor's horizon, σ_p^2 is the variance of the portfolio's return, and τ is the investor's risk tolerance. This utility function, favored by Markowitz (1952) and Sharpe (1991), provides a good approximation of other, more general, functions and has the agreeable characteristics of providing more utility as expected return increases and less utility as risk increases.

Portfolio construction consists of two interrelated tasks: (1) an asset allocation task for choosing how to allocate the investor's wealth between a risk-free security and a set of N risky securities and (2) a risky portfolio construction task for choosing how to distribute wealth among the N risky securities.

Let h_R represent the fraction of wealth that the investor specifically allocates to the risky portfolio, and let h_i represent the fraction of wealth invested in the ith risky security. There are three components of capital that earn interest at the risk-free rate. The first is the wealth that the investor specifically allocates to the risk-free security, and this has a magnitude of $1 - h_R$. The second is the balance of the deposit made with the broker after paying for the purchase of shares long, and this has a magnitude of $h_R - \sum_{i \in L} h_i$, where L is the set of securities held long. The third is the proceeds of the short sales, and this has a magnitude of $\sum_{i \in S} |h_i| = -\sum_{i \in S} h_i$, where S is the set of securities sold short. (For simplicity, we assume no haircut on the short rebate.)

Summing these three components gives the total amount of capital h_F that earns interest at the risk-free rate as

$$h_F = 1 - \sum_{i=1}^{N} h_i$$

A number of interesting observations can be made about h_F. First, note that it is independent of h_R. Second, observe that, in the case of short-only management in which $\sum_{i=1}^{N} h_i = -1$, the quantity h_F is equal to 2; that is, the investor earns the risk-free rate twice. Third, in the case of dollar-balanced long-short management in which $\sum_{i=1}^{N} h_i = 0$, the investor earns the risk-free rate only once.

Let r_F represent the return on the risk-free security, and let R_i represent the expected return on the ith risky security. The expected return on the investor's total portfolio is

$$r_P = h_F r_F + \sum_{i=1}^{N} h_i R_i.$$

Substituting the expression derived above for h_F into this equation gives the total portfolio return as the sum of a risk-free return component and a risky return component, expressed as $r_p = r_F + r_R$. The risky return component is

$$r_R = \sum_{i=1}^{N} h_i r_i \qquad (14.2a)$$

where $r_i = R_i - r_F$ is the expected return on the ith risky security in excess of the risk-free rate. The risky return component can also be expressed in matrix notation as

$$r_R = \mathbf{h}^T \mathbf{r} \qquad (14.2b)$$

where $\mathbf{h} = [h_1, h_2, \ldots, h_N]^T$ and $\mathbf{r} = [r_1, r_2, \ldots, r_N]^T$. It can be shown that the variance of the risky return component, σ_R^2, is

$$\sigma_R^2 = \mathbf{h}^T \mathbf{Q} \mathbf{h} \qquad (14.3)$$

where $\mathbf{Q}$ is the covariance matrix of the risky securities' returns. The variance of the overall portfolio is $\sigma_P^2 = \sigma_R^2$.

With these expressions, the utility function in Eq. (14.1) can be expressed in terms of controllable variables. We determine the optimal portfolio by maximization of the utility function through appropriate choice of these variables. This maximization is performed subject to the appropriate constraints. A minimal set of appropriate constraints consists of: (1) the Regulation T margin requirement and (2) the requirement that all the wealth allocated to the risky securities is fully utilized. The solution (providing $\mathbf{Q}$ is nonsingular) gives the optimal risky portfolio as

$$\mathbf{h} = \tau \mathbf{Q}^{-1} \mathbf{r} \qquad (14.4)$$

where $\mathbf{Q}^{-1}$ is the inverse of the covariance matrix. We refer to the portfolio in Eq. (14.4) as the minimally constrained portfolio.

The optimal portfolio weights depend on predicted statistical properties of the securities. Specifically, the expected returns and their covariances must be quantities that the investor expects to be realized over the portfolio's holding period. As no investor knows the true statistical distribution of the returns, expected returns and covariances are likely to differ between investors. Optimal portfolio holdings will thus differ from investor to investor, even if all investors possess the same utility function.

The optimal holdings given in Eq. (14.4) have a number of important properties. First, they define a portfolio that permits short positions because no nonnegativity constraints are imposed during its construction. Second, they define a *single* portfolio that exploits the characteristics of *individual* securities in a single integrated optimization. Even though the single portfolio can be partitioned artificially into one subportfolio of only stocks held long and another subportfolio of only stocks sold short, there is no benefit to doing so. Third, the holdings need not satisfy any arbitrary balance conditions; dollar- or beta-neutrality is not required.

Because optimal portfolio weights are determined in a single integrated optimization, without regard to any index or benchmark weights, the portfolio has no inherent benchmark. This means that there exists no *inherent* measure of portfolio excess return or residual risk; rather, the portfolio will exhibit an absolute return and an absolute variance of return. This return can be calculated as the weighted spread between the returns to the securities held long and the returns to the securities sold short.

Performance attribution cannot distinguish between the contributions of the securities held long and those sold short; the contributions of the long and short positions are inextricably linked. Separate long and short alphas (and their correlation) are meaningless.

Neutral Portfolios

The flexibility afforded by the ability to short stocks allows investors to construct long-short portfolios that are insensitive to chosen exogenous factors. In practice, for example, most long-short portfolios are designed to be insensitive to the return of the equity market. This may be accomplished by constructing the portfolio so that the beta of the short positions equals and offsets the beta of the long positions, or (more problematically) the dollar amount of securities sold short equals the dollar amount of securities held long.[7]

Market neutrality, whether achieved through a balance of dollars or betas, may exact costs in terms of forgone utility. If more opportunities exist on the short than the long side of the market, for example, one might expect some return sacrifice from a portfolio that is required to hold equal-dollar or equal-beta positions long and short. Market neutrality could be achieved by using the appropriate amount of stock index futures, without requiring that long and short security positions be balanced.

Investors may nevertheless prefer long-short balances for "mental accounting" reasons. That is, investors may prefer to hold long-short portfolios that have no systematic risk, without requiring seemingly separate management of derivatives overlays. Even if separate managers are used for long-short and for derivatives, however, there is no necessity for long-short balance; the derivatives manager can be instructed to augment or offset the long-short portfolio's market exposure.

Imposing the condition that the portfolio be insensitive to the equity market return (or to any other factor) constitutes an additional constraint on the portfolio. The optimal neutral portfolio is the one that maximizes the investor's utility subject to all constraints, including that of neutrality.

This optimal neutral portfolio need not be, and generally is not, the same as the portfolio given by Eq. (14.4) that maximizes the minimally constrained utility function. To the extent that the optimal neutral portfolio differs from the minimally constrained optimal portfolio, it will involve a sacrifice in investor utility. In fact, a neutral long-short portfolio will maximize the investor's minimally constrained utility function only under the very limited conditions discussed next.

Dollar-Neutral Portfolios

We consider first the conditions under which a dollar-neutral portfolio maximizes the minimally constrained utility function. By definition, the risky portfolio is dollar-neutral if the net holding H of risky securities is zero, meaning that

$$H = \sum_{i=1}^{N} h_i = 0. \tag{14.5}$$

This condition is independent of h_R, the fraction of wealth held in the risky portfolio. Applying the condition given in Eq. (14.5) to the optimal weights from Eq. (14.4), together with a simplifying assumption regarding the covariance matrix, it can be shown that the dollar-neutral portfolio is equal to the minimally constrained optimal portfolio when:[8]

$$H \propto \sum_{i=1}^{N} \left(\xi_i - \bar{\xi} \right) \frac{r_i}{\sigma_i} = 0. \tag{14.6}$$

where σ_i is the standard deviation of the return of stock i, $\xi_i = 1/\sigma_i$ is a measure of the stability of the return of stock i, and $\bar{\xi}$ is the average return stability of all stocks in the investor's universe. The term r_i / σ_i is a risk-adjusted return, and the term $\xi_i - \bar{\xi}$ can be regarded as an excess stability, or a stability weighting. Highly volatile stocks will have low stabilities, so their excess stabilities will be negative. Conversely, low-volatility stocks will have high stabilities, so their excess stabilities will be positive.

The condition shown in Eq. (14.6) states that the optimal net holding of risky securities is proportional to the universe's net stability-weighted risk-adjusted expected return. If this quantity is positive, the net holding should be long; if it is negative, the net holding should be short. The optimal risky portfolio will be dollar-neutral only under the relatively unlikely condition that this quantity is zero.

Beta-Neutral Portfolios

We next consider the conditions under which a beta-neutral portfolio maximizes the minimally constrained utility function. Once the investor has chosen a benchmark, each security can be modeled in terms of its expected excess return α_i and its beta β_i with respect to that benchmark. Specifically, if r_B is the expected return of the benchmark, then the expected return of the ith security is

$$r_i = \alpha_i + \beta_i r_B. \tag{14.7}$$

The expected return of the portfolio can be modeled in terms of its expected excess return α_p and beta β_p with respect to the benchmark

$$r_p = \alpha_p + \beta_p r_B.$$ (14.8)

where the beta of the portfolio is expressed as a linear combination of the betas of the individual securities, as follows:

$$\beta_P = \sum_{i=1}^{N} h_i \beta_i.$$ (14.9)

From Eq. (14.8), it is clear that any portfolio that is insensitive to changes in the expected benchmark return must satisfy the condition

$$\beta_P = 0.$$ (14.10)

Applying the condition given in Eq. (14.10) to the optimal weights from Eq. (14.4), together with the model given in Eq. (14.7), it can be shown that the beta-neutral portfolio is equal to the optimal minimally constrained portfolio when:

$$\sum_{i=1}^{N} \frac{\beta_i r_i}{\omega_i^2} = 0$$ (14.11)

where ω_i^2 is the variance of the excess return of security i.

Equation (14.11) describes the condition that a universe of securities must satisfy in order for an optimal portfolio constructed from that universe to be unaffected by the return of the chosen benchmark. The summation in Eq. (14.11) can be regarded as the portfolio's net beta-weighted risk-adjusted expected return. Only under the relatively unlikely condition that this quantity is zero will the optimal portfolio be beta-neutral.

Optimal Equitization

Using various benchmark return vectors, one can construct an orthogonal basis for a portfolio's returns.[9] The portfolio can then be characterized as a sum of components along (or exposures to) the orthogonal basis vectors.

Consider a two-dimensional decomposition. The expected return of the chosen benchmark can be used as the first basis vector and an orthogonalized cash return as the second. The expected return of a beta-neutral portfolio is independent of the returns of the chosen benchmark. That is, its returns are orthogonal to the returns of the benchmark, and can therefore be treated as being equivalent to an orthogonalized cash component. In this sense, the beta-neutral portfolio appears to belong to a completely different asset class from the benchmark. It can be "transported" to the benchmark asset class by using a derivatives overlay, however.

A long-short portfolio can be constructed to be close to orthogonal to a benchmark from any asset class, and can be transported to any other asset class by use of appropriate derivatives overlays. But because long-short portfolios comprise existing underlying securities, they inhabit the same vector space as existing asset classes; they do not constitute a separate asset class in the sense of adding a new dimension to the existing asset class vector space.

Some practitioners nevertheless treat long-short portfolios as though they represent a separate asset class. They do this, for example, when they combine an optimal neutral long-short portfolio with a separately optimized long-only portfolio so as to optimize return and risk relative to a chosen benchmark. The long-only portfolio is, in effect, used as a surrogate benchmark to transport the neutral long-short portfolio toward the desired risk and return profile.

Although unlikely, it is possible that the resulting combined portfolio can optimize the investor's original utility function. It can do so, however, only if the portfolio $\mathbf{h}$ that maximizes that utility can be constructed from a linear combination of the long-only portfolio and the neutral long-short portfolio.

Specifically, if h_{LO} represents the holdings of the long-only portfolio and h_{NLS} those of the neutral long-short portfolio, the combined portfolio can be optimal if $\mathbf{h}$ belongs to the range of the transformation induced by vectors $\mathbf{h}_{LO}$ and $\mathbf{h}_{NLS}$; that is, if

$$\mathbf{h} \in R[\mathbf{h}_{LO}\,\mathbf{h}_{NLS}]. \qquad (14.12)$$

In general, however, there is nothing forcing the three portfolios to satisfy such a condition.

How, then, should one combine individual securities and a benchmark security to arrive at an optimal portfolio? The answer is straightforward: One includes the benchmark security explicitly in the formulation of the investor's utility function and performs a single integrated optimization to obtain the optimal individual security and benchmark security holdings simultaneously.

Consider the problem of maximizing a long-short portfolio's return with respect to a benchmark while simultaneously controlling for residual risk. The variables that can be controlled in this problem are $\mathbf{h}$ and the benchmark holding denoted by h_B. We make the simplifying assumption that benchmark holdings consume no capital. This is approximately true for benchmark derivatives such as futures and swaps. The portfolio's expected excess return is thus

$$r_E = r_F + \sum_{i=1}^{N} h_i r_i + h_B r_B - r_B. \tag{14.13}$$

It can be shown [see Jacobs, Levy, and Starer (1998)] that the optimal risky portfolio $\mathbf{h}$ in this case is

$$\mathbf{h} = (\boldsymbol{\phi} + m\boldsymbol{\Psi})\tau$$

where $\boldsymbol{\phi} = \mathbf{Q}^{-1}\mathbf{r}$ is the standard portfolio that would be chosen by an idealized investor with unit risk tolerance who optimizes Eq. (14.1) without any constraints; $\boldsymbol{\Psi} = \mathbf{Q}^{-1}\mathbf{q}$ is the minimum-residual-risk (MRR) portfolio; $\mathbf{q} = \text{cov}(\mathbf{r}, r_B)$ is a vector of covariances between the risky securities' returns and the benchmark return; and m is the ratio of the expected excess return of the MRR portfolio to the variance of that return.

Clearly, as the expected excess return to the MRR portfolio increases, or the variance of that return decreases, the ratio m increases, and a larger proportion of the risky portfolio should be assigned to the MRR portfolio. Conversely, as m decreases, more of the risky portfolio should be assigned to the standard portfolio $\boldsymbol{\phi}$. As the investor's risk tolerance increases, the amount of wealth assigned to the risky portfolio increases.

The exposure to the benchmark that maximizes the investor's utility is

$$h_B = 1 - m\tau.$$

This exposure decreases as the MRR portfolio becomes more attractive and as the investor's risk tolerance increases. The exposure may be negative, under which condition the investor sells the benchmark security short. Conversely, as the investor's risk tolerance or the attractiveness of the MRR portfolio decreases, the benchmark exposure should increase.

In the limit, as either m or τ tends toward zero, the optimal benchmark exposure reaches 100 percent of the invested wealth. An optimally equitized portfolio, however, will generally not include a full exposure to the benchmark security. In the limit, as m approaches zero (and h_B approaches 1), the risky portfolio $\mathbf{h}$ becomes proportional to the standard portfolio; for this risky portfolio to be optimally beta- or dollar-neutral, the same conditions must be satisfied as those given in Eq. (14.6) and (14.11) for the unequitized portfolio defined by Eq. (14.4).

The risky part of the equitized portfolio is optimally dollar-neutral when

$$\sum_{i=1}^{N}\left(\xi_i - \overline{\xi}\right)\frac{r_i + mq_i}{\sigma_i} = 0. \qquad (14.14)$$

The term on the left-hand side of Eq. (14.14) can be interpreted as a net stability-weighted risk-adjusted expected return. The risky part of the optimally equitized portfolio should be net long if this quantity is positive and net short if it is negative. This is analogous to the condition given in Eq. (14.6) for an unequitized long-short portfolio. The equitized case includes an additional term, mq_i, that captures the attractiveness of the MRR portfolio and the correlations between the risky securities' and the benchmark's returns.

Similarly, the risky part of the optimally equitized portfolio is beta-neutral when

$$\sum_{i=1}^{N}\frac{\beta_i}{\omega_i^2}\left(r_i + mq_i\right) = 0.$$

This is analogous to the condition given in Eq. (14.11) for an unequitized portfolio. Again, the condition for the equitized portfolio to be beta-neutral includes the additional term mq_i.

CONCLUSION

The freedom to sell stocks short allows the investor to benefit from stocks with negative expected returns as well as from those with positive expected returns. The advantages of combining long and short portfolio positions, however, depend critically on the way the portfolio is constructed. Traditionally, long-short portfolios have been run as two-portfolio strategies, where a short-only portfolio is added to a long-only portfolio. This is suboptimal compared with an integrated, single-portfolio approach that considers the expected returns, risks, and correlations of all securities simultaneously. Such an approach maximizes the investor's ability to trade-off risk and return for the best possible performance.

Also generally suboptimal are construction approaches that constrain the short and long positions of the portfolio to be dollar- or beta-neutral. Only under very limited conditions will such a constrained portfolio provide the same utility as an unconstrained portfolio. In general, rather than using long-short balance to achieve a desired exposure (including no exposure at all) to a particular benchmark, investors will be better off considering benchmark exposure as an explicit element of their utility functions.

Long-short management is often perceived as substantially riskier or costlier than long-only management. Much of any incremental cost or risk, however, reflects either the long-short portfolio's degree of leverage or its degree of "activeness"; both of these parameters are under the explicit control of the investor. Additionally, proper optimization ensures that expected returns compensate the investor for risks incurred.

Given the added flexibility that a long-short portfolio affords the investor, it can be expected to perform better than a long-only portfolio based on the same set of insights.

ENDNOTES

The authors thank Clarence C. Y. Kwan for helpful comments, and Judith Kimball for editorial assistance.

1. As the median-capitalization stock in the Russell 3000 index has a weighting of 0.01 percent.
2. The ability to short will be particularly valuable in a market in which short-selling is restricted and investment opinion diverse. When investors hold diverse opinions, some will be more pessimistic than others. With short-selling restricted, however, this pessimism will

not be fully reflected in security prices. In such a world, there are likely to be more profitable opportunities for selling overpriced stocks short than there are profitable opportunities for purchasing underpriced stocks. See Miller (1977).

3. This assumes symmetry of inefficiencies across attractive and unattractive stocks. It also assumes that portfolio construction proceeds identically and separately for the long and short sides as it does in long-only portfolio construction. Although these assumptions may appear unduly restrictive, they have often been invoked. See Jacobs, Levy, and Starer (1998) for a discussion of this literature and our counterpoints.

4. In deriving the formula, it is assumed that the beta of the short side equals the beta of the long side.

5. Furthermore, under Regulation T, a long-only portfolio can engage in leverage to the same extent as a long-short portfolio. Long-short has an advantage here, however, because purchasing stock on margin can give rise to a tax liability for tax-exempt investors. According to Internal Revenue Service Ruling 95-8, borrowing shares to initiate short sales does not constitute debt financing, so any profits realized when short positions are closed out do not give rise to unrelated business taxable income.

6. For analytical tractability and expositional simplicity, we use the traditional mean-variance utility function, although it is only a single-period formulation and is not sensitive to investor wealth. Also, behavioral research may question the use of an analytic utility function in the presence of apparently irrational investor behavior. Nevertheless, we believe our conclusions hold for more elaborate descriptions of investor behavior.

7. A dollar balance may appear to provide tangible proof of the market neutrality of the portfolio. But unless a dollar-balanced portfolio is also beta-balanced, it is not market-neutral.

8. The simplifying assumption applied is the constant-correlation model of Elton, Gruber, and Padberg (1976).

9. One could, for example, use the Gram-Schmidt procedure [see Strang (1988)].

REFERENCES

Elton, Edwin J., Martin J. Gruber, and Manfred W. Padberg. 1976. "Simple criteria for optimal portfolio selection." *Journal of Finance* 31 (5): 1341–1357.

Jacobs, Bruce I. 1998. "Controlled risk strategies." In *ICFA Continuing Education: Alternative Assets.* Charlottesville, Virginia: Association for Investment Management and Research.

Jacobs, Bruce I., Kenneth N. Levy, and David Starer. 1998. "On the optimality of long-short strategies." *Financial Analysts Journal* 54 (2): 40–51.

Markowitz, Harry. 1952. "Portfolio selection." *Journal of Finance* 7 (1): 77–91.

Miller, Edward M. 1977. "Risk, uncertainty, and divergence of opinion." *Journal of Finance* 32 (4): 1151–1168.

Sharpe, William F. 1991. "Capital asset prices with and without negative holdings." *Journal of Finance* 46 (2): 489–509.

Strang, Gilbert. 1988. *Linear Algebra and Its Applications.* 3d ed. New York: Harcourt Brace Jovanovich.

CHAPTER 15

Alpha Transport
with Derivatives*

Separating security selection from asset allocation.

Beam me up, Scotty! Alpha transport enables investors to obtain the best from both security selection and asset allocation.

Of all the futuristic devices dreamed up by science fiction, certainly one of the most useful is the "transporter" from the *Star Trek* series, used to "beam" characters instantaneously to their desired destinations. No long train commutes, no missed airline connections, just a little dematerialization; then, zip, you're rematerialized (most of the time) right where you want to be.

Unfortunately, science hasn't yet mastered the technology to get us from here to there instantaneously, at least in the physical universe. In the investment universe, however, the development of markets for derivatives provides some inkling of what the future may hold.

Derivatives can be used, like the transporter on the starship *U.S.S. Enterprise*, to beam the performance available from one set of securities to virtually any desired alternative set. When used in conjunction with underlying asset class portfolios in a strategy known as "alpha transport," derivatives can help solve one of the thorniest issues investors face—how to maximize the returns available from

---

* Originally published in the *Journal of Portfolio Management*, Special 25th Anniversary Issue, May 1999, pp. 55–60.

security selection while also achieving an asset allocation that meets desired return and risk goals.

ASSET ALLOCATION OR SECURITY SELECTION

Empirical research has suggested that asset allocation has the greatest impact on an investment fund's returns. Over 90 percent of an average pension fund's total return variance can be traced to its investment policy—the long-term allocation of its investments across asset classes [Brinson, Singer, and Beebower (1991)]. Even within asset classes, the allocation of a portfolio across subsets of the asset class can explain a large portion of the portfolio's return. For 1985 to 1989, for example, over 97 percent of the returns to a fund known for stock selection—Fidelity Magellan Fund—were mirrored by a passive fund invested in large-cap growth stocks (46 percent), medium-size stocks (31 percent), small-cap stocks (19 percent), and European stocks (4 percent) [Sharpe (1992)].

These findings have helped to fuel the popularity of passive, or indexed, management. Index funds designed to offer risk-return profiles that match the risk-return profile of a given asset class or subset benchmark can be combined at the overall fund level so as to maximize expected return at a desired level of risk. As the trading required to keep portfolios in line with underlying indexes is generally modest, transaction costs for passive management are generally low. As much of the portfolio construction problem can be relegated to computers, the management fees for passive management are also modest.

Passive management is essentially insightless, however. It does not attempt to pursue alpha—return in excess of the return on the relevant benchmark. Rather, its appeal lies in its ability to deliver with consistency the asset class return or the return of a subset of the asset class. In practice, of course, trading costs and management fees, however modest, diminish this performance.

Active management does attempt to achieve returns above the asset class benchmark, by selecting from the benchmark individual securities that have higher expected returns. Even modest levels of success in active management can add meaningfully to portfolio value. Given the size of most institutional portfolios, even a small percentage increase in portfolio return translates into a large dollar gain. The opportunity cost of using passive management has nevertheless tended to be viewed as low. This is certainly the case when passive management is measured against the performance of traditional active managers, who, as a group, have tended to underperform their asset class benchmarks.

Traditional active management, however, suffers from at least two disadvantages when measured against the performance of the asset class underlying it. First, it is highly labor-intensive, involving in-depth examinations of companies' financial statements, management, product lines, and facilities. To make the stock selection task tractable, active managers generally focus on only a limited number of stocks; this can result in loss of potentially valuable information and loss of profit opportunity.

Second, traditional active management is highly subjective. Subjectivity in the process of selecting stocks can lead to cognitive biases resulting in suboptimal decision making [Jacobs and Levy (1998)]. Furthermore, the qualitative nature of the stock selection process makes for ad hoc portfolio construction. The risk-return profile of the traditional active manager's portfolio may vary greatly relative to the underlying asset class (or subclass) from which its constituents are selected.

Skillful quantitative active management can combine the potential benefits of traditional active management—value-added relative to an underlying benchmark—with the benefits of passive management—tight control of risk and return relative to the underlying benchmark. Computerized information-gathering and adept statistical modeling can expand the scope of analysis and improve the quality of the selection process while reducing the risk of cognitive biases. Furthermore, the resulting numerical estimates for expected returns and risks are eminently suitable for portfolio construction via optimization techniques. The goal of optimization is to maximize portfolio return while controlling portfolio risk relative to the underlying benchmark [Jacobs and Levy (1995)].

Quantitatively managed active portfolios offer investors the potential to benefit from skilled security selection while retaining the performance available from underlying asset classes. Investors can seek out active managers who offer value-added relative to a chosen asset class. Ideally, skilled managers can be found for each of the asset classes the investor chooses to hold. The investor can thus maximize performance from both security selection and asset allocation.

In practice, however, the task of combining asset allocation with security selection often involves a trade-off. Even with active management of portfolios tied to underlying asset classes or subclasses, the goals of asset allocation and security selection sometimes conflict. Given the presumed priority of the asset allocation choice, it is often the return from security selection that is sacrificed.

Consider the case of an investor who has both large- and small-cap equity managers. On the one hand, to the extent that small-cap stocks are less efficiently priced than their large-cap counterparts, the potential of the small-cap manager to add value relative to an underlying small-cap universe may be greater than the potential of the large-cap manager to add value relative to an underlying large-cap universe. The investor may thus want to allocate more to the small-cap than the large-cap manager.

On the other hand, small-cap stocks may be considered too risky in general, or may be expected to underperform larger-cap stocks. In the interest of optimizing overall fund return and risk, the investor may wish to limit the allocation to the small-cap manager and allocate significantly more to the large-cap manager. In this case, however, the investor sacrifices the potential alpha from small-cap security selection in exchange for overall asset class return and risk.

The investor's asset allocation decision comes down to a choice between sacrificing security selection return in favor of asset class performance, or sacrificing asset class performance in favor of security selection return. In the new world of derivatives, however, investors need no longer face such Solomonic decisions.

Derivatives can be used to liberate managers, and manager performance, from their underlying asset classes. Investors, or managers, can deploy derivatives to transport the security selection alpha of any manager to any asset class. Alpha transport enables the overall fund to add value from both asset and manager allocation.

ASSET ALLOCATION AND SECURITY SELECTION

Suppose an active small-cap manager has been able to add value relative to the Russell 2000 small-cap universe, but small-cap stocks are expected to underperform large-cap stocks. If the investor maintains his or her allocation to the small-cap manager, the incremental return expected to be earned by large-cap stocks relative to small-cap stocks will be given up. If the investor shifts funds from the small-cap to a large-cap manager to capture the expected incremental asset class return, he or she will be giving up the superior alpha from the small-cap manager's ability to select securities within the small-cap universe.

The investor, or the small-cap manager, can use derivatives to: (1) neutralize the portfolio's exposure to small-cap stocks in general and (2) transport any excess return (and residual risk) from the small-cap portfolio to the large-cap universe. The incremental returns from both security selection and asset allocation are retained.

In order to neutralize the portfolio's exposure to the small-cap universe, the portfolio manager or investor can sell short futures contracts on the Russell 2000 small-cap index in an amount approximately equal to the portfolio's value. Changes in the value of the futures contracts will offset the changes in the value of the portfolio in response to movements in the small-cap universe underlying the futures.

The short derivatives position thus eliminates the fund's exposure to the small-cap universe. What remains is the differential between the portfolio's return (and risk) and the small-cap universe return (and risk) represented by the index. This excess return, or alpha, and its associated residual risk, reflect the manager's stock selection efforts.

Simultaneously, the manager takes a long position in futures contracts on a desired universe—say, the large-cap universe represented by the S&P 500. This long derivatives position provides exposure to the desired asset class, in this case the large-cap equity universe. The fund can thus benefit from any positive performance of the large-cap asset class while retaining the small-cap manager's performance in excess of the small-cap universe.

The combined derivatives positions, one short and one long, effectively allow the fund to transport alpha from the underlying small-cap portfolio to the large-cap asset class.

As an alternative to the two futures trades, the portfolio or fund manager can look to the over-the-counter (OTC) derivatives market, contracting with a swaps dealer to exchange small-cap equity returns for large-cap equity returns. The swap contract might specify, for example, that the fund pay quarterly over the term of the contract an amount equal to the return on the Russell 2000 index times an underlying notional amount, say, the value of the underlying small-cap portfolio. The swaps dealer pays in exchange an amount equal to the return on the S&P 500 times the value of the portfolio.

Consider, for example, a $100 million portfolio invested in small-cap stocks. Assume the Russell 2000 returns 10 percent over the period, the S&P 500 returns 13 percent, and the small-cap portfolio returns 12 percent. The small-cap portfolio grows from $100 to $112 million. The fund pays out 10 percent of $100 million, or $10 million, to the swaps dealer. The fund receives 13 percent of $100 million, or $13 million, from the dealer.

The fund winds up with $115 million for the period. It benefits from both the superior return on the large-cap asset class in excess of the small-cap asset class return and the superior return of the active small-cap manager in excess of the small-cap asset class benchmark.

An active equity portfolio's value-added can even be transported to a bond universe with the use of futures or swaps. For example, futures contracts on an appropriate equity index can be sold short to neutralize the portfolio's equity exposure, while bond futures are simultaneously purchased to establish the desired bond exposure. Alternatively, the fund could enter into a swap to pay an equity index return times a notional value approximating the value of the underlying equity portfolio and receive an amount equal to a bond return times the portfolio value.

TRANSPORTER MALFUNCTIONS

When the transporter on the starship *Enterprise* malfunctioned, the results were generally not pretty. Sometimes the transporter failed to rematerialize its subjects, leaving a character's atoms lost in space. Sometimes it transported them to the wrong place, so they materialized within a bulkhead or, less fatally (usually), in an alternative universe. And sometimes, despite the utmost efforts of engineer Scotty, the transporter simply couldn't be made to cut through the interference raised by gamma radiation or Captain Kirk's bombast. Alpha transport faces a not dissimilar set of difficulties, but their effects are rarely as critical.

Alpha transport may face interference in the form of unavailability or illiquidity of derivatives instruments. In particular, futures contracts are not traded on all asset class benchmarks that may be of interest to investors, and even when available the contracts may not have enough liquidity to support institutional-size needs. While futures contracts on the S&P 500 enjoy excellent liquidity, liquidity drops off considerably for contracts on smaller-cap U.S. and on some non-U.S. equity indexes. When investors face insurmountable interference in transporting via futures, however, they can turn to the OTC swaps market. Swaps can be customized to meet most investor needs.

Alpha transport with futures contracts may also deposit investors at a location slightly removed from their desired destination. Although the futures price will converge to the underlying index price at expiration, futures-based strategies may not always provide the exact performance of the underlying index, for several reasons.

First, although futures are fairly priced to reflect the current value of the underlying spot index adjusted for the forward interest rate over the time to contract expiration and the value of dividends on the underlying index, actual futures prices can diverge from fair price. The S&P 500 futures contract usually tracks the underlying index closely, but less-liquid contracts tend to experience greater tracking error. This type of basis risk can add to or subtract from derivative performance relative to the underlying index.

Futures performance may also differ from underlying index performance because of frictions introduced by margin costs and by the need to roll over the more-liquid short-term futures contracts. Because the purchase or short sale of futures contracts involves a deposit of initial margin (generally about 5 percent of the value of the underlying stocks) plus daily marks to market, a small portion of investment funds will have to be retained in cash. This will earn interest at the short-term rate, but will represent a drag on performance when the rate earned is below the interest rate implicit in the futures contract (and add to performance when the rate earned exceeds the implicit futures rate).

Swaps reduce some of the risks of missing the target index. Swaps generally require no initial margin or deposit (although one may be required by the terms of a specific swap contract), and the term of the swap contract can be specified to match the investor's horizon. Furthermore, swap counterparties are obligated to exchange payments according to the terms in the contract; payments are not subject to fluctuations about the value of the underlying benchmark, as is the case with futures.

Swaps do entail price risk. A swaps dealer will generally extract a charge in the form of a spread. For example, a party wanting to exchange the Russell 2000 return for the S&P 500 return may be required to pay the Russell 2000 plus some basis points.

In general, the price of a swap will depend upon the ease with which the swap dealer can hedge it. If a swap dealer knows it can lay off a swap immediately with a counterparty demanding the other side, it will charge less than if it knows it will have to incur the risks associated with hedging its exposure. Swap prices may vary depending upon a specific dealer's knowledge of potential counterparties, as well as its ability to exploit tax advantages and access to particular markets.

Swaps also entail some risk of "dematerialization," which comes in the form of credit risk. Swaps are not backed, as are futures contracts, by exchange clearinghouses. The absence of initial margin deposit and daily marking to market further increases credit risk. Although credit risk will generally be minimal for the investor or manager swapping with a large well-capitalized investment bank, the credit quality of counterparties must be closely monitored to minimize exposure to potential default. Default may prove costly, and as swaps are essentially illiquid, it may be difficult or impossible to find a replacement for a defaulting counterparty.

The potential benefits of alpha transport, in terms of flexibility and value-added, are nevertheless substantial for both investors and managers. By liberating the security selection return from the universe to which the securities belong, alpha transport allows investors to maximize both manager selection and asset class allocation. The decision to maximize alpha need no longer be subservient to the investor's asset allocation decision; the investor can pursue the best opportunities in both asset allocation and security selection.

Alpha transport may also liberate portfolio managers. This will certainly be the case if managers have neglected their own areas of expertise in order to pursue returns from those types of securities favored by clients. Alpha transport frees managers to focus on the universes within which they feel they have the greatest skill, hence the greatest potential to add value. This freedom should ultimately translate into enhanced performance for their clients.

Alpha transport, by decoupling the security selection decision from the asset allocation decision, affords investors increased flexibility in structuring an overall fund. This added flexibility should translate into enhanced performance. In much the same way, the manner in which an individual portfolio is constructed can afford the portfolio manager increased flexibility to pursue excess returns from security selection.

MATTER–ANTIMATTER WARP DRIVE

In searching for alpha, most managers (and investors) focus on "winning" securities, those expected to outperform their benchmark. But "losing" securities, those expected to underperform, have as much potential to contribute to excess return. Just as the warp engine of the *Enterprise* combined matter and antimatter for propulsion, the portfolio manager can combine securities with positive and negative expected returns to propel the pursuit of alpha. The ability to sell short securities with negative expected returns releases a portfolio from constraints imposed by underlying benchmark weights, enhancing its potential return.

A portfolio that can only hold securities long is restricted in its ability to pursue alpha. On a basic level, the long-only portfolio may not be able to reflect fully the manager's views about a particular stock. Consider a long-only equity manager who has a strong negative view about a company. The largest position this manager can take is to exclude the stock from the portfolio. As the typical U.S. stock constitutes only 0.01 percent of the capitalization of the U.S. equity universe, not holding this typical stock translates into a portfolio underweight of 0.01 percent relative to the underlying broad market benchmark. Such a minute underweight can hardly be expected to contribute a great deal to the portfolio's excess return.

The manager is restricted in a more general sense, however, by the weights of the stocks in the underlying index. Departures from benchmark weights, needed to produce excess returns, introduce residual risk relative to the benchmark. The more the portfolio departs from securities' weights in the benchmark, the greater the probability that its return will diverge from the return on the benchmark. Controlling the portfolio's residual risk means controlling the portfolio's weighting of each security relative to its index weighting.

In contrast, risk control in long-short investment uses a balance of security weightings. The ability to short in and of itself affords the manager greater flexibility to implement negative insights [see Jacobs and Levy (1996)]. Furthermore, within the context of an integrated portfolio optimization that considers the risks and returns of all candidate securities (both potential outperformers and potential underperformers), the ability to short frees the portfolio from a benchmark's security weights. Rather than converging to benchmark weights, the portfolio can use offsetting long and short positions to control risk.

In fact, the manager can eliminate the portfolio's systematic risk entirely by holding offsetting long and short positions of approximately equal beta. Such a market-neutral portfolio incurs only the risk associated with the individual securities held long and sold short, which is controlled by the optimization process. The manager's ability to go long or short individual securities (or exclude individual securities) is limited only by the investor's taste for risk and the need to balance long and short betas.

Such a benchmark-neutral long-short portfolio offers an active return (and associated risk) from the specific securities selected to be held long or sold short. Given the added flexibility that the long-short manager enjoys in implementing insights, this active return should exceed the excess return to a long-only portfolio based on the same set of insights. The neutral portfolio does not reflect either the return or the risk of the underlying equity benchmark. In benchmark-neutral long-short portfolios, the value added from the manager's stock selection skill, represented by the spread between the returns on the portfolio's long and short positions, is independent of the performance of the equity asset class from which the securities are selected.

The value-added from security selection in a long-short portfolio can be transported to a desired asset class through the use of derivatives, just as with long-only alpha transport. As the long-short portfolio is already benchmark-neutral, however, there will be no need to short futures in order to establish neutrality, as is the case with a long-only portfolio. By purchasing futures in an amount approximately equal to the investment in the long-short strategy, the manager or investor can establish exposure to a desired asset class. (Alternatively, the manager can enter into a swap to obtain a desired asset class exposure.)

An equity index futures position will, for example, impart to the overall portfolio the return and risk of the underlying equity benchmark [see Jacobs and Levy (1997)]. In addition, the portfolio will retain the return and risk of the long-short manager's active security selection—the long-short spread. This return should benefit from the long-short manager's added flexibility, attributable to the absence of restrictions on portfolio construction imposed by securities' benchmark weights, to pursue return and control risk.

Performance may be further enhanced by relaxation of additional constraints. For example, optimal long-short portfolio construction does not necessarily require benchmark neutrality [see Jacobs, Levy, and Starer (1999)]. Rather, the optimal exposure to the benchmark arises naturally from an integrated optimization that takes the characteristics of the benchmark security explicitly into account, along with the risks and returns of the individual securities.

TO BOLDLY GO

Long-short portfolio construction affords flexibility in pursuit of return and control of risk at the individual portfolio level. Alpha transport affords flexibility in pursuit of return and control of risk at the overall fund level. By improving the manager's ability to implement investment insights, long-short construction can lead to better performance from security selection. Alpha transport can, in turn, enable the investor to capture that enhanced performance while maintaining the performance from the desired asset allocation.

Enhanced flexibility in asset allocation and enhanced potential for adding value from security selection should embolden both investors and managers in the pursuit of active returns. As new derivatives instruments are introduced, and existing ones develop liquidity (perhaps as the result of increased use by alpha transporters), opportunities for adding value should increase.

Derivatives and portfolio construction techniques, such as long-short, are essentially tools, however. They may be able to enhance good performance, but they cannot turn bad performance into good performance; in fact, both derivatives and long-short can magnify an investor's exposure to poor performance. In the end, the ability of either alpha transport or long-short construction to add value rests on the quality of the insights going into the investment process.

Live long and prosper!

ENDNOTE

The authors thank Judith Kimball for editorial assistance.

REFERENCES

Brinson, G. P., B. D. Singer, and G. L. Beebower. 1991. "Determinants of portfolio performance II: An update." *Financial Analysts Journal* 47 (3): 40–48.

Jacobs, B. I. and K. N. Levy. 1995. "Engineering portfolios: A unified approach." *Journal of Investing* 4 (4): 8–14.

——— and ———. 1996. "20 myths about long-short." *Financial Analysts Journal* 52 (5): 81–85.

——— and ———. 1997. "The long and short on long-short." *Journal of Investing* 6 (1): 73–86.

——— and ———. 1998. "Investment management: An architecture for the equity market." In *Active Equity Portfolio Management*, F. J. Fabozzi, ed. New Hope, Pennsylvania: Frank J. Fabozzi Associates.

Jacobs, B. I., K. N. Levy, and D. Starer. 1999. "Long-short portfolio management: An integrated approach." *Journal of Portfolio Management* 26 (2): 23–32.

Sharpe, W. F. 1992. "Asset allocation: Management style and performance measurement." *Journal of Portfolio Management* 18 (2): 7–19.

Admati, A., 153
Aiyagari, S., 126, 128
Akaike, H., 184, 186
Akerlof, G., 126, 129
Alavi, A., 185, 189
Amihud, Y., 87, 93, 150, 153, 161, 183, 186
Arbel, A., 48, 49, 52, 56, 90, 92, 93, 126, 129, 137, 139, 153, 164, 167, 183, 186
Ariel, R., 140, 141, 146, 147, 153
Arnott, R. D., 53, 57, 88, 90, 92, 93, 109, 125, 126, 128, 129, 320
Arrow, K., 91, 93, 107, 109, 126, 129

Bachelier, L., 186
Bachrach, B., 56, 93
Ball, R., 88, 94
Banz, R., 49, 87, 89, 90, 94, 128, 129, 159, 160, 162, 165, 186
Barone-Adesi, G., 57, 86, 94, 101, 151, 156, 168, 191
Barry, C., 52, 94, 163, 164, 186
Bartlett, M., 174, 186
Basu, S., 49, 50, 59, 86, 90, 94, 165, 186
Bauman, S., 52, 53, 90, 96
Bayes, T., 185, 186
Beaton, A. W., 224, 227
Beckers, S., 86, 94
Beebower, G. L., 263, 282, 370, 380
Belsley, D. A., 226, 227
Benesh, G., 53, 57, 58, 94
Benston, G., 88, 94
Bernheim, Alfred L., 309
Bernstein, P., 107, 126, 129

Bethke, W., 127, 129
Bildersee, J., 138, 153
Black, F., 87, 94, 105, 107, 109, 129
Blume, M., 50, 56, 86, 87, 89, 94, 160, 186
Bohan, J., 88, 94
Boles, K., 88, 95
Booth, J., 87, 94, 162, 186
Box, G., 92, 93, 95, 99, 174, 175, 183, 186, 187, 189
Boyd, S., 127, 129
Branch, B., 88, 95, 167, 187
Breen, W., 49, 86, 89, 90, 94, 95, 128, 129, 165, 186
Brinson, G. P., 263, 282, 370, 380
Brown, K., 127, 129
Brown, P., 86, 87, 89, 90, 94, 151, 153, 160, 161, 167, 187
Brown, S., 52, 94, 163, 164, 186
Brush, J., 88, 92, 95
Bucy, R., 177, 189
Buffett, Warren, 249

Camerer, C., 107, 126, 129, 327, 348
Carleton, W., 87, 95
Carvell, S., 49, 52, 57, 93, 95, 126, 129, 164, 183, 186, 187
Chamberlin, S., 57, 97
Chan, K., 87, 88, 90, 92, 95, 126, 129, 138, 153, 162, 163, 168, 176, 184, 187
Chang, E., 138, 153
Chari, V., 92, 95, 139, 154, 167, 187
Chen, N., 85, 87, 90, 95, 162, 163, 176, 184, 187
Cheung, S., 50, 94
Chiang, R., 161, 187

Clarke, Roger G., 251, 252, 261
Clasing, H., 54, 101, 118, 132
Cochran, W., 89, 90, 101
Cohn, R., 106, 131
Connor, G., 85, 95, 163, 187
Conover, W. J., 224, 227
Constantinides, G., 50, 88, 95, 138, 154, 168, 187
Cook, T., 49, 51, 74, 90, 95, 165, 187
Copeland, T., 85, 90, 92, 93, 95, 125, 128, 129
Corhay, A., 139, 154
Cornell, B., 152, 154
Coursey, D., 145, 154
Cragg, J., 57, 96
Cross, F., 152, 154

Dadachanji, N., 319
Daniel, W., 57, 97
Davis, P., 105, 127, 128, 131
DeBondt, W., 88, 96, 106, 109, 126, 127, 129
DeLong, B., 109, 126, 129
Dimson, E., 161, 187
Doan, T., 185, 187
Dodd, David L., 2
Donnelly, B., 103, 129
Douglas, G., 88, 96
Dowen, R., 52, 53, 90, 96
Dreman, D., 87, 96, 127, 129
Dyl, E., 88, 96, 144, 145, 152, 154, 167, 187

Edmister, R., 56, 96
Einhorn, S., 86, 96, 125, 130
Elton, Edwin J., 53, 96, 108, 109, 127, 130, 366
Estep, T., 124, 125, 130

Fabozzi, Frank J., 43, 261, 310, 380
Fama, E., 51, 85, 88, 89, 92, 96, 103, 106, 109, 126, 130, 183, 184, 185, 188
Farrell, James L., Jr., 91, 96, 236, 246
Ferris, S., 152, 154

Ferson, W., 87, 96, 127, 130, 162, 188
Fields, M., 135, 154
Fielitz, B., 88, 97
Flannery, M., 143, 154
Foerster, S., 127, 130
Ford, Henry, 236
Fosback, N., 135, 154
Foster, G., 51, 96
Frankel, J., 126, 130
Freeman, R., 51, 96
French, K., 51, 88, 92, 96, 106, 109, 126, 130, 144, 147, 154, 183, 184, 185, 188
Friedman, B., 107, 130
Friend, I., 57, 88, 97
Fuller, R. J., 327, 348

Galai, D., 56, 93
Garcia, C. B, 319, 320
Gardner, E., 173, 188
Gibbons, M., 152, 154, 183, 188
Gilmer, R., 183, 188
Givoly, D., 50, 97, 137, 154
Goodman, D., 49, 52, 87, 97, 100
Goppi, H., 94
Gordon, M., 124, 130, 159, 188
Gould, F. J., 319, 320
Graham, Benjamin, 2
Granger, C., 175, 185, 188
Granito, M., 97
Grant, J., 92, 97, 183, 188
Greene, J., 56, 96
Greene, M., 88, 97
Grinold, Richard C., 89, 97, 246, 252, 259, 261
Gruber, Martin J., 53, 96, 108, 109, 127, 130, 366
Gultekin, B., 53, 85, 86, 94, 97, 137, 138, 151, 154, 168, 188
Gultekin, M., 53, 85, 86, 94, 97, 108, 109, 127, 130, 137, 138, 151, 154, 168, 188

Hagerman, R., 88, 94
Hagin, R., 58, 97

Handa, P., 87, 97, 162, 188
Hannan, E., 184, 188
Harlow, W., 127, 129
Harris, L., 53, 54, 97, 142, 148, 149, 150, 154, 183, 188
Haugen, R., 152, 154
Hausch, D., 126, 130
Hawawini, G., 139, 152, 154, 155
Hawkins, E., 57, 97
Hawthorne, F., 47, 97
Henn, R., 94
Hess, P., 152, 154, 183, 188
Hirsch, Y., 135, 141, 142, 147, 153, 155
Hoffman, G. Wright, 290, 309
Hogarth, R., 105, 130, 131, 132
Howe, J., 127, 130
Hsiao, C., 184, 188
Hsieh, D., 90, 95, 176, 184, 187
Huber, P. J., 224, 227
Huberts, L. C., 327, 348
Husic, F., 56, 94

Iman, R. L., 224, 227

Jacobs, Bruce I., 29, 32, 33, 40, 44, 45, 54, 73, 86, 97, 108, 110, 117, 118, 121, 123, 124, 125, 126, 127, 130, 136, 138, 151, 155, 159, 166, 168, 169, 183, 184, 185, 188, 224, 227, 236, 239, 240, 243, 244, 245, 249, 250, 268, 276, 281, 282, 292, 293, 309, 319, 320, 354, 363, 367, 371, 378, 379, 380
Jaffe, J., 152, 155
Jagannathan, R., 92, 95, 139, 154, 167, 187
Jain, P., 153, 155
James, W., 91, 98
Jenkins, G., 92, 95, 174, 175, 183, 185, 186, 189
Joh, G., 153, 155
Jones, C., 51, 88, 98, 100, 127, 131, 132, 151, 155, 168, 189
Jones, Robert C., 86, 96, 128, 131, 236, 246

Joy, O., 86, 98
Judge, G., 89, 98

Kahn, N., 138, 153
Kahn, Ronald N., 246, 252, 261
Kahneman, D., 98, 109, 131
Kalman, R., 177, 189
Kandel, S., 87, 96, 162, 188
Kato, K., 86, 98, 139, 155
Kawaller, I. G., 347, 348
Keim, D, 50, 51, 52, 54, 85, 87, 90, 92, 98, 127, 130, 137, 142, 143, 144, 152, 155, 166, 183, 188
Kerrigan, T., 57, 98
Keynes, John Maynard, 14, 108, 131
Kinney, W., 88, 101, 137, 156, 166, 190
Kleidon, A., 86, 87, 89, 90, 94, 160, 161, 187
Klemkosky, R., 57, 98
Kling, J., 179, 189
Kmenta, J., 62, 89, 98, 281, 282
Koch, T. W., 347, 348
Kolb, R., 147, 155
Korajczyk, R., 85, 95, 163, 187
Kothari, S., 87, 97, 162, 188
Krase, Scott, 251, 252, 261
Krask, Mitchell C., 193
Kraus, A., 57, 98
Kuh, E., 226, 227
Kuhn, Thomas, 26, 45
Kwan, Clarence C. Y., 365

Lakonishok, J., 50, 51, 81, 87, 88, 89, 90, 95, 136, 137, 140, 142, 144, 145, 146, 147, 151, 155
Lanstein, R., 54, 60, 62, 66, 88, 91, 101, 108, 131
Latane, H., 51, 88, 98, 100, 127, 131, 132
Lehmann, B., 85, 99, 163, 189
Leinweber, D. J., 320
Lerman, Z., 87, 99
Leroy, A. M., 224, 227
Levi, M. D., 144, 146, 155, 226, 227

Levis, M., 174, 175, 189
Levy, H., 87, 99, 126, 131
Levy, Kenneth N., 29, 32, 33, 40, 44, 45, 108, 110, 117, 118, 121, 123, 124, 127, 128, 130, 136, 138, 151, 155, 159, 166, 168, 169, 183, 184, 185, 188, 224, 227, 236, 239, 240, 243, 244, 245, 249, 250, 268, 276, 281, 282, 292, 293, 309, 319, 320, 363, 367, 371, 378, 379, 380
Litterman, R., 178, 179, 185, 187, 189
Litzenberger, R., 57, 87, 89, 98, 99
Ljung, G., 93, 99, 174, 189
Lo, A., 92, 99, 174, 189

Maberly, E., 152, 154
MacBeth, J., 88, 89, 96
MacKinlay, C., 92, 99, 174, 189
Maddala, G. S., 89, 99, 226, 227
Makhija, A., 152, 154
Makridakis, S., 184, 189
Malkiel, B., 57, 96
Marathe, V., 54, 90, 99, 100, 108, 132
Markowitz, Harry M., 345, 356, 367
Marsh, T., 86, 87, 89, 90, 94, 160, 161, 187
Martin, C., 185, 189
Martin, J., 52, 57, 87, 98, 101
Martin, S., 144, 154
Mayers, D., 85, 95
Mayshar, J., 87, 99
McElreath, R., 89, 99
McEnally, R., 88, 99
McGee, V., 184, 189
McGwire, Mark, 6
McInish, T., 150, 157
McKibben, W., 93, 101
McNees, S., 185, 189
McNichols, M., 141, 156
McWilliams, J., 86, 99
Meese, R., 126, 130
Mencken, H. L., 15
Mendelson, H., 87, 93, 150, 153, 161, 183, 186

Merrill, A., 135, 156
Merton, R., 86, 87, 99, 109, 131, 163, 164, 189
Michaud, R., 105, 127, 128, 131, 319, 320, 347, 348
Michel, P., 139, 154
Miller, Edward M., 109, 131, 152, 156, 183, 190, 292, 293, 310, 327, 348, 366, 367
Miller, M., 87, 99, 104, 131
Miller, P., 86, 99
Modest, D., 85, 99, 163, 189
Modigliani, F., 104, 106, 131
Morgan, A., 92, 99, 174, 190
Morgan, I., 92, 99, 174, 190

Nakamura, T., 86, 101
Newbold, P., 185, 188
Nicholson, F., 86, 100
Niederhoffer, V., 126, 131

O'Brien, J., 107, 131
O'Hanlon, J., 126, 131
Ofer, A., 92, 95, 139, 154, 167, 187
Ogden, J., 141, 156
Ohlson, J., 127, 131
Olsen, C., 51, 96
Ord, K., 150, 157
Ovadia, A., 50, 97, 137, 154

Padberg, Manfred W., 366
Pagels, Heinz, 45
Palm, F., 185, 191
Pearce, D., 88, 98, 151, 155, 168, 189
Peavy, J., 49, 52, 87, 97, 100
Penman, S., 54, 100, 109, 127, 131, 141, 145, 156
Peterson, D., 152, 156
Peterson, P., 53, 57, 58, 94
Pfleiderer, P., 153
Phillips-Patrick, F., 152, 156
Pierce, D., 174, 187
Pinegar, M., 138, 153
Plott, C., 126, 131
Poterba, J., 107, 132
Protopapadakis, A., 143, 154

Quenouille, M., 176, 190

Rainville, H., 58, 100
Ramaswamy, K., 87, 89, 99
Ratcliffe, J., 89, 100
Reder, M., 105, 130, 131, 132
Regan, P. J., 327, 348
Reid, K., 54, 60, 62, 65, 66, 68, 70,
  86, 90, 91, 93, 100, 101
Reilly, F., 144, 157
Reinganum, M., 49, 50, 85, 87, 90,
  92, 100, 160, 161, 162, 163, 164,
  167, 190
Rendleman, R., 51, 88, 98, 100, 127,
  131, 132
Renshaw, E., 126, 132
Rentzler, J., 53, 96
Rissanen, J., 184, 188
Ritter, J., 138, 156
Rodriguez, R., 147, 155
Rogalski, R., 50, 51, 100, 147, 152,
  156, 167, 190
Roll, R., 50, 54, 87, 93, 100, 126, 130,
  137, 143, 156, 160, 161, 162, 167,
  184, 187, 190
Rosenberg, B., 54, 60, 62, 66, 70, 78,
  86, 88, 91, 93, 94, 100, 101, 108,
  132
Ross, S., 163, 184, 187, 190
Rousseeuw, P. J., 224, 227
Rozeff, M., 49, 51, 74, 88, 90, 95,
  101, 137, 156, 165, 166, 183, 187,
  190
Rubinstein, M., 126, 130
Rudd, A., 54, 70, 78, 86, 88, 94, 101,
  118, 132
Runkle, D., 184, 190
Russell, T., 132

Samuelson, Paul, 124, 131
Savage, J., 86, 95
Schallheim, J., 86, 98, 139, 155
Schneeweis, T., 152, 156
Schneider, Margaret Grant, 309
Scholes, M., 87, 88, 94, 99
Schramm, Sabine, 252, 261

Schultz, P., 50, 87, 101, 161, 168,
  190
Schwartz, R., 88, 101
Schwert, G., 83, 101, 160, 191
Senchack, A., 52, 87, 101
Seyhun, H., 167, 191
Shangkuan, P., 86, 96, 125, 130
Shapiro, A., 51, 81, 89, 90, 98
Shapiro, E., 124, 130
Sharpe, William F., 54, 68, 72, 86,
  90, 93, 101, 103, 125, 127, 132, 260,
  261, 263, 264, 267, 276, 282, 290,
  310, 319, 344, 348, 356, 367, 370,
  380
Shefrin, H., 77, 87, 88, 101, 109, 126,
  132, 152, 156, 164, 168, 191
Shevlin, T., 51, 96
Shiller, R., 106, 125, 126, 127, 132,
  185, 191
Simon, Herbert, 43, 45, 109, 124,
  132
Sims, C., 184, 185, 187, 191
Singer, B. D., 263, 282, 370, 380
Singleton, C., 88, 101
Smidt, S., 50, 88, 98, 136, 137, 140,
  142, 145, 147, 151, 155
Smirlock, M., 53, 54, 101, 149, 152,
  156
Smith, R., 87, 94, 162, 186
Snedecor, G., 89, 90, 101
Sorensen, E., 132
Stambaugh, R., 50, 87, 89, 90, 94,
  96, 98, 142, 144, 152, 155, 160, 162,
  183, 186, 188, 189
Starer, David, 349, 363, 366, 367,
  379, 380
Starks, L., 53, 54, 101, 149, 152, 156
Statman, Meir, 77, 87, 88, 101, 109,
  126, 132, 152, 156, 164, 168, 191,
  251, 252, 261
Stein, C., 91, 98
Stoll, H., 87, 101, 160, 191
Strang, Gilbert, 366, 367
Strebel, P., 49, 52, 57, 93, 95, 126,
  129, 164, 183, 186, 187
Summers, L., 106, 107, 132

Swanson, H., 183, 188

Terada, N., 86, 101
Thaler, R., 88, 96, 106, 109, 126, 127, 129, 131
Theil, H., 60, 101, 170, 191, 226, 227
Tinic, S., 50, 51, 53, 57, 86, 88, 90, 92, 100, 101, 102, 138, 151, 152, 156, 167, 168, 190, 191
Treynor, J., 107, 132
Trittin, Dennis, 246
Tukey, J. W., 224, 227
Tversky, A., 98, 109, 131

Umstead, D., 175, 191

Vasicek, O., 57, 102
Venkatesh, P., 161, 187
Verrecchia, R., 125, 133
VonGermeten, J., 125, 129

Wachtel, S., 88, 102, 135, 156
Wagner, W., 97
Ward, C., 126, 131
Warga, A., 89, 102

Wasley, C., 87, 97, 162, 188
Weigelt, K., 107, 126, 129
Welsch, R. E., 226, 227
West, R., 51, 53, 57, 86, 88, 90, 92, 101, 102, 151, 152, 156, 168, 191
Westerfield, R., 57, 88, 97, 152, 155
Whaley, R., 87, 101, 160, 191
Wheelwright, S., 184, 189
Whitcomb, D., 88, 101
White, James A., 309, 310
Whitford, D., 144, 157
Widmann, E., 86, 99
Wiggins, D., 89, 99
Williams, John, 104, 133
Williams, Terry, 309, 310
Williamson, D., 132
Wilson, J., 88, 98, 151, 155, 168, 189
Wingender, J., 88, 101
Wood, R., 150, 157

Yellen, J., 126, 129

Zacks, L., 108, 133
Zellner, A., 59, 102, 185, 191
Ziemba, W., 126, 130

SUBJECT INDEX

Active management, 4, 370
  (*See also* Traditional active
    management)
Alpha transport, 369–380
Analyst coverage, 212–221
Anomalies, 26, 27
  (*See also* Return effects)
Anomalous pockets of inefficiency
  (API), 35–39
Anomaly capture strategies, 73
API strategies, 35–39
Arbitrage pricing theory (APT),
  10, 19, 27, 163, 291
ARMA processes, 173, 184n
Asset allocation, 263, 370–373
Autocorrelation, 77–81, 174
Autoregresive/moving-average
  (ARMA) processes, 173, 184n

BARRA model, 54, 86n
Bayesian random walk, 41–43, 179
Bayesian vector time-series
  models, 179–182
Benchmark weights, 285
Beta, 56, 57, 111
Bid/ask spread, 161
Binary industry variables, 61
Blue Monday effect, 142
Book/price, 56, 111, 273–275
Breadth of insights, 5, 6, 9, 229–231

Calendar anomalies, 31, 135–157
  day-of-the-week effect, 141–145
  holiday effect, 145–148
  January effect, 136–140
  size effect, and, 166–168

Calendar anomalies *(Con'd)*
  time-of-day effect, 148–150
  turn-of-the-month effect, 140,
    141
Capital Asset Pricing Model
  (CAPM), 12, 19, 25, 27, 32, 33, 291
Cashflow/price, 56, 111
Chaos theory, 43n
Close-of-day anomaly, 149
Closing prices, 150
Co-skewness, 57, 111
Complex systems, 12, 20, 25, 43
  (*See also* Market complexity)
Consensus vs. flash data, 196–209
Correlogram, 174
Current asset pricing theories, 32,
  33
Current yield, 104
Customized optimization, 13

Database biases, 165
Day-end effect, 149, 150
Day-of-the-week effect, 54, 141–145
DDM (*see* Value modeling)
Default spread, 40
Depth of insights, 5, 6, 229
Derivatives, 369–380
Dimson betas, 161
Disentangling equity return
  regularities, 21, 47–102
    advantages of disentangling, 30,
      31
    autocorrelation, 77–81
    January effect, 73–77
    methodology, 59–61
    P/E and size effects, 62–64

Disentangling equity return
  regularities *(Con'd)*
    previous research, 48–54, 59
    return regularities considered,
      55–59
    study implications, 72, 73
    time-series regressions, 81–84
    trends/reversals, 67–71
    yield/neglect/price/risk, 65–67
Distributed effects, 216–221
Dividend discount model (DDM)
  (see Value modeling)
Dividend yield, 55
Don't Sell Stocks on Monday
  (Hirsch), 141

Earnings controversy, 57, 111
Earnings surprise, 30, 38, 58, 112
Earnings torpedo, 38, 58, 111
Econometric models, 41, 178
Efficient Market Hypothesis
  (EMH), 3, 4, 11, 19, 25–27, 32, 33,
  72
Electronic trading, 2, 14, 232
EMH, 3, 4, 11, 19, 25–27, 32, 33, 72
Empirical Bayes, 73
Empirical return regularities
  (ERRs), 37, 39–41
Engineering strategies, 9–10,
  242–243
Enhanced passive portfolios, 252
Equitized long-short portfolio,
  290, 295, 296, 299–302, 308,
  331–334
Equity attributes, 108–114
  (See also Return effects)
Equity return regularities *(see*
  Return effects)
ERRs, 37, 39–41
Ex post selection bias, 165
Excess return, 251
Exponential smoothing, 173
Extrapolation techniques, 171–173

Fads, 106–108
Feedback, 175

Financial ratios, 104
Flash vs. consensus data, 196–209
Ford shares, 22
Forecast E/P, 194
Forecast earnings trend, 196
Forecasting techniques:
  Bayesian vector time-series
    models, 179–182
  DDM returns, 121–123
  simple extrapolation techniques,
    171–173
  structural macroeconomic
    models, 178
  time-series techniques, 173–175
  transfer functions, 175, 176
  vector time-series models,
    176–178
  (See also Methodology)
Friday the 13th, 147
Fundamental analysis, 2, 3, 236
Futures, 373–375

Generalized least-squares (GLS)
  regression, 60, 113
Goodness of insights, 5, 6
Gram-Schmidt procedure, 366n
Growth managers, 230, 235
Growth stocks, 22

Hands-on oversight, 233
Hard-to-borrow shares, 305, 341
Hedge long-short portfolio, 290,
  297, 309
Herd opinions/decisions, 107
High-definition style rotation,
  263–282
High-IR managers, 260
Holiday effect, 145–148
Holistic approach to investing,
  235–250
Human psychology, 105–109, 123,
  276

IC, 169
Impulse analysis, 180
Index-plus portfolios, 252

Information coefficient (IC), 5, 6, 169
Information ratio (IR), 253
Innovations, 185n
Intel shares, 22
Investor psychology, 105–109, 123, 276
Investor utility, 253
IR, 253

January effect, 59, 73–77, 136–140

Lagging price, 60
Large-cap stocks, 23, 264–265, 266, 372–374
Late reporter anomaly, 55
Law of one alpha, 247–250
Leverage, 317, 342
Leverage points, 226n
Liquidity buffer, 324, 331
Long-short equity investing, 244, 245, 283–367
  advantages, 290, 293, 328–331, 350–352
  alpha transport, 377–379
  asset class, 307, 314
  beta-neutral portfolio, 360, 361
  borrowability, 341, 353
  building market-neutral portfolio, 322–326
  costs, 318, 341–343, 353–355
  custody issues, 306
  dollar-neutral portfolio, 359, 360
  equitized strategy, 290, 295, 296, 299–302, 308, 331–334
  ERISA, 306, 344, 345
  hard-to-borrow shares, 305, 341
  hedge strategy, 290, 297, 309
  impediments to short selling, 291
  implementation, 303, 304
  integrated approach, 349–367
  integrated optimization, 328–331, 344
  legal issues, 306

Long-short equity investing (Con'd)
  leverage, 317, 342
  liquidity buffer, 324, 331
  management fees, 318, 343, 354, 355
  market-neutral strategy, 289, 295, 296, 299, 301, 308, 322–326
  mechanics, 297–300
  morality issues, 307
  myths, 311–320
  optimal equitized portfolio, 361–364
  optimal neutral portfolio, 358, 359
  optimal portfolio, 355–364
  portfolio construction techniques, 303, 304
  portfolio payoff patterns, 294–296
  practical issues/concerns, 304
  prime broker, 297, 306, 341
  principal packages, 342
  quantitative vs. judgmental approach, 303
  residual risk, 343, 344
  risk, 316, 317, 343, 344, 355
  short rebate, 298
  short squeeze, 305, 348n
  shorting issues, 304, 305
  tax treatment, 306, 317
  theoretical tracking error, 300, 301
  trading, 334–339
  trading costs, 354
  trading issues, 305, 306
  uptick rules, 341, 342
Look-ahead bias, 60, 165
Low P/E, 27, 31, 55, 111, 272
Low price, 56, 112, 268–272

MA terms, 177
Macroeconomic events, 39, 63, 81–84, 239, 276
  (See also Empirical return regularities)

MAE, 170, 182
Market complexity, 12, 15, 20,
    25–45, 236–238
    anomalies, 26, 27
    anomalous pockets of
        inefficiency (API), 35–39
    Bayesian random walk
        forecasting, 41–43
    empirical return regularities
        (ERRs), 37, 39–41
    modeling empirical return
        regularities, 40, 41
    pure returns, 21, 22, 29–31, 35
    return effects (*see* Return
        effects)
Market inefficiency, 31, 32
Market-neutral long-short
    portfolio, 289, 295, 296, 299, 301,
    308, 322–326
Market psychology, 105–109, 123,
    276
ME, 169, 182
Mean absolute error (MAE), 170,
    182
Mean error (ME), 169, 182
Measurement error, 193–196
    (*See also* Predictor specification)
Measures of central tendency, 194,
    195
Methodology:
    disentangling, 59–61
    forecasting techniques (*see*
        Forecasting techniques)
    value modeling (DDM), 110, 113
Mispriced securities, 19
Missing data values, 209–212
Modeling empirical return
    regularities, 40, 41
Molecular biology, 25
Monotone regression, 224n, 225n
Moving-average (MA) terms, 177
Multicollinearity, 62
Multifactor CAPM, 33, 64
Multivariate regression, 110
Multivariate time series
    techniques, 40

nth-order autocorrelation, 183n
Naïve returns, 21–22, 29, 62, 110,
    268–272, 274
Negative surprises, 38, 58
Neglect, 56, 111
Newton's laws of motion, 25
Nonlinearity, 22, 239
    (*See also* Distributed effects)
Noise, 107, 171
Nonzero intercepts, 44n

OLS regression, 170
One unit of exposure, 113
One-way causality, 175
Opening prices, 150
Optimization techniques, 9, 13,
    231, 232, 241
Ordered systems, 20, 25
Ordinary least-squares (OLS)
    regression, 170
Out-of-sample tests, 40, 170, 171
Overfitting, 41, 177
Overpricing, 327
Overreaction, 109

p value, 224n
Pairs trading, 303
Passive management, 4, 10, 26,
    370
Pearson correlation, 224n
Performance attribution, 233
Portfolio construction, 2, 241–242,
    229–282
    high-definition style rotation,
        263–282
    holistic approach, 235–250
    residual risk, 251–261
    unified approach, 235–246
    (*See also* Long-short equity
        investing)
Portfolio optimization, 2, 13, 231,
    232, 241
Portmanteau Q statistic, 174
Predictor specification, 193–227
    alternative specifications for
        portfolio screening, 196–204

Predictor specification *(Con'd)*
  alternative specifications for
    return modeling, 204–209
  analyst coverage, and, 212–221
  effect of measurement error on
    regression coefficients, 222, 223
  measurement error, and,
    194–209
  missing data values, and,
    209–212
Price/book ratio, 104
Price/cashflow ratio, 104
Price/earnings ratio, 27, 31, 55,
  111, 272
Prime broker, 297, 306, 341
Principal packages, 342
Procedural Rationality, 109, 139
Prospect Theory, 109, 139
Proxying, 30, 31
Psychology, 22
  (See also Market psychology)
Pure returns, 21, 22, 29–31, 35, 62,
  110, 239, 270–272, 274
  (See also Disentangling equity
    return regularities)

Q statistic, 174
Quantitative management, 9, 10,
  19, 231, 236, 371–372
Quintiling procedures, 29

Random systems, 25
Random walk, 3, 19, 20, 41, 79
Relative strength, 112
Residual reversal, 58, 112
Residual risk, 56, 251–261
Residual risk tolerance, 260
Responsibility effect, 164
Retrospective inclusion bias, 165
Return effects:
  beta, 56, 57
  book/price, 56
  calendar anomalies, 135–157
    (See also Calendar anomalies)
  cashflow/price, 56
  co-skewness, 57

Return effects *(Con'd)*
  dividend yield, 55
  earnings controversy, 57
  earnings surprise, 58
  earnings torpedo, 58
  January effect, 59, 136–140
  low P/E, 55
  low price, 56
  neglect, 56
  relative strength, 58
  residual reversal, 58
  return reversal effect, 30
  sales/price, 56
  sigma, 56
  small size, 55 *(See also* Size
    effect)
  trends in analysts' earnings
    estimates, 57
  (See also Disentangling equity
    return regularities)
Return modeling, 35
Return-predictor relationships, 22,
  23
Return reversal effect, 30, 159
Risk constraints, 251–261
Risk modeling, 34
RMSE, 170, 182
Robust regressions, 224n
Root-mean-squared error (RMSE),
  170, 182

Sales/price, 56, 111
Screening procedures, 29
Security analysis, 19–227
  disentangling equity return
    regularities, 47–102
    (See also Disentangling equity
      return regularities)
  dividend discount model
    (DDM), 103–133
  market complexity, 25–45
    (See also Market complexity)
  problems in predictor
    specification, 193–227
    (See also Predictor
      specification)

Security analysis *(Con'd)*
  time-related anomalies, 135–157
    (See also Calendar anomalies)
  value modeling, 103–133
Security Analysis (Graham and
  Dodd), 2
Sharpe ratio, 281n
Short rebate, 298
Short selling, 244, 283–285
  (See also Long-short equity
    investing)
Short squeeze, 305, 348n
Sigma, 56, 111
Simple averaging, 173
Simple extrapolation technique,
  171–173
Size effect, 27, 40, 41, 159–191
  Bayesian vector time-series
    models, 179–182
  calendar effects, and, 166–168
  default spread, and, 40
  foreign exchange rates, and, 39
  other return effects, and,
    164–166
  risk measurement, and, 161–163
  risk premiums, and, 163, 164
  simple extrapolation techniques,
    171–173
  structural macroeconomic
    models, 178
  time-series techniques, 173–175
  transaction costs, and, 160, 161
  transfer functions, 175, 176
  vector time-series models,
    176–178
Small-cap stocks, 23, 263–264, 266,
  268–272, 274, 276–277, 372–374
Small-capitalization managers,
  230, 235
Small-firm effect *(see* Size effect)
Spearman rank correlation, 224n
Specialization, 236, 237
Specification problem *(see*
  Predictor specification)
Statistical arbitrage, 304
Stein-James estimators, 73

Structural macroeconomic models,
  178
Style rotation, 263–282
SURM, 89n
Survivorship bias, 60, 165
Swaps, 373–376
Tax-loss measures, 38, 39, 112, 137,
  138, 167, 168
Theil U, 170, 182
Theoretical tracking error, 300, 301
3000-stock universe, 224n
Time-of-day effect, 148–150
Time-related anomalies *(see*
  Calendar anomalies)
Time-series techniques, 81–84,
  173–175
Trading, 2, 13–14, 73
  (See also Long-short equity
    investing)
Trading-time hypothesis, 152n
Traditional active management,
  4–8, 229, 371
Transfer functions, 175, 176
Trends in analysts' earnings
  estimates, 37, 38, 57, 112
Turn-of-the-month effect, 140, 141
2 percent curtain, 252, 258

UBTI, 306, 317, 342–343, 366n
Underweighting, 284
Unified model, 235–246
  common evaluation framework,
    240
  economies, 245, 246
  engineering benchmark
    strategies, 242, 243
  flexibility, 243–245
  market segmentation/
    integration, 236–238
  performance measurement, 241,
    242
Univariate forecasting techniques,
  40, 110
Unrelated business taxable
  income (UBTI), 306, 317, 342–343,
  366n

Uptick rules, 341, 342
Utility function, 356

Value managers, 229, 230, 235
Value modeling, 33, 34, 103–133, 272, 273
  actual returns, 118–121
  equity attributes, 108–114
  expected returns, 114–118
  forecasting DDM returns, 121–123
  market psychology, 105–109
  methodology, 110, 113
  naïve expected returns, 116
  pure expected returns, 117, 118
Value stocks, 22, 263–265, 267–268

VAR model, 40, 41, 176, 177
VARMA models, 44n, 178
Vector autoregression (VAR) model, 40, 41, 176, 177
Vector autoregression moving-average (VARMA) models, 44n, 178
Vector time-series models, 176–178

Week-of-the-month effect, 55
Weekend effect, 142, 149
White noise, 174
Window dressing, 39, 138
Winsorization, 89n, 204

Yield, 111, 272–273

Bruce I. Jacobs and **Kenneth N. Levy** are cofounders and principals of Jacobs Levy Equity Management. Based in Roseland, New Jersey, Jacobs Levy Equity Management currently manages over $5 billion for more than 20 institutions, among them many of the world's largest corporate pension plans, public retirement systems, multi-employer funds, endowments and foundations.

Bruce Jacobs holds a Ph.D. in finance from the Wharton School of the University of Pennsylvania. He is the author of *Capital Ideas and Market Realities: Option Replication, Investor Behavior, and Stock Market Crashes* (1999), and serves on the advisory board of the *Journal of Portfolio Management.*

Ken Levy holds an M.B.A. and M.A. in applied economics from the Wharton School of the University of Pennsylvania. He is a Chartered Financial Analyst, and served on the Institute of Chartered Financial Analysts' candidate curriculum committee. He is currently on the advisory board of POSIT.